# The Layman's QUICK REFERENCE CONCORDANCE

Published by Barbour Publishing, Inc., P.O. Box 719,
Uhrichsville, Ohio 44683, www.barbourbooks.com

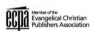 Member of the
Evangelical Christian
Publishers Association

Printed in the United States of America.
5 4 3

# The *Layman's* QUICK REFERENCE CONCORDANCE

### Edited by
## George W. Knight

BARBOUR
PUBLISHING

# Introduction

What do you get when you combine the best features of a biblical concordance, a Bible dictionary, and a guide to the major events and key passages of the Bible into one handy book? You get the book you are now holding . . . *The Layman's Quick Reference Concordance.* Based on the familiar King James Version, its purpose is to provide essential biblical information to lay students of the Bible in a format that is compact, convenient, and easy to use and understand.

The heart of this book is the concordance, which helps you find full passages in the Bible by looking under key words which the passages contain. Only selected Bible words, included because of their biblical significance, are listed as concordance entries. Under each concordance entry, only the most important verses from the Bible that contain these key words appear. This selective process makes *The Layman's Quick Reference Concordance* easier to use than an exhaustive concordance such as *Strong's,* which tends to overwhelm lay Bible students with too much information.

Another handy feature of this book's concordance is the listing of all forms of the same root word under one entry. For example, see the entry **CONVERT [ED, ETH, ING].** Bible verses containing the words *Convert, Converted, Converteth,* and *Converting* are listed under this one concordance entry. Key phrases from the Bible, such as **BEAR FALSE WITNESS, ETERNAL LIFE,**

**PREACH THE GOSPEL,** and **SEEK THE LORD,** also appear as concordance entries throughout the book.

The names of important people and places in the Bible appear as dictionary entries in this book. Most of these people or places have brief, thumbnail definitions, followed by passages in the Bible where pertinent information about these people or places can be found. Bible passages printed in **bold type** identify the most important sources of information about this biblical person or place. For a more complete narrative description of important people, places, and theological concepts in the Bible, see the companion volume to this book, *The Layman's Bible Dictionary,* issued by Barbour Publishing in 1998.

Throughout *The Layman's Quick Reference Concordance,* you will also find many key Bible events and major biblical passages listed for your convenience. For example, let's assume you are looking for the "Fruit of the Spirit" passage in the New Testament. Perhaps you cannot recall any of the key words in this passage from the King James Version that would help you find it through the concordance route. You simply look under **FRUIT OF THE SPIRIT** in this book, and it directs you to the passage in question: Galatians 5:22–26. Other important biblical passages and events that can be located through this same approach include **BURNING BUSH REVEALED TO MOSES, FAITH CHAPTER OF THE BIBLE,** and **PLAGUES AGAINST EGYPT.**

My thanks to Paul Muckley of Barbour Publishing for his encouragement and counsel in this book project. I am also grateful to my wife, Dorothy, for her assistance with the word processing and proofreading of the manuscript. I send the book forth with the prayer that it will help lay Bible students in the important work of studying and teaching God's Word.

George W. Knight
Nashville, Tennessee

# Abbreviations Used for Books of the Bible

## OLD TESTAMENT

| Abbreviation | Bible Book | Abbreviation | Bible Book |
|---|---|---|---|
| Gen | Genesis | Eccl | Ecclesiastes |
| Ex | Exodus | Song | Song of Solomon |
| Lev | Leviticus | Isa | Isaiah |
| Num | Numbers | Jer | Jeremiah |
| Deut | Deuteronomy | Lam | Lamentations |
| Josh | Joshua | Ezek | Ezekiel |
| Judg | Judges | Dan | Daniel |
| Ruth | Ruth | Hos | Hosea |
| 1 Sam | 1 Samuel | Joel | Joel |
| 2 Sam | 2 Samuel | Amos | Amos |
| 1 Kgs | 1 Kings | Obad | Obadiah |
| 2 Kgs | 2 Kings | Jon | Jonah |
| 1 Chr | 1 Chronicles | Mic | Micah |
| 2 Chr | 2 Chronicles | Nah | Nahum |
| Ezra | Ezra | Hab | Habakkuk |
| Neh | Nehemiah | Zeph | Zephaniah |
| Esth | Esther | Hag | Haggai |
| Job | Job | Zech | Zechariah |
| Ps, Pss | Psalm(s) | Mal | Malachi |
| Prov | Proverbs | | |

# Abbreviations Used for Books of the Bible

## NEW TESTAMENT

| Abbreviation | Bible Book | Abbreviation | Bible Book |
|---|---|---|---|
| Matt | Matthew | 1 Tim | 1 Timothy |
| Mark | Mark | 2 Tim | 2 Timothy |
| Luke | Luke | Titus | Titus |
| John | John | Phlm | Philemon |
| Acts | Acts | Heb | Hebrews |
| Rom | Romans | Jas | James |
| 1 Cor | 1 Corinthians | 1 Pet | 1 Peter |
| 2 Cor | 2 Corinthians | 2 Pet | 2 Peter |
| Gal | Galatians | 1 John | 1 John |
| Eph | Ephesians | 2 John | 2 John |
| Phil | Philippians | 3 John | 3 John |
| Col | Colossians | Jude | Jude |
| 1 Thes | 1 Thessalonians | Rev | Revelation |
| 2 Thes | 2 Thessalonians | | |

# -A-

**AARON** (brother of Moses and first high priest of Israel). For a description of Aaron's life and work, see **Ex 4:14; 5:1; 7:10–20; 17:12; 28:1; 32:3–5,35 • Lev 8:2–27; 10:8 • Num 4:19; 16:3; 17:3–10; 20:12,28.** Aaron is also mentioned in 1 Chr 6:49 • Pss 105:26; 133:2 • Luke 1:5 • Acts 7:40 • Heb 5:4; 7:11; 9:4.

**ABANA RIVER** (a river of Syria). 2 Kgs 5:12.

**ABASE [D]**
*Ezek 21:26* exalt him that is low, and *a* him that is high
*Luke 18:14* every one that exalteth himself shall be *a'd*
*Phil 4:12* I [Paul] know…how to be *a'd*…how to abound

**ABATED**
*Gen 8:3* hundred and fifty days the waters were *a*
*Deut 34:7* his [Moses'] eye was not dim, nor…natural force *a*

**ABBA** (an Aramaic word for "Father"). Mark 14:36 • Rom 8:15 • Gal 4:6.

**ABDON** (a judge of Israel). Judg 12:13,15.

**ABED-NEGO** (a companion of Daniel). Dan 2:49; 3:12–30. *Azariah:* Dan 1:7.

**ABEL** (a son of Adam). **Gen 4:2–25** • Matt 23:35 • Luke 11:51 • Heb 11:4; 12:24.

**ABIA.** See *Abijah.*

**ABIATHAR** (a high priest in David's time). 1 Sam 22:20–22; 23:6,9; 30:7 • 2 Sam 8:17; 15:24–35; 17:15; 19:11; 20:25 • 1 Kgs 1:7–42; 2:22–35; 4:4 • 1 Chr 15:11; 18:16; 24:6; 27:34 • Mark 2:26.

**ABIDE [ING, TH]**
*1 Kgs 8:13* the earth a settled place for thee [God] to *a* in
*Ps 15:1* LORD, who shall *a* in thy tabernacle?
*Ps 91:1* *a* under the shadow of the Almighty
*Ps 119:90* thou [God] hast established the earth…it *a'th*
*Eccl 1:4* another generation cometh…earth *a'th* for ever
*Nah 1:6* who can *a* in…fierceness of his [God's] anger?
*Luke 2:8* shepherds *a'ing* in the field, keeping watch
*Luke 9:4* whatsoever house ye enter into, there *a*
*Luke 19:5* Zacchaeus…to day I [Jesus] must *a* at thy house
*John 3:36* believeth not the Son…wrath…*a'th* on him

*John 12:46* whosoever believeth on me [Jesus]…not *a* in darkness

*John 14:16* another Comforter…may *a* with you for ever

*John 15:4 A* in me [Jesus], and I in you

*John 15:5* He that *a'th* in me [Jesus]…bringeth…fruit

*John 15:10* keep my [Jesus'] commandments…*a* in my love

*1 Cor 3:14* any man's work *a* which he hath built

*1 Cor 13:13 a'th* faith, hope, charity … greatest … is charity

*Phil 1:25* I [Paul] shall *a*…with you all for your…joy

*1 Pet 1:23* Born…by the word of God…*a'th* for ever

*1 John 2:10* He that loveth his brother *a'th* in the light

*1 John 2:17* but he that doeth the will of God *a'th* for ever

*1 John 2:28 a* in him [Jesus]… confidence…at his coming

*1 John 3:14* He that loveth not his brother *a'th* in death

*1 John 3:15* no murderer hath eternal life *a'ing* in him

**ABIGAIL** (a wife of David). 1 Sam 25:3–42; 27:3; 30:5 • 2 Sam 2:2; 3:3 • 1 Chr 3:1.

**ABIJAH** (son and successor of Rehoboam as king of Judah).

2 Chr 11:20–22. *Abia:* Matt 1:7. *Abijam:* 1 Kgs 14:31; **15:1–8.**

**ABIJAIM.** See *Abijah.*

**ABILENE** (a Roman section of Palestine). Luke 3:1.

**ABIMELECH**
1. A Philistine king in Abraham's time. Gen 20:2–18; 21:22–32; 26:1–31.
2. A son of Gideon. Judg 8:31; **9:1–56;** 10:1 • 2 Sam 11:21.

**ABIRAM** (leader of a rebellion against Moses). **Num 16:1–27;** 26:9 • Deut 11:6 • Ps 106:17.

**ABISHAG** (David's nurse in his old age). 1 Kgs 1:3–4,15; 2:17,21–22.

**ABISHAI** (deputy commander in David's army). 1 Sam 26:6–9 • 2 Sam 2:18,24; 3:30; 10:10–14; 16:9–11; 18:2–12; 19:21; 20:6,10; 21:17; 23:18 • 1 Chr 2:16; 11:20; 18:12; 19:11,15.

**ABISHALOM.** See *Absalom.*

**ABLE TO DELIVER**
*Isa 36:14* Let not Hezekiah deceive…not be *a-t-d* you
*Ezek 7:19* gold…not be *a-t-d* them in the day of the…LORD

*Dan 3:17* God…is **a-t-d** us [Daniel's friends]

**ABNER** (commander of King Saul's army). 1 Sam 14:50–51; 17:55–57; 20:25; 26:5–15 • 2 Sam 2:8–30; 3:6–37; 4:1,12 • 1 Kgs 2:5,32 • 1 Chr 26:28; 27:21.

## ABOLISH [ED]

*Isa 2:18* the idols he [God] shall utterly **a**

*Isa 51:6* my [God's] righteousness shall not be **a'ed**

*Eph 2:15* **a'ed** in his [Jesus'] flesh … enmity … making peace

*2 Tim 1:10* Jesus Christ, who hath **a'ed** death

## ABOMINATION OF DESOLATION

*Matt 24:15* see the **a-o-d**… stand in the holy place

*Mark 13:14* see the **a-o-d**… standing where it ought not

## ABOMINATION TO THE LORD, THINGS CONSIDERED AN

1. Graven images (Deut 7:25)

2. The froward, or wicked (Prov 3:32)

3. A false balance (Prov 11:1)

4. Lying lips (Prov 12:22)

5. Sacrifice of the wicked (Prov 15:8)

6. Thoughts of the wicked (Prov 15:26)

7. Every one that is proud in heart (Prov 16:5)

## ABOUND [ED]

*Rom 5:15* the grace of God… hath **a'ed** unto many

*Rom 5:20* sin **a'ed,** grace did much more **a**

*Rom 6:1* Shall we continue in sin, that grace may **a?**

*Rom 15:13* **a** in hope, through the power of the Holy Ghost

*2 Cor 8:7* in your love…see that ye **a** in this grace also

*Eph 1:8* he [God] hath **a'ed** toward us in all wisdom

*Phil 4:12* I [Paul] know…how to be abased…how to **a**

*1 Thes 3:12* increase and **a** in love one toward another

## ABOVE

*Gen 1:7* God…divided the waters…**a** the firmament

*Ex 19:5* a peculiar treasure unto me [God] **a** all people

*Ex 20:4* not make…likeness of any thing…in heaven **a**

*Deut 7:6* chosen thee to be a special people…**a** all people

*1 Kgs 8:23* no God like thee, in heaven **a,** or on earth beneath

*1 Chr 16:25* great is the LORD… to be feared **a** all gods

*1 Chr 29:11* thou [God] art exalted as head **a** all

11

*2 Chr 2:5* for great is our God *a* all gods

*Esth 2:17* the king loved Esther *a* all the women

*Ps 8:1* who [God] hast set thy glory *a* the heavens

*Ps 57:5* Be thou exalted, O God, *a* the heavens

*Ps 95:3* For the LORD is…a great King *a* all gods

*Ps 99:2* The LORD…is high *a* all the people

*Prov 31:10* a virtuous woman? For her price is far *a* rubies

*Jer 17:9* The heart is deceitful *a* all things

*Dan 6:3* Daniel was preferred *a* the…princes

*Matt 10:24* The disciple is not *a* his master

*John 8:23* Ye are from beneath; I [Jesus] am from *a*

*1 Cor 10:13* God…not suffer you…tempted *a*…ye are able

*Eph 1:21* Far *a* all principality, and power, and might

*Eph 3:20* unto him [Jesus]… able to do…*a* all that we ask

*Eph 4:6* One God…who is *a* all, and through all

*Eph 6:16* *A* all, taking the shield of faith

*Phil 2:9* given him [Jesus] a name…*a* every name

*Col 3:1* seek those things which are *a*

*Col 3:2* Set your affection on things *a,* not on…the earth

*Jas 1:17* Every good…and… perfect gift is from *a*

*Jas 3:17* Wisdom…from *a* is first pure, then…gentle

**ABRAHAM** (father of the nation of Israel). Also known as *Abram.* See **Gen 11:26–25:10** for a sketch of Abraham.

1. Called by the Lord to a new land (Gen 12:1–6)

2. Promised many descendants (Gen 12:1–7; 13:14–18; 15:5–21; 17:1–9; 22:15–19)

3. Separated from Lot (Gen 13:1–12)

4. Blessed by Melchizekek (Gen 14:17–20)

5. Son Ishmael born to Hagar (Gen 16:15–16)

6. Name changed from Abram to Abraham (Gen 17:5)

7. Circumcised with his household (Gen 17:10–27)

8. Interceded for Sodom and Gomorrah (Gen 18:23–33)

9. Son Isaac born to Sarah (Gen 21:1–8)

10. Prevented from sacrificing Isaac (Gen 22:1–14)

11. Death of Sarah (Gen 23:1–20)

12. Death of Abraham (Gen 25:7–10)

Abraham is mentioned several times in the New Testament: Matt 1:1–2,17; 3:9; 8:11; 22:32 • Mark 12:26 • Luke 1:55,73; 3:8,34; 13:16,28; 16:23–25, 29–30; 19:9; 20:37 • John

8:39–58 • Acts 3:13,25; 7:2–32; 13:26 • Rom 4:1–16; 9:7; 11:1 • 2 Cor 11:22 • Gal 3:6–18; 4:22 • Heb 2:16; 6:13; 7:1–9; 11:8,17 • Jas 2:21,23 • 1 Pet 3:6.

**ABRAM.** See *Abraham.*

**ABSALOM** (a son of King David who tried to seize his father's throne). 2 Sam 3:3; 13:1,4,20–39; 14:1–33; **15:1–18:33;** 19:1–10; 20:6 • 1 Kgs 1:6; 2:7 • 1 Chr 3:2 • 2 Chr 11:20–21. *Abishalom:* 1 Kgs 15:2–10.

## ABUNDANCE
*1 Kgs 18:41* Elijah said … there is a sound of *a* of rain
*Ps 37:11* meek shall … delight … in the *a* of peace
*Eccl 5:12 a* of the rich will not suffer him to sleep
*Matt 12:34* out of the *a* of the heart the mouth speaketh
*Luke 12:15* life consisteth not in the *a* … he possesseth

## ABUNDANT
*1 Cor 12:24* more *a* honour to that part which lacked
*2 Cor 4:15 a* grace might … redound to the glory of God
*2 Cor 11:23* in labours more *a,* in stripes above measure
*1 Tim 1:14* grace of our Lord was exceeding *a* with faith

*1 Pet 1:3* according to his [God's] *a* mercy … hath begotten us … a lively hope

## ACCEPT [ED]
*Job 42:9* the LORD also *a'ed* Job
*Jer 14:12* I [God] will not *a* them … consume them by the sword
*Jer 37:20* let my supplication … be *a'ed* before thee [God]
*Amos 5:22* burnt offerings … I [God] will not *a* them
*Mal 1:10* neither will I [God] *a* an offering at your hand
*Luke 4:24* No prophet is *a'ed* in his own country
*Acts 10:35* feareth him [God] … is *a'ed* with him

## ACCEPTABLE
*Ps 19:14* meditation of my heart … *a* in thy [God's] sight
*Prov 21:3* To do justice … is more *a* … than sacrifice
*Isa 61:2* To proclaim the *a* year of the LORD
*Luke 4:19* To preach the *a* year of the Lord
*Rom 12:1* bodies a living sacrifice … *a* unto God
*Eph 5:10* Proving what is *a* unto the Lord
*1 Tim 2:3* good and *a* in the sight of God
*1 Pet 2:5* spiritual sacrifices, *a* to God by Jesus Christ

## ACCESS

*Rom 5:2* By whom [Jesus] …we have *a*…into this grace

*Eph 2:18* through him [Jesus] we…have *a*…unto the Father

*Eph 3:12* In whom [Jesus] we have…*a* with confidence

## ACCOMPLISHED

*Isa 40:2* Speak…to Jerusalem…her warfare is *a*

*Jer 25:12* seventy years are *a,* that I [God] will punish the king of Babylon

*Luke 2:6* days were *a* that she [Mary] should be delivered

*Luke 12:50* how am I [Jesus] straitened till it be *a*

*Luke 18:31* things…concerning the Son of man shall be *a*

*John 19:28* Jesus knowing that all things were now *a*

## ACCORD

*Acts 1:14* These all continued with one *a* in prayer

*Acts 2:1* Pentecost was…come, they were all with one *a*

*Acts 2:46* one *a*…and breaking bread from house to house

*Phil 2:2* having the same love, being of one *a*

## ACCOUNT [ED]

*Ps 144:3* the son of man, that thou makest *a* of him!

*Matt 12:36* idle word that men…speak, they shall give *a*

*Luke 16:2* *a* of thy stewardship…thou mayest be no longer steward

*Luke 20:35* *a'ed* worthy…neither marry, nor are given in marriage

*Luke 21:36* *a'ed* worthy to… stand before the Son of man

*Luke 22:24* strife among them, which…be *a'ed* the greatest

*Rom 14:12* every one…shall give *a* of himself to God

*Gal 3:6* Abraham believed God…*a'ed*…for righteousness

*Phil 4:17* I [Paul] desire fruit that may abound to your *a*

*Phlm 1:18* oweth thee ought, put that on mine [Paul's] *a*

*1 Pet 4:5* give *a* to him…ready to judge…the dead

## ACCURSED

*Josh 6:18* keep yourselves from the *a* thing

*Josh 7:1* For Achan…took of the *a* thing

*Rom 9:3* myself [Paul] were *a* from Christ for…kinsmen

*1 Cor 12:3* no man speaking by the Spirit…calleth Jesus *a*

## ACCUSATION

*Matt 27:37* over his head his *a*…JESUS THE KING OF THE JEWS

*Luke 6:7* Pharisees watched him [Jesus]…find an *a* against him

*John 18:29* Pilate … said, What *a* bring ye against this man?

## ACCUSE [D]
*Matt 12:10* heal on the sabbath day … they might *a* him [Jesus]

*Matt 27:12* *a'd* of the chief priests … he [Jesus] answered nothing

*Luke 3:14* neither *a* any falsely … content with … wages

*Luke 11:54* catch something out of his [Jesus'] mouth, that they might *a* him

*Luke 23:2* *a* him [Jesus] … We found this fellow perverting the nation

**ACELDAMA** (a burial ground purchased with Judas's betrayal money). Acts 1:19.

**ACHAIA** (a Roman province of Greece visited by Paul). Acts 18:12,27; **19:21** • Rom 15:26; 16:5 • 1 Cor 16:15 • 2 Cor 1:1; 9:2; 11:10 • 1 Thes 1:7–8.

**ACHAN** (a warrior under Joshua executed for his disobedience). **Josh 7:1–26;** 22:20. *Achar:* 1 Chr 2:7.

**ACHAZ.** See *Ahaz.*

**ACHISH** (a Philistine king who aided David). 1 Sam 21:10–14; 27:2–12; 28:1–2; 29:6–9.

## ACKNOWLEDGE
*Ps 51:3* I *a* my transgressions … my sin is ever before me

*Prov 3:6* ways *a* him [God], and he shall direct thy paths

*Jer 3:13* *a* thine iniquity … that thou hast transgressed against the LORD

*Jer 14:20* *a,* O LORD, our wickedness … sinned against thee

## ACQUAINTED
*Ps 139:3* Thou [God] … art *a* with all my ways

*Isa 53:3* a man of sorrows, and *a* with grief

## ACTS
*Deut 11:7* eyes have seen all the great *a* of the LORD

*1 Sam 12:7* reason with you … righteous *a* of the LORD

*Ps 103:7* his [God's] *a* unto the children of Israel

*Ps 106:2* *a* of the LORD? who can show forth all his praise?

*Ps 145:4* One generation shall declare thy [God's] mighty *a*

*Ps 150:2* Praise him [God] for his mighty *a*

**ACTS OF THE APOSTLES, BOOK OF.** The one book of history in the New Testament that traces the expansion of the early church from the ascension of Jesus to Paul's imprisonment in Rome—a period of about thirty-five years. Acts shows how the Christian witness spread in accordance with the Great Commission of Jesus (see Acts 1:8).

**ADAM** (the first person created by God). **Gen 2:19–5:5** • Deut 32:8 • 1 Chr 1:1 • Job 31:33 • Luke 3:38 • Rom 5:14 • 1 Cor 15:22,45 • 1 Tim 2:13–14 • Jude 14.

**ADMAH** (a city destroyed with Sodom and Gomorrah). Gen 10:19; 14:2,8 • Deut 29:23 • Hos 11:8.

**ADMONISH [ING]**
*Rom 15:14* ye also are…able also to *a* one another
*Col 3:16* *a'ing* one another in psalms and hymns
*2 Thes 3:15* not as an enemy, but *a* him as a brother

**ADONIJAH** (a son of King David and rival of Solomon for the throne). 2 Sam 3:4 • **1 Kgs 1:5–53;** 2:13–28 • 1 Chr 3:2.

**ADOPTION**
*Rom 8:15* Spirit of *a,* whereby we cry, Abba, Father
*Rom 8:23* waiting for the *a*… the redemption of our body

*Gal 4:5* them…under the law…receive the *a* of sons
*Eph 1:5* predestinated us unto the *a* of children by Jesus

**ADRIA** (the Adriatic Sea). Acts 27:27.

**ADULTERY**
*Ex 20:14* Thou shalt not commit *a*
*Lev 20:10* *a*…neighbour's wife…adulterer…put to death
*Deut 5:18* Neither shalt thou commit *a*
*Prov 6:32* whoso committeth *a*…destroyeth his own soul
*Jer 7:9* and commit *a*…and walk after other gods
*Matt 5:28* looketh on a woman to lust…hath committed *a*
*Mark 10:11* put away his wife, and marry another, committeth *a*
*John 8:3* brought unto him [Jesus] a woman taken in *a*
*Gal 5:19* works of the flesh are…*A,* fornication
*2 Pet 2:14* eyes full of *a*…cannot cease from sin

**ADVERSARY [IES]**
*Deut 32:43* he [God] will…render vengeance to his *a'ies*
*1 Sam 2:10* *a'ies* of the LORD shall be broken
*1 Kgs 5:4* hath given me rest… there is neither *a* nor evil

**16**

*Esth 7:6* The *a* and enemy is this wicked Haman

*Ps 69:19* mine *a'ies* are all before thee [God]

*Ps 74:10* how long shall the *a* reproach?

*Ps 109:29* Let mine *a'ies* be clothed with shame

*Nah 1:2* LORD will take vengeance on his *a'ies*

*Matt 5:25* Agree with thine *a* ... in the way with him

*Luke 18:3* widow ... came ... saying, Avenge me of mine *a*

*Luke 21:15* wisdom, which all your *a'ies* shall not ... resist

*1 Cor 16:9* great door ... is opened ... many *a'ies*

*1 Pet 5:8* *a* the devil ... seeking whom he may devour

**ADVERSITY**

*Ps 35:15* mine *a* they rejoiced, and gathered ... together

*Prov 17:17* a brother is born for *a*

*Prov 24:10* faint in the day of *a,* thy strength is small

*Isa 30:20* bread of *a,* and the water of affliction

**ADVOCATE**

*1 John 2:1* we have an *a* with the Father, Jesus Christ

**AFFECTION**

*Rom 1:31* Without understanding ... without natural *a*

*Col 3:2* Set your *a* on things above, not ... on the earth

*Col 3:5* uncleanness, inordinate *a,* evil concupiscence

*2 Tim 3:3* Without natural *a,* trucebreakers, false accusers

**AFFLICT [ED]**

*Ex 1:11* taskmasters to *a* them [Israelites] with their burdens

*Ex 1:12* more they *a'ed* them [Israelites] ... more they ... grew

*Ex 22:22* not *a* any widow, or fatherless child

*Ruth 1:21* Almighty hath *a'ed* me [Naomi]

*1 Kgs 11:39* I [God] will for this *a* the seed of David

*2 Kgs 17:20* LORD rejected ... Israel, and *a'ed* them

*Job 34:28* he [God] heareth the cry of the *a'ed*

*Ps 44:2* thou [God] didst *a* the people, and cast them out

*Ps 88:15* I am *a'ed* and ready to die

*Ps 90:15* the days wherein thou [God] hast *a'ed* us

*Ps 119:71* I have been *a'ed* ... learn thy [God's] statutes

*Ps 140:12* maintain the cause of the *a'ed*

*Isa 49:13* the LORD ... will have mercy upon his *a'ed*

*Isa 53:4* esteem him [God's servant] stricken ... smitten ... *a'ed*

*Lam 1:12* LORD hath *a'ed* me in ... his fierce anger

*Lam 3:33* he [God] doth not *a* willingly nor grieve

*Nah 1:12* Though I have *a'ed* thee [God], I will *a* thee no more

*Matt 24:9* *a'ed,* and shall kill you...for my [Jesus']...sake

*Heb 11:37* wandered about in sheepskins...*a'ed,* tormented

*Jas 4:9* Be *a'ed*...your laughter be turned to mourning

*Jas 5:13* *a'ed?* let him pray. Is any merry...sing psalms

## AFFLICTION [S]

*Gen 29:32* the LORD hath looked upon my [Leah's] *a*

*Ex 3:7* I [God] have...seen the *a* of my people

*Deut 16:3* unleavened bread... the bread of *a*

*Deut 26:7* the LORD...looked on our *a*...and our oppression

*Job 30:16* days of *a* have taken hold upon me

*Ps 25:18* Look upon mine *a* and my pain

*Ps 34:19* Many are the *a's* of the righteous

*Ps 119:153* mine *a*...for I do not forget thy [God's] law

*Ps 132:1* LORD, remember David, and all his *a's*

*Isa 30:20* bread of adversity, and the water of *a*

*Lam 1:3* Judah is gone into captivity because of *a*

*2 Cor 4:17* light *a*...worketh for us...exceeding...glory

*Col 1:24* fill up that...behind of the *a's* of Christ

*2 Tim 4:5* endure *a's*...make full proof of thy ministry

*Jas 1:27* visit the fatherless and widows in their *a*

## AFRAID

*Gen 3:10* I [Adam] was *a*...and I hid myself

*Gen 28:17* he [Jacob] was *a*... How dreadful is this place

*Ex 3:6* Moses...was *a* to look upon God

*Ex 14:10* Egyptians marched after them [Israelites]... they were sore *a*

*Num 22:3* Moab was sore *a* of the people [Israelites]

*Deut 7:18* not be *a*...remember what the LORD...did

*Deut 31:6* nor be *a*...thy God... will not fail thee

*Josh 1:9* be not *a*...for the LORD...is with thee

*1 Sam 18:12* Saul was *a* of David...the LORD was with him

*Esth 7:6* Haman was *a* before the king and the queen

*Job 3:25* that which I was *a* of is come unto me

*Job 5:21* neither shalt thou be *a* of destruction

*Ps 27:1* LORD...strength of my life; of whom shall I be *a?*

*Ps 56:3* What time I am *a,* I will trust in thee [God]

*Ps 56:11* In God have I put my trust … I will not be *a* what man can do unto me

*Ps 91:5* Thou shalt not be *a* for the terror by night

*Isa 12:2* not be *a* … Jehovah is my strength

*Jer 1:8* be not *a* … I [God] am with thee to deliver thee

*Jer 2:12* Be astonished … be horribly *a* … saith the LORD

*Jer 42:11* not *a* of the king of Babylon … I [God] … with you

*Jer 42:16* famine, whereof ye were *a*, shall follow

*Dan 4:5* a dream … made me [Daniel] *a* … visions … troubled me

*Jon 1:5* mariners were *a*, and cried every man unto his god

*Matt 14:27* Jesus spake … it is I; be not *a*

*Matt 17:7* Jesus … said, Arise, and be not *a*

*Matt 25:25* I was *a*, and … hid thy talent in the earth

*Matt 28:10* Be not *a:* go tell my [Jesus'] brethren that they go into Galilee

*Mark 6:50* Be of good cheer: it is I [Jesus]; be not *a*

*Mark 9:32* they [the disciples] understood not … and were *a* to ask him [Jesus]

*Luke 2:9* and they [shepherds] were sore *a*

*Luke 12:4* Be not *a* of them that kill the body

*John 14:27* Let not your heart be troubled, neither let it be *a*

*Acts 9:26* they [apostles] were all *a* of him [Paul]

*Gal 4:11* I [Paul] am *a* of you, lest I … labour in vain

**AGABUS** (a prophet who warned of a famine and foretold Paul's arrest in Jerusalem). Acts 11:28; 21:10.

**AGAG** (a king of Amalek who was killed by Samuel). Num 24:7 • **1 Sam 15:8–33.**

**AGAR.** See *Hagar.*

**AGREE [D]**

*Amos 3:3* Can two walk together, except they be *a'd*

*Matt 5:25* *A* with … adversary quickly … in the way with him

*Matt 20:13* didst not thou *a* with me for a penny?

*Mark 14:56* false witness against him [Jesus], but their witness *a'd* not

**AGRIPPA** (a ruler before whom Paul made his defense at Caesarea). Acts 25:13–26; **26:1–32.**

**AHAB** (a king of Israel whose wicked reign led to idol worship). **1 Kgs 16:28–22:40** • 2 Kgs 1:1; 3:1,5; 9:7–29;

10:1–30; 21:3,13 • **2 Chr 18:1–34;** 21:6,13; 22:3–8 • Mic 6:16.

**AHASUERUS** (a king of Persia who married Esther). Esth 1:1–3:12; 6:2–10:3.

**AHAVA** (a town or river in Babylonia). Ezra 8:15,21,31.

**AHAZ** (a king of Judah who practiced idol worship). **2 Kgs 15:38–16:20** • 2 Chr 28:1–27 • Isa 1:1; 7:1–3,10–12; 14:28; 38:8 • Hos 1:1 • Mic 1:1. *Achaz:* Matt 1:9.

**AHAZIAH**
   1. A king of Israel who worshiped the pagan god Baal. 1 Kgs 22:40,49–51 • 2 Kgs 1:2,18 • 1 Chr 3:11 • 2 Chr 20:35–37.
   2. A king of Judah who fell into idol worship. 2 Kgs 8:24–9:28 • 2 Chr 22:1–9. *Azariah:* 2 Chr 22:6.

**AHIJAH** (a prophet in Solomon's time who foretold the division of the kingdom). **1 Kgs 11:29–39;** 14:2,18; 15:29 • 2 Chr 9:29; 10:15.

**AHIMAAZ** (a person who kept David informed about Abslom's rebellion). **2 Sam 15:27,36;** 17:17,20; 18:19–29 • 1 Chr 6:8–9,53.

**AHIMELECH** (high priest during King Saul's reign). 1 Sam 21:1–2,8; 22:9–20; 23:6 • 2 Sam 8:17 • 1 Chr 24:3,6,31.

**AHITHOPHEL** (one of David's aides who joined Absalom's rebellion against the king). 2 Sam 15:12–34; **16:15–23; 17:1–23** • 2 Sam 23:34 • 1 Chr 27:33–34.

**AI** (a Canaanite city captured by Joshua). **Josh 7:2–8:29;** 9:3; 10:1–2; 12:9 • Ezra 2:28 • Neh 7:32 • Jer 49:3. *Aiath:* Isa 10:28. *Aija:* Neh 11:31. *Hai:* Gen 12:8.

**AIATH.** See *Ai.*

**AIJA.** See *Ai.*

**ALARM**
*Jer 4:19* the sound of the trumpet, the *a* of war
*Joel 2:1* an *a*…for the day of the LORD cometh

**ALIEN**
*Ex 18:3* I have been an *a* in a strange land
*Job 19:15* a stranger: I [Job] am an *a* in their sight
*Ps 69:8* stranger…*a* unto my mother's children

**ALIVE**
*Gen 7:23* Noah only remained *a,* and they…with him

*Ps 41:2* The LORD will preserve him, and keep him *a*

*Mark 16:11* heard that he [Jesus] was *a*...had been seen

*Luke 15:24* my son was dead, and is *a* again

*Acts 1:3* he [Jesus] showed himself *a* after his passion

*Rom 6:11* dead...unto sin, but *a* unto God through Jesus

*1 Cor 15:22* even so in Christ shall all be made *a*

*1 Thes 4:17* are *a*...caught up together...to meet the Lord

*Rev 1:18* I [Jesus] am *a*...and have the keys...of death

*Rev 2:8* first and the last, which was dead, and is *a*

## ALMIGHTY GOD

*Gen 17:1* I am the *A-G*...be thou perfect

*Rev 19:15* treadeth the winepress of the...wrath of *A-G*

## ALMS

*Matt 6:1* do not your *a* before men, to be seen of them

*Luke 12:33* give *a;* provide...a treasure...that faileth not

*Acts 10:4* thine [Cornelius's] *a* are come up...before God

## ALONE

*Gen 2:18* not good that the man should be *a*

*Gen 32:24* Jacob was left *a*...wrestled a man with him

*Ex 24:2* Moses *a* shall come near the LORD

*Num 11:14* I [Moses] am not able to bear all this people *a*

*Job 7:16* let me *a;* for my [Job's] days are vanity

*Ps 86:10* thou art great...thou art God *a*

*Ps 148:13* praise the...LORD... his name *a* is excellent

*Eccl 4:10* woe to him that is *a* when he falleth

*Isa 2:11* the LORD *a* shall be exalted

*Dan 10:7* And I Daniel *a* saw the vision

*Matt 4:4* It is written, Man shall not live by bread *a*

*Matt 14:23* a mountain...to pray...he [Jesus] was there *a*

*Mark 1:24* Let us *a;* what have we to do with thee...Jesus

*Mark 14:6* Let her *a*...she hath wrought a good work

*Luke 5:21* Who can forgive sins, but God *a?*

*John 12:24* a corn of wheat fall...and die, it abideth *a*

*John 17:20* Neither pray I [Jesus] for these *a*

*Jas 2:17* faith, if it hath not works, is dead, being *a*

## ALPHA AND OMEGA (the first and last letters of the Greek alphabet). Rev 1:8,11; 21:6; 22:13.

21

**ALPHAEUS.** See *Cleophas.*

**ALTAR [S]**

*1 Kgs 1:50* Adonijah...caught hold on the horns of the *a*

*1 Kgs 8:22* Solomon stood before the *a*...in the presence of all...Israel

*Ezek 6:4* *a's* shall be desolate, and...images...broken

*Luke 1:11* angel...standing on the right side of the *a*

*Acts 17:23* an *a* with this inscription, TO THE UN-KNOWN GOD

**ALTARS BUILT BY OLD TESTAMENT PERSONALI-TIES**

1. Noah (Gen 8:20)
2. Abraham (Gen 12:7)
3. Isaac (Gen 26:25)
4. Jacob at Shalem (Gen 33:20)
5. Jacob at Bethel (Gen 35:7)
6. Moses (Ex 17:15)
7. Joshua (Josh 8:30)
8. Gideon (Judg 6:24)
9. Saul (1 Sam 14:35)
10. David (2 Sam 24:25)

**ALWAYS**

*Gen 6:3* My [God's] spirit shall not *a* strive with man

*1 Chr 16:15* mindful *a* of his [God's] covenant

*Ps 16:8* LORD *a* before me...he is at my right hand

*Ps 103:9* He [God] will not *a* chide: neither...keep his anger for ever

*Prov 5:19* be thou ravished *a* with her love

*Mark 14:7* the poor with you *a*...me [Jesus] ye have not *a*

*Luke 18:1* men ought *a* to pray, and not to faint

*Acts 7:51* ye do *a* resist the Holy Ghost

*Rom 1:9* I [Paul] make mention of you *a* in my prayers

*1 Cor 1:4* I [Paul] thank my God *a* on your behalf

*1 Cor 15:58* *a* abounding in the work of the Lord

*2 Cor 4:10* *A* bearing about... the dying of the Lord

*Eph 5:20* Giving thanks *a* for all things unto God

**AMALEKITES** (tribal enemies of the Israelites). Gen 14:7 • Num 13:29; 14:25,43–45 • Judg 6:3,33; 7:12; 10:12; 12:15 • 1 Sam 14:48; 15:6–8,15–32; 27:8; 30:1,18 • 2 Sam 1:1 • 1 Chr 4:43.

**AMASA** (commander of Absalom's rebel army). 2 Sam 17:25; 19:13; 20:4–12 • 1 Kgs 2:5,32 • 2 Chr 2:17.

**AMAZED**

*Ex 15:15* dukes of Edom shall be *a*...inhabitants of Canaan shall melt away

*Matt 12:23* people were ***a*** ... Is not this the son of David?

*Matt 19:25* disciples heard it, they were exceedingly ***a***

*Mark 1:27* all ***a,*** insomuch that they questioned

*Mark 2:12* all ***a*** ... We never saw it on this fashion

*Mark 6:51* they were sore ***a*** ... beyond measure

*Mark 9:15* people ... were ... ***a,*** and ... saluted him [Jesus]

*Mark 10:32* Jesus went before them: and they were ***a***

*Luke 9:43* they were all ***a*** at the ... power of God

*Acts 2:7* they were all ***a*** ... are not all these ... Galilaeans?

*Acts 2:12* were all ***a*** ... saying ... What meaneth this?

**AMAZIAH** (a king of Judah who worshiped the false gods of Edom). 2 Kgs 12:21; 13:12; 14:1–20 • **2 Chr 25:1–28.**

**AMMONITES** (tribal enemies of the Israelites). Deut 2:20 • 1 Sam 11:11 • 1 Kgs 11:1,5 • 2 Chr 20:1; 26:8; 27:5 • Ezra 9:1 • Neh 4:7 • Jer 27:3; 40:11,14; 41:10,15; 49:1–2 • Ezek 21:20,28; 25:2–10.

**AMNON** (a son of David who was murdered by his half brother Absalom). 2 Sam 3:2; **13:1–39.**

**AMON** (an evil king of Judah who was assassinated by his own servants). **2 Kgs 21:18–25** • **2 Chr 33:20–25** • Jer 1:2; 25:3 • Zeph 1:1 • Matt 1:10.

**AMORITES** (tribal enemies of the Israelites). Gen 10:16; 14:13; 15:16,21; 48:22 • Ex 3:8,17; 13:5; 23:23; 33:2; 34:11 • Num 13:29; 21:13–34; 22:2; 32:33,39; • Deut 1:4–44; 2:24; 3:2–9; 4:46–47; 7:1; 20:17; 31:4 • Josh 2:10; 3:10; 5:1; 7:7; 9:1,10; 10:5–12; 12:2,8; 13:4,10,21; 24:8–18 • Judg 1:34–36; 3:5; 6:10; 10:8,11; 11:19–23 • 1 Sam 7:14 • 2 Sam 21:2 • 1 Kgs 4:19; 9:20; 21:26 • 2 Kgs 21:11 • 1 Chr 1:14 • 2 Chr 8:7 • Ezra 9:1 • Neh 9:8 • Pss 135:11; 136:19 • Ezek 16:3,45 • Amos 2:9,10.

**AMOS** (a prophet against the Northern Kingdom and author of the book that bears his name). Amos is not mentioned outside the Book of Amos.

**AMOS, BOOK OF.** A prophetic book of the Old Testament written to call the people of the Northern Kingdom (Israel) back to worship of the one true God. According to Amos, true religion consists of following God's commands and treating others with justice (see Amos 5:24).

**AMRAPHEL** (a king of Shinar in Abraham's time). Gen 14:1,9.

**ANAK** (ancestor of a tribe of giants). **Num 13:22–33** • Deut 9:2 • Josh 15:13–14; 21:11 • Judg 1:20.

**ANAKIMS** (a tribe of giants). Deut 1:28; 2:10–11,21; 9:2 • Josh 11:21–22; 14:12,15.

**ANAMMELECH** (a pagan god of the Babylonians). 2 Kgs 17:31.

**ANANIAS**
1. A believer in the early church struck dead for lying. Acts 5:1–5.
2. A believer who befriended Paul after his conversion. Acts 9:10–17; 22:12.

**ANATHOTH** (a village north of Jerusalem). Josh 21:18 • 1 Kgs 2:26 • 1 Chr 6:60 • Ezra 2:23 • Neh 7:27; 11:32 • Isa 10:30 • Jer 1:1; 11:21,23; 29:27; 32:7–9.

**ANCIENT OF DAYS** (a title of God). Dan 7:9,13,22.

**ANDREW** (one of the twelve disciples of Jesus). Matt 4:18; 10:2 • Mark 1:16,29; 3:18; 13:3 • Luke 6:14 • John 1:40,44; 6:8; 12:22 • Acts 1:13.

**ANGEL APPEARANCES**
1. To Hagar during her pregnancy with Ishmael (Gen 16:7–11)
2. To Lot (Gen 19:1)
3. To Hagar and Ishmael in the wilderness (Gen 21:17)
4. To Abraham (Gen 22:11,15)
5. To Jacob at Haran (Gen 28:12; 31:11)
6. To Jacob at Mahanaim (Gen 32:1)
7. To Moses (Ex 3:2)
8. To Balaam (Num 22:22–35)
9. To Gideon (Judg 6:11–22)
10. To Samson's mother and father (Judg 13:3–21)
11. To Elijah (1 Kgs 19:5,7 • 2 Kgs 1:3,15)
12. To David (1 Chr 21:16)
13. To Gad (1 Chr 21:18)
14. To Ornan (1 Chr 21:20,27)
15. To Shadrach, Meshach, and Abed-nego (Dan 3:24–28)
16. To Zechariah (Zech 1:9)
17. To Joseph in Nazareth (Matt 1:20)
18. To Joseph in Bethlehem (Matt 2:13)
19. To Joseph in Egypt (Matt 2:19)
20. To Zacharias (Luke 1:11–29)
21. To Mary (Luke 1:26–38)
22. To shepherds at Jesus' birth (Luke 2:9–14)
23. To Jesus in the Garden of Gethsemane (Luke 22:43)

24. To Jesus at the resurrection (Matt 28:2)

25. To women at the tomb (Matt 28:5)

26. To Mary Magdalene at the empty tomb (John 20:11–12)

27. To the apostles (Acts 5:19)

28. To Philip (Acts 8:26)

29. To Cornelius (Acts 10:3)

30. To Peter in prison (Acts 12:7–11)

31. To Paul (Acts 27:23–24)

32. To John on the isle of Patmos (Rev 1:1)

## ANGELS

*Ps 8:5* thou [God] hast made him [man] a little lower than the *a*

*Ps 148:2* Praise ye him, all his [God's] *a*

*Matt 22:30* nor are given in marriage, but are as the *a*

*Matt 25:31* Son of man shall come…holy *a* with him

*Luke 15:10* joy in the presence of the *a*…over one sinner that repenteth

*Rom 8:38* death, nor life, nor *a,* nor principalities

*1 Cor 13:1* tongues of men and of *a,* and have not charity

*Heb 13:2* some have entertained *a* unawares

## ANGER

*Gen 30:2* Jacob's *a* was kindled against Rachel

*1 Sam 11:6* spirit of God came upon Saul…*a* was kindled

*1 Sam 20:30* Saul's *a* was kindled against Jonathan

*2 Sam 12:5* David's *a* was… kindled against the man

*Ps 6:1* O LORD, rebuke me not in thine *a,* neither chasten

*Ps 30:5* For his [God's] *a* endureth but a moment

*Ps 78:58* provoked him [God] to *a* with their high places

*Ps 103:8* LORD is merciful and gracious, slow to *a*

*Prov 15:1* but grievous words stir up *a*

*Prov 16:32* He that is slow to *a* is better than the mighty

*Prov 21:14* A gift…pacifieth *a:* and a reward…wrath

*Isa 63:6* I [God] will tread down the people in mine *a*

*Jer 4:8* the fierce *a* of the LORD is not turned back

*Lam 4:16* the *a* of the LORD hath divided them

*Mic 5:15* I [God] will execute vengeance in *a* and fury upon the heathen

*Nah 1:3* LORD is slow to *a*… will not…acquit the wicked

*Mark 3:5* he [Jesus] looked… with *a*…for the hardness of their hearts

*Eph 4:31* wrath, and *a*…and evil speaking, be put away

*Col 3:8* put off all these; *a,* wrath, malice

*Col 3:21* Fathers, provoke not your children to *a*

## ANGER OF THE LORD

*Ex 4:14* the *a-o-t-L* was kindled against Moses

*Num 11:10* *a-o-t-L* was kindled…Moses also was displeased

*Num 25:3* the *a-o-t-L* was kindled against Israel

*2 Sam 6:7* the *a-o-t-L* was kindled against Uzzah

*2 Sam 24:1* the *a-o-t-L* was… against Israel and he moved David against them

*2 Kgs 24:20* through the *a-o-t-L*…Zedekiah rebelled against…Babylon

*2 Chr 25:15* the *a-o-t-L* was kindled against Amaziah

*Jer 4:8* the fierce *a-o-t-L* is not turned back

*Jer 12:13* be ashamed…because of the fierce *a-o-t-L*

*Jer 51:45* deliver ye every man his soul from the…*a-o-t-L*

## ANGUISH

*Job 15:24* *a* shall make him afraid; they shall prevail

*Ps 119:143* *a* have taken…me: yet thy [God's] commandments are my delights

*John 16:21* delivered of the child, she remembereth no more the *a*

*Rom 2:9* and *a,* upon every soul of man that doeth evil

*2 Cor 2:4* and *a*…I [Paul] wrote…with many tears

**ANNA** (a prophetess who praised the infant Jesus). Luke 2:36–38.

**ANNAS** (a high priest during Jesus' ministry). Luke 3:2 • John 18:13,24 • Acts 4:6.

## ANNUNCIATION OF JESUS' BIRTH TO JOSEPH. Matt 1:18–25.

## ANNUNCIATION OF JESUS' BIRTH TO MARY. Luke 1:26–38.

## ANOINT [ED, EST, ING]

*Ex 30:30* *a* Aaron and his sons, and consecrate them

*Ex 40:15* *a* them [Aaron's sons]…that they may minister…in the priest's office

*Lev 8:10* Moses…*a'ed* the tabernacle…and sanctified them

*Lev 8:12* the *a'ing* oil upon Aaron's head…sanctify him

*Judg 9:8* trees went forth…to *a* a king over them

*1 Sam 15:1* LORD sent me [Samuel] to *a* thee [Saul]

*1 Sam 16:13* Samuel…*a'ed* him [David] in the midst of his brethren

*2 Sam 2:4* they *a'ed* David king over the house of Judah

*1 Kgs 19:15* *a* Hazael to be king over Syria

26

*2 Chr 6:42* turn not away...
thine **a'ed:** remember...
David

*Ps 20:6* LORD saveth his **a'ed;**
he will hear...from...
heaven

*Ps 23:5* thou [God] **a'est** my
head with oil

*Isa 45:1* Thus saith the LORD to
his **a'ed,** to Cyrus

*Isa 61:1* LORD hath **a'ed** me
[God's servant]...to pro-
claim liberty

*Mark 14:8* come...to **a** my
[Jesus'] body to...burying

*Mark 16:1* bought...spices,
that they [women] might...
**a** him [Jesus]

*Luke 7:46* this woman hath
**a'ed** my [Jesus'] feet

*John 9:6* he [Jesus] **a'ed** the
eyes of the blind man

*John 12:3* Mary...**a'ed** the feet
of Jesus

*Heb 1:9* hath **a'ed** thee with
the oil of gladness

*Jas 5:14* **a'ing** him with oil in
the name of the Lord

**ANSWER**

*Job 31:35* that the Almighty
would **a** me [Job]

*Ps 27:7* have mercy...upon me,
and **a** me

*Ps 86:7* I will call upon thee
[God]...thou wilt **a** me

*Prov 15:1* A soft **a** turneth
away wrath

*Prov 26:4* **A** not a fool according to his folly

*Jer 33:3* I [God] will **a** thee, and
show thee great...things

*Luke 21:14* not to meditate
before what ye shall **a**

*1 Pet 3:15* give an **a** to every
man that asketh you a reason

*1 Pet 3:21* baptism...the **a** of a
good conscience toward God

**ANTICHRIST** (the archen-
emy of Christ). 1 John 2:18,22;
4:3 • 2 John 7.

**ANTIOCH**
1. A city in Syria. Acts 6:5;
11:19–27; 13:1; 14:26; 15:22–35;
18:22 • Gal 2:11.
2. A city in Pisidia. Acts
13:14; 14:19,21 • 2 Tim 3:11.

**APOLLOS** (a Jewish believer
from Alexandria, Egypt). Acts
18:24; 19:1 • 1 Cor 3:4–6,22; 4:6;
16:12 • Titus 3:13.

**APOSTLE [S]**

*Matt 10:2* names of the twelve
**a's** are these

*Mark 6:30* **a's** gathered...and
told him [Jesus] all things

*Luke 6:13* he [Jesus] chose
twelve...he named **a's**

*Acts 1:26* Matthias...num-
bered with the eleven **a's**

*Acts 2:42* they continued stedfastly in the **a's'** doctrine

*Acts 2:43* many wonders and
signs were done by the **a's**

*Acts 5:18* laid their hands on the *a's* ... put them in ... prison

*Acts 8:1* they [believers] were ... scattered ... except the *a's*

*Rom 1:1* Paul, a servant ... called to be an *a*

*Rom 11:13* I [Paul] am the *a* of the Gentiles

*1 Cor 1:1* Paul, called to be an *a* of Jesus Christ

*1 Cor 9:1* Am I [Paul] not an *a?* am I not free?

*1 Cor 12:28* in the church, first *a's,* secondarily prophets

*1 Cor 12:29* Are all *a's?* are all prophets? are all teachers?

*1 Cor 15:9* I [Paul] am the least of the *a's*

*2 Cor 11:13* transforming themselves into ... *a's* of Christ

*2 Cor 12:12* signs of an *a* were wrought among you

*Eph 2:20* built upon the foundation of the *a's*

*Eph 4:11* gave some, *a's;* and some, prophets

*Heb 3:1* *A* and High Priest of our profession, Christ Jesus

## APPEAR [ED, ETH, ING]

*Gen 1:9* let the dry land *a:* and it was so

*Gen 12:7* the LORD *a'ed* unto Abram ... Unto thy seed will I give this land

*Gen 35:9* God *a'ed* unto Jacob ... and blessed him

*Ex 3:2* Angel ... *a'ed* unto him [Moses] in a flame

*Ex 16:10* the glory of the LORD *a'ed* in the cloud

*1 Sam 3:21* LORD *a'ed* again ... revealed himself to Samuel

*1 Kgs 9:2* LORD *a'ed* to Solomon ... as he had ... at Gibeon

*2 Kgs 2:11* *a'ed* a chariot ... Elijah went ... by a whirlwind

*Ps 42:2* when shall I come and *a* before God?

*Ps 102:16* the LORD ... shall *a* in his glory

*Song 2:12* The flowers *a* on the earth

*Mal 3:2* who shall stand when he [God] *a'eth?*

*Matt 2:13* *a'eth* ... take the ... child ... and flee into Egypt

*Matt 2:19* Herod was dead ... the Lord *a'eth* ... to Joseph

*Matt 17:3* *a'ed* ... Moses and Elias talking with him [Jesus]

*Matt 23:27* whited sepulchres, which ... *a* beautiful outward

*Matt 24:30* then shall *a* the sign of the Son of man

*Mark 16:9* Jesus ... *a'ed* first to Mary Magdalene

*Mark 16:12* he [Jesus] *a'ed* in another form ... two of them

*Mark 16:14* he [Jesus] *a'ed* unto ... eleven as they sat at meat

*Luke 1:11* there *a'ed* unto him [Zacharias] an angel

*Luke 24:34* The Lord ... hath *a'ed* to Simon

*Acts 2:3* there *a'ed* unto them cloven tongues like as of fire

*2 Cor 5:10* all *a* before the judgment seat of Christ

*Col 3:4* then shall ye also *a* with him [Jesus]

*1 Tim 6:14* keep this commandment…until the *a'ing* of our Lord Jesus Christ

*2 Tim 1:10* made manifest by the *a'ing* of our Saviour

*2 Tim 4:1* judge the quick and the dead at his *a'ing*

*2 Tim 4:8* unto all them…that love his [Jesus'] *a'ing*

*Titus 2:13* the glorious *a'ing* of…our Saviour

*Jas 4:14* It [life] is…a vapour, that *a'eth* for a little time

*1 Pet 5:4* chief Shepherd shall *a,* ye shall receive a crown

**APPII FORUM** (a place south of Rome where believers greeted Paul). Acts 28:15.

**APPOINT [ED]**

*Num 1:50* **a** the Levites over the tabernacle of testimony

*Josh 20:2* **A** out for you cities of refuge

*Job 14:5* thou hast *a'ed* his bounds that he cannot pass

*Ps 104:19* He [God] *a'ed* the moon for seasons

*Isa 1:14* your *a'ed* feasts my [God's] soul hateth

*Luke 10:1* Lord *a'ed* other… and sent them two and two

*Acts 6:3* seven men…whom we may *a* over this business

*1 Thes 5:9* God hath not *a'ed* us to wrath, but to…salvation

*2 Tim 1:11* I [Paul] am *a'ed* a preacher, and an apostle

*Heb 1:2* whom he [God] hath *a'ed* heir [Jesus] of all things

*Heb 9:27* *a'ed*…once to die, but after this the judgment

**APPROVED**

*Acts 2:22* Jesus of Nazareth, a man *a*…by miracles

*2 Tim 2:15* Study to show thyself *a* unto God

**AQUILA** (a believer who worked with Paul at Corinth). Acts 18:2,18,26 • Rom 16:3 • 1 Cor 16:19 • 2 Tim 4:19.

**ARABAH** (the Jordan River valley). Josh 18:18.

**ARAM.** See *Syria*.

**ARARAT** (a mountainous region in Armenia where Noah's ark came to rest). **Gen 8:4** • Jer 51:27.

**ARAUNAH** (a Jebusite from whom David bought a threshing floor). 2 Sam 24:16–24. *Ornan:* 1 Chr 21:15–28 • 2 Chr 3:1.

**ARCHANGEL** (a chief angel).
1 Thes 4:16 • Jude 9.

**AREOPAGUS** (a meeting place in Athens). Acts 17:19.

**ARIEL** (a name for Jerusalem). Isa 29:1–7.

**ARIMATHAEA** (a city northwest of Jerusalem). Matt 27:57 • Mark 15:43 • Luke 23:51 • John 19:38.

**ARISE**
*Josh 1:2* now therefore *a,* go over this Jordan
*Ps 7:6* **A,** O LORD...because of the rage of mine enemies
*Ps 82:8* **A,** O God, judge the earth...inherit all nations
*Prov 31:28* Her children *a* up, and call her blessed
*Isa 60:1* **A,** shine; for thy light is come
*Jer 18:2* **A**...go down to the potter's house...hear my [God's] words
*Dan 7:17* Beasts...are four kings...*a* out of the earth
*Jon 1:2* **A,** go to Nineveh, that great city...cry against it
*Mal 4:2* shall the Sun of righteousness *a* with healing in his wings
*Matt 2:13* angel...appeareth to Joseph...saying, **A**...take the young child
*Matt 24:24* there shall *a* false Christs, and false prophets

*Mark 5:41* Damsel, I [Jesus] say unto thee, *a*
*Luke 5:24* I [Jesus] say...**A**...take up thy couch
*Luke 15:18* *a* and go to my father...I have sinned
*Luke 17:19* he [Jesus] said...**A,** go thy way: thy faith hath made thee whole
*Acts 11:7* **A,** Peter; slay and eat
*Acts 20:30* men *a,* speaking perverse things

**ARISTARCHUS** (a companion of Paul). Acts 19:29; 20:4; 27:2 • Col 4:10 • Phlm 24.

**ARK OF MOSES** (a basket in which the infant Moses was placed). Ex 2:3,5.

**ARK OF NOAH** (a wooden ship in which Noah's family escaped from the flood). **Gen 6:12–9:18** • Matt 24:38 • Luke 17:27 • 1 Pet 3:20.

**ARK OF THE COVENANT** (a wooden chest containing a pot of manna, Aaron's rod that budded, and stone tablets on which the Ten Commandments were inscribed). **Ex 25:10–22** • Num 10:33 • Deut 10:8; 31:9,25 • Josh 3:3–17; 4:7–18; 6:6–8; 8:33 • Judg 20:27 • 1 Sam 4:3–5 • 2 Sam 15:24 • 1 Kgs 3:15; 6:19; 8:1,6 • 1 Chr 15:25–29; 16:6,37; 17:1; 22:19; 28:2,18 • 2 Chr 5:2–7 • Jer

3:16. *Ark of the testimony:* Ex 25:22 • Num 7:89 • Josh 4:16.

**ARK OF THE TESTIMONY.** See *Ark of the Covenant.*

**ARM OF THE LORD**

*Isa 51:9* O *a-o-t-L;* awake, as in the ancient days

*Isa 53:1* to whom is the *a-o-t-L* revealed?

**ARMAGEDDON** (scene of the final conflict between God and the forces of evil). Rev 16:16.

**ARNON** (a river in southern Palestine). Num 21:13–28; 22:36 • Deut 2:24,36; 3:12,16; 4:48 • Josh 12:1–2; 13:9,16 • Judg 11:13–26 • 2 Kgs 10:33 • Isa 16:2 • Jer 48:20.

**ARTAXERXES I** (the Persian king in whose court Ezra and Nehemiah served). Ezra 4:7–23; 8:1 • Neh 2:1; 5:14; 13:6.

**ASA** (a king of Judah who led a religious revival). 1 Kgs 15:8–33; 16:8–29 • **2 Chr 14:1–13;** 15:2–19; 16:1–13 • Jer 41:9 • Matt 1:7–8.

**ASAHEL** (a captain in David's army). 2 Sam 2:18–32; 3:27,30; 23:24 • 1 Chr 2:16; 11:26; 27:7.

**ASCEND [ED, ING]**

*Gen 28:12* ladder ... the angels ... *a'ing* and descending

*Josh 10:7* Joshua *a'ed* from Gilgal, he ... all the people of war

*Ps 24:3* who shall *a* into the hill of the LORD

*Ps 68:18* Thou hast *a'ed* on high ... led captivity captive

*Luke 19:28* he [Jesus] went before, *a'ing* up to Jerusalem

*John 1:51* angels of God *a'ing* ... upon the Son of man

*John 6:62* see the Son of man *a* up where he was before

*John 20:17* I [Jesus] am not yet *a'ed* to my Father

*Eph 4:8* he [Jesus] *a'ed* up on high, he led captivity captive

**ASCENSION OF JESUS.** See *Jesus, Life and Ministry of.*

**ASENATH** (Joseph's Egyptian wife). Gen 41:45,50; 46:20.

**ASER.** See *Asher.*

**ASHAMED**

*Gen 2:25* both naked, the man and his wife, and were not *a*

*Ps 31:17* Let me not be *a* ... for I have called upon thee [God]

*Joel 2:27* your God ... and my people shall never be *a*

*Mark 8:38* of him also shall the Son of man be *a*

*Rom 1:16* I [Paul] am not *a* of the gospel of Christ

*Rom 10:11* Whosoever believeth on him [Jesus] shall not be *a*

*2 Tim 2:15* a workman that needeth not to be *a*

*1 John 2:28* not be *a* before him [Jesus] at his coming

**ASHDOD** (a major Philistine city). Josh 11:22; 15:46–47 • 1 Sam 5:1–7; 6:17 • 2 Chr 26:6 • Neh 13:23–24 • Isa 20:1 • Jer 25:20 • Amos 1:8; 3:9 • Zeph 2:4 • Zech 9:6.

**ASHER** (a son of Jacob and ancestor of one of the twelve tribes of Israel). Gen 30:13; 35:26; 46:17; 49:20 • Ex 1:4 • Num 26:46 • 1 Chr 2:2; 7:30,40. The tribe of Asher settled in northern Canaan. Josh 19:24–31. *Aser:* Luke 2:36.

**ASHES**

*Job 2:8* he [Job] took… a potsherd to scrape himself… among the *a*

*Isa 61:3* to give unto them beauty for *a*

*Jer 25:34* Howl, ye shepherds… and wallow… in the *a*

**ASHIMA** (a pagan god of Hamath). 2 Kgs 17:30.

**ASHKELON** (a major Philistine city). Judg 14:19 • Jer 25:20; 47:5,7 • Amos 1:8 • Zeph 2:4,7 • Zech 9:5. *Askelon:* Judg 1:18.

**ASHTAROTH** (a pagan goddess of the Philistines). Judg 2:13; 10:6 • 1 Sam 7:3–4; 12:10; 31:10. *Ashtoreth:* 1 Kgs 11:33.

**ASIA** (a Roman province in Asia Minor). Acts 2:9; 6:9; 16:6; 19:10,22,26–27,31; 20:4,16,18 • 1 Cor 16:19 • 2 Cor 1:8 • 2 Tim 1:15 • 1 Pet 1:1 • Rev 1:4,11.

**ASK [ED]**

*Josh 4:6* your children *a*… What mean… these stones?

*Judg 1:1* Israel *a'ed*… Who shall go up… against the Canaanites

*1 Kgs 3:5* LORD appeared to Solomon in a dream… *A* what I shall give thee

*Ps 105:40* people *a'ed,* and he [God] brought quails

*Jer 37:17* king *a'ed* him [Jeremiah]… Is there any word from the LORD

*Matt 6:8* Father knoweth what … ye … need … before ye *a*

*Matt 7:7* *A,* and it shall be given you

*Matt 7:9* if his son *a* bread, will he give him a stone

*Matt 18:19* any thing… they shall *a,* it shall be done

*Matt 21:22* ye shall *a*… believing, ye shall receive

*Mark 14:61* high priest *a'ed* him [Jesus] ... Art thou the Christ

*Mark 15:2* Pilate *a'ed* him [Jesus], Art thou the King of the Jews

*Luke 11:13* Your ... Father give the Holy Spirit to them that *a* him

*John 14:14 a* any thing in my [Jesus'] name, I will do it

*John 16:24 a,* and ye shall receive ... your joy may be full

*Eph 3:20* exceeding abundantly above all that we *a*

*Jas 1:5* If any of you lack wisdom, let him *a* of God

*Jas 4:2* yet ye have not, because ye *a* not

*1 John 5:14 a* ... according to his [God's] will, he heareth

**ASKELON.** See *Ashkelon.*

**ASNAPPER** (an Assyrian king). Ezra 4:10.

**ASSHUR.** See *Assyria.*

**ASSUR.** See *Assyria.*

**ASSYRIA** (a dominant power in the ancient world which overthrew the Northern Kingdom, enslaved many of its inhabitants, and resettled the region with foreigners). **2 Kgs 18:9–37;** 19:35–37 • Isa 7–8; 10:12; 14:24–25 • Hos 10:6 •

Nah 3:1–19. *Asshur:* Gen 10:11; Num 24:22–24. *Assur:* Ezra 4:2.

**ATHALIAH** (a daughter of Ahab and Jezebel who seized the throne as queen of Judah). 2 Kgs 8:26; **11:1–20** • 2 Chr 22:2–12; 23:12–21.

**ATHENS** (capital city of ancient Greece and the idolatrous city where Paul preached to the philosophers). **Acts 17:15–22;** 18:1 • 1 Thes 3:1.

**ATONEMENT**

*Ex 29:36* offer ... a bullock for a sin offering for *a*

*Num 15:25* priest shall make an *a* for all ... Israel

**ATTAIN [ED]**

*Ps 139:6* knowledge is too wonderful ... I cannot *a* ... it

*Phil 3:11* I [Paul] might *a* unto the resurrection of the dead

*Phil 3:12* as though I [Paul] had already *a'ed*

*Phil 3:16* already *a'ed,* let us walk by the same rule

*1 Tim 4:6* nourished up in ... faith and of good doctrine whereunto thou hast *a'ed*

**ATTEND**

*Ps 17:1* O LORD, *a* unto my cry, give ear unto my prayer

*Ps 86:6* O LORD ... *a* to ... my supplications

33

*Prov 4:1* Hear…the instruction of a father, and *a* to know understanding

**AUGUSTUS** (emperor of the Roman Empire at the time when Jesus was born). **Luke 2:1** • Acts 25:21,25; 27:1.

**AUTHORITY**
*Prov 29:2* When the righteous are in *a,* the people rejoice
*Matt 8:9* I am a man under *a,* having soldiers under me
*Matt 20:25* they that are great exercise *a* upon them
*Matt 21:23* who gave thee [Jesus] this *a*
*Matt 21:27* Neither tell I you by what *a* I [Jesus] do these things

*Mark 1:22* he [Jesus] taught them as one that had *a*
*Luke 9:1* he [Jesus] called his … disciples … gave them…*a* over all devils
*1 Cor 15:24* when he [Jesus] shall have put down…all *a*
*1 Tim 2:12* suffer not a woman…to usurp *a* over the man

**AVEN.** See *On,* No. 2.

**AZARIAH.** See *Abed-nego; Ahaziah,* No. 2; *Uzziah.*

**AZZAH.** See *Gaza.*

# -B-

**BAAL** (a pagan Canaanite god of rain thought to provide fertility for crops and livestock and worshiped on occasion during Old Testament times by the Israelites). Num 22:41 • Judg 2:13; 6:25–32 • 1 Kgs 16:31–32; 18:19–40; 19:18; 22:53 • 2 Kgs 10:18–28; 11:18; 17:16; 21:3–4 • 2 Chr 23:17 • Jer 2:8; 7:9; 11:13,17; 12:16; 19:5; 23:13; 32:29,35 • Hos 2:8; 13:1 • Zeph 1:4. *Baalim:* 1 Sam 12:10.

**BAALAH.** See *Kirjath-jearim.*

**BAAL-BERITH** (a name under which the Canaanite god Baal was worshiped at Shechem). Judg 8:33; 9:4. *Berith:* Judg 9:46.

**BAAL-PEOR** (a name under which the Canaanite god Baal was worshiped by the Moabites). Num 25:1–9 • Deut 4:3–4 • Ps 106:28–29 • Hos 9:10. *Peor:* Num 31:1–18 • Josh 22:17.

**BAAL-ZEBUB** (a name under which the Canaanite god Baal was worshiped by the Philistines). 2 Kgs 1:2–16. *Beelzebub:* Matt 10:25; 12:24.

**BAASHA** (a king of the Northern Kingdom who gained the throne by murdering the heirs of King Jeroboam). **1 Kgs 15:16–33;** 16:1–13 • 2 Kgs 9:9 • 2 Chr 16:1–6 • Jer 41:9.

**BABEL, TOWER OF.** See *Tower of Babel.*

**BABE [S]**
*Ps 8:2* Out of the mouth of *b's* and sucklings hast thou [God] ordained strength
*Matt 21:16* Out of the mouth of *b's* and sucklings thou [God] hast perfected praise
*Luke 1:41* when Elisabeth heard...Mary, the *b* leaped in her womb
*Luke 2:16* Mary, and Joseph, and the *b* lying in a manger
*1 Pet 2:2* As newborn *b's,* desire the...milk of the word

**BABYLON** (capital city of the Babylonian Empire). Citizens of the Southern Kingdom (Judah) were taken to Babylon as captives after the fall of Jerusalem in 587 B.C. (2 Chr 36:5–21). Most references to Babylon appear in the books of 2 Kings, Jeremiah, Ezekiel, and Daniel. In the Book of Revelation, Babylon is a symbol of evil and wickedness (Rev 14:8; 16:19; 17:5; 18:2,10,21).

**BABYLON** (a powerful nation that carried the Southern Kingdom (Judah) into exile about 587 B.C.). The Babylonians were defeated by the Persians about 539 B.C., fulfilling the prophecies of Isaiah and Jeremiah. **2 Chr 36:5–21** • Isa 14:22 • Jer 50:9. *Land of the Chaldeans:* Ezek 12:13. *Sheshach:* Jer 25:26. *Shinar:* Isa 11:11.

**BACK [S]**

*Gen 19:26* But his [Lot's] wife looked *b*...and she became a pillar of salt

*Ex 14:21* LORD caused the sea to go *b* by a strong...wind

*Josh 7:8* Israel turneth their *b's* before their enemies

*2 Sam 12:23* can I [David] bring him [David's child] *b*

*Neh 9:26* they [the Israelites] were disobedient...cast thy [God's] law behind their *b's*

*Job 39:22* neither turneth he [God] *b* from the sword

*Ps 35:4* let them be turned *b* and brought to confusion

*Ps 44:18* Our heart is not turned *b*

*Prov 10:13* a rod is for the *b* of him...void of understanding

*Prov 26:3* a bridle for the ass, and a rod for the fool's *b*

*Isa 14:27* who shall turn it [God's hand] *b*

*Isa 38:17* thou [God] hast cast all my sins behind thy *b*

*Jer 4:8* anger of the LORD is not turned *b* from us

*Ezek 23:35* thou hast...cast me [God] behind thy *b*

*Dan 7:6* a leopard, which had upon the *b* of it four wings

*Matt 24:18* Neither let him... return *b* to take his clothes

*Luke 9:62* No man...looking *b,* is fit for the kingdom

*John 6:66* many of his [Jesus'] disciples went *b*

*Acts 20:20* I [Paul] kept *b* nothing...profitable unto you

**BACKSLIDER**

*Prov 14:14* The *b* in heart shall be filled with his own ways

**BACKSLIDING [S]**

*Jer 3:14* Turn, O *b* children, saith the LORD

*Jer 14:7* our *b's* are many; we have sinned

*Hos 4:16* For Israel slideth back as a *b* heifer

*Hos 14:4* I [God] will heal their *b*...love them freely

**BALAAM** (a soothsayer or wizard hired by King Balak of Moab to curse the Israelites). **Num 22:1–24:25** • Deut 23:4–5 • Josh 13:22; 24:9–10 • Mic 6:5 • 2 Pet 2:15 • Jude 11 • Rev 2:14.

**BALAC.** See *Balak.*

**BALAK** (a king of Moab who hired Balaam the soothsayer to curse the Israelites). **Num 22:1–24:25** • Josh 24:9 • Judg 11:25 • Mic 6:5. *Balac:* Rev 2:14.

**BALANCE [S]**
*Lev 19:36* Just *b's,* just weights, a just ephah
*Job 31:6* Let me be weighed in an even *b*
*Prov 11:1* A false *b* is abomination to the LORD
*Isa 40:12* Who [God] hath measured … the hills in a *b*
*Dan 5:27* Thou [Belshazzar] art weighed in the *b's,* and art found wanting
*Amos 8:5* making the ephah small … falsifying the *b's*
*Rev 6:5* he that sat on him [a black horse] had a pair of *b's* in his hand

**BALM OF GILEAD** (an aromatic gum, used for medicinal purposes, exported from Gilead in Arabia). Jer 8:22.

**BAND [S]**
*Lev 26:13* I [God] have broken the *b's* of your yoke
*Ps 119:61* The *b's* of the wicked have robbed me
*Jer 2:20* I [God] have broken thy yoke, and burst thy *b's*

*Hos 11:4* I [God] drew them … with *b's* of love
*Matt 27:27* the soldiers … gathered unto him [Jesus] the whole *b* of soldiers
*Luke 8:29* he [wild man among the tombs] brake the *b's*
*John 18:12* the *b* … took Jesus, and bound him
*Acts 10:1* Cornelius, a centurion of the *b* called … Italian *b*
*Acts 16:26* prison … doors were opened, and every one's *b's* were loosed

**BAPTISM**
*Matt 20:22* Are ye [James and John] able … to be baptized with the *b* that I [Jesus] am baptized with
*Matt 21:25* The *b* of John, whence was it
*Mark 1:4* John did … preach the *b* of repentance
*Luke 12:50* I [Jesus] have a *b* to be baptized with
*Rom 6:4* we are buried with him [Jesus] by *b* into death
*Eph 4:5* One Lord, one faith, one *b*
*Col 2:12* Buried with him [Jesus] in *b*
*1 Pet 3:21* The like figure whereunto even *b* doth also now save us

**BAPTISM OF JESUS.** See *Jesus, Life and Ministry of.*

37

## BAPTISM OF REPENTANCE

*Luke 3:3* he [John the Baptist] came...preaching the ***b-o-r*** for the remission of sins

*Acts 13:24* John...preached... the ***b-o-r*** to all the people

*Acts 19:4* Then said Paul, John verily baptized with the ***b-o-r***

## BAPTIZE [D, ING]

*Matt 3:11* he [Jesus] shall ***b*** you with the Holy Ghost

*Matt 3:13* Then cometh Jesus...unto John, to be ***b'd*** of him

*Matt 28:19* Go...and teach all nations, ***b'ing*** them in the name of the Father

*Mark 1:8* but he [Jesus] shall ***b*** you with the Holy Ghost

*Mark 16:16* He that believeth and is ***b'd*** shall be saved

*Luke 3:7* Then said he [John the Baptist] to the multitude that came forth to be ***b'd***

*John 1:28* Bethabara beyond Jordan...John was ***b'ing***

*John 3:22* he [Jesus] tarried... and ***b'd***

*John 3:23* John also was ***b'ing*** in Aenon near to Salim

*John 4:1* Jesus made and ***b'ed*** more disciples than John

*Acts 1:5* ye shall be ***b'd*** with the Holy Ghost

*Acts 2:38* Repent, and be ***b'd***... in the name of Jesus

*Acts 2:41* they that gladly received his [Peter's] word were ***b'd***

*Acts 8:12* they [the Samaritans] were ***b'd,*** both men and women

*Acts 8:36* what doth hinder me [the eunuch] to be ***b'd***

*Acts 9:18* he [Paul] received sight...arose, and was ***b'd***

*Acts 16:15* she [Lydia] was ***b'd,*** and her household

*Acts 16:33* he [Philippian jailer]...was ***b'd,*** he and all his

*Acts 22:16* arise, and be ***b'd,*** and wash away thy sins

*Rom 6:3* so many of us as were ***b'd*** into Jesus Christ were ***b'd*** into his death

*1 Cor 1:13* or were ye ***b'd*** in the name of Paul

*1 Cor 1:17* Christ sent me [Paul] not to ***b,*** but to preach the gospel

*1 Cor 12:13* by one Spirit are we all ***b'd*** into one body

*1 Cor 15:29* what shall they do which are ***b'd*** for the dead

*Gal 3:27* as many of you as have been ***b'd*** into Christ have put on Christ

**BARABBAS** (a notorious murderer and insurrectionist released by Pilate during the trial of Jesus). Matt 27:16–26 • Mark 15:7–15 • Luke 23:18 • John 18:40.

**BARAK** (a general who led the judge Deborah to victory over the Canaanites). **Judg 4:1–24** • Heb 11:32.

**BARBARIAN** (a word used by the Greeks to designate uncouth foreigners or citizens of other nations besides Greece). Acts 28:4 • Rom 1:14 • 1 Cor 14:11 • Col 3:11.

**BAR-JESUS** (a false prophet who opposed Paul and Silas). Acts 13:6–12. *Elymas:* Acts 13:8.

**BARNABAS** (a believer who befriended Paul and accompanied him on the first missionary journey). Acts 4:36–37; 9:27; 11:22–30; 12:25; **13:1–14:28;** 15:2–39 • 1 Cor 9:6 • Gal 2:1,9,13. *Joses:* Acts 4:36.

**BARREN**
*Gen 11:30* But Sarai was *b;* she had no child
*Gen 29:31* he [God] opened her [Leah's] womb ... Rachel was *b*
*Ps 113:9* He [God] maketh the *b* woman to keep house
*Luke 1:7* Elisabeth was *b,* and ... well stricken in years
*Luke 23:29* Blessed are the *b* ... wombs that never bare
*2 Pet 1:8* ye shall neither be *b* nor unfruitful in the knowledge of our Lord

**BARTHOLOMEW** (one of the twelve apostles of Jesus). Matt 10:3 • Mark 3:18 • Luke 6:14 • Acts 1:13. Probably the same person as *Nathanael:* John 1:45–46.

**BARTIMAEUS** (a blind beggar healed by Jesus). Mark 10:46–52.

**BARUCH** (friend and scribe of the prophet Jeremiah). Jer 32:12–16; 36:4–32; 43:1–7; 45:1–2.

**BARZILLAI** (a friend who helped King David during his flight from Absalom). **2 Sam 17:27–29;** 19:31–39 • 1 Kgs 2:7.

**BASHAN** (a fertile plain east of the Jordan River allotted to the half-tribe of Manasseh after the conquest of Canaan). Num 21:33–35 • Deut 3:13; 29:7 • Josh 13:11–12 • 2 Kgs 10:32–33 • Neh 9:22 • Ps 22:12 • Ezek 39:18 • Amos 4:1.

**BASKET [S]**
*Gen 40:18* Joseph answered ... The three *b's* are three days
*Jer 24:2* One *b* had very good figs ... like ... figs ... first ripe
*Amos 8:1* and behold a *b* of summer fruit
*Matt 14:20* they [the disciples] took up of the fragments

that remained twelve *b's* full

*Mark 8:20* how many *b's* full of fragments took ye [the disciples] up

*Acts 9:25* the disciples...let him [Paul] down...in a *b*

**BATH-SHEBA** (wife of Uriah who committed adultery with David and became his wife). **2 Sam 11:1–27; 12:24** • 1 Kgs 1:11,15–31; 2:13–25. *Bath-shua:* 1 Chr 3:5.

**BATH-SHUA.** See *Bath-sheba.*

**BE STRONG**

*Deut 31:6* **B-s** and of a good courage, fear not

*Josh 10:25* Joshua said...**b-s** and of good courage

*1 Chr 28:10* chosen thee [Solomon] to build an house for the sanctuary: *b-s*...do it

*Isa 35:4* **B-s**...your God will come with vengeance

*Hag 2:4* **b-s,** all ye people of the land, saith the LORD

*1 Cor 16:13* stand fast in the faith...**b-s**

*Eph 6:10* **b-s** in the Lord, and in the power of his might

*2 Tim 2:1* **b-s** in the grace that is in Christ Jesus

**BEAM**

*1 Sam 17:7* the staff of his [Goliath's] spear was like a weaver's *b*

*Matt 7:3* why...considerest not the *b*...in thine own eye

*Luke 6:42* cast out first the *b* out of thine own eye

**BEAR [ETH, ING]**

*Gen 4:13* Cain said unto the LORD, My punishment is greater than I can *b*

*Gen 16:11* thou [Hagar]... shalt *b* a son...Ishmael

*Gen 17:19* Sarah thy [Abraham's] wife shall *b*...a son

*Ex 20:16* shalt not *b* false witness against thy neighbour

*Ex 37:5* he [Bezaleel] put... staves into...rings by... sides of...ark, to *b* the ark

*Lev 16:22* the goat shall *b* upon him all their iniquities

*Lev 19:18* Thou shalt not avenge, nor *b* any grudge

*Num 11:14* I [Moses] am not able to *b* all this people alone

*Num 14:27* How long shall I [God] *b* with this evil congregation

*Deut 5:20* Neither shalt thou *b* false witness against thy neighbour

*Deut 32:11* As an eagle...**b'eth** them [her young] on her wings

*Ps 91:12* They shall *b* thee up...lest thou dash thy foot against a stone

*Ps 126:6* goeth forth and weepeth, **b'ing** precious seed

*Prov 25:18* A man that *b'eth* false witness against his neighbour is a maul

*Isa 7:14* a virgin shall...*b* a son...call his name Immanuel

*Isa 46:4* I [God] will *b*...and will deliver you

*Ezek 4:6* thou [Ezekiel] shalt *b* the iniquity of...Judah

*Ezek 18:20* neither shall the father *b*...iniquity of the son

*Ezek 36:7* the heathen...shall *b* their shame

*Mic 7:9* I will *b* the indignation of the LORD

*Matt 3:11* whose [Jesus'] shoes I [John the Baptist] am not worthy to *b*

*Mark 15:21* compel one Simon...to *b* his [Jesus'] cross

*Luke 4:11* they [angels] shall *b* thee [Jesus] up, lest...thou dash thy foot against a stone

*Luke 13:9* if it *b* fruit, well: and if not...cut it down

*Luke 14:27* whosoever doth not *b* his cross...cannot be my disciple

*Luke 22:10* there shall a man meet you [the disciples], *b'ing* a pitcher

*John 1:7* came for a witness, to *b* witness of the Light

*John 5:31* If I [Jesus] *b* witness of myself, my witness is not true

*John 8:18* Father that sent me [Jesus] *b'eth* witness of me

*John 10:25* the works that I [Jesus] do...*b* witness of me

*John 15:8* Herein is my [Jesus'] Father glorified, that ye *b* much fruit

*John 16:12* many things to say unto you, but ye cannot *b* them

*John 19:17* he [Jesus] *b'ing* his cross went forth into...the place of a skull

*Acts 9:15* he [Paul] is a chosen vessel...to *b* my [Jesus'] name before the Gentiles

*Rom 8:16* The Spirit itself *b'eth* witness with our spirit

*Rom 15:1* We then that are strong ought to *b* the infirmities of the weak

*1 Cor 13:7* [charity] *b'eth* all things, believeth all things

*2 Cor 4:10* *b'ing* about...the dying of the Lord Jesus

*2 Cor 11:1* Would to God ye could *b* with me [Paul] a little in my folly

*Gal 6:2* *B* ye one another's burdens, and so fulfil the law of Christ

*Gal 6:17* I [Paul] *b* in my body the marks of the Lord Jesus

*Heb 9:28* Christ was once offered to *b* the sins of many

*Heb 13:13* Let us go forth... *b'ing* his [Jesus'] reproach

**41**

*1 John 5:6* it is the Spirit that ***b'eth*** witness, because the Spirit is truth

*1 John 5:7* three that ***b*** record in heaven, the Father, the Word, and the Holy Ghost

## BEAR FALSE WITNESS

*Ex 20:16* Thou shalt not ***b-f-w*** against thy neighbour

*Deut 5:20* Neither shalt thou ***b-f-w*** against thy neighbour

*Matt 19:18* Thou shalt not steal, Thou shalt not ***b-f-w***

*Rom 13:9* Thou shalt not ***b-f-w,*** Thou shalt not covet

## BEAR FRUIT

*Isa 37:31* remnant…of the house of Judah shall…***b-f***

*Luke 13:9* if it ***b-f,*** well: and if not…cut it down

*John 15:4* branch cannot ***b-f*** of itself, except it abide in… vine

## BEAT [ETH, ING]

*Prov 23:14* ***b*** him with the rod…deliver his soul from hell

*Isa 2:4* they shall ***b*** their swords into plowshares

*Isa 3:15* What mean ye that ye ***b*** my [God's] people to pieces…grind the…poor

*Joel 3:10* ***B*** your plowshares into swords

*Jon 4:8* the sun ***b*** upon the head of Jonah

*Matt 7:25* the winds blew, and ***b*** upon that house

*Mark 4:37* the waves ***b*** into the ship, so that it was now full

*Mark 12:5* him they killed, and many others; ***b'ing*** some

*Acts 16:22* the magistrates… commanded to ***b*** them [Paul and Silas]

*Acts 22:19* I [Paul] imprisoned and ***b***…them that believed on thee [Jesus]

*1 Cor 9:26* so fight I [Paul], not as one that ***b'eth*** the air

## BEATITUDES. Matt 5:3–11.

## BEAUTIFUL

*1 Sam 16:12* he [David] was… of a ***b*** countenance

*2 Sam 11:2* David…saw a woman…and the woman was very ***b***

*Eccl 3:11* He [God] hath made every thing ***b*** in his time

*Isa 52:7* How ***b*** upon the mountains are the feet of him that bringeth good tidings

*Matt 23:27* ye [scribes and Pharisees]…indeed appear ***b*** outward

*Rom 10:15* as it is written, How ***b*** are the feet of them

## BECKONED

*Luke 5:7* they ***b*** unto their partners…in the other ship

*Acts 21:40* Paul…***b*** with the hand unto the people

*Acts 24:10* Paul, after that the governor had *b* unto him to speak, answered

**BEELZEBUB.** See *Baal-zebub.*

**BEER-SHEBA** (a well that Abraham and Abimelech dug to seal their covenant and a city that grew up around the well). **Gen 21:31–33;** 26:32–33 • Judg 20:1 • 2 Sam 3:10 • Amos 5:5.

**BEFOREHAND**
*Mark 13:11* take no thought *b* what ye shall speak
*1 Tim 5:25* the good works of some are manifest *b*

**BEGAN**
*Gen 6:1* men *b* to multiply on the face of the earth
*2 Sam 5:4* David was thirty years old when he *b* to reign
*2 Chr 3:1* Solomon *b* to build the house of the LORD
*Jon 3:4* Jonah *b* to enter into the city a day's journey
*Matt 4:17* Jesus *b* to preach, and to say, Repent
*Matt 26:22* they [the disciples]…*b* every one of them to say unto him, Lord, is it I
*Mark 6:7* he [Jesus] called… the twelve…*b* to send them forth
*Mark 8:31* he [Jesus] *b* to teach them, that the Son of man must suffer

*Luke 14:18* they all with one consent *b* to make excuse
*Luke 15:14* famine…and he [the prodigal son] *b* to be in want
*Luke 19:45* he [Jesus]…*b* to cast out them that sold therein
*John 13:5* he [Jesus]…*b* to wash the disciples' feet

**BEGINNING [S]**
*Gen 1:1* In the *b* God created the heaven and the earth
*Job 42:12* the LORD blessed the latter end of Job more than his *b*
*Ps 111:10* The fear of the LORD is the *b* of wisdom
*Prov 1:7* The fear of the LORD is the *b* of knowledge
*Eccl 7:8* Better is the end of a thing than the *b* thereof
*Isa 40:21* hath it not been told you from the *b*
*Isa 48:3* I have declared the former things from the *b*
*Matt 19:4* Have ye not read… he which made them at the *b* made them male and female
*Matt 20:8* give them their hire, *b* from the last unto the first
*Mark 13:8* famines and troubles: these are the *b's* of sorrows
*Luke 24:27* *b* at Moses…he [Jesus] expounded…the things concerning himself

*John 1:1* In the *b* was the Word...Word was with God

*John 6:64* Jesus knew from the *b* who...believed not

*Col 1:18* he [Jesus] is the *b,* the firstborn from the dead

*2 Thes 2:13* God hath from the *b* chosen you to salvation

*Heb 7:3* [Melchisedec] having neither *b* of days

*2 Pet 3:4* all things continue as they were from the *b*

*1 John 1:1* That which was from the *b*...we have heard

*1 John 2:13* ye have known him [Jesus] that is from the *b*

*1 John 3:11* heard from the *b*... we should love one another

*Rev 1:8* Alpha and Omega, the *b* and the ending

*Rev 22:13* Alpha and Omega, the *b* and the end

**BEGOTTEN**

*Ps 2:7* Thou art my Son; this day have I *b* thee

*John 1:14* we beheld his [Jesus'] glory, the glory as of the only *b* of the Father

*John 1:18* the only *b* Son...he hath declared him [God]

*John 3:16* God so loved the world...gave his only *b* Son

*1 Cor 4:15* for in Christ Jesus I [Paul] have *b* you through the gospel

*1 Pet 1:3* God...hath *b* us again unto a lively hope

**BEHAVE [D]**

*1 Sam 18:14* David *b'd* himself wisely...LORD was with him

*Ps 101:2* I will *b* myself wisely in a perfect way

*Ps 131:2* I have *b'd* and quieted myself, as a child

*1 Cor 13:5* [charity] doth not *b* itself unseemly

*2 Thes 3:7* we *b'd* not ourselves disorderly among you

**BEHIND**

*Matt 9:20* behold, a woman... with an issue of blood... came *b* him [Jesus]

*Matt 16:23* he [Jesus]...said unto Peter, Get thee *b* me

*Phil 3:13* forgetting those things which are *b*

*Col 1:24* fill up that which is *b* of the afflictions of Christ

*Rev 1:10* I was in the Spirit... and heard *b* me a great voice

**BEHOLD [EST, ETH, ING]**

*Gen 1:31* God saw every thing that he had made, and, *b,* it was very good

*Ps 33:13* The LORD...*b'eth* all the sons of men

*Ps 119:18* that I may *b* wondrous things out of thy [God's] law

*Ps 133:1* *B,* how...pleasant it is for brethren to dwell together in unity

*Prov 15:3* The eyes of the LORD are in every place, ***b'ing*** the evil and the good

*Isa 7:14* ***B,*** a virgin shall conceive, and bear a son

*Isa 40:26* ***b*** who hath created these things

*Isa 42:1* ***B*** my [God's] servant, whom I uphold

*Isa 59:1* ***B,*** the LORD's hand is not shortened, that it cannot save

*Jer 32:27* ***B,*** I am the LORD, the God of all flesh

*Jer 44:11* ***B,*** I [God] will set my face against you for evil

*Mal 4:5* ***B,*** I [God] will send you Elijah the prophet

*Matt 10:16* ***B,*** I [Jesus] send you forth as sheep in the midst of wolves

*Matt 12:18* ***B*** my [God's] servant, whom I have chosen

*Matt 12:49* ***B*** my [Jesus'] mother and my brethren

*Mark 10:21* Then Jesus ***b'ing*** him [young ruler] loved him

*Luke 1:38* Mary said, ***B*** the handmaid of the Lord

*Luke 6:41* why ***b'est*** thou the mote … in thy brother's eye

*John 1:36* he [John the Baptist] saith, ***B*** the Lamb of God

*John 19:14* and he [Pilate] saith unto the Jews, ***B*** your King

*1 Cor 15:51* ***B*** … We shall not all sleep … shall all be changed

*2 Cor 5:17* ***b,*** all things are become new

*Jas 1:23* a hearer … and not a doer … is like … a man ***b'ing*** his … face in a glass

*1 John 3:1* ***B,*** what manner of love the Father hath bestowed upon us

*Rev 3:11* ***B,*** I [Jesus] come quickly: hold … fast

*Rev 3:20* ***B,*** I [Jesus] stand at the door, and knock

*Rev 21:5* ***B,*** I [Jesus] make all things new

**BELA.** See *Zoar.*

**BELIAL.** See *Satan.*

**BELIEVE [D, ING, TH]**

*Gen 15:6* he [Abraham] ***b'd*** in the LORD; and he counted it to him for righteousness

*Ex 4:1* they will not ***b*** me [Moses], nor hearken unto my voice

*Ps 119:66* I have ***b'd*** thy [God's] commandments

*Jon 3:5* the people of Nineveh ***b'd*** God … put on sackcloth

*Matt 18:6* whoso shall offend one of these little ones which ***b*** in me

*Matt 21:22* whatsoever ye shall ask in prayer, ***b'ing,*** ye shall receive

*Mark 5:36* he [Jesus] saith … Be not afraid, only ***b***

*Mark 9:23* If thou canst ***b,*** all things are possible

*Mark 9:24* Lord, I ***b;*** help thou mine unbelief

45

*Mark 11:24 **b*** that ye receive them, and ye shall have them

*Luke 24:25* O fools, and slow of heart to ***b***

*John 3:12* how shall ye ***b,*** if I tell you of heavenly things

*John 3:16* whosoever ***b'th*** in him [Jesus] should not perish

*John 3:18* he hath not ***b'd*** in the name of the only begotten Son of God

*John 3:36* He that ***b'th*** on the Son hath everlasting life

*John 4:48* Except ye see signs and wonders, ye will not ***b***

*John 6:29* This is the work of God, that ye ***b*** on him whom he hath sent

*John 6:35* he that ***b'th*** on me [Jesus] shall never thirst

*John 6:64* Jesus knew…who they were that ***b'd*** not

*John 9:36* Who is he, Lord, that I might ***b*** on him

*John 11:25* he that ***b'th*** in me [Jesus], though he were dead, yet shall he live

*John 11:26* whosoever…***b'th*** in me [Jesus] shall never die

*John 11:27* Yea, Lord: I ***b*** that thou art the Christ

*John 12:46* whosoever ***b'th*** on me [Jesus] should not abide in darkness

*John 14:1* ye ***b*** in God, ***b*** also in me [Jesus]

*John 20:25* Except I [Thomas]…thrust my hand into his [Jesus'] side, I will not ***b***

*John 20:29* blessed are they that have not seen, and yet have ***b'd***

*John 20:31* that ye might ***b*** that Jesus is the Christ

*Acts 4:32* multitude of them that ***b'd*** were of one heart

*Acts 8:37* And he [the eunuch] said, I ***b*** that Jesus Christ is the Son of God

*Acts 16:31* ***B*** on the Lord Jesus Christ…thou shalt be saved

*Rom 1:16* it [the gospel] is the power of God unto salvation to every one that ***b'th***

*Rom 4:3* Abraham ***b'd*** God, and it was counted unto him for righteousness

*Rom 6:8* we ***b*** that we shall also live with him [Jesus]

*Rom 10:4* Christ is the end of the law for righteousness to every one that ***b'th***

*Rom 10:9* ***b***…that God hath raised him [Jesus] from the dead, thou shalt be saved

*Rom 10:14* How then shall they call on him in whom they have not ***b'd***

*Rom 13:11* now is our salvation nearer than when we ***b'd***

*Rom 15:13* the God of hope fill you with all joy…in ***b'ing***

*1 Cor 1:21* it pleased God by the foolishness of preaching to save them that *b*

*1 Cor 13:7* [charity] beareth all things, *b'th* all things

*2 Tim 1:12* I [Paul] know whom I have *b'd*

*Heb 11:6* he that cometh to God must *b* that he is

*Jas 2:19* thou doest well: the devils also *b,* and tremble

*1 John 3:23* we should *b* on the name of his Son Jesus

*1 John 5:1* Whosoever *b'th* that Jesus is the Christ is born of God

*1 John 5:10* He that *b'th* on the Son of God hath the witness in himself

## BELIEVERS

*Acts 5:14* *b* were the more added to the Lord

*1 Tim 4:12* be thou an example of the *b,* in word…faith

## BELONG [ED, ETH]

*Ps 3:8* Salvation *b'eth* unto the LORD

*Ps 94:1* O LORD God, to whom vengeance *b'eth,* show thyself

*Dan 9:9* To the Lord our God *b* mercies and forgivenesses

*Luke 23:7* he [Pilate] knew that he [Jesus] *b'ed* unto Herod's jurisdiction

*1 Cor 7:32* He that is unmarried careth for the things that *b* to the Lord

## BELOVED SON

*Matt 3:17* This is my *b-S,* in whom I am well pleased

*Matt 17:5* This is my *b-S,* in whom I am well pleased; hear ye him

*Mark 1:11* Thou art my *b-S,* in whom I am well pleased

*Mark 9:7* This is my *b-S:* hear him

*Luke 3:22* Thou art my *b-S;* in thee I am well pleased

*Luke 9:35* This is my *b-S:* hear him

*Luke 20:13* send my *b-s:* it may be they will reverence him

*1 Cor 4:17* I [Paul] sent unto you Timotheus, who is my *b-s*

*2 Tim 1:2* To Timothy, my [Paul's] dearly *b-s:* Grace, mercy

**BELSHAZZAR** (last king of the Babylonian Empire whose fall was foretold by a mysterious hand writing on the wall). **Dan 5:1–31;** 7:1; 8:1.

**BELTESHAZZAR.** See *Daniel.*

**BENAIAH** (a loyal supporter of David who later became commander-in-chief of Solomon's army). 2 Sam 8:18; 20:23; 23:20,22 • 1 Kgs 1:8–44; 2:25–46; 4:4 • 1 Chr 11:22,24; 18:17; 27:5–6.

**BEN-AMMI** (a son of Lot and ancestor of the Ammonites). Gen 19:30–38.

**BENEFITS**

*Ps 68:19* Blessed be the Lord, who daily loadeth us with *b*

*Ps 103:2* Bless the LORD, O my soul…forget not all his *b*

*Ps 116:12* What shall I render unto the LORD for all his *b*

**BEN-HADAD** (a title for three different kings of Damascus, Syria).

1. Ben-hadad I, who invaded the Northern Kingdom in league with King Asa of Judah. 1 Kgs 15:18–21 • 2 Chr 16:2–4.

2. Ben-hadad II, who waged war against King Ahab of Israel. 1 Kgs 20:1–34 • 2 Kgs 6:24; 8:7–9.

3. Ben-hadad III, who was defeated by the Assyrians, as the prophet Amos predicted. 2 Kgs 13:3,24–25 • Amos 1:4.

**BENJAMIN** (a son of Jacob and ancestor of one of the twelve tribes of Israel). Gen 35:18,24; 42:4,36; 43:14–29; 45:12–14,22; 46:19,21 • Ex 1:3 • 1 Chr 2:2; 7:6; 8:1. The tribe of Benjamin settled in central Canaan. Josh 18:11–28.

**BEREA** (a city of Macedonia visited by Paul). Acts 17:10–14.

**BEREAVE [D]**

*Gen 42:36* Me [Jacob] have ye *b'd* of my children

*Jer 15:7* I [the LORD] will *b* them of children

*Jer 18:21* let their wives be *b'd* of their children

**BERITH.** See *Baal-berith.*

**BERNICE** (a sister of Herod Agrippa II, Roman governor of Palestine before whom Paul appeared). Acts 25:13,23; 26:1–32.

**BERODACH-BALADAN** (a king of Babylon whose ambassadors viewed the treasures of King Hezekiah of Judah). 2 Kgs 20:12–19. *Merodach-baladan:* Isa 39:1.

**BESEECH [ING]**

*1 Chr 21:8* *b* thee [God], do away…iniquity of thy servant

*Ps 116:4* O LORD, I *b* thee, deliver my soul

*Isa 64:9* see, we *b* thee [God], we are all thy people

*Jer 38:20* Obey, I [Jeremiah] *b* thee, the voice of the LORD

*Dan 9:16* I [Daniel] *b* thee [God], let thine anger…be turned away

*Jon 4:3* O LORD, take, I [Jonah] *b* thee, my life from me

*Matt 8:5* came unto him [Jesus] a centurion, *b'ing* him

*Luke 7:3* he sent unto him [Jesus]…*b'ing* him that he would…heal his servant

*Luke 9:38* Master, I *b* thee, look upon my son

*Rom 12:1* I [Paul] *b* you therefore, brethren

*1 Cor 4:16* I [Paul] *b* you, be ye followers of me

*2 Cor 2:8* I [Paul] *b* you…confirm your love toward him

*2 Cor 5:20* we are ambassadors for Christ, as though God did *b* you by us

*Eph 4:1* I [Paul]…*b* you that ye walk worthy of the vocation wherewith ye are called

*Phlm 10* I [Paul] *b* thee for my son Onesimus

*1 Pet 2:11* I [Peter] *b* you… abstain from fleshly lusts

**BEST**

*1 Sam 8:14* he [the king] will take your fields…the *b* of them

*Luke 15:22* Bring forth the *b* robe, and put it on him

*1 Cor 12:31* But covet earnestly the *b* gifts

**BESTOW [ED]**

*Luke 12:17* What shall I do… no room where to *b* my fruits

*John 4:38* I [Jesus] sent you to reap that whereon ye *b'ed* no labour

*1 Cor 13:3* though I [Paul] *b* all my goods to feed the poor

*Gal 4:11* I [Paul] am afraid of you, lest I have *b'ed* upon you labour in vain

*1 John 3:1* what manner of love the Father hath *b'ed* upon us

**BETHABARA** (a place along the Jordan River where John the Baptist baptized). John 1:28.

**BETHANY** (a village outside Jerusalem where Lazarus, Mary, and Martha lived and the site from which Jesus ascended to heaven). Matt 21:17; 26:6 • Mark 11:1,11–12; 14:3 • Luke 19:29; 24:50–51 • John 11:1,18; 12:1.

**BETHEL** (a city where Jacob had a vision of angels on a staircase). Gen 12:8; 13:3–4; **28:10–19**; 35:1–15 • Josh 16:2 • 1 Sam 7:15–16; 10:3 • 1 Kgs 12:28–33 • 2 Kgs 23:4,15–20 • Jer 48:13 • Hos 10:15 • Amos 7:10–13. *El-bethel:* Gen 35:7. *Luz:* Gen 28:19.

**BETHESDA** (a pool in Jerusalem where Jesus healed a lame man). John 5:2–8.

**49**

**BETH-HORON** (twin towns— Upper and Lower—in the territory of Ephraim which served as important military outposts). Josh 10:10–14; 16:3–5 • 1 Sam 13:18 • 1 Chr 7:24 • 2 Chr 8:5.

**BETHLEHEM** (a town in southern Palestine near Jerusalem where Jesus was born in fulfillment of prophecy). Gen 35:19; 48:7 • Ruth 1:19,22; 2:4; 4:11 • 1 Sam 16:4; 17:15; 20:6,28 • 2 Sam 2:32; 23:14–16,24 • 1 Chr 11:16–26 • 2 Chr 11:6 • Ezra 2:21 • Neh 7:26 • **Mic 5:2** • Matt 2:1–16 • **Luke 2:4–7.** *Beth-lehem-judah:* Judg 19:18. *Ephratah:* Ruth 4:11. *Ephrath:* Gen 35:16–19.

**BETH-LEHEM-JUDAH.** See *Bethlehem.*

**BETHPHAGE** (a village outside Jerusalem mentioned in connection with Jesus' triumphal entry into the city). Matt 21:1 • Mark 11:1 • Luke 19:29.

**BETHSAIDA** (a fishing village on the Sea of Galilee; the home of Andrew, Peter, and Philip—apostles of Jesus). Matt 11:21 • Mark 6:45 • Luke 10:13 • **John 1:44; 12:21.**

**BETRAY [ED, EST, ETH]**
*Matt 17:22* Son of man shall be *b'ed* into the hands of men
*Matt 26:2* the Son of man is *b'ed* to be crucified
*Matt 26:16* he [Judas] sought opportunity to *b* him [Jesus]
*Matt 26:45* the Son of man is *b'ed* into the hands of sinners
*Mark 14:10* Judas...went unto the chief priests, to *b* him [Jesus] unto them
*Mark 14:21* but woe to that man by whom the Son of man is *b'ed*
*Luke 22:21* the hand of him that *b'eth* me [Jesus] is with me on the table
*Luke 22:48* Judas, *b'est* thou the Son of man with a kiss
*John 6:64* Jesus knew...who should *b* him
*1 Cor 11:23* the Lord Jesus the same night in which he was *b'ed* took bread

**BETTER**
*1 Sam 15:22* Behold, to obey is *b* than sacrifice
*2 Kgs 5:12* Are not Abana and Pharpar...*b* than all the waters of Israel
*Ps 37:16* A little that a righteous man hath is *b* than the riches of many wicked
*Ps 84:10* a day in thy [God's] courts is *b* than a thousand
*Ps 118:8* *b* to trust in the LORD than to put confidence in man

50

*Prov 8:11* For wisdom is *b* than rubies

*Prov 15:16* *B* is little with the fear of the LORD than great treasure and trouble

*Prov 16:16* How much *b* is it to get wisdom than gold

*Prov 19:22* a poor man is *b* than a liar

*Prov 27:5* Open rebuke is *b* than secret love

*Prov 27:10* *b* is a neighbour… near than a brother far off

*Eccl 4:9* Two are *b* than one; because they have a good reward for their labour

*Eccl 4:13* *B* is a poor and a wise child than an old and foolish king

*Eccl 6:9* *B* is the sight of the eyes than the wandering of the desire

*Eccl 7:1* A good name is *b* than precious ointment

*Eccl 7:8* *B* is the end of a thing than the beginning thereof

*Eccl 9:18* Wisdom is *b* than weapons of war

*Song 4:10* how much *b* is thy love than wine

*Dan 1:20* found them [Daniel and his friends] ten times *b* than all the magicians

*Jon 4:8* Jonah… said, It is *b* for me to die than to live

*Matt 12:12* How much then is a man *b* than a sheep

*Matt 18:8* it is *b* for thee to enter into life halt or maimed

*1 Cor 7:9* for it is *b* to marry than to burn

*Phil 1:23* having a desire… to be with Christ; which is far *b*

*Heb 1:4* Being made so much *b* than the angels

*Heb 7:22* was Jesus made a surety of a *b* testament

**BEULAH** (a symbolic name for Israel after the Exile in Babylon when the nation would be in a fruitful relationship with God). Isa 62:4.

**BEZER** (a city of refuge in the territory of Reuben). Deut 4:43 • Josh 20:8; 21:36 • 1 Chr 6:78.

**BILDAD** (one of the three friends who comforted Job). His speeches appear in Job 8:1–22; 18:1–21; 25:1–6.

**BILHAH** (a wife of Jacob and mother of two of his sons, Dan and Naphtali). Gen 29:29; 30:3–7; 35:22,25; 37:2; 46:25 • 1 Chr 7:13.

**BIND [ETH, ING]**

*Gen 37:7* we [Joseph and his brothers] were *b'ing* sheaves in the field

*Deut 6:8* thou shalt *b* them for a sign upon thine hand

*Ps 147:3* He [God] healeth the broken in heart, and *b'eth* up their wounds

*Prov 3:3* **b** them [mercy and truth] about thy neck

*Isa 61:1* the LORD…hath sent me to **b** up the broken-hearted

*Dan 3:20* he [the king] commanded…to **b** Shadrach, Meshach, and Abednego

*Matt 12:29* how can one enter into a strong man's house… except he first **b**…man

*Matt 16:19* whatsoever thou shalt **b** on earth shall be bound in heaven

*Matt 23:4* they [Pharisees] **b** heavy burdens

*Mark 5:3* no man could **b** him [demon-possessed man]

*Acts 22:4* I [Paul] persecuted… **b'ing** and delivering…both men and women

**BIRTH**

*Eccl 7:1* good name is better than…ointment…day of death than…day of…**b**

*Matt 1:18* the **b** of Jesus Christ was on this wise

*John 9:1* Jesus…saw a man which was blind from his **b**

*Rev 12:2* she being with child cried, travailing in **b**

**BIRTH OF JESUS.** See *Jesus, Life and Ministry of.*

**BIRTHRIGHT**

*Gen 25:31* Jacob said, Sell me this day thy [Esau's] **b**

*Heb 12:16* Esau, who for one morsel of meat sold his **b**

**BISHOP [S]**

*Phil 1:1* to all the saints…at Philippi, with the **b's**

*1 Tim 3:1* If a man desire the office of a **b,** he desireth a good work

*1 Tim 3:2* A **b** then must be blameless…husband of one wife

*Titus 1:7* a **b** must be blameless, as the steward of God

*1 Pet 2:25* ye are now returned unto the Shepherd and **B** of your souls

**BITHYNIA** (a Roman province of Asia Minor that Paul was prevented from entering). Acts 16:7.

**BITTER**

*Ex 1:14* they [the Egyptians] made…lives **b** with… bondage

*Ex 12:8* with **b** herbs they shall eat it [the Passover meal]

*Ex 15:23* could not drink of the waters of Marah…they were **b**

*Isa 24:9* strong drink shall be **b** to them that drink it

*Jer 31:15* A voice was heard in Ramah…**b** weeping

*Hab 1:6* I raise up the Chaldeans, that **b** and hasty nation

*Jas 3:11* Doth a fountain send forth … sweet water and *b*

**BITTER HERBS** (herbs eaten by the Israelites during their Passover celebrations to help them remember their enslavement years in Egypt). Ex 12:8 • Num 9:11.

**BITTERNESS**

*Job 9:18* He [God] … filleth me [Job] with *b*

*Job 21:25* another dieth in the *b* of his soul

*Acts 8:23* thou art in the gall of *b,* and in the bond of iniquity

*Rom 3:14* Whose mouth is full of cursing and *b*

*Eph 4:31* Let all *b,* and wrath … be put away from you

**BLAMELESS**

*1 Cor 1:8* ye may be *b* in the day of our Lord Jesus

*1 Tim 3:2* A bishop then must be *b,* the husband of one wife

*1 Tim 3:10* use the office of a deacon, being found *b*

*Titus 1:7* a bishop must be *b,* as the steward of God

**BLASPHEME [D]**

*Ps 74:10* shall the enemy *b* thy [God's] name for ever

*Ps 74:18* the foolish people have *b'd* thy [God's] name

*Mark 3:29* he that shall *b* against the Holy Ghost hath never forgiveness

*Rev 13:6* he opened his mouth … against God, to *b* his name

**BLASPHEMY [IES]**

*Matt 12:31* *b* against the Holy Ghost shall not be forgiven

*Matt 26:65* He [Jesus] hath spoken *b;* what further need have we of witnesses

*Mark 2:7* Why doth this man [Jesus] thus speak *b'ies*

*Col 3:8* put off all these; anger, wrath, malice, *b*

*Rev 13:1* I [John] … saw a beast … and upon his heads the name of *b*

**BLESS [ED, ING, INGS]**

*Gen 1:22* God *b'ed* them … Be fruitful, and multiply

*Gen 2:3* God *b'ed* the seventh day, and sanctified it

*Gen 9:1* And God *b'ed* Noah and his sons

*Gen 12:2* I [God] will *b* thee [Abraham], and make thy name great

*Gen 22:18* in thy [Abraham's] seed shall all the nations of the earth be *b'ed*

*Gen 27:34* Esau … said unto his father, *B* me, even me also

*Gen 39:5* the LORD *b'ed* the Egyptian's house for Joseph's sake

*Ex 20:11* the LORD *b'ed* the sabbath day, and hallowed it

*Num 6:24* The LORD *b* thee, and keep thee

*Num 24:1* Balaam saw that it pleased the LORD to *b* Israel

*Deut 8:10* thou shalt *b* the LORD... for the good land... he hath given thee

*Deut 11:26* I set before you this day a *b'ing* and a curse

*Deut 33:1* Moses... *b'ed* the children of Israel

*Job 1:21* the LORD hath taken away; *b'ed* be the name of the LORD

*Job 42:12* the LORD *b'ed* the latter end of Job more than his beginning

*Ps 1:1* *B'ed* is the man that walketh not in the counsel of the ungodly

*Ps 28:6* *B'ed* be the LORD, because he hath heard... my supplications

*Ps 29:11* the LORD will *b* his people with peace

*Ps 32:1* *B'ed* is he whose transgression is forgiven

*Ps 33:12* *B'ed* is the nation whose God is the LORD

*Ps 41:13* *B'ed* be the LORD God... from everlasting

*Ps 66:20* *B'ed* be God, which hath not turned away my prayer, nor his mercy

*Ps 67:1* God... *b* us; and cause his face to shine upon us

*Ps 84:4* *B'ed* are they that dwell in thy [God's] house

*Ps 94:12* *B'ed* is the man whom thou [God] chastenest

*Ps 96:2* Sing unto the LORD, *b* his name

*Ps 106:48* *B'ed* be the LORD God of Israel from everlasting to everlasting

*Ps 115:18* we will *b* the LORD from this time forth

*Ps 119:2* *B'ed* are they that keep his [God's] testimonies

*Ps 128:1* *B'ed* is every one that feareth the LORD

*Ps 145:1* I will *b* thy [God's] name for ever and ever

*Prov 10:6* *B'ings* are upon the head of the just

*Prov 31:28* Her children arise up, and call her *b'ed*

*Ezek 34:26* there shall be showers of *b'ing*

*Matt 5:3* *B'ed* are the poor in spirit

*Matt 5:4* *B'ed* are they that mourn

*Matt 5:5* *B'ed* are the meek

*Matt 5:6* *B'ed* are they which do hunger... after righteousness

*Matt 5:7* *B'ed* are the merciful

*Matt 5:8* *B'ed* are the pure in heart

*Matt 5:9* *B'ed* are the peacemakers

*Matt 5:10* *B'ed* are they which are persecuted for righteousness' sake

*Matt 5:11* *B'ed* are ye, when men shall revile you, and persecute you

*Matt 5:44* Love your enemies, *b* them that curse you

*Matt 16:17* *B'ed* art thou, Simon Barjona

*Matt 26:26* Jesus took bread, and *b'ed* it, and brake it

*Mark 10:16* he [Jesus]…put his hands upon them [the children], and *b'ed* them

*Luke 1:28 b'ed* art thou [Mary] among women

*Luke 11:28* Yea rather, *b'ed* are they that hear the word of God, and keep it

*John 20:29 b'ed* are they that have not seen, and yet have believed

*Rom 12:14 B* them which persecute you: *b,* and curse not

*1 Cor 4:12* being reviled, we *b*

*1 Cor 10:16* The cup of *b'ing*… is it not the communion of the blood of Christ

*Gal 3:9* they which be of faith are *b'ed* with…Abraham

*Eph 1:3* who [God] hath *b'ed* us with all spiritual *b'ings*

*1 Tim 6:15* who [Jesus] is the *b'ed* and only Potentate

*Titus 2:13* that *b'ed* hope, and the glorious appearing of… our Saviour

*Jas 1:12 B'ed* is the man that endureth temptation

*Jas 3:10* Out of the same mouth proceedeth *b'ing* and cursing

*Rev 1:3 B'ed* is he that readeth, and they that hear the words of this prophecy

*Rev 5:12* Worthy is the Lamb… to receive…honour, and glory, and *b'ing*

*Rev 22:7 b'ed* is he that keepeth the sayings of the prophecy of this book

## BLESS THE LORD

*Ps 16:7* I will *b-t-L,* who hath given me counsel

*Ps 34:1* I will *b-t-L* at all times: his praise shall continually be in my mouth

*Ps 103:1 B-t-L,* O my soul: and all that is within me, bless his holy name

*Ps 103:2 B-t-L,* O my soul, and forget not all his benefits

*Ps 134:2* Lift up your hands in the sanctuary, and *b-t-L*

## BLIND [ED]

*Job 29:15* I was eyes to the *b,* and feet was I to the lame

*Ps 146:8* The Lord openeth the eyes of the *b*

*Isa 35:5* the eyes of the *b* shall be opened

*Isa 42:7* To open the *b* eyes, to bring out the prisoners

*Isa 43:8* Bring forth the *b* people that have eyes

*Lam 4:14* They have wandered as *b* men in the streets

*Mal 1:8* if ye offer the *b* for sacrifice, is it not evil

*Matt 11:5* The *b* receive their sight, and the lame walk

*Matt 20:30* two *b* men sitting by the way side…cried out

*Matt 23:24* Ye *b* guides [Pharisees], which strain at a gnat

*Mark 8:22* they bring a *b* man unto him [Jesus], and besought him

*Mark 10:46* *b* Bartimaeus, the son of Timaeus, sat by the highway

*Luke 4:18* Spirit...anointed me [Jesus] to preach...recovering of sight to the *b*

*Luke 6:39* Can the *b* lead the *b*

*Luke 7:22* tell John...that the *b* see, the lame walk

*John 9:2* who did sin, this man, or his parents, that he was born *b*

*John 12:40* He [God] hath *b'ed* their eyes...hardened their heart

*Acts 13:11* thou [Elymas the sorcerer]...shalt be *b*

*1 John 2:11* he that hateth his brother is in darkness, and...darkness hath *b'ed* his eyes

## BLINDNESS

*Gen 19:11* they [angels] smote the men...with *b,* both small and great

*2 Kgs 6:18* And he [God] smote them with *b* according to the word of Elisha

*Eph 4:18* being alienated from the life of God...because of the *b* of their heart

## BLOOD

*Gen 4:10* the voice of thy [Cain's] brother's *b* crieth unto me [God]

*Gen 9:6* Whoso sheddeth man's *b,* by man shall his *b* be shed

*Ex 7:21* there was *b* throughout all the land of Egypt

*Ex 12:23* when he seeth the *b* upon the lintel...the LORD will pass over the door

*Ex 24:8* Moses took the *b,* and sprinkled it on the people

*Lev 7:27* Whatsoever soul eateth...*b*...shall be cut off

*Lev 15:19* if...her issue in her flesh be *b,* she shall be put apart seven days

*Lev 17:11* For the life of the flesh is in the *b*

*Lev 20:9* he hath cursed his father or his mother; his *b* shall be upon him

*Num 35:19* The revenger of *b*... shall slay the murderer

*1 Kgs 18:28* they [the priests of Baal]...cut themselves... till the *b* gushed out

*1 Kgs 22:38* the dogs licked up his [Ahab's] *b*

*2 Kgs 9:33* her [Jezebel's] *b* was sprinkled on the wall

*1 Chr 22:8* thou [David] hast shed much *b* upon the earth

*Ps 30:9* What profit is there in my *b,* when I go...to the pit

*Prov 1:16* their feet...make haste to shed *b*

*Prov 6:17* a lying tongue, and hands that shed innocent *b*

*Isa 1:11* I [God] delight not in the *b* of bullocks

*Isa 1:15* I [God] will not hear: your hands are full of *b*

*Isa 59:3* hands are defiled with *b*...fingers with iniquity

*Ezek 9:9* land is full of *b,* and the city full of perverseness

*Joel 2:31* The sun shall be turned into darkness, and the moon into *b*

*Matt 9:20* a woman...with an issue of *b* twelve years, came behind him [Jesus]

*Matt 16:17* for flesh and *b* hath not revealed it unto thee [Peter]

*Matt 26:28* this is my [Jesus'] *b* of the new testament, which is shed for many

*Matt 27:8* that field was called, The field of *b,* unto this day

*Matt 27:24* Pilate...washed his hands...saying, I am innocent of the *b* of this...person [Jesus]

*Matt 27:25* Then answered all the people...His [Jesus'] *b* be on us

*Luke 11:50* the *b* of all the prophets...may be required of this generation

*Luke 22:44* his [Jesus'] sweat was as...great drops of *b*

*John 6:53* Except ye...drink his [Jesus'] *b,* ye have no life

*John 19:34* one of the soldiers...pierced his [Jesus'] side...came there out *b* and water

*Acts 2:20* sun shall be turned into darkness...moon into *b*

*Acts 17:26* And [God] hath made of one *b* all nations of men

*Acts 18:6* Your *b* be upon your own heads

*Acts 20:28* feed the church of God, which he [Jesus] hath purchased with his own *b*

*Rom 5:9* now justified by his [Jesus'] *b,* we shall be saved from wrath

*1 Cor 10:16* The cup of blessing...is it not the communion of the *b* of Christ

*1 Cor 15:50* flesh and *b* cannot inherit the kingdom of God

*Eph 2:13* ye who sometimes were far off are made nigh by the *b* of Christ

*Eph 6:12* we wrestle not against flesh and *b*

*Col 1:14* In whom we have redemption through his [Jesus'] *b*

*Heb 9:12* by his [Jesus'] own *b* he entered in once into the holy place

*Heb 10:4* not possible that the *b* of bulls...should take away sins

*Heb 13:12* he [Jesus] might sanctify...with his own *b*

*1 John 1:7* the *b* of Jesus Christ his Son cleanseth us from all sin

*Rev 6:12* the sun became black...and the moon became as *b*

*Rev 7:14* they … have washed their robes, and made them white in the *b* of the Lamb

*Rev 16:3* the sea … became as the *b* of a dead man

## BLOT [TED, TETH]

*Ex 32:33* Whosoever hath sinned against me [God], him will I *b* out of my book

*Ps 51:1* according unto … thy [God's] tender mercies *b* out my transgressions

*Ps 51:9* Hide thy [God's] face from my sins, and *b* out all mine iniquities

*Ps 69:28* Let them be *b'ted* out of the book of the living

*Isa 43:25* I [God], even I, am he that *b'teth* out thy transgressions for mine own sake

*Isa 44:22* I [God] have *b'ted* out … thy transgressions

*Acts 3:19* Repent … that your sins may be *b'ted* out

*Rev 3:5* I [God] will not *b* out his name out of the book of life … will confess his name

## BOANERGES (a name, meaning "sons of thunder," given by Jesus to His disciples James and John). Mark 3:17.

## BOAST [ETH, ING, INGS]

*Ps 44:8* In God we *b* all the day long

*Prov 25:14* Whoso *b'eth* himself of a false gift is like clouds … without rain

*Prov 27:1* *B* not thyself of to morrow

*2 Cor 9:3* lest our *b'ing* of you should be in vain

*Eph 2:9* Not of works, lest any man should *b*

*Jas 3:5* the tongue is a little member … *b'eth* great things

*Jas 4:16* ye rejoice in your *b'ings:* all such rejoicing is evil

## BOAZ (the husband of Ruth and an ancestor of Christ). Ruth 2:1–23; 3:2,7; 4:1–21 • 1 Chr 2:11–12. *Booz:* Matt 1:5 • Luke 3:32.

## BODY

*Num 19:11* He that toucheth the dead *b* … shall be unclean

*Deut 21:23* His *b* shall not remain all night upon the tree

*Mic 6:7* give … the fruit of my *b* for the sin of my soul

*Matt 6:23* eye be evil, thy whole *b* shall be full of darkness

*Matt 26:26* Jesus took bread … Take, eat; this is my *b*

*Mark 15:43* Joseph of Arimathaea … craved the *b* of Jesus

*Luke 12:22* Take no thought … for the *b,* what ye … put on

*Luke 23:55* the women … beheld … how his [Jesus'] *b* was laid

*Rom 6:12* Let not sin therefore reign in your mortal *b*

*Rom 7:24* who shall deliver me from the *b* of this death

*Rom 12:5* we, being many, are one *b* in Christ

*1 Cor 6:18* he that committeth fornication sinneth against his own *b*

*1 Cor 10:17* we being many are one bread, and one *b*

*1 Cor 12:12* the *b* is one, and hath many members

*1 Cor 13:3* though I [Paul] give my *b* to be burned

*1 Cor 15:44* It is sown a natural *b;* it is raised a spiritual *b*

*2 Cor 5:8* absent from the *b*... present with the Lord

*Gal 6:17* I [Paul] bear in my *b* the marks of the Lord Jesus

*Phil 1:20* Christ shall be magnified in my [Paul's] *b*

*Col 1:18* he [Christ] is the head of the *b,* the church

*Jas 3:6* it [the tongue] defileth the whole *b*

*1 Pet 2:24* Who [Jesus]...bare our sins in his own *b* on the tree

## BODY OF CHRIST

*Rom 7:4* ye also are become dead to the law by the *b-o-C*

*1 Cor 10:16* The bread which we break, is it not the communion of the *b-o-C*

*1 Cor 12:27* ye are the *b-o-C,* and members in particular

*Eph 4:12* for the work of the ministry...edifying of the *b-o-C*

## BOLD [LY]

*Prov 28:1* The wicked flee... righteous are *b* as a lion

*Acts 9:29* he [Paul] spake *b'ly* in the name of the Lord Jesus

*Acts 19:8* he [Paul] went into the synagogue, and spake *b'ly*

*Phil 1:14* many of the brethren...are much more *b* to speak the word without fear

*Heb 4:16* Let us...come *b'ly* unto the throne of grace

## BOLDNESS

*Acts 4:13* they saw the *b* of Peter and John

*Acts 4:31* they [the apostles]... prayed...spake the word of God with *b*

*Eph 3:12* In whom [Jesus] we have *b*...with confidence

*Phil 1:20* with all *b*...Christ... magnified in my [Paul's] body

*1 John 4:17* that we may have *b* in the day of judgment

## BOND [S]

*Ps 116:16* thou [God] hast loosed my *b's*

*Jer 27:2* Make thee *b's* and yokes, and put them upon thy [Jeremiah's] neck

*Acts 26:29* that...all that hear me this day, were...such as I [Paul] am, except these *b's*

*Gal 3:28* There is neither Jew nor Greek…*b* nor free

*Eph 4:3* keep the unity of the Spirit in the *b* of peace

*Eph 6:20* I [Paul] am an ambassador in *b's*

*Phil 1:13* my [Paul's] *b's* in Christ are manifest in… palace

*Col 3:11* there is neither…*b* nor free: but Christ is all

*Col 3:14* put on charity, which is the *b* of perfectness

*Phlm 10* son Onesimus, whom I [Paul] have begotten in my *b's*

**BONDAGE**

*Ex 1:14* they [the Egyptians] made…lives bitter with hard *b*

*Ex 6:6* I [God] will rid you [the Israelites] out of their *b*

*John 8:33* We be Abraham's seed…never in *b* to any man

*Rom 8:15* ye have not received the spirit of *b* again to fear

*Gal 4:9* how turn ye…to… desire again to be in *b*

*Gal 5:1* be not entangled again with the yoke of *b*

**BOOK OF LIFE**

*Phil 4:3* help those…fellow-labourers, whose names are in the *b-o-l*

*Rev 3:5* I will not blot out his name out of the *b-o-l*

*Rev 20:12* another book was opened, which is the *b-o-l*

*Rev 20:15* whosoever was not found written in the *b-o-l* was cast into the lake of fire

**BOOZ.** See *Boaz.*

**BORN**

*Gen 17:17* Shall a child be *b* unto him [Abraham] that is an hundred years old

*Gen 21:5* Abraham was an hundred years old, when his son Isaac was *b*

*Job 3:3* Let the day perish wherein I [Job] was *b*

*Job 5:7* man is *b* unto trouble, as the sparks fly upward

*Job 14:1* Man that is *b* of a woman is of few days

*Ps 58:3* The wicked…go astray as soon as they be *b*

*Prov 17:17* A friend loveth at all times, and a brother is *b* for adversity

*Eccl 3:2* A time to be *b,* and a time to die

*Isa 9:6* unto us a child is *b,* unto us a son is given

*Jer 20:14* Cursed be the day wherein I [Jeremiah] was *b*

*Matt 2:1* when Jesus was *b* in Bethlehem of Judaea

*Luke 1:35* that holy thing…*b* of thee [Mary] shall be called the Son of God

*Luke 2:11* unto you is *b* this day…a Saviour

*Luke 7:28* Among those…*b* of women…not a greater

prophet than John the Baptist

*John 9:2* sin, this man, or his parents, that he was *b* blind

*John 18:37* Thou sayest that I [Jesus] am a king. To this end was I *b*

*Acts 22:28* And Paul said, But I was free *b*

*1 Cor 15:8* he [Jesus] was seen of me [Paul] also, as of one *b* out of due time

*1 John 3:9* Whosoever is *b* of God doth not commit sin

*1 John 4:7* every one that loveth is *b* of God

## BORN AGAIN

*John 3:3* Jesus…said…Except a man be *b-a,* he cannot see the kingdom of God

*John 3:7* Marvel not that I [Jesus] said unto thee [Nicodemus], Ye must be *b-a*

*1 Pet 1:23* *b-a,* not of corruptible seed, but of incorruptible

## BOSOM

*Ex 4:6* he [Moses] put his hand into his *b:* and…his hand was leprous as snow

*Prov 5:20* why wilt thou… embrace the *b* of a stranger

*Isa 40:11* He [God] shall… carry them [lambs] in his *b*

*Luke 16:22* the beggar died… carried…into Abraham's *b*

*John 1:18* the only begotten Son…in the *b* of the Father

*John 13:23* leaning on Jesus' *b* one of his disciples

## BOTTLE [S]

*Job 32:19* my belly…is ready to burst like new *b's*

*Ps 56:8* put thou my tears into thy [God's] *b*

*Luke 5:37* no man putteth new wine into old *b's*

## BOTTOMLESS PIT

*Rev 9:1* to him was given the key of the *b-p*

*Rev 11:7* the beast that ascendeth out of the *b-p* shall make war

*Rev 20:1* I saw an angel…having the key of the *b-p*

## BOUGHT

*Lev 27:24* the field shall return unto him of whom it was *b*

*Jer 32:9* I [Jeremiah] *b* the field of Hanameel

*Matt 13:46* he [merchant]… sold all…he had, and *b* it [pearl]

*Mark 11:15* Jesus…began to cast out them that sold and *b* in the temple

*Luke 14:18* I have *b* a piece of ground, and I must needs go and see it

*1 Cor 6:20* ye are *b* with a price…glorify God

*1 Cor 7:23* Ye are *b* with a price; be not ye the servants of men

## BOUND

*Gen 22:9* Abraham...laid the wood...and *b* Isaac his son

*Judg 16:21* the Philistines took him [Samson]...and *b* him with fetters of brass

*Dan 3:23* Shadrach, Meshach, and Abednego, fell down *b* into the...fiery furnace

*Matt 14:3* Herod had laid hold on John, and *b* him

*Matt 18:18* Whatsoever ye shall bind on earth shall be *b* in heaven

*Mark 5:4* he [a demon-possessed man] had been often *b*

*Luke 10:34* *b*...wounds...took care of him [wounded traveler]

*John 11:44* he [Lazarus] came forth, *b*...with graveclothes

*Acts 20:22* I [Paul] go *b* in the spirit unto Jerusalem

*2 Tim 2:9* but the word of God is not *b*

*Rev 20:2* he [an angel] laid hold on the dragon...and *b* him a thousand years

## BOUNTIFUL [LY]

*Ps 13:6* the LORD...hath dealt *b'ly* with me

*Prov 22:9* He that hath a *b* eye shall be blessed

*2 Cor 9:6* he which soweth *b'ly* shall reap also *b'ly*

## BOWED

*Ps 38:6* I am troubled; I am *b* down greatly

*Ps 57:6* They...prepared a net for my steps...soul is *b* down

*Isa 2:11* the haughtiness of men shall be *b* down

*Matt 27:29* they *b* the knee before him [Jesus]...mocked him

*Luke 13:11* a woman which had a spirit of infirmity... was *b* together

*John 19:30* Jesus...*b* his head, and gave up the ghost

## BOZRAH (ancient capital of Edom). Gen 36:33 • 1 Chr 1:44 • Isa 34:6; 63:1 • Jer 49:13,22 • Amos 1:12 • Mic 2:12.

## BREAD OF LIFE, JESUS AS. See *"I Am" Statements of Jesus.*

## BREAK [EST, ETH, ING]

*Gen 32:24* there wrestled a man with him [Jacob] until the *b'ing* of the day

*Job 9:17* For he [God] *b'eth* me with a tempest

*Job 19:2* How long will ye [God]...*b* me...with words

*Job 34:24* He [God] shall *b* in pieces mighty men

*Ps 2:9* Thou shalt *b* them with a rod of iron

*Ps 29:5* the LORD *b'eth* the cedars of Lebanon

*Ps 46:9* he [God] *b'eth* the bow, and cutteth the spear

*Ps 48:7* Thou [God] **b'est** the ships of Tarshish

*Ps 58:6* **b** out the great teeth of the young lions, O LORD

*Ps 89:34* My covenant will I [God] not **b**

*Ps 94:5* They **b** in pieces thy people, O LORD

*Eccl 3:3* a time to **b** down, and a time to build up

*Isa 14:7* The whole earth is at rest...**b** forth into singing

*Isa 42:3* A bruised reed shall he [God's servant] not **b**

*Jer 1:14* Out of the north an evil shall **b** forth

*Jer 19:11* Even so will I [God] **b** this people and this city

*Jer 23:29* Is not my [God's] word like...a hammer that **b'eth** the rock

*Hos 1:5* I [God] will **b** the bow of Israel

*Matt 6:20* lay up...treasures in heaven...where thieves do not **b** through nor steal

*Matt 12:20* A bruised reed shall he [Jesus] not **b**

*Luke 24:35* he [Jesus] was known of them in **b'ing** of bread

*Acts 2:42* they [believers] continued stedfastly in the apostles' doctrine...**b'ing** of bread

*1 Cor 10:16* The bread which we **b,** is it not the communion of the body of Christ

**BRIBE [S]**

*1 Sam 12:3* of whose hand have I received any **b**

*Ps 26:10* and their right hand is full of **b's**

*Amos 5:12* they afflict the just, they take a **b**

**BUILDER [S]**

*Ps 118:22* stone which the **b's** refused is become the head stone of the corner

*Mark 12:10* The stone which the **b's** rejected is become the head of the corner

*Acts 4:11* This is the stone... set at nought of you **b's**

*Heb 11:10* he [Abraham] looked for a city...whose **b** and maker is God

*1 Pet 2:7* the stone which the **b's** disallowed...is made the head of the corner

**BUILDING [S]**

*1 Kgs 7:1* Solomon was **b** his own house thirteen years

*2 Chr 3:3* Solomon was instructed for the **b** of the house of God

*Mark 13:2* Seest thou these great **b's?** there shall not be left one stone upon another

*1 Cor 3:9* ye are God's husbandry, ye are God's **b**

*2 Cor 5:1* we have a **b** of God, an house not made with hands, eternal

*Eph 2:21* the **b** fitly framed together groweth unto an holy temple

**BURDEN [S]**

*Ex 1:11* they [the Egyptians] did set over them taskmasters to afflict them with their **b's**

*Ps 38:4* as an heavy **b** they [sins] are too heavy for me

*Ps 55:22* Cast thy **b** upon the LORD...he shall sustain thee

*Jer 17:22* Neither carry forth a **b**...on the sabbath day

*Matt 11:30* my [Jesus'] yoke is easy, and my **b** is light

*Matt 20:12* we have borne the **b** and heat of the day

*Matt 23:4* they [the Pharisees] bind heavy **b's**

*Gal 6:2* Bear ye one another's **b's**...fulfil the law of Christ

*Gal 6:5* For every man shall bear his own **b**

**BURIAL OF JESUS.** See *Jesus, Life and Ministry of.*

**BURN [ED, ETH, ING]**

*Ex 3:2* the bush **b'ed** with fire, and...was not consumed

*Ex 30:8* when Aaron lighteth the lamps...shall **b** incense

*Neh 2:17* the gates [of Jerusalem] thereof are **b'ed**

*Job 30:30* my [Job's] bones are **b'ed** with heat

*Job 41:19* Out of his [God's] mouth go **b'ing** lamps

*Ps 79:5* shall thy [God's] jealousy **b** like fire

*Ps 97:3* A fire goeth before him [God], and **b'eth** up his enemies round about

*Prov 6:27* Can a man take fire in his bosom, and his clothes not be **b'ed**

*Jer 7:9* Will ye steal, murder... and **b** incense unto Baal

*Jer 20:9* his [God's] word was in mine [Jeremiah's] heart as a **b'ing** fire

*Jer 39:8* the Chaldeans **b'ed** the king's house

*Dan 3:17* our God...is able to deliver us from the **b'ing** fiery furnace

*Luke 3:17* the chaff he [God] will **b** with fire

*Luke 24:32* Did not our heart **b** within us

*Rom 1:27* the men...**b'ed** in their lust one toward another

*1 Cor 3:15* If any man's work shall be **b'ed**...suffer loss

*1 Cor 7:9* for it is better to marry than to **b**

*1 Cor 13:3* though I [Paul] give my body to be **b'ed,** and have not charity

*2 Pet 3:10* the earth also and the works...shall be **b'ed** up

*Rev 19:20* beast...false prophet ...were cast...into a lake... **b'ing** with brimstone

**BURNING BUSH RE-VEALED TO MOSES.** Ex 3:1–5.

**BURNT OFFERING, IN-STRUCTIONS FOR.** Lev 1:1–17.

**BUY [ETH]**

*Gen 42:3* Joseph's ten brethren went…to *b* corn in Egypt

*Prov 23:23* *B* the truth, and sell it not; also wisdom

*Prov 31:16* She considereth a field, and *b'eth* it

*Amos 8:6* *b* the poor for silver… needy for a pair of shoes

*Matt 13:44* a man…selleth all…he hath, and *b'eth* that field

*John 6:5* he [Jesus] saith… Whence shall we *b* bread, that these may eat

**BUYER**

*Isa 24:2* as with the *b,* so with the seller

*Ezek 7:12* let not the *b* rejoice, nor the seller mourn

**BYWORD**

*Deut 28:37* thou shalt become… a *b,* among all nations

*1 Kgs 9:7* Israel shall be…a *b* among all people

*Job 17:6* He [God] hath made me [Job] also a *b*

*Ps 44:14* Thou [God] makest us a *b* among the heathen

# -C-

**CAESAREA** (a city of Judah on the coast of the Mediterranean Sea where Paul was held as a prisoner). Acts 8:40; 9:30; 10:1,24; 11:11; 12:19; 18:22; 21:8–16; **23:23,33; 25:1–16.**

**CAESAREA PHILIPPI** (a city in northern Palestine where Peter confessed Jesus as the Messiah). Matt 16:13–20.

**CAIAPHAS** (high priest of the Jews before whom Jesus and the apostles Peter and John appeared). Matt 26:3,57 • Luke 3:2 • John 11:49; 18:13–14,24, 28 • Acts 4:6.

**CAIN** (oldest son of Adam and Eve who murdered his brother Abel). **Gen 4:1–25** • Heb 11:4 • 1 John 3:12 • Jude 11.

**CAINAN.** See *Kenan.*

**CALEB** (one of the twelve spies who scouted Canaan and recommended that Israel attack the Canaanites). **Num 13:6,30;** 14:6,24,30,38; 26:65; 32:12; 34:19 • Deut 1:36 • Josh 14:6,13–14; 15:13–18; 21:12 • Judg 1:12–20 • 1 Sam 25:3; 30:14 • 1 Chr 4:15; 6:56.

## CALF

*Ex 32:24* I [Aaron] cast it into the fire … there came out this *c*

*Deut 9:16* ye had sinned … and had made you a molten *c*

*Ps 106:19* They made a *c* in Horeb, and worshipped the molten image

*Isa 11:6* shall lie down with … *c* and the young lion

*Jer 34:18* they cut the *c* in twain, and passed between the parts thereof

*Luke 15:23* bring hither the fatted *c,* and kill it

*Acts 7:41* they made a *c* … and offered sacrifice unto the idol

## CALL [ED, EST, ING]

*Gen 1:5* God *c'ed* the light Day … the darkness … Night

*Gen 2:19* whatsoever Adam *c'ed* every living creature, that was the name

*Gen 12:8* he [Abraham] builded an altar … and *c'ed* upon the name of the LORD

*Gen 17:5* Neither shall thy name any more be *c'ed* Abram, but … Abraham

*Gen 17:19* thou [Abraham] shalt *c* his name Isaac

*Gen 32:30* Jacob *c'ed* the name of the place Peniel

*Gen 35:10* thy name shall not be *c'ed* any more Jacob

*Gen 49:1* Jacob *c'ed* unto his sons, and said, Gather yourselves together

*Ex 2:7* *c* to thee a nurse of the Hebrew women

*Ex 2:10* she *c'ed* his name Moses ... Because I drew him out of the water

*Ex 3:4* God *c'ed* unto him [Moses] out of the midst of the bush

*Ex 19:20* the LORD *c'ed* Moses up to the top of the mount

*Deut 4:26* I [Moses] *c* heaven ... to witness against you

*Deut 28:10* all people ... shall see that thou art *c'ed* by the name of the LORD

*Judg 16:25* *C* for Samson, that he may make us sport

*1 Sam 3:8* the LORD *c'ed* Samuel again the third time

*1 Sam 12:18* So Samuel *c'ed* unto the LORD

*1 Kgs 18:25* Elijah said ... *c* on the name of your gods, but put no fire under

*2 Kgs 5:11* I [Naaman] thought, He [Elisha] will surely ... *c* on ... the LORD

*1 Chr 11:7* they *c'ed* it [Jerusalem] the city of David

*1 Chr 16:8* *c* upon his [God's] name, make known his deeds

*2 Chr 7:14* If my [God's] people, which are *c'ed* by my name, shall ... pray

*Job 27:10* will he always *c* upon God

*Ps 4:1* Hear me when I *c*, O God of my righteousness

*Ps 18:3* *c* upon the LORD, who is worthy to be praised

*Ps 18:6* In my distress I *c'ed* upon the LORD

*Ps 50:15* *c* upon me [God] in the day of trouble

*Ps 72:17* all nations shall *c* him [God] blessed

*Ps 86:5* thou, Lord, art ... plenteous in mercy unto all them that *c* upon thee

*Ps 105:1* give thanks unto the LORD; *c* upon his name

*Ps 145:18* The LORD is nigh unto all them that *c* upon him

*Prov 31:28* Her children arise up, and *c* her blessed

*Isa 7:14* and bear a son, and shall *c* his name Immanuel

*Isa 9:6* his [Messiah's] name shall be *c'ed* Wonderful

*Isa 45:3* I, the LORD, which *c* thee by thy name, am the God of Israel

*Isa 49:1* The LORD hath *c'ed* me from the womb

*Isa 55:6* *c* ye upon him [God] while he is near

*Isa 62:2* thou shalt be *c'ed* by a new name

*Isa 62:4* but thou shalt be *c'ed* Hephzibah, and thy land Beulah

*Isa 65:24* before they *c*, I [God] will answer

*Jer 3:17* they shall *c* Jerusalem the throne of the LORD

*Jer 33:3* *C* unto me [God], and I will answer thee

*Dan 2:2* the king commanded to *c* the magicians

*Hos 1:6* God said unto him [Hosea], *C* her name Loruhamah

*Hos 11:1* then I [God]...*c'ed* my son out of Egypt

*Joel 1:14* Sanctify ye a fast, *c* a solemn assembly

*Joel 2:32* whosoever shall *c* on the name of the LORD shall be delivered

*Jon 1:6* O sleeper [Jonah]? arise, *c* upon thy God

*Matt 1:21* thou [Joseph] shalt *c* his name JESUS

*Matt 1:25* and he [Joseph] *c'ed* his name JESUS

*Matt 2:23* He [Jesus] shall be *c'ed* a Nazarene

*Matt 5:9* the peacemakers... shall be *c'ed*...children of God

*Matt 9:13* I [Jesus] am not come to *c* the righteous, but sinners to repentance

*Matt 11:16* children sitting in the markets, and *c'ing* unto their fellows

*Matt 18:2* Jesus *c'ed* a little child unto him

*Matt 19:17* Why *c'est* thou me [Jesus] good

*Matt 20:16* many be *c'ed,* but few chosen

*Matt 21:13* My [God's] house shall be *c'ed*...house of prayer

*Matt 23:9* *c* no man your father upon the earth

*Matt 27:22* What shall I [Pilate] do then with Jesus which is *c'ed* Christ

*Luke 1:13* thou [Zacharias] shalt *c* his name John

*Luke 1:32* He [Jesus]...shall be *c'ed*...Son of the Highest

*Luke 6:46* And why *c* ye me, Lord, Lord

*Luke 9:1* he [Jesus] *c'ed* his twelve disciples together, and gave them...authority

*Luke 14:13* *c* the poor, the maimed, the lame

*Luke 15:21* I [prodigal son] have sinned...no more worthy to be *c'ed* thy son

*John 1:42* thou [Peter] shalt be *c'ed* Cephas...a stone

*Acts 2:21* whosoever shall *c* on...the Lord shall be saved

*Acts 10:15* What God hath cleansed, that *c* not thou [Peter] common

*Acts 11:26* disciples were *c'ed* Christians first in Antioch

*Acts 13:2* Separate me Barnabas and Saul for the work whereunto I have *c'ed* them

*Rom 1:1* Paul, a servant...*c'ed* to be an apostle

*Rom 8:28* all things work together for good...to them who are the *c'ed*

*Rom 10:12* the same Lord…is rich unto all that *c* upon him

*Rom 10:13* whosoever shall *c* upon…the Lord shall be saved

*Rom 10:14* How then shall they *c* on him in whom they have not believed

*1 Cor 1:26* not many mighty, not many noble, are *c'ed*

*1 Cor 7:20* Let every man abide in the same *c'ing*

*Gal 5:13* brethren, ye have been *c'ed* unto liberty

*Eph 4:1* walk worthy of the vocation…ye are *c'ed*

*Phil 3:14* I [Paul] press toward the mark for the prize of the high *c'ing* of God

*1 Thes 4:7* For God hath not *c'ed* us unto uncleanness, but unto holiness

*2 Tim 2:22* follow righteousness…with them that *c* on the Lord out of a pure heart

*Heb 11:8* Abraham, when he was *c'ed*…obeyed

*Jas 5:14* Is any sick among you? let him *c* for the elders

*1 Pet 2:9* the praises of him [Jesus] who hath *c'ed* you out of darkness

*1 John 3:1* that we should be *c'ed* the sons of God

## CALL ON THE LORD

*2 Sam 22:4* I will *c-o-t-L,* who is worthy to be praised

*2 Tim 2:22* follow righteousness…with them that *c-o-t-L* out of a pure heart

**CALVARY** (a hill near Jerusalem where Jesus was crucified). Luke 23:33. The word is from a Latin word which means "skull," thus "place of the skull." *Golgotha:* Mark 15:22 • John 19:17.

**CANA OF GALILEE** (a village where Jesus performed His first miracle—the turning of water into wine). **John 2:1–11;** 4:46–54; 21:2.

## CANAAN

1. A son of Ham whose descendants founded several tribal peoples in and around Palestine. Gen 9:18–27; 10:6,15–18 • 1 Chr 1:8,13.

2. The region where Canaan's descendants settled and the territory that God promised to Abraham. Gen 15:3–7. *Chanaan:* Acts 7:11.

**CANDACE** (a title of the queens of Ethiopia in New Testament times). Acts 8:27.

## CANDLE

*Ps 18:28* For thou [God] wilt light my *c*

*Matt 5:15* Neither do men light a *c,* and put it under a bushel

*Rev 22:5* they need no *c,* neither light of the sun

**CAPERNAUM** (a city on the shore of the Sea of Galilee which served as the headquarters for Jesus during His Galilean ministry). **Matt 4:13–17;** 8:5; 11:23; 17:24 • Mark 1:21; 2:1; 9:33 • Luke 4:23,31; 7:1; 10:15 • John 2:12; 4:46; 6:17,24,59.

**CAPHTOR** (the original home of the Philistines, probably the island of Crete). Deut 2:23 • Jer 47:4 • Amos 9:7.

**CAPPADOCIA** (a Roman province of Asia Minor). Acts 2:9 • 1 Pet 1:1.

**CAPTIVE [S]**
*Ps 68:18* Thou hast ascended on high, thou hast led captivity *c*
*Isa 61:1* LORD hath anointed me [God's servant] ... to proclaim liberty to the *c's*
*Jer 13:19* Judah shall be carried away *c*
*Jer 39:9* Nebuzaradan ... carried away *c* into Babylon the remnant of the people
*Ezek 1:1* as I [Ezekiel] was among the *c's* by the river
*Luke 4:18* he [God] hath anointed me [Jesus] ... to preach deliverance to the *c's*

*Eph 4:8* When he [Jesus] ascended ... he led captivity *c*

**CARCHEMISH** (an ancient city in Mesopotamia where the Assyrian army defeated the Egyptians). Isa 10:9 • Jer 46:2. *Charchemish:* 2 Chr 35:20–24.

**CARE [S, ST, TH]**
*Mark 4:19* the *c's* of this world ... choke the word
*Mark 4:38* *c'st* thou [Jesus] not ... we [the disciples] perish
*John 10:13* he is an hireling, and *c'th* not for the sheep
*1 Cor 7:33* he that is married *c'th* for the things that are of the world
*2 Cor 11:28* that which cometh upon me [Paul] daily, the *c* of all the churches
*1 Tim 3:5* how shall he take *c* of the church of God
*1 Pet 5:7* all your *c* upon him [Jesus]; for he *c'th* for you

**CARMEL, MOUNT** (a mountain where the prophet Elijah demonstrated the authority of God over the priests of the pagan god Baal). Josh 12:22; 19:26 • 1 Sam 15:12 • **1 Kgs 18:19–45** • 2 Kgs 2:25; 4:25; 19:23 • 2 Chr 26:10 • Song 7:5 • Isa 33:9; 35:2; 37:24 • Jer 46:18; 50:19 • Amos 1:2; 9:3 • Mic 7:14 • Nah 1:4.

**CASLUHIM** (an ancient people descended from Mizraim, son of Ham; Casluhim was the Hebrew word for Egypt). Gen 10:14 • 1 Chr 1:12.

**CAST [ING]**

*Gen 37:20* slay him [Joseph], and *c* him into some pit

*Ex 4:3* he [Moses] *c* it [his rod] on the ground, and it became a serpent

*Ex 32:24* I [Aaron] *c* it into the fire…there came out this calf

*Lev 16:8* Aaron shall *c* lots upon the two goats

*Josh 18:10* Joshua *c* lots for them in Shiloh

*Job 8:20* God will not *c* away a perfect man

*Job 30:19* He [God] hath *c* me into the mire

*Ps 37:24* Though he fall, he shall not be utterly *c* down

*Ps 42:11* Why art thou *c* down, O my soul

*Ps 51:11* *C* me not away from thy [God's] presence

*Ps 55:22* *C* thy burden upon the LORD…he shall sustain thee

*Ps 71:9* *C* me not off in the time of old age

*Ps 77:7* Will the Lord *c* off for ever…be favourable no more

*Ps 94:14* the LORD will not *c* off his people

*Eccl 3:5* A time to *c* away stones, and a time to gather

*Eccl 11:1* *C* thy bread upon the waters

*Isa 31:7* every man shall *c* away his idols of silver

*Jer 7:15* I [God] will *c* you out of my sight

*Dan 3:21* these men…were *c* into the…fiery furnace

*Dan 6:16* brought Daniel…*c* him into the den of lions

*Jon 1:15* they [mariners]…*c* him [Jonah] forth into the sea

*Zech 11:13* thirty pieces of silver, and *c* them to the potter

*Matt 3:10* tree…bringeth not forth good fruit is…*c* into the fire

*Matt 15:26* take the children's bread, and *c* it to dogs

*Matt 21:12* Jesus…*c* out all them that sold and bought in the temple

*Matt 27:5* And he [Judas] *c* down the pieces of silver

*Matt 27:35* crucified him [Jesus], and parted his garments, *c'ing* lots

*Mark 1:39* he [Jesus] preached…throughout all Galilee, and *c* out devils

*Mark 12:43* this poor widow hath *c* more in

*Luke 9:49* Master, we saw one *c'ing* out devils in thy name

*John 8:7* He that is without sin…let him first *c* a stone

*Rom 13:12* let us therefore *c* off the works of darkness

*1 Pet 5:7* *C'ing* all your care upon him [Jesus]; for he careth for you

*Rev 12:9* the great dragon was *c* out, that old serpent

*Rev 20:15* not found...in the book of life was *c* into the lake of fire

## CASTOR AND POLLUX

(pagan gods who were considered protectors of sailors). Paul's ship to Rome featured a carving of these two gods. Acts 28:11.

## CAUGHT

*2 Sam 18:9* his [Absalom's] head *c* hold of the oak

*Eccl 9:12* as the birds...*c* in the snare; so are the sons of men

*Matt 14:31* Jesus stretched... his hand, and *c* him [Peter]

*Acts 8:39* the Spirit of the Lord *c* away Philip

*1 Thes 4:17* we...shall be *c* up together...in the clouds

## CEASE [D, ING]

*Gen 8:22* While the earth remaineth...day and night shall not *c*

*Josh 5:12* And the manna *c'd* on the morrow

*Neh 6:3* why should the work *c*...I [Nehemiah] leave it

*Job 32:1* these three men *c'd* to answer Job

*Ps 37:8* *C* from anger, and forsake wrath

*Ps 85:4* O God...cause thine anger toward us to *c*

*Prov 23:4* Labour not to be rich: *c* from thine...wisdom

*Eccl 12:3* the grinders *c* because they are few

*Ezek 26:13* I will cause the noise of thy songs to *c*

*Jon 1:15* they...cast him [Jonah] forth...and the sea *c'ed* from her raging

*Mark 4:39* the wind *c'd,* and there was a great calm

*Acts 5:42* they [the apostles] *c'd* not to teach and preach Jesus Christ

*Acts 12:5* prayer was made without *c'ing* of the church unto God for him [Peter]

*Rom 1:9* without *c'ing* I [Paul] make mention of you always in my prayers

*1 Cor 13:8* whether there be tongues, they shall *c*

*Col 1:9* since the day we heard it, do not *c* to pray for you

*1 Thes 5:17* Pray without *c'ing*

## CEDARS OF LEBANON

*Judg 9:15* let fire come out... and devour the *c-o-L*

*Ps 29:5* yea, the LORD breaketh the *c-o-L*

*Ps 104:16* trees...are full of sap; the *c-o-L,* which he [God] hath planted

*Isa 2:13* upon all the *c-o-L,* that are high and lifted up

*Isa 14:8* the fir trees rejoice at thee, and the *c-o-L*

**CEDRON.** See *Kidron.*

**CENCHREA** (a harbor of Corinth through which Paul passed during his second missionary journey). **Acts 18:18** • Rom 16:1.

**CHALDEANS, LAND OF THE.** See *Babylonia.*

**CHANAAN.** See *Canaan,* No. 2.

**CHANGE [D, TH]**
*Jer 2:11* Hath a nation *c'd* their gods, which are … no gods
*Jer 13:23* Can the Ethiopian *c* his skin … the leopard his spots
*Dan 2:21* he [God] *c'th* the times and the seasons
*Dan 5:6* the king's countenance was *c'd*
*Hos 4:7* therefore will I [God] *c* their glory into shame
*Rom 1:23* *c'd* the glory of the uncorruptible God
*Rom 1:26* their women did *c* the natural use into that which is against nature
*1 Cor 15:51* We shall not all sleep, but we shall all be *c'd*
*Phil 3:21* Who shall *c* our vile body … like … his glorious body

**CHARCHEMISH.** See *Carchemish.*

**CHARGE [D]**
*Deut 3:28* *c* Joshua, and encourage him
*1 Kgs 2:1* David … *c'd* Solomon his son
*Ps 91:11* For he [God] shall give his angels *c* over thee
*Matt 16:20* Then *c'd* he … that they should tell no man that he was Jesus the Christ
*Mark 8:15* And he [Jesus] *c'd* them, saying … beware of the leaven of the Pharisees
*Luke 8:56* he [Jesus] *c'd* them … tell no man what was done
*Acts 7:60* Lord, lay not this sin to their *c*
*1 Tim 6:17* *C* them that are rich … they be not high-minded

**CHARITY**
*1 Cor 13:3* and have not *c,* it profiteth me nothing
*Col 3:14* And above all these things put on *c*
*1 Tim 4:12* be thou an example … in conversation, in *c*
*1 Pet 4:8* *c* shall cover the multitude of sins
*Rev 2:19* I [Jesus] know thy works, and *c,* and service

**CHARRAN.** See *Haran.*

74

## CHASTEN [ED, EST, ETH, ING]

*Ps 38:1* O LORD, rebuke me not…neither *c* me in thy hot displeasure

*Ps 73:14* all the day long have I been…*c'ed* every morning

*Ps 94:12* Blessed is the man whom thou *c'est,* O LORD

*Prov 3:11* My son, despise not the *c'ing* of the LORD

*1 Cor 11:32* we are judged, we are *c'ed* of the Lord

*Heb 12:6* whom the Lord loveth he *c'eth*

*Rev 3:19* As many as I love, I rebuke and *c*

**CHEBAR** (a river or canal of Babylonia where the prophet Ezekiel received his visions during the Exile). Ezek 1:1,3; 3:15,23; 10:15,20,22; 43:3.

**CHEDORLAOMER** (a king of Elam who invaded Canaan in Abraham's time). Gen 14:1–17.

## CHEER

*Matt 9:2* Son [man with palsy], be of good *c*

*John 16:33* be of good *c;* I [Jesus] have overcome the world

*Acts 23:11* Be of good *c,* Paul… so must thou bear witness also at Rome

## CHEERFUL

*Prov 15:13* A merry heart maketh a *c* countenance

*Zech 9:17* corn shall make the young men *c*

*2 Cor 9:7* let him give…for God loveth a *c* giver

**CHEMOSH** (chief pagan god of the Moabites and Ammonites to which children were sacrificed). Num 21:29 • Judg 11:24 • 1 Kgs 11:7,33 • 2 Kgs 23:13 • Jer 48:7,13,46.

**CHERETHIMS.** See *Cherethites.*

**CHERETHITES** (a tribe of the Philistines in southwest Palestine). 1 Sam 30:14 • Zeph 2:5. *Cherethims:* Ezek 25:16.

**CHERITH** (a brook where the prophet Elijah was fed by ravens during a famine). 1 Kgs 17:3–6.

## CHILD

*Gen 17:17* a *c* be born unto him…an hundred years old

*Ex 22:22* Ye shall not afflict any widow, or fatherless *c*

*1 Kgs 3:25* king [Solomon] said, Divide the living *c* in two

*1 Kgs 17:22* the soul of the *c* came into him…he revived

*2 Kgs 5:14* his [Naaman's] flesh came again like unto the flesh of a little *c*

*Prov 22:6* Train up a *c* in the way he should go

*Isa 9:6* unto us a *c* is born, unto us a son is given

*Jer 1:6* behold, I [Jeremiah] cannot speak: for I am a *c*

*Hos 11:1* When Israel was a *c,* then I [God] loved him

*Matt 1:23* a virgin shall be with *c*…bring forth a son

*Matt 2:21* he [Joseph]…took the young *c*…and came into the land of Israel

*Matt 18:4* Whosoever…shall humble himself as this little *c,* the same is greatest

*Mark 10:15* not receive the kingdom…as a little *c,* he shall not enter

*Luke 2:17* they made known abroad the saying…concerning this *c*

*Luke 2:40* the *c* [Jesus] grew, and waxed strong in spirit

*1 Cor 13:11* When I [Paul] was a *c,* I spake as a *c*

*2 Tim 3:15* from a *c* thou [Timothy] hast known the holy scriptures

## CHILDREN

*Gen 3:16* in sorrow thou [Eve] shalt bring forth *c*

*Gen 37:3* Israel loved Joseph more than all his *c*

*Ex 1:7* the *c* of Israel were fruitful, and increased

*Ex 12:26* when your *c* shall say…What mean ye by this service

*Ex 20:5* visiting the iniquity of the fathers upon the *c*

*Num 8:17* the firstborn of the *c* of Israel are mine [God's]

*Deut 24:16* The fathers shall not be put to death for the *c*

*Josh 4:6* when your *c* ask their fathers…What mean ye by these stones

*Josh 18:10* Joshua divided the land unto the *c* of Israel

*Job 19:18* Yea, young *c* despised me [Job]

*Ps 14:2* The LORD looked down…upon the *c* of men

*Ps 34:11* Come, ye *c*…I will teach…the fear of the LORD

*Ps 103:7* He [God] made known…acts unto the *c* of Israel

*Ps 103:13* as a father pitieth his *c,* so the LORD pitieth them that fear him

*Ps 115:14* The LORD shall increase…you and your *c*

*Ps 127:3* Lo, *c* are an heritage of the LORD

*Ps 127:4* As arrows are in the hand of a mighty man; so are *c* of the youth

*Prov 4:1* Hear, ye *c,* the instruction of a father

*Prov 13:22* A good man leaveth an inheritance to his children's *c*

*Prov 20:7* his *c* are blessed after him [the just man]

*Prov 31:28* Her *c* arise up, and call her blessed

*Isa 54:13* all thy *c* shall be taught of the LORD

*Jer 3:22* Return, ye backsliding *c* ... I [God] will heal

*Jer 31:15* Rahel weeping for her *c* refused to be comforted

*Lam 1:16* my *c* are desolate, because the enemy prevailed

*Hos 2:4* they be the *c* of whoredoms

*Matt 2:16* Herod ... slew all the *c* ... in Bethlehem

*Matt 7:11* know how to give good gifts unto your *c*

*Matt 18:3* Except ye ... become as little *c,* ye shall not enter into the kingdom

*Matt 23:37* how often would I [Jesus] have gathered thy *c*

*Matt 27:25* His [Jesus'] blood be on us, and on our *c*

*Mark 10:13* they brought young *c* to him [Jesus]

*Luke 16:8* the *c* of this world ... wiser than the *c* of light

*John 8:39* If ye were Abraham's *c,* ye would do the works of Abraham

*John 12:36* that ye may be the *c* of light

*1 Cor 14:20* Brethren, be not *c* in understanding

*Gal 4:28* we, brethren ... are the *c* of promise

*Eph 4:14* That we henceforth be no more *c*

*Eph 6:1* **C,** obey your parents in the Lord

*Eph 6:4* fathers, provoke not your *c* to wrath

*1 Thes 5:5* Ye are all the *c* of light ... children of the day

*1 John 2:1* My little *c* ... write I unto you, that ye sin not

*1 John 3:18* little *c,* let us not love in word ... but in deed

*1 John 5:21* Little *c,* keep yourselves from idols

*3 John 4* no greater joy than to hear that my [John's] *c* walk in truth

**CHILDREN OF GOD**

*Matt 5:9* Blessed are the peacemakers: for they shall be called the *c-o-G*

*Rom 8:16* The Spirit ... beareth witness ... we are the *c-o-G*

*Gal 3:26* ye are all the *c-o-G* by faith in Christ Jesus

*1 John 5:2* know that we love the *c-o-G,* when we love God

**CHILDREN WELCOMED BY JESUS.** Matt 19:13–15 • Mark 10:13–16 • Luke 18:15–17.

**CHINNEROTH, SEA OF.** See *Galilee, Sea of.*

**CHITTIM.** See *Cyprus.*

**CHLOE** (a believer in Corinth). 1 Cor 1:11.

## CHOOSE [ING]

*Deut 7:7* The LORD did not...*c* you, because ye were more in number

*Deut 30:19* *c* life, that both thou and thy seed may live

*Josh 24:15* *c* you this day whom ye will serve

*Neh 9:7* Thou art the LORD the God, who didst *c* Abram

*Phil 1:22* yet what I [Paul] shall *c* I wot not

*Heb 11:25* **C'ing** rather to suffer affliction

## CHORAZIN (a city near the Sea of Galilee upon which Jesus pronounced a woe because of its unbelief). Matt 11:21 • Luke 10:13.

## CHOSEN

*Deut 7:6* God hath *c* thee to be a special people

*Judg 10:14* Go and cry unto the gods which ye have *c*

*1 Chr 16:13* ye children of Jacob, his [God's] *c* ones

*1 Chr 28:5* he [God] hath *c* Solomon my [David's] son to sit upon the throne

*Ps 33:12* Blessed is...the people whom he [God] hath *c* for his own inheritance

*Prov 22:1* A good name is rather to be *c* than great riches

*Isa 43:10* Ye are...my [God's] servant whom I have *c*

*Matt 12:18* Behold my [God's] servant, whom I have *c*

*Matt 20:16* for many be called, but few *c*

*Luke 10:42* Mary hath *c* that good part

*John 15:16* Ye have not *c* me [Jesus], but I have *c* you

*Acts 9:15* he [Paul] is a *c* vessel unto me [Jesus]

*1 Cor 1:27* God hath *c* the foolish things of the world to confound the wise

*2 Thes 2:13* God hath...*c* you to salvation

*1 Pet 2:9* ye are a *c* generation, a royal priesthood

## CHRONICLES, BOOKS OF FIRST AND SECOND. Two historical books of the Old Testament that cover several centuries of history, beginning with a genealogy of Adam and his descendants (1 Chr 1–9) and ending with the return of Jewish captives to their homeland about 538 B.C. following a period of exile (2 Chr 36).

## CHURCH [ES]

*Matt 16:18* thou art Peter, and upon this rock I [Jesus] will build my *c*

*Matt 18:17* if he shall neglect to hear them, tell it unto the *c*

*Acts 2:47* Lord added to the *c* daily such as should be saved

*Acts 5:11* great fear came upon all the *c*

*Acts 8:3* As for Saul, he made havock of the *c*

*Acts 14:23* when they [Paul and Barnabas] had ordained them elders in every *c*

*Acts 20:28* the Holy Ghost hath made you overseers, to feed the *c* of God

*Rom 16:16* The *c'es* of Christ salute you

*1 Cor 14:4* he that prophesieth edifieth the *c*

*1 Cor 14:35* it is a shame for women to speak in the *c*

*2 Cor 11:28* cometh upon me [Paul] daily, the care of all the *c'es*

*Gal 1:13* I [Paul] persecuted the *c* of God

*Eph 3:21* Unto him be glory in the *c* by Christ Jesus

*Eph 5:25* Christ also loved the *c,* and gave himself for it

*Col 1:18* he [Christ] is the head of the body, the *c*

*1 Tim 3:5* how shall he take care of the *c* of God

*1 Tim 3:15* *c* of the living God ... pillar and ground of ... truth

*Jas 5:14* elders of the *c;* and let them pray over him

*Rev 1:4* John to the seven *c'es* which are in Asia

*Rev 2:1* Unto the angel of the *c* of Ephesus

*Rev 2:8* unto the angel of the *c* in Smyrna

*Rev 2:12* to the angel of the *c* in Pergamos

*Rev 2:18* unto the angel of the *c* in Thyatira

*Rev 3:1* unto the angel of the *c* in Sardis

*Rev 3:7* to the angel of the *c* in Philadelphia

*Rev 3:14* unto the angel of the *c* of the Laodiceans

**CHUSHAN-RISHATHAIM** (a king of Mesopotamia who was defeated by the judge Othniel). Judg 3:8–10.

**CILICIA** (a province of Asia Minor whose major city was Tarsus, the apostle Paul's hometown). Acts 6:9; 15:23,41; 21:39; 22:3; 23:34; 27:5 • Gal 1:21.

**CIRCUMCISE [D]**

*Gen 17:11* ye shall *c* the flesh of your foreskin

*Gen 17:24* Abraham was ninety years old and nine, when he was *c'd*

*Lev 12:3* eighth day the flesh of his foreskin shall be *c'd*

*Josh 5:2* *c* again the children of Israel the second time

*Jer 4:4* *C* yourselves to the LORD, and take away the foreskins of your heart

*Acts 15:1* certain men ... from Judaea ... said, Except ye be *c'd* ... ye cannot be saved

*Gal 5:2* if ye be *c'd,* Christ shall profit you nothing

*Phil 3:5* **C'd** the eighth day, of the stock of Israel

## CIRCUMCISION

*Acts 10:45* they of the **c** which believed were astonished

*Rom 3:1* or what profit is there of **c**

*Rom 15:8* Christ was a minister of the **c** for the truth of God

*1 Cor 7:19* **C** is nothing, and uncircumcision is nothing

*Col 3:11* neither Greek nor Jew, **c** nor uncircumcision

**CITIES OF REFUGE** (six cities—Bezer, Golan, Hebron, Kedesh, Ramoth-gilead, and Shechem—set aside as sanctuaries for those who killed other persons by accident). Num 35:11,14 • Josh 20:2,8; 21:13, 21,27,32,38 • 1 Chr 6:57,67.

**CLAUDA** (a small island near Crete where Paul's ship anchored during a storm). Acts 27:16.

**CLAUDIUS LYSIAS** (a Roman military officer who protected Paul from his enemies). Acts 21:30–35; 23:22–30.

**CLEAN AND UNCLEAN ANIMALS.** Lev 11:1–47.

## CLEANSE [D, TH]

*Lev 16:30* shall the priest make an atonement…to **c** you

*Neh 13:22* I [Nehemiah] commanded the Levites that they should **c** themselves

*Ps 51:2* Wash me thoroughly… and **c** me from my sin

*Ps 73:13* Verily I have **c'd** my heart in vain

*Matt 11:5* the lepers are **c'd,** and the deaf hear

*Matt 23:26* **c** first that which is within the cup

*Mark 1:42* the leprosy departed…and he was **c'd**

*Luke 17:17* Were there not ten **c'd?** but where are the nine

*Acts 10:15* What God hath **c'd,** that call not thou [Peter] common

*2 Cor 7:1* let us **c** ourselves from all filthiness

*1 John 1:7* the blood of Jesus Christ…**c'th** us from all sin

*1 John 1:9* he [Jesus] is faithful and just…to **c** us from all unrighteousness

## CLEAVE [D, TH]

*Gen 2:24* shall a man leave his father and his mother, and shall **c** unto his wife

*Deut 10:20* to him [God] shalt thou **c**…swear by his name

*Josh 23:8* But **c** unto the LORD your God

*Job 19:20* My bone **c'th** to my skin and to my flesh

*Job 29:10* their tongue *c'd* to the roof of their mouth

*Ps 102:5* By reason...of my groaning my bones *c* to my skin

*Ps 137:6* let my tongue *c* to the roof of my mouth; if I prefer not Jerusalem

*Mark 10:7* shall a man leave his father and mother, and *c* to his wife

*Rom 12:9* Abhor that which is evil; *c* to that which is good

**CLEOPAS** (a Christian believer to whom the resurrected Christ appeared on the road to Emmaus). Luke 24:18.

**CLEOPHAS** (the husband of Mary, one of the women who was present at the crucifixion of Jesus). John 19:25. *Alphaeus:* Matt 10:3.

**CLOTHE [D, ING]**

*Gen 3:21* Unto Adam...wife did...God make coats of skins, and *c'd* them

*2 Chr 6:41* O LORD God, be *c'd* with salvation

*Job 7:5* My [Job's] flesh is *c'd* with worms

*Ps 93:1* The LORD...is *c'd* with majesty

*Ps 132:9* Let thy priests be *c'd* with righteousness

*Prov 31:25* Strength and honour are her *c'ing*

*Isa 50:3* I [God] *c* the heavens with blackness

*Isa 61:10* For he [God] hath *c'd* me with the garments of salvation

*Matt 7:15* Beware of false prophets...in sheep's *c'ing*

*Matt 25:36* Naked, and ye *c'd* me; sick...ye visited me

*Mark 1:6* John was *c'd* with camel's hair

*Mark 12:38* the scribes...love to go in long *c'ing*

*Mark 15:17* they *c'd* him [Jesus] with purple

*Luke 12:28* how much more will he [God] *c* you, O ye of little faith

*Luke 16:19* a certain rich man...*c'd* in purple

*1 Pet 5:5* be subject one to another...*c'd* with humility

*Rev 19:13* he was *c'd* with a vesture dipped in blood

**CLOTHES**

*Gen 37:34* Jacob rent his *c*... put sackcloth upon his loins

*Num 8:21* the Levites were purified...washed their *c*

*Josh 7:6* Joshua rent his *c,* and fell to the earth

*1 Kgs 1:1* covered him [David] with *c,* but he gat no heat

*Prov 6:27* Can a man take fire in his bosom, and his *c* not be burned

*Mark 5:28* she [woman with issue of blood] said, If I...

touch but his [Jesus'] *c,* I shall be whole

*Luke 2:7* wrapped him [Jesus] in swaddling *c*

*John 19:40* wound it [Jesus' body] in linen *c*

*Acts 7:58* laid down...*c* at a young man's [Paul's] feet

## CLOUD [S]

*Gen 9:13* I [God] do set my bow in the *c*

*Ex 13:21* LORD went before them [Israel]...pillar of a *c*

*Ex 40:34* a *c* covered the tent of the congregation

*1 Kgs 8:10* the *c* filled the house of the LORD

*1 Kgs 18:44* there ariseth a little *c* out of the sea

*Job 26:8* He [God] bindeth up the waters in his thick *c's*

*Ps 78:14* he [God] led them [Israel] with a *c*

*Ps 108:4* and thy [God's] truth reacheth unto the *c's*

*Prov 3:20* By his [God's] knowledge...the *c's* drop down the dew

*Isa 14:14* I will ascend above the heights of the *c's*

*Isa 19:1* the LORD rideth upon a swift *c*

*Isa 44:22* I [God] have blotted out, as a thick *c,* thy transgressions

*Lam 3:44* Thou [God] hast covered thyself with a *c*

*Joel 2:2* A day of darkness and...gloominess, a day of *c's*

*Matt 24:30* the Son of man coming in the *c's*

*Mark 9:7* voice came out of the *c,* saying, This is my beloved Son [Jesus]

*Luke 21:27* Son of man coming in a *c* with power and great glory

*Acts 1:9* he [Jesus] was taken up; and a *c* received him out of their sight

*1 Thes 4:17* we...shall be caught up together with them in the *c's*

*Heb 12:1* we also are compassed about with so great a *c* of witnesses

*Rev 1:7* Behold, he [Jesus] cometh with *c's;* and every eye shall see him

## COCK

*Matt 26:34* before the *c* crow, thou [Peter] shalt deny me [Jesus] thrice

*Mark 14:68* he [Peter] went out...and the *c* crew

*Luke 22:61* Peter remembered...Before the *c* crow, thou shalt deny me [Jesus]

## COLD

*Ps 147:17* who can stand before his [God's] *c*

*Prov 25:25* As *c* waters to a thirsty soul, so is good news

*Matt 24:12* the love of many shall wax *c*

*Rev 3:15* thou [church at Laodicea] art neither *c* nor hot

**COLOSSE** (a city near Ephesus and the site of a church to which Paul wrote one of his epistles). Col 1:2.

**COLOSSIANS, EPISTLE TO THE.** A short epistle of the apostle Paul on the theme of Christ's glory and majesty and His work of redemption (chaps. 1–2). Paul also challenged the Colossian Christians to express the love of Christ in their relationships with others (chaps. 3–4).

**COMFORT [ED, ETH]**
*Job 2:11* Job's three friends... came... to *c* him

*Ps 23:4* thy [God's] rod and thy staff they *c* me

*Isa 40:1 C* ye, *c* ye my people, saith your God

*Isa 49:13* the LORD hath *c'ed* his people

*Isa 61:2* To proclaim the acceptable year of the LORD... to *c* all that mourn

*Jer 31:15* Rahel weeping for her children refused to be *c'ed* for her children

*Lam 1:21* there is none to *c* me

*Matt 5:4* Blessed are they that mourn: for they shall be *c'ed*

*Luke 8:48* be of good *c*...faith hath made thee [woman with issue of blood] whole

*2 Cor 1:3* Blessed be God...the Father of mercies, and the God of all *c*

*2 Cor 1:4* Who *c'eth* us in all our tribulation

*Phil 2:1* If there be therefore any consolation in Christ, if any *c* of love

*1 Thes 4:18 c* one another with these words

**COMFORTER**
*John 14:26* the *C*...shall teach you all things

*John 15:26* the *C*...shall testify of me [Jesus]

*John 16:7* if I [Jesus] go not away, the *C* will not come unto you

**COMMAND [ED, ETH, ING]**
*Gen 7:5* Noah did...all that the LORD *c'ed* him

*Gen 21:4* Abraham circumcised his son Isaac...as God had *c'ed* him

*Gen 49:33* Jacob had made an end of *c'ing* his sons

*Ex 19:7* Moses...laid before their faces all these words which the LORD *c'ed*

*Deut 4:2* Ye shall not add unto the word...I [God] *c* you

*Deut 5:12* Keep the sabbath day to sanctify it, as the LORD...hath *c'ed*

*Josh 1:9* Have not I [God] *c'ed* thee? Be strong and of a good courage

*1 Sam 13:13* thou [Saul] hast not kept the command-ment...which he [God] *c'ed* thee

*1 Chr 16:15* the word which he [God] *c'ed* to a thousand generations

*Ps 33:9* he [God] *c'ed,* and it stood fast

*Ps 105:8* He [God] hath remem-bered...the word...he *c'ed*

*Jer 1:17* speak unto them all that I [God] *c* thee [Jere-miah]

*Dan 6:16* the king *c'ed,* and they...cast him [Daniel] into the den of lions

*Matt 28:20* observe all things whatsoever I [Jesus] have *c'ed* you

*Mark 1:27* with authority *c'eth* he [Jesus]...the unclean spirits

*Mark 6:8* [Jesus] *c'ed* them that they should take noth-ing for their journey

*Luke 4:3* *c* this stone that it be made bread

*Luke 8:25* for he [Jesus] *c'eth* even the winds and water

*John 8:5* Moses in the law *c'ed* us...such should be stoned

*John 15:17* These things I [Jesus] *c* you...love one another

## COMMANDMENT [S]

*Ex 16:28* How long refuse ye to keep my [God's] *c's*

*Ex 34:28* he [Moses] wrote upon the tables...the ten *c's*

*Lev 27:34* These are the *c's*... for the children of Israel in mount Sinai

*Deut 28:9* thou shalt keep the *c's* of the LORD thy God

*1 Kgs 2:3* keep his [God's]...*c's,* and his judgments

*2 Kgs 17:16* they left all the *c's* of the LORD

*Ezra 9:10* for we have forsaken thy [God's] *c's*

*Ps 111:7* all his [God's] *c's* are sure

*Ps 119:10* let me not wander from thy [God's] *c's*

*Ps 119:115* I will keep the *c's* of my God

*Ps 147:15* He [God] sendeth forth his *c* upon earth

*Prov 6:20* My son, keep thy father's *c*

*Prov 10:8* The wise in heart will receive *c's:* but a prat-ing fool shall fall

*Eccl 12:13* keep his [God's] *c's*...this is the...duty of man

*Amos 2:4* they have...not kept his [God's] *c's*

*Matt 15:3* ye [Pharisees] also transgress the *c* of God by your tradition

*Matt 22:40* On these two *c's* hang...the law and the prophets

*Mark 12:28* Which is the first *c* of all

*Mark 12:29* The first of all the *c's* is ... The Lord our God is one Lord

*John 13:34* A new *c* I [Jesus] give unto you, That ye love one another

*John 14:15* If ye love me [Jesus], keep my *c's*

*John 15:10* If ye keep my [Jesus'] *c's,* ye shall abide in my love

*John 15:12* This is my [Jesus'] *c* ... love one another, as I have loved you

*1 Cor 7:19* Circumcision is nothing ... but the keeping of the *c's* of God

*Eph 6:2* Honour thy father and mother; which is the first *c* with promise

*1 John 2:3* we know him [Jesus], if we keep his *c's*

*2 John 6* this is love, that we walk after his [God's] *c's*

*Rev 22:14* Blessed are they that do his [God's] *c's*

## COMMANDMENT [S] OF THE LORD

*Num 9:18* At the *c-o-t-L* the children of Israel journeyed

*Num 14:41* Wherefore now do ye transgress the *c-o-t-L*

*Deut 4:2* keep the *c's-o-t-L* your God

*Deut 8:6* thou shalt keep the *c's-o-t-L* thy God

*1 Sam 15:24* I [Saul] have transgressed the *c-o-t-L*

*2 Kgs 17:16* they left all the *c's-o-t-L* ... and made them molten images

*Ps 19:8* the *c-o-t-L* is pure, enlightening the eyes

## COMMEND [ED, ETH]

*Prov 12:8* A man shall be *c'ed* according to his wisdom

*Luke 16:8* the lord *c'ed* the unjust steward, because he had done wisely

*Luke 23:46* Father, into thy hands I [Jesus] *c* my spirit

*Rom 5:8* God *c'eth* his love toward us ... Christ died for us

*Rom 16:1* I [Paul] *c* unto you Phebe our sister

## COMMIT [TED, TETH]

*Gen 39:22* the keeper of the prison *c'ted* to Joseph's hand all the prisoners

*Ex 20:14* Thou shalt not *c* adultery

*Lev 18:29* the souls that *c* them shall be cut off

*Lev 20:10* the man that *c'teth* adultery ... shall surely be put to death

*Josh 22:20* Did not Achan the son of Zerah *c* a trespass

*Ps 31:5* Into thine [God's] hand I *c* my spirit

*Prov 6:32* whoso *c'teth* adultery with a woman lacketh understanding

*Prov 16:3 C* thy works unto the Lord

*Jer 2:13* my [God's] people have *c'ted* two evils

*Matt 5:28* whosoever looketh on a woman to lust after her hath *c'ted* adultery

*Matt 5:32* whosoever shall marry her that is divorced *c'teth* adultery

*Mark 10:11* Whosoever shall put away his wife, and marry another, *c'teth* adultery

*Mark 10:19* Thou knowest the commandments, Do not *c* adultery, Do not kill

*John 5:22* Father…hath *c'ted* all judgment unto the Son

*John 8:34* Whosoever *c'teth* sin is the servant of sin

*1 Cor 6:18* he that *c'teth* fornication sinneth against his own body

*1 Cor 10:8* Neither let us *c* fornication, as some of them

*2 Cor 5:19* God…in Christ… hath *c'ted* unto us the word of reconciliation

*1 Tim 6:20* Timothy, keep that which is *c'ted* to thy trust

*2 Tim 1:12* he [Jesus] is able to keep that which I [Paul] have *c'ted*…against that day

*2 Tim 2:2* the same *c* thou to faithful men

*1 John 3:9* Whosoever is born of God doth not *c* sin

**COMMON**

*Mark 12:37* the *c* people heard him [Jesus] gladly

*Acts 2:44* all that believed… had all things *c*

*Acts 10:14* I [Peter] have never eaten any thing that is *c* or unclean

*1 Cor 10:13* There hath no temptation taken you but such as is *c* to man

**COMMUNICATION [S]**

*Matt 5:37* let your *c* be, Yea, yea; Nay, nay

*Luke 24:17* What manner of *c's* are these

*Eph 4:29* Let no corrupt *c* proceed out of your mouth

**COMMUNION**

*1 Cor 10:16* cup of blessing which we bless, is it not the *c* of the blood of Christ

*2 Cor 6:14* what *c* hath light with darkness

*2 Cor 13:14* and the *c* of the Holy Ghost, be with you all

**COMPASSION [S]**

*Ex 2:6* she had *c* on him [Moses], and said, This is one of the Hebrews' children

*Ps 86:15* thou, O Lord, art a God full of *c*

*Ps 145:8* The LORD is gracious, and full of *c*

*Jer 12:15* I [God] will return, and have *c* on them

*Zech 7:9* show mercy and *c's* every man to his brother

*Matt 14:14* Jesus…was moved with *c* toward them

*Matt 18:27* the lord of that servant was moved with *c,* and loosed him

*Mark 9:22* if thou canst do any thing, have *c* on us

*Luke 10:33* a certain Samaritan…when he saw him, he had *c* on him

*Luke 15:20* his father…had *c,* and ran, and fell on his neck

*1 Pet 3:8* be ye all of one mind, having *c* one of another

*1 John 3:17* seeth his brother have need, and shutteth up his bowels of *c* from him

## COMPEL

*Matt 5:41* *c* thee to go a mile, go with him twain

*Mark 15:21* they *c* one Simon a Cyrenian…to bear his [Jesus'] cross

*Luke 14:23* Go out into the highways and hedges, and *c* them to come in

## CONCEIT [S]

*Prov 26:5* Answer a fool…lest he be wise in his own *c*

*Prov 28:11* The rich man is wise in his own *c*

*Rom 12:16* Be not wise in your own *c's*

## CONCEIVE [D]

*Gen 21:2* Sarah *c'd,* and bare Abraham a son

*Job 3:3* the day perish…in which it was said, There is a man child *c'd*

*Ps 51:5* shapen in iniquity, and in sin did my mother *c* me

*Isa 7:14* a virgin shall *c,* and bear a son

*Matt 1:20* that…*c'd* in her [Mary] is of the Holy Ghost

*Luke 1:31* thou [Mary] shalt *c*…and bring forth a son

*Luke 1:36* thy [Mary's] cousin Elisabeth, she hath also *c'd* a son in her old age

*Heb 11:11* Sara herself received strength to *c* seed

## CONCERNING

*Luke 2:17* they [shepherds] made known abroad the saying…*c* this child

*Luke 18:31* all things that are written…*c* the Son of man shall be accomplished

*Luke 24:27* he [Jesus] expounded…the things *c* himself

*Acts 28:22* for as *c* this sect…it is spoken against

*1 Cor 12:1* Now *c* spiritual gifts, brethren

*Eph 5:32* I [Paul] speak *c* Christ and the church

*1 Thes 5:18* this is the will of God in Christ Jesus *c* you

*1 Pet 4:12* *c* the fiery trial which is to try you

87

*2 Pet 3:9* The Lord is not slack *c* his promise

## CONDEMN [ED, ETH]
*Job 15:6* Thine own mouth *c'eth* thee
*Prov 12:2* a man of wicked devices will he [God] *c*
*Matt 12:37* by thy words thou shalt be *c'ed*
*Luke 6:37* *c* not, and ye shall not be *c'ed*
*John 3:17* God sent not his Son...to *c* the world
*John 8:11* Neither do I [Jesus] *c* thee: go...sin no more

## CONDEMNATION
*John 3:19* the *c*...men loved darkness rather than light
*Rom 8:1* no *c* to them which are in Christ Jesus
*Jas 3:1* knowing that we shall receive the greater *c*
*Jas 5:12* let your yea be yea... lest ye fall into *c*

## CONFESS [ETH, ING]
*Ps 32:5* I will *c* my transgressions unto the LORD
*Mark 1:5* were all baptized of him [John the Baptist]... *c'ing* their sins
*Luke 12:8* him shall the Son of man also *c*
*Rom 10:9* if thou shalt *c* with thy mouth the Lord Jesus
*Phil 2:11* every tongue should *c* that Jesus Christ is Lord

*Jas 5:16* *C* your faults one to another
*1 John 1:9* If we *c* our sins, he is faithful and just to forgive
*1 John 4:2* Every spirit that *c'eth* that Jesus Christ is come in the flesh is of God
*1 John 4:15* Whosoever shall *c* that Jesus is the Son of God, God dwelleth in him
*Rev 3:5* I [Jesus] will *c* his name before my Father

## CONFIDENCE
*Ps 118:9* better to trust in the LORD than to put *c* in princes
*Prov 14:26* In the fear of the LORD is strong *c*
*Isa 30:15* in quietness and in *c* shall be your strength
*Mic 7:5* put ye not *c* in a guide
*Eph 3:12* In whom [Jesus] we have...access with *c*
*1 John 2:28* when he [Jesus] shall appear, we may have *c*

## CONFIDENT
*Prov 14:16* but the fool rageth, and is *c*
*2 Cor 5:8* We are *c*...willing... to be absent from the body
*Phil 1:6* Being *c*...that he which hath begun a good work...will perform it

## CONFIRM [ED, ETH, ING]
*Deut 27:26* Cursed be he that *c'eth* not all the words of this law to do them

*1 Chr 14:2* David perceived… LORD had *c'ed* him king

*Mark 16:20* the Lord working with them, and *c'ing* the word with signs

*Acts 15:41* And he [Paul] went through Syria and Cilicia, *c'ing* the churches

*Rom 15:8* Jesus Christ was a minister… to *c* the promises made unto the fathers

*1 Cor 1:6* as the testimony of Christ was *c'ed* in you

*1 Cor 1:8* Who [Jesus] shall also *c* you unto the end

*2 Cor 2:8* *c* your love toward him [Jesus]

## CONFORMED

*Rom 8:29* he [God] also did predestinate to be *c* to the image of his Son

*Rom 12:2* be not *c* to this world: but be ye transformed

**CONIAH.** See *Jehoiachin.*

**CONQUEST OF CANAAN BY ISRAEL.** Josh 6–12.

## CONSCIENCE

*John 8:9* they [scribes and Pharisees]… being convicted by their own *c,* went out

*Acts 23:1* I [Paul] have lived in all good *c* before God

*1 Cor 8:12* when ye… wound their weak *c,* ye sin

*1 Cor 10:27* eat, asking no question for *c* sake

*1 Tim 1:5* charity out of a pure heart, and of a good *c*

*1 Tim 3:9* mystery of the faith in a pure *c*

*Heb 9:14* the blood of Christ… purge… *c* from dead works

## CONSENT [ING]

*Prov 1:10* if sinners entice thee, *c* thou not

*Luke 14:18* all with one *c* began to make excuse

*Acts 8:1* Saul was *c'ing* unto his [Stephen's] death

*Acts 22:20* I [Paul]… was… *c'ing* unto his [Stephen's] death

*1 Cor 7:5* Defraud ye not… except it be with *c* for a time

## CONSIDER [ED, EST, ETH, ING]

*1 Sam 12:24* *c* how great things he [God] hath done

*Job 1:8* Hast thou [Satan] *c'ed* my [God's] servant Job

*Job 37:14* stand still, and *c* the wondrous works of God

*Ps 8:3* When I *c* thy [God's] heavens, the work of thy fingers… moon and… stars

*Ps 25:19* *C* mine enemies; for they are many

*Ps 41:1* Blessed is he that *c'eth* the poor

*Ps 119:153* *C* mine affliction, and deliver me

*Prov 6:6* Go to the ant, thou sluggard; *c* her ways

*Prov 31:16* She *c'eth* a field, and buyeth it

*Isa 43:18* neither *c* the things of old

*Hag 1:5* thus saith the LORD of hosts; *C* your ways

*Matt 6:28 C* the lilies of the field, how they grow

*Matt 7:3* but *c'est* not the beam that is in thine own eye

*Gal 6:1 c'ing* thyself, lest thou also be tempted

*Heb 3:1 c* the…High Priest of our profession, Christ Jesus

## CONSOLATION

*Luke 2:25* man [Simeon] was just and devout, waiting for the *c* of Israel

*Luke 6:24* But woe unto you that are rich! for ye have received your *c*

*Acts 4:36* Barnabas…being interpreted, The son of *c*

*Rom 15:5* the God of…*c* grant you to be likeminded

*Phil 2:1* If there be therefore any *c* in Christ

## CONTENT

*Phil 4:11* whatsoever state I [Paul] am, therewith to be *c*

*1 Tim 6:8* having food and raiment let us be therewith *c*

*Heb 13:5* be *c* with such things as ye have

## CONTINUE [D, ING, TH]

*Luke 6:12* he [Jesus]…*c'd* all night in prayer

*John 8:31* If ye *c* in my [Jesus'] word, then are ye my disciples indeed

*John 15:9* so have I [Jesus] loved you: *c* ye in my love

*Acts 1:14* These all *c'd* with one accord in prayer

*Acts 2:46* they [the believers], *c'ing* daily with one accord

*Acts 18:11* he [Paul] *c'd* there… teaching the word of God

*Rom 6:1* Shall we *c* in sin, that grace may abound

*Rom 12:12* patient in tribulation; *c'ing* instant in prayer

*Gal 3:10* Cursed is every one that *c'th* not in all things… in the book of the law

*Phil 1:25* I [Paul]…shall abide and *c* with you all for your… joy of faith

*1 Tim 4:16* Take heed…unto the doctrine; *c* in them

*Heb 13:1* Let brotherly love *c*

*2 Pet 3:4* all things *c* as they were from the beginning

*1 John 2:19* they would no doubt have *c'd* with us

## CONVERSATION

*Gal 1:13* ye have heard of my [Paul's] *c* in time past

*Phil 3:20* our *c* is in heaven; from whence also we look for the Saviour

*1 Tim 4:12* be thou an example…in *c,* in charity

*Heb 13:5* Let your *c* be without covetousness

*2 Pet 3:11* what manner of persons ought ye to be in all holy *c* and godliness

## CONVERSION

*Acts 15:3* they [Paul and Barnabas] passed through …declaring the *c* of the Gentiles

## CONVERSION OF PAUL.
Acts 9:1–16.

## CONVERT [ED, ETH, ING]

*Ps 19:7* The law of the LORD is perfect, *c'ing* the soul

*Ps 51:13* sinners shall be *c'ed* unto thee [God]

*Matt 18:3* Except ye be *c'ed,* and become as little children

*Acts 3:19* Repent ye therefore, and be *c'ed*

*Jas 5:19* if any of you do err… and one *c* him

*Jas 5:20* he which *c'eth* the sinner…shall save a soul

**CORE.** See *Korah.*

**CORINTH** (a major city in Greece where Paul lived for eighteen months and established a church). **Acts 18:1–18;** 19:1 • 1 Cor 1:2 • 2 Cor 1:1,23 • 2 Tim 4:20.

## CORINTHIANS, FIRST AND SECOND EPISTLES TO THE.
Two letters of the apostle Paul to the church at Corinth, dealing mainly with problems in the church, including divisions (1 Cor. 1–4), sexual immorality (1 Cor. 5–6), and abuses of the Lord's Supper and spiritual gifts (1 Cor. 11–12; 14).

**CORNELIUS** (a Roman soldier who became one of the first Gentile converts to Christianity). Acts 10:1–48.

## CORRUPT [ED]

*Gen 6:11* The earth also was *c* before God

*Ex 8:24* land [Egypt] was *c'ed* by…swarm of flies

*Job 17:1* My [Job's] breath is *c,* my days are extinct

*Matt 6:20* treasures in heaven…neither moth nor rust doth *c*

*Luke 6:43* a good tree bringeth not forth *c* fruit

*2 Cor 7:2* we have wronged no man, we have *c'ed* no man

*Eph 4:29* no *c* communication proceed out of your mouth

*Jas 5:2* Your riches are *c'ed*… garments are motheaten

## CORRUPTION

*Isa 38:17* thou [God] hast in love…delivered it [my soul] from the pit of *c*

*Rom 8:21* delivered from…*c* into the glorious liberty of the children of God

*1 Cor 15:42* It [the body] is sown in *c*…raised in incorruption

*Gal 6:8* he that soweth to his flesh shall of the flesh reap *c*

## COUNSEL OF THE LORD

*Ps 33:11* The *c-o-t-L* standeth for ever

*Prov 19:21* nevertheless the *c-o-t-L,* that shall stand

## COUNT [ED, ETH]

*Gen 15:6* and he [God] *c'ed* it… for righteousness

*Job 31:4* Doth not he [God] see my ways…*c* all my steps

*Ps 44:22* we are *c'ed* as sheep for the slaughter

*Prov 17:28* a fool, when he holdeth his peace, is *c'ed* wise

*Luke 14:28* sitteth not down first, and *c'eth* the cost

*Acts 5:41* *c'ed* worthy to suffer shame for his [Jesus'] name

*Rom 4:3* it was *c'ed* unto him [Abraham] for righteousness

*Phil 3:7* gain to me [Paul], those I *c'ed* loss for Christ

*Phil 3:8* I [Paul] *c* all things but loss

*Phil 3:13* I [Paul] *c* not myself to have apprehended

*2 Thes 1:5* that ye may be *c'ed* worthy of the kingdom of God

*1 Tim 5:17* Let the elders that rule well be *c'ed* worthy

*Jas 1:2* *c* it all joy when ye fall into divers temptations

*2 Pet 3:9* The Lord is not slack concerning his promise, as some men *c* slackness

## COURAGE

*Deut 31:6* Be strong and of a good *c,* fear not

*Ps 31:24* Be of good *c,* and he [God] shall strengthen your heart

*Isa 41:6* every one said to his brother, Be of good *c*

## COVENANT [S]

*Gen 9:9* I [God] establish my *c* with you [Noah]

*Gen 9:13* bow in the cloud… shall be for a token of a *c*

*Gen 15:18* the Lord made a *c* with Abram

*Ex 2:24* God remembered his *c* with Abraham

*Ex 19:5* keep my [God's] *c,* then ye shall be a peculiar treasure

*Ex 34:28* he [Moses] wrote… the words of the *c,* the ten commandments

*Deut 4:23* Take heed…lest ye forget the *c* of the Lord

*Deut 29:9* Keep therefore the words of this *c*

*1 Sam 18:3* Jonathan and David made a *c*

*Jer 11:3* Cursed be the man that obeyeth not…this *c*

*Jer 31:31* I [God] will make a new *c* with...Israel

*Ezek 16:62* I [God] will establish my *c* with thee

*Rom 11:27* For this is my [God's] *c*...when I shall take away their sins

*Eph 2:12* aliens...and strangers from the *c's* of promise

*Heb 8:6* he [Jesus] is the mediator of a better *c*

*Heb 13:20* through the blood of the everlasting *c*

## COVET [ED, ETH]

*Ex 20:17* Thou shalt not *c* thy neighbour's house

*Prov 21:26* He *c'eth* greedily all the day long

*Acts 20:33* I [Paul] have *c'ed* no man's silver

*1 Cor 12:31* But *c* earnestly the best gifts

*1 Tim 6:10* some *c'ed* after... erred from the faith

## COVETOUSNESS

*Ps 119:36* Incline my heart unto thy [God's] testimonies, and not to *c*

*Luke 12:15* Take heed, and beware of *c*

*Heb 13:5* Let your conversation be without *c*

## CREATE [D]

*Gen 1:1* In the beginning God *c'd* the heaven and the earth

*Gen 1:27* God *c'd* man in his own image

*Gen 6:7* I [God] will destroy man whom I have *c'd*

*Ps 51:10* *C* in me a clean heart, O God...renew a right spirit

*Ps 148:5* for he [God] commanded, and they were *c'd*

*Isa 45:12* I [God] have made the earth...*c'd* man upon it

*Isa 65:17* I [God] *c* new heavens and a new earth

*Jer 31:22* the LORD hath *c'd* a new thing in the earth

*Mal 2:10* Have we not all one father? hath not one God *c'd* us

*1 Cor 11:9* Neither was the man *c'd* for the woman

*Eph 2:10* we are his workmanship, *c'd* in Christ Jesus

*Col 1:16* all things were *c'd* by him [Jesus], and for him

*Rev 4:11* for thou [God] hast *c'd* all things

## CREATION

*Mark 10:6* beginning of the *c* God made...male and female

*Rom 1:20* invisible things of him [God] from the *c* of the world are clearly seen

*Rom 8:22* the whole *c* groaneth and travaileth in pain

**CREATION OF MAN.** Gen 1:26–2:7.

**CREATION OF WORLD.**
Gen 1:1–25.

**CREATION OF WOMAN.**
Gen 2:18–25.

**CROOKED**
*Deut 32:5* they are a perverse and *c* generation
*Eccl 7:13* make that straight, which he [God] hath made *c*
*Isa 40:4* the *c* shall be made straight...rough places plain
*Luke 3:5* the *c* shall be made straight...rough ways... smooth
*Phil 2:15* sons of God...in the midst of a *c*...nation

**CROSS**
*Matt 27:32* they compelled [Simon] to bear his [Jesus'] *c*
*Matt 27:42* let him [Jesus] now come down from the *c*
*Luke 9:23* take up his *c* daily, and follow me [Jesus]
*John 19:17* And he [Jesus] bearing his *c* went forth into...the place of a skull
*1 Cor 1:18* the preaching of the *c* is to them that perish foolishness
*Gal 6:14* forbid that I [Paul] should glory, save in the *c*
*Phil 2:8* he [Jesus]...became obedient unto...death of the *c*

*Heb 12:2* who [Jesus] for the joy that was set before him endured the *c*

**CROSSING OF JORDAN RIVER INTO CANAAN.**
Josh 3:1–17.

**CROSSING OF RED SEA.**
Ex 14:21–31.

**CROWN [ED, EDST]**
*Ps 8:5* thou [God]...hast *c'ed* him [man] with...honour
*Prov 17:6* Children's children are the *c* of old men
*Mark 15:17* platted a *c* of thorns, and put it about his [Jesus'] head
*Phil 4:1* my joy and *c,* so stand fast in the Lord
*2 Tim 4:8* laid up for me [Paul] a *c* of righteousness
*Heb 2:7* thou *c'edst* him [Jesus] with glory and honour
*Heb 2:9* But we see Jesus... *c'ed* with glory and honour

**CROWN OF GLORY**
*Prov 16:31* The hoary head is a *c-o-g*
*Isa 28:5* shall the LORD of hosts be for a *c-o-g*
*Isa 62:3* Thou shalt...be a *c-o-g* in the hand of the LORD
*1 Pet 5:4* chief Shepherd... appear, ye shall receive a *c-o-g*

**CROWN OF LIFE**

*Jas 1:12* when he is tried, he shall receive the *c-o-l*

*Rev 2:10* faithful unto death, and I will give thee a *c-o-l*

**CRUCIFIXION OF JESUS.** See *Jesus, Life and Ministry of.*

**CURSE [D, DST, ING, TH]**

*Gen 3:14* thou [the serpent] art *c'd* above all cattle

*Gen 12:3* I [God] will…*c* him that *c'th* thee [Abraham]

*Lev 20:9* one that *c'th* his father…shall be…put to death

*Num 23:11* I [Balak] took thee [Balaam] to *c* mine enemies

*Deut 11:26* I [Moses] set before you [Israel] this day a blessing and a *c*

*Deut 27:15* *C'd* be the man that maketh any graven or molten image

*Deut 30:19* I [Moses] have set before you life and death, blessing and *c'ing*

*Josh 6:26* *C'd* be the man… that…buildeth…Jericho

*Job 2:9* Dost thou [Job] still retain thine integrity? *c* God, and die

*Jer 20:14* *C'd* be the day…I [Jeremiah] was born

*Matt 5:44* Love your enemies, bless them that *c* you

*Matt 15:4* He that *c'th* father…let him die

*Matt 25:41* Depart from me [Jesus], ye *c'd,* into everlasting fire

*Mark 11:21* fig tree which thou [Jesus] *c'dst* is withered

*Mark 14:71* But he [Peter] began to *c*…saying, I know not this man [Jesus]

*Acts 23:14* bound ourselves under a great *c*…eat nothing until we have slain Paul

*Rom 12:14* Bless them which persecute you: bless…*c* not

*Gal 3:13* Christ hath redeemed us from the *c* of the law

*Jas 3:10* Out of the same mouth proceedeth blessing and *c'ing*

**CUSTOM**

*Matt 9:9* he [Jesus] saw… Matthew…at the receipt of *c*

*John 18:39* a *c,* that I [Pilate] should release unto you one at the passover

*Rom 13:7* Render…to all their dues…*c* to whom *c*

**CUTH** (a Babylonian district whose citizens settled the Northern Kingdom [Israel] after it fell to the Assyrians). 2 Kgs 17:30. *Cuthah:* 2 Kgs 17:24.

**CUTHAH.** See *Cuth.*

**CYPRUS** (a large island in the Mediterranean Sea that Paul and Barnabas visited during the first missionary journey). Acts 4:36; 11:19–20; **13:4–13;** 15:39; 21:3,16; 27:4. *Chittim:* Jer 2:10. *Kittim:* Gen 10:4.

**CYRENE** (a city in Africa and home of the Simon who carried the cross of Jesus). Matt 27:32 • Mark 15:21 • Luke 23:26 • Acts 2:10; 6:9; 11:20; 13:1.

**CYRENIUS** (Roman governor of Syria at the time of Jesus' birth). Luke 2:1–4.

**CYRUS** (a king of the Persian empire who allowed the Jewish captives to return to their homeland about 536 B.C.). 2 Chr 36:22–23 • **Ezra 1:1–8;** 3:7; 4:3,5; 5:13–14,17; 6:3,14 • Isa 44:28; 45:1 • Dan 1:21; 6:28; 10:1.

# -D-

**DAGON** (chief pagan god of the Philistines). Judg 16:23 • 1 Sam 5:1–7.

**DALMANUTHA** (a place near the Sea of Galilee visited by Jesus). Mark 8:10.

**DALMATIA** (a Roman province along the Adriatic Sea visited by Titus). 2 Tim 4:10.

**DAMASCUS** (capital city of Syria and the city to which Paul was traveling when he was converted). Gen 14:15 • 2 Sam 8:5–6 • 1 Kgs 15:18 • 2 Kgs 8:7–15 • Isa 8:4 • **Acts 9:1–8** • 2 Cor 11:32–33 • Gal 1:17. *Syria-damascus:* 1 Chr 18:6.

**DAMNATION**

*Mark 3:29* blaspheme against the Holy Ghost…is in danger of eternal *d*

*John 5:29* that have done evil, unto the resurrection of *d*

*1 Cor 11:29* he…eateth and drinketh *d* to himself

**DAN**

1. A son of Jacob and ancestor of one of the twelve tribes of Israel. Gen 30:6; 35:25; 46:23; 49:16–17 • Ex 1:4 • Josh 19:47–48 • 1 Chr 2:2 • Ezek 27:19. The tribe of Dan settled in central Palestine and along the Mediterranean Sea. Judg 1:34; 5:17; 13:25; 18:2–30.

2. A village in the territory of Dan. Gen 14:14 • Judg 20:1 • 1 Chr 21:2 • 2 Chr 30:5. *Laish:* Isa 10:30.

**DANIEL** (a prophet who remained faithful to God among the pagan Babylonians and Persians). References to Daniel outside the Book of Daniel are found in Ezek 14:14, 20; 28:3 • Matt 24:15 • Mark 13:14. His Babylonian name was *Belteshazzar:* Dan 1:7.

**DANIEL, BOOK OF.** An apocalyptic book of the Old Testament known for its imagery that is similar to that in the Book of Revelation in the New Testament. The book describes the trials and tribulations suffered by Daniel and his three friends as captives of the Babylonians and Persians (Dan 1–7) and Daniel's visions and dreams about the future (Dan 8–12).

**DARIUS** (a title for four different kings of Persia).

1. Darius I or Darius the Great, who continued Cyrus's policy of restoring the Jewish people to their homeland. Ezra 6:1–12.

2. Darius II or Darius the Persian. Neh 12:22.

3. Darius III or Darius Codomannus, who is probably the "fourth" king of Persia mentioned by the prophet Daniel. Dan 11:2.

4. Darius the Mede, who made Daniel a ruler over several provincial leaders. Dan 6:1–2.

## DARKENED

*Isa 24:11* all joy is *d,* the mirth of the land is gone

*Joel 3:15* The sun and the moon shall be *d*

*Mark 13:24* after that tribulation, the sun shall be *d*

*Rom 1:21* they [ungodly]… became vain…heart was *d*

## DARKNESS

*Gen 1:2* and *d* was upon the face of the deep

*Ex 10:22* a thick *d* in all the land of Egypt three days

*2 Sam 22:29* the LORD will lighten my *d*

*Job 34:22* There is no *d,* nor shadow of death

*Ps 18:9* He [God]…came down…*d* was under his feet

*Isa 5:20* Woe unto them that… put *d* for light, and light for *d*

*Isa 9:2* people that walked in *d* have seen a great light

*Joel 2:31* sun shall be turned into *d*…moon into blood

*Matt 4:16* people which sat in *d* saw great light

*Luke 23:44* a *d* over all the earth until the ninth hour

*John 1:5* the *d* comprehended it [the light] not

*John 3:19* men loved *d* rather than light

*John 12:46* whosoever believeth…not abide in *d*

*Acts 2:20* The sun shall be turned into *d*

*Acts 26:18* To open their eyes, and to turn them from *d* to light

*2 Cor 4:6* God, who commanded the light to shine out of *d*… shined in our hearts

*Eph 6:12* we wrestle…against the rulers…*d* of this world

*1 Pet 2:9* who [Jesus] hath called you out of *d* into his marvellous light

*1 John 1:5* God is light, and in him is no *d* at all

*1 John 2:11* he that hateth his brother is in *d*

**DAVID** (a popular king of Judah and an earthly ancestor of the promised Messiah, Jesus Christ). See **1 Sam 16–31 • 2 Sam 1–24 • 1 Kgs 1:1–2:11 • 1 Chr 11–29** for a sketch of David.

1. Anointed as a boy by Samuel (1 Sam 16:1–13)

2. Musician and armor-bearer for King Saul (1 Sam 16:14–23)

3. Killed the Philistine Goliath (1 Sam 17:1–54)

4. Hid from King Saul as a fugitive (1 Sam 19:1–30:31)

5. King over Judah (2 Sam 2:1–4:12)

6. Captured Jerusalem (Jebus) and turned it into his capital city (1 Chr 11:4–9)

7. King over all Israel (2 Sam 5:1–6:16)

8. His throne established by the Lord forever (2 Sam 7:1–29)

9. Committed adultery with Bathsheba (2 Sam 11:1–27)

10. Survived rebellion by his son Absalom (2 Sam 15:7–23)

11. Not allowed to build the temple (1 Chr 17:1–15)

12. Death of David (1 Kgs 2:10–11 • 1 Chr 29:26–28)

13. Succeeded by his son Solomon (1 Kgs 1:10–35)

The phrase "a psalm of David" appears in the titles of many psalms in the Book of Psalms, indicating either that David wrote these psalms or that they were written in his honor. Pss 2–9; 11–41; 51–65; 68–70; 86; 101–103; 108–110; 122; 124; 131–133; 138–145.

The prophets of the Old Testament often spoke of the promised Messiah who would fulfill God's promise to David. Isa 9:7; 55:3 • Jer 17:25; 33:17 • Ezek 37:24 • Zech 12:8.

In the New Testament, Jesus was called "the son of David" or "seed of David." Matt 9:27; 20:31 • Luke 18:38–39 • John 7:42 • Rom 1:3 • 2 Tim 2:8.

## DAY

*Gen 1:5* evening and the morning were the first *d*

*Ex 13:3* Remember this *d* ... ye came out from Egypt

*Ex 20:11* LORD blessed the sabbath *d,* and hallowed it

*Deut 4:4* ye that did cleave unto the LORD your God are alive ... this *d*

*Deut 11:26* Behold, I [Moses] set before you this *d* a blessing and a curse

*Josh 4:14* On that *d* the LORD magnified Joshua

*Josh 10:13* the sun stood still ... and hasted not to go down about a whole *d*

*Josh 24:15* choose you this *d* whom ye will serve

*1 Kgs 18:36* known this *d* that thou art God in Israel

*1 Chr 16:23* show forth from *d* to *d* his [God's] salvation

*Job 3:3* the *d* perish wherein I [Job] was born

*Job 19:25* he shall stand at the latter *d* upon the earth

*Ps 1:2* in his [God's] law doth he meditate *d* and night

*Ps 19:2* *D* unto *d* uttereth speech

*Ps 50:15* call upon me [God] in the *d* of trouble

*Ps 84:10* For a *d* in thy [God's] courts is better than a thousand

*Ps 86:7* In the *d* of my trouble I will call upon thee [God]

*Ps 91:5* shalt not be afraid... for the arrow that flieth by *d*

*Ps 118:24* This is the *d* which the LORD hath made

*Ps 121:6* sun shall not smite thee by *d*

*Prov 27:1* knowest not what a *d* may bring forth

*Isa 13:6* Howl ye, for the *d* of the LORD is at hand

*Isa 60:19* sun shall be no more thy light by *d*

*Jer 1:10* I [God] have this *d* set thee over the nations

*Jer 9:1* I [Jeremiah] might weep *d* and night for the slain of my people

*Jer 20:14* Cursed be the *d*...I [Jeremiah] was born

*Joel 2:31* before...the terrible *d* of the LORD come

*Amos 5:18* Woe unto you that desire the *d* of the LORD

*Zech 2:11* many nations...be joined to the LORD in that *d*

*Zech 14:6* in that *d,* that the light shall not be clear

*Mal 3:2* who may abide the *d* of his [God's] coming

*Matt 6:11* Give us this *d* our daily bread

*Matt 7:22* Many will say to me in that *d,* Lord, Lord

*Matt 25:13* know neither the *d* nor the hour wherein the Son of man cometh

*Mark 14:25* I [Jesus] will drink no more of the fruit of the vine, until that *d*...I drink it new

*Luke 2:11* born this *d* in the city of David a Saviour

*Luke 9:22* Son of man must... be slain...raised the third *d*

*Luke 19:9* This *d* is salvation come to this house

*Luke 24:46* it behoved Christ to suffer...to rise from the dead the third *d*

*John 9:4* I [Jesus] must work... while it is *d*

*John 11:24* he [Lazarus] shall rise again...at the last *d*

*1 Cor 16:2* Upon the first *d* of the week let every one of you lay by him in store

*2 Cor 6:2* behold, now is the *d* of salvation

*Phil 3:5* Circumcised the eighth *d*...stock of Israel

*2 Tim 1:12* keep that...committed unto him [Jesus] against that *d*

*Heb 13:8* Jesus Christ the same yesterday, and to *d*

*2 Pet 3:8* one *d* is with the Lord as a thousand years

*Rev 1:10* I [John] was in the Spirit on the Lord's *d*

*Rev 6:17* the great *d* of his [God's] wrath is come

## DAY OF ATONEMENT

*Lev 23:27* a *d-o-a:* it shall be an holy convocation

*Lev 23:28* a *d-o-a,* to make an atonement…before the LORD

*Lev 25:9* in the *d-o-a* shall ye make the trumpet sound

## DAY OF JUDGMENT

*Matt 11:22* It shall be more tolerable for Tyre…at the *d-o-j,* than for you

*Matt 12:36* every idle word… men…shall give account thereof in the *d-o-j*

*1 John 4:17* that we may have boldness in the *d-o-j*

## DAY OF THE LORD

*Isa 2:12* the *d-o-t-L* of hosts… upon every one that is proud

*Joel 1:15* Alas…for the *d-o-t-L* is at hand

*Amos 5:20* Shall not the *d-o-t-L* be darkness, and not light? even very dark

*Obad 15* the *d-o-t-L* is near upon all the heathen

*Zech 14:1* Behold, the *d-o-t-L* cometh

*Mal 4:5* send you Elijah the prophet before the…dreadful *d-o-t-L*

*Acts 2:20* sun shall be turned into darkness…before that great…*d-o-t-L* come

*1 Thes 5:2* the *d-o-t-L* so cometh as a thief in the night

*2 Pet 3:10* the *d-o-t-L* will come as a thief in the night

## DEACON [S]

*1 Tim 3:10* use the office of a *d,* being found blameless

*1 Tim 3:12* Let the *d's* be the husbands of one wife

*1 Tim 3:13* used the office of a *d* well purchase to themselves a good degree

## DEAD

*Ex 12:30* great cry in Egypt… not a house where there was not one *d*

*Josh 1:2* Moses my [God's] servant is *d*…therefore arise

*2 Kgs 4:32* when Elisha was come into the house, behold, the child was *d*

*Eccl 9:5* but the *d* know not any thing

*Jer 22:10* Weep ye not for the *d,* neither bemoan him

*Matt 2:19* when Herod was *d*… an angel…appeareth in a dream to Joseph

*Matt 8:22* Follow me [Jesus]; and let the *d* bury their *d*

*Matt 10:8* Heal the sick, cleanse the lepers, raise the *d*

*Mark 6:16* I [Herod] beheaded: he [John the Baptist] is risen from the *d*

*Mark 15:44* Pilate marvelled if he [Jesus] were already *d*

*Luke 15:24* this my son was *d,* and is alive again

*Luke 20:38* he is not a God of the *d,* but of the living

*Luke 24:46* it behoved Christ to suffer...rise from the *d*

*John 11:25* though he were *d,* yet shall he live

*John 20:9* they knew not... that he [Jesus] must rise again from the *d*

*Acts 17:32* when they heard of the resurrection of the *d,* some mocked

*Acts 26:8* thought a thing incredible with you, that God should raise the *d*

*Rom 1:4* declared to be the Son of God with power...by the resurrection from the *d*

*Rom 6:4* Christ was raised up from the *d* by...the Father

*Rom 10:9* if thou...shalt believe...that God hath raised him [Jesus] from the *d*

*1 Cor 15:13* no resurrection of the *d,* then is Christ not risen

*Gal 2:19* I [Paul] through the law am *d* to the law

*Eph 2:1* you hath he [Jesus] quickened, who were *d* in trespasses and sins

*Col 1:18* who [Jesus] is...the firstborn from the *d*

*1 Thes 4:16* the *d* in Christ shall rise first

*2 Tim 2:8* Jesus Christ...was raised from the *d* according to my gospel

*Jas 2:17* Even so faith, if it hath not works, is *d*

*1 Pet 4:5* to him that is ready to judge the quick and the *d*

*Rev 1:17* I [John] saw him [Jesus], I fell at his feet as *d*

*Rev 14:13* Blessed are the *d* which die in the Lord

**DEAD SEA.** See *Salt Sea.*

**DEAF**

*Isa 35:5* the ears of the *d* shall be unstopped

*Mark 7:32* they bring unto him [Jesus] one that was *d*

*Luke 7:22* tell John...lepers are cleansed, the *d* hear

**DEATH**

*Deut 30:15* I [Moses] have set before thee...*d* and evil

*Deut 33:1* Moses...blessed the children of Israel before his *d*

*2 Kgs 4:40* man of God, there is *d* in the pot

*Job 16:16* on my [Job's] eyelids is the shadow of *d*

*Ps 13:3* lighten mine eyes, lest I sleep the sleep of *d*

*Ps 23:4* walk through the valley of the shadow of *d*

*Ps 48:14* For this God...will be our guide even unto *d*

*Ps 107:14* He [God] brought them out of...shadow of *d*

*Ps 116:15* Precious in the sight of the LORD...*d* of his saints

*Prov 14:12* but the end thereof are the ways of *d*

*Isa 9:2* they that dwell in … the shadow of *d,* upon them hath the light shined

*Isa 53:9* he [God's servant] made his grave with the wicked, and … rich in his *d*

*Jer 21:8* I [God] set before you the way of life, and … *d*

*Matt 4:16* to them which sat in the … shadow of *d* light is sprung up

*Mark 14:34* My [Jesus'] soul is exceeding sorrowful unto *d*

*Luke 2:26* he [Simon] should not see *d,* before he had seen the Lord's Christ

*John 5:24* He that … believeth … is passed from *d* unto life

*John 11:4* sickness is not unto *d,* but for the glory of God

*Acts 8:1* Saul was consenting unto his [Stephen's] *d*

*Rom 5:12* so *d* passed upon all men, for that all have sinned

*Rom 6:4* we are buried with him [Jesus] by baptism into *d*

*Rom 6:23* the wages of sin is *d*

*Rom 7:24* who shall deliver me [Paul] from the body of … *d*

*Rom 8:38* neither *d,* nor life, nor angels

*1 Cor 11:26* ye do show the Lord's *d* till he come

*1 Cor 15:26* The last enemy that shall be destroyed is *d*

*1 Cor 15:55* O *d,* where is thy sting

*Phil 2:8* he [Jesus] humbled himself … obedient unto *d*

*Phil 3:10* being made conformable unto his [Jesus'] *d*

*Heb 11:5* Enoch was translated that he should not see *d*

*1 John 3:14* we have passed from *d* unto life, because we love the brethren

*Rev 1:18* I [Jesus] am alive for evermore … and have the keys of hell and of *d*

*Rev 20:14* *d* and hell were cast into the lake of fire

*Rev 21:4* there shall be no more *d,* neither sorrow

**DEATH OF JESUS.** See *Jesus, Life and Ministry of.*

**DEBORAH** (a prophetess and judge of Israel who defeated the Canaanites). **Judg 4:4–16; 5:1–31.**

**DEBT [S]**

*Matt 6:12* forgive us our *d's,* as we forgive our debtors

*Matt 18:27* the lord of that servant … forgave him the *d*

*Rom 4:4* to him that worketh is the reward … of *d*

**DEBTOR [S]**

*Rom 1:14* I [Paul] am *d* both to the Greeks, and to the Barbarians

*Rom 8:12* we are *d's,* not to the flesh, to live after the flesh

**DECAPOLIS** (a district with a large Greek population east of the Jordan River). Jesus visited this area several times. Matt 4:25 • Mark 5:20; 7:31.

## DECEIVE [D, ING, TH]
*Deut 11:16* Take heed…that your heart be not **d'd**

*Prov 20:1* Wine is a mocker… and whosoever is **d'd** thereby is not wise

*Luke 21:8* Take heed that ye be not **d'd:** for many shall come in my [Jesus'] name

*Gal 6:3* think himself to be something, when he is nothing, he **d'th** himself

*Gal 6:7* Be not **d'd;** God is not mocked

*Eph 5:6* Let no man **d** you with vain words

*Jas 1:22* be ye doers of the word, and not hearers only, **d'ing** your own selves

*1 John 1:8* If we say that we have no sin, we **d** ourselves

## DECEIVER [S]
*Matt 27:63* **d** said…After three days I [Jesus] will rise again

*2 John 7* many **d's** are entered into the world

## DECLARE [D, ING]
*1 Chr 16:24* **D** his [God's] glory among the heathen

*Ps 9:11* **d** among the people his [God's] doings

*Ps 19:1* The heavens **d** the glory of God

*Ps 66:16* **d** what he [God] hath done for my soul

*Ps 71:17* hitherto have I **d'd** thy [God's] wondrous works

*Ps 96:3* **D** his [God's] glory among the heathen

*Isa 12:4* Praise the Lord…**d** his doings among the people

*Isa 48:3* I have **d'd** the former things from the beginning

*John 1:18* the only begotten Son…he hath **d'd** him [God]

*Acts 15:12* **d'ing** what miracles…God had wrought among the Gentiles

*Acts 17:23* Whom therefore ye ignorantly worship, him [God] **d** I [Paul] unto you

*Rom 1:4* **d'd** to be the Son of God with power

*1 Cor 15:1* I [Paul] **d** unto you the gospel…I preached

*1 John 1:3* That which we have seen…**d** we unto you

*1 John 1:5* the message which we…**d** unto you

## DEED [S]
*1 Chr 16:8* Call upon his [God's] name, make known his **d's** among the people

*Luke 23:41* we receive the due reward of our **d's**

*John 3:19* men loved darkness… because their **d's** were evil

*Rom 2:6* render to every man according to his **d's**

*Rom 3:28* justified by faith without the *d's* of the law

*Col 3:17* And whatsoever ye do in word or *d*

*1 John 3:18* not love in word... but in *d* and in truth

## DEFILE [D, TH]

*Ezek 20:7* *d* not yourselves with the idols of Egypt

*Dan 1:8* Daniel...would not *d* himself with...king's meat

*Matt 15:20* to eat with unwashen hands *d'th* not a man

*Mark 7:2* saw some of his [Jesus'] disciples eat bread with *d'd*...hands

*Mark 7:18* thing from without entereth into the man, it cannot *d* him

*John 18:28* went not into the judgment hall, lest they [Pharisees] should be *d'd*

*1 Cor 3:17* If any man *d* the temple of God

*Jas 3:6* the tongue...*d'th* the whole body

**DEHAVITES** (a tribe which settled in Samaria after the Northern Kingdom fell to the Assyrians). Ezra 4:9–16.

**DELILAH** (a woman who betrayed Samson to the Philistines). Judg 16:4–21.

## DELIVER [ED, EDST, ETH, ING]

*Ex 18:10* Jethro said...the LORD...hath *d'ed* you out of the hand of the Egyptians

*Deut 1:27* the LORD...hath brought us forth...to *d* us into the hand of the Amorites

*Deut 9:10* LORD *d'ed* unto me [Moses] two tables of stone

*Josh 10:8* I [God] have *d'ed* them into thine hand

*Judg 6:1* the LORD *d'ed* them into the hand of Midian

*Judg 10:13* ye have forsaken me [God] and served other gods...I will *d* you no more

*1 Sam 17:37* he [God] will *d* me [David] out of the hand of this Philistine

*Job 16:11* God hath *d'ed* me [Job] to the ungodly

*Job 33:28* He [God] will *d* his [man's] soul from...the pit

*Ps 17:13* O LORD, *d* my soul from the wicked

*Ps 25:20* keep my soul and *d* me: let me not be ashamed

*Ps 34:4* the LORD...*d'ed* me from all my fears

*Ps 34:17* the LORD...*d'eth* them out of all their troubles

*Ps 41:1* the LORD will *d* him in time of trouble

*Ps 72:12* he [God] shall *d* the needy when he crieth

*Ps 107:6* and he [God] *d'ed* them out of their distresses

*Ps 116:8* thou [God] hast **d'ed** my soul from death

*Ps 120:2* **D** my soul, O LORD, from lying lips

*Prov 11:4* righteousness **d'eth** from death

*Isa 19:20* he [God] shall send them a saviour ... and he shall **d** them

*Isa 46:4* even I [God] will carry, and will **d** you

*Jer 1:8* I am with thee to **d** thee, saith the LORD

*Jer 20:13* he [God] hath **d'ed** ... the poor from ... evildoers

*Dan 3:17* our God ... is able to **d** us from the ... furnace

*Dan 6:20* is thy [Daniel's] God ... able to **d** thee

*Hos 11:8* how shall I [God] **d** thee, Israel

*Joel 2:32* whosoever shall call on ... the LORD shall be **d'ed**

*Zeph 1:18* nor their gold shall ... **d** them in the day of the LORD'S wrath

*Matt 6:13* lead us not into temptation ... **d** us from evil

*Matt 24:9* Then shall they **d** you up to be afflicted

*Matt 25:20* Lord, thou **d'edst** unto me five talents

*Mark 10:33* Son of man shall be **d'ed** unto the chief priests

*Mark 15:1* the chief priests ... **d'ed** him [Jesus] to Pilate

*Luke 2:6* days were accomplished that she [Mary] should be **d'ed**

*Luke 9:44* Son of man shall be **d'ed** into the hands of men

*Acts 22:4* I [Paul] persecuted ... **d'ing** into prisons both men and women

*Rom 7:24* who shall **d** me [Paul] from ... this death

*Gal 1:4* he [Jesus] might **d** us from this present evil world

*Col 1:13* Who [Jesus] ... **d'ed** us from the power of darkness

*2 Tim 4:18* Lord shall **d** me from every evil work

*2 Pet 2:9* Lord ... knoweth how to **d** ... out of temptations

**DEMAS** (a believer who deserted Paul). Col 4:14 • 2 Tim 4:10 • Phlm 24.

**DEMETRIUS**
1. A silversmith at Ephesus who incited a riot against the apostle Paul. Acts 19:24–38.
2. A believer commended by the apostle John. 3 John 12.

**DENY [IED, IETH, ING]**
*Matt 10:33* him will I also **d** before my Father

*Matt 26:72* And again he [Peter] **d'ied** with an oath, I do not know the man [Jesus]

*Mark 14:30* thou [Peter] shalt **d** me [Jesus] thrice

*Luke 9:23* let him **d** himself, and take up his cross daily

*Luke 12:9* he that **d'ieth** me [Jesus] before men shall be **d'ied** before ... God

*1 Tim 5:8* hath **d'ied** the faith, and is worse than an infidel

*2 Tim 2:12* if we **d** him [Jesus], he also will **d** us

*Titus 2:12* **d'ing** ... worldly lusts, we should live soberly

*1 John 2:23* Whosoever **d'ieth** the Son ... hath not the Father

## DEPTH [S]

*Ps 106:9* so he [God] led them through the **d's**

*Ps 130:1* Out of the **d's** have I cried unto thee, O LORD

*Jon 2:5* the **d** closed me [Jonah] round about

*Mic 7:19* thou [God] wilt cast ... their sins into ... **d's** of the sea

*Rom 8:39* Nor height, nor **d** ... shall be able to separate us from the love of God

*Rom 11:33* **d** of the riches both of the wisdom and knowledge of God

**DERBE** (a village in the province of Lycaonia visited by Paul and Barnabas). **Acts 14:6–20;** 16:1; 20:4.

## DESCEND [ED, ING]

*Gen 28:12* and behold ... angels of God ascending and **d'ing** on it [a ladder]

*Prov 30:4* Who hath ascended up into heaven, or **d'ed**

*Matt 7:27* the rain **d'ed,** and the floods came

*Matt 28:2* angel ... **d'ed** from heaven ... rolled back the stone

*Mark 15:32* Let Christ ... **d** now from the cross

*Luke 3:22* Holy Ghost **d'ed** ... like a dove

*John 1:32* I [John] saw the Spirit **d'ing** from heaven like a dove

*Rom 10:7* Who shall **d** into the deep ... to bring up Christ

*Eph 4:10* He [Jesus] that **d'ed** ... also ... ascended up far above all heavens

*1 Thes 4:16* Lord himself shall **d** from heaven with a shout

*Rev 21:10* that great city ... holy Jerusalem, **d'ing** out of heaven from God

## DESIRE [D, ING, S, TH]

*Gen 3:16* **d** shall be to thy [Eve's] husband

*Deut 5:21* Neither shalt thou **d** thy neighbour's wife

*Ps 27:4* One thing have I **d'd** of the LORD

*Ps 37:4* and he [God] shall give thee the **d's** of thine heart

*Ps 38:9* all my **d** is before thee [God] ... my groaning ... not hid

*Ps 73:25* none upon earth that I **d** beside thee [God]

*Ps 145:16* Thou [God] ... satisfiest the **d** of every living thing

*Prov 21:25* The *d* of the slothful killeth him

*Song 7:10* I am my beloved's, and his *d* is toward me

*Isa 26:9* With my soul have I *d'd* thee in the night

*Ezek 24:16* I take away from thee the *d* of thine eyes

*Hos 6:6* I [God] *d'd* mercy, and not sacrifice

*Amos 5:18* Woe unto you that *d* the day of the LORD

*Matt 12:46* his [Jesus'] mother... stood without, *d'ing* to speak with him

*Mark 9:35* any man *d* to be first, the same shall be last

*Mark 11:24* What things soever ye *d,* when ye pray

*Luke 22:31* Simon, behold, Satan hath *d'd* to have you

*Rom 10:1* my [Paul's] heart's *d*...for Israel is, that they might be saved

*2 Cor 5:2* *d'ing* to be clothed upon with our house which is from heaven

*Phil 1:23* having a *d* to depart, and to be with Christ

*1 Tim 3:1* *d* the office of a bishop, he *d'th* a good work

*Heb 11:16* now they *d* a better country, that is, an heavenly

*1 Pet 2:2* As newborn babes, *d* the sincere milk of the word

**DESTRUCTION [S]**

*Job 5:22* At *d* and famine thou shalt laugh

*Ps 90:3* Thou [God] turnest man to *d*

*Ps 107:20* He [God]...delivered them from their *d's*

*Prov 16:18* Pride goeth before *d,* and a haughty spirit before a fall

*Isa 13:6* day of the LORD... shall come as a *d* from the Almighty

*Matt 7:13* broad is the way, that leadeth to *d*

**DEUTERONOMY, BOOK OF.** An Old Testament book that contains a series of speeches delivered by Moses to the Israelites as they prepared to enter the land of Canaan. This book repeats many of the laws of God revealed to Moses on Mt. Sinai about two generations earlier—thus its name Deuteronomy, which means "second law."

**DEVOUT**

*Luke 2:25* Simeon...was just and *d,* waiting for the consolation of Israel

*Acts 2:5* there was dwelling at Jerusalem Jews, *d* men

**DIANA** (a pagan goddess to whom a shrine was erected at Ephesus, a center of Diana worship). Acts 19:24–35.

**DIE [D, ST, TH]** *See also*
**DYING**

*Gen 2:17* day that thou eatest
thereof [the forbidden tree]
thou shalt surely *d*

*Gen 45:28* I [Jacob] will...see
him [Joseph] before I *d*

*Ex 16:3* Would to God we had
*d'd*...in the land of Egypt

*Deut 4:22* I [Moses] must *d* in
this land, I must not go over
Jordan...ye shall go over

*Deut 14:21* not eat of any thing
that *d'th* of itself

*Judg 16:30* Samson said, Let
me *d* with the Philistines

*Ruth 1:17* Where thou [Naomi]
*d'st,* will I [Ruth] die

*2 Sam 12:5* he [David] said...
the man that hath done this
thing shall surely *d*

*2 Chr 25:4* every man shall *d*
for his own sin

*Job 2:9* Dost thou [Job] still
retain thine integrity? curse
God, and *d*

*Job 3:11* Why *d'd* I [Job] not
from the womb

*Job 14:14* If a man *d,* shall he
live again

*Prov 10:21* but fools *d* for want
of wisdom

*Eccl 3:2* A time to be born, and
a time to *d*

*Isa 6:1* In the year that king
Uzziah *d'd* I [Isaiah] saw
also the Lord

*Jer 16:6* the great and the
small shall *d* in this land

*Jer 31:30* every one shall *d* for
his own iniquity

*Ezek 18:32* I [God] have no
pleasure in the death of him
that *d'th*

*Jon 4:3* it is better for me
[Jonah] to *d* than to live

*Matt 26:35* Though I [Peter]
should *d* with thee [Jesus],
yet will I not deny thee

*John 6:50* bread...from heaven,
that a man may eat...and
not *d*

*John 11:16* said Thomas...Let
us also go, that we may *d*
with him [Jesus]

*John 11:21* Lord, if thou hadst
been here, my [Martha's]
brother had not *d'd*

*John 11:50* it is expedient for
us, that one man should *d*
for the people

*John 12:24* if it [grain of wheat]
*d,* it bringeth forth much
fruit

*Acts 21:13* I [Paul] am ready...
to *d* at Jerusalem for the
name of...Jesus

*Rom 5:6* in due time Christ *d'd*
for the ungodly

*Rom 5:7* scarcely for a righteous man will one *d*

*Rom 5:8* while we were yet sinners, Christ *d'd* for us

*Rom 6:9* Christ being raised
from the dead *d'th* no more

*Rom 14:7* none...liveth to himself...no man *d'th* to himself

*Rom 14:8* whether we live ... or **d,** we are the Lord's

*1 Cor 15:3* how that Christ **d'd** for our sins according to the scriptures

*1 Cor 15:22* in Adam all **d** ... in Christ ... all be made alive

*2 Cor 5:14* if one **d'd** for all, then were all dead

*2 Cor 5:15* he [Jesus] **d'd** for all, that they ... should not ... live unto themselves

*Phil 1:21* to me [Paul] to live is Christ, and to **d** is gain

*Heb 9:27* it is appointed unto men once to **d**

*Rev 14:13* Blessed are the dead which **d** in the Lord

**DINAH** (Jacob's daughter who was assaulted by Shechem). Gen 30:20–21; **34:1–31.**

**DINAITES** (a tribe which settled in Samaria after the Northern Kingdom fell to the Assyrians). Ezra 4:9–16.

**DIOTREPHES** (a believer condemned for his false teachings by the apostle John). 3 John 9–10.

**DISCERN [ING]**

*1 Kgs 3:9* that I [Solomon] may **d** between good and bad

*Ezek 44:23* cause them to **d** between ... unclean and ... clean

*Matt 16:3* ye hypocrites, ye can **d** the face of the sky

*1 Cor 11:29* drinketh damnation to himself, not **d'ing** the Lord's body

*1 Cor 12:10* another prophecy; to another **d'ing** of spirits

**DISCIPLE**

*Matt 10:24* The **d** is not above his master

*Luke 14:26* If any man ... hate not his father ... he cannot be my [Jesus'] **d**

*John 19:38* Joseph of Arimathaea, being a **d** of Jesus

**DISOBEDIENCE**

*Rom 5:19* For as by one man's [Adam's] **d** many were made sinners

*Eph 5:6* cometh the wrath of God upon the children of **d**

**DISOBEDIENT**

*Acts 26:19* I [Paul] was not **d** unto the heavenly vision

*2 Tim 3:2* boasters, proud, blasphemers, **d** to parents

*Titus 1:16* they deny him [God], being abominable, and **d** and ... reprobate

*1 Pet 2:7* unto them which be **d,** the stone ... is made the head of the corner

**DISTRESS [ED, ES]**

*Ps 18:6* In my **d** I called upon the LORD

*Ps 107:13* he [God] saved them out of their ***d'es***

*Zeph 1:15* That day is...a day of trouble and ***d***

*Luke 21:23* for there shall be great ***d*** in the land

*Rom 8:35* shall separate us from the love of Christ? shall tribulation, or ***d***

*2 Cor 4:8* troubled on every side, yet not ***d'ed***

*2 Cor 12:10* I [Paul] take pleasure...in ***d'es*** for Christ's sake

*1 Thes 3:7* comforted over you [Thessalonians] in all our ... ***d*** by your faith

## DIVIDE [D, ING, TH]

*Gen 1:6* let it [the firmament] ***d*** the waters from the waters

*Ex 14:16* stretch out thine [Moses'] hand over the sea, and ***d*** it

*Ex 14:21* the LORD...made the sea dry land...waters were ***d'd***

*Num 33:54* ye shall ***d*** the land by lot for an inheritance

*Judg 7:16* he [Gideon] ***d'd***... men into three companies

*Job 26:12* He [God] ***d'th*** the sea with his power

*Ps 78:13* He [God] ***d'd*** the sea... caused them to pass through

*Prov 16:19* Better it is to be... with the lowly, than to ***d*** the spoil with the proud

*Dan 5:28* Thy [Belshazzar's] kingdom is ***d'd,*** and given to the Medes and Persians

*Zech 14:1* thy spoil shall be ***d'd*** in the midst of thee

*Matt 25:32* he [Jesus] shall separate them...as a shepherd ***d'd*** his sheep from the goats

*Luke 11:17* kingdom ***d'd*** against itself is brought to desolation

*Luke 12:13* speak to my brother, that he ***d*** the inheritance with me

*Luke 12:53* The father shall be ***d'd*** against the son

*Luke 15:12* And he [prodigal son's father] ***d'd*** unto them his living

*1 Cor 1:13* Is Christ ***d'd?*** was Paul crucified for you

*2 Tim 2:15* a workman...not... ashamed, rightly ***d'ing*** the word of truth

## DIVISION [S]

*Luke 12:51* I [Jesus] tell you, Nay; but rather ***d***

*John 9:16* How can a man...do such miracles? And there was a ***d*** among them

*Rom 16:17* mark them which cause ***d's*** and offences

*1 Cor 3:3* there is among you envying, and strife, and ***d's***

**DIVISION OF CANAAN AMONG THE ISRAELITE TRIBES.** Josh 14:1–19:51.

111

## DIVORCE [D]

*Lev 21:14* a widow, or a ***d'd*** woman...these shall he [a priest] not take

*Jer 3:8* I [God] had put her [Israel] away, and given her a bill of ***d***

*Matt 5:32* whosoever shall marry her that is ***d'd*** committeth adultery

## DOCTRINE [S]

*Mark 11:18* the people was astonished at his [Jesus'] ***d***

*John 7:16* My [Jesus'] ***d*** is not mine, but his that sent me

*Acts 2:42* they continued stedfastly in the apostles' ***d***

*Eph 4:14* be no more children... carried about with every wind of ***d***

*1 Tim 4:13* give attendance to reading, to exhortation, to ***d***

*2 Tim 3:16* All scripture is... profitable for ***d***

*2 Tim 4:3* For the time will come when they will not endure sound ***d***

*Heb 13:9* Be not carried about with divers and strange ***d's***

*2 John 9* He that abideth in the ***d*** of Christ

**DOEG** (a shepherd for King Saul who betrayed David). 1 Sam 21:7; **22:9–22.**

## DOER [S]

*Prov 17:4* A wicked ***d*** giveth heed to false lips

*Rom 2:13* the ***d's*** of the law shall be justified

*Jas 1:22* be ye ***d's*** of the word, and not hearers only

*Jas 1:23* if any be a hearer of the word, and not a ***d***

## DOMINION [S]

*Gen 1:28* God said...have ***d*** over the fish of the sea

*Job 25:2* ***D*** and fear are with him [God]

*Ps 8:6* Thou [God] madest him [man] to have ***d*** over the works of thy hands

*Ps 72:8* He [God] shall have ***d*** also from sea to sea

*Dan 4:3* his [God's] ***d*** is from generation to generation

*Zech 9:10* and his [God's] ***d*** shall be from sea even to sea

*Matt 20:25* princes of the Gentiles exercise ***d***

*Rom 6:9* death hath no more ***d*** over him [Jesus]

*Col 1:16* by him [Jesus] were all things created...whether they be thrones, or ***d's***

*1 Pet 4:11* to whom [Jesus] be...***d*** for ever and ever

*Jude 25* To...God our Saviour, be...***d*** and power

**DOOR OF THE SHEEP, JESUS AS.** See *"I Am" Statements of Jesus.*

**DORCAS.** See *Tabitha.*

**DOTHAN** (a city where Joseph was sold into slavery by his brothers). **Gen 37:17–28** • 2 Kgs 6:8–23.

## DOUBT [ED, ING]

*Matt 14:31* thou of little faith, wherefore didst thou *d*

*Matt 28:17* they worshipped him [Jesus]: but some *d'ed*

*1 Tim 2:8* men pray every where lifting up holy hands, without wrath and *d'ing*

## DREAM

*Gen 37:5* Joseph dreamed a *d,* and he told it his brethren

*Gen 40:9* the chief butler told his *d* to Joseph

*Gen 41:25* Joseph said…The *d* of Pharaoh is one

*Dan 2:3* I [Nebuchadnezzar] have dreamed a *d,* and my spirit was troubled

*Joel 2:28* pour out my [God's] spirit…old men shall *d* dreams

*Acts 2:17* and your old men shall *d* dreams

## DREAMS THROUGH WHICH GOD SPOKE TO PEOPLE

1. To Abimelech, king of Gerar (Gen 20:3)

2. To Jacob, son of Isaac (Gen 28:10–12)

3. To Laban, father-in-law of Jacob (Gen 31:24)

4. To Solomon, king of Judah (1 Kgs 3:5)

5. To Joseph, husband of Mary (Matt 1:20; 2:12–13,22)

## DRINK [ETH, ING]

*Ex 15:24* the people murmured against Moses, saying, What shall we *d*

*Job 1:13* when his [Job's] sons and his daughters were eating and *d'ing* wine

*Ps 69:21* in my thirst they gave me vinegar to *d*

*Ps 78:15* He [God]…gave them *d* as out of the great depths

*Prov 5:15* *D* waters out of thine own cistern

*Prov 20:1* Wine is a mocker, strong *d* is raging

*Prov 25:21* and if he [your enemy] be thirsty, give him water to *d*

*Eccl 2:24* There is nothing better for a man, than that he should eat and *d*

*Eccl 9:7* *d* thy wine with a merry heart

*Isa 5:11* Woe unto them that rise up early…that they may follow strong *d*

*Ezek 12:18* *d* thy water with trembling

*Dan 1:12* give us [Daniel and his friends] pulse to eat, and water to *d*

*Matt 6:31* What shall we eat? or, What shall we *d*

*Matt 25:42* I was thirsty, and ye gave me no *d*

113

*Mark 2:16* he [Jesus] eateth and *d'eth* with...sinners

*Mark 10:38* can ye *d* of the cup that I [Jesus] *d* of

*Mark 15:23* they gave him [Jesus] to *d* wine...with myrrh

*Luke 5:30* Why do ye [Jesus] eat and *d* with publicans

*Luke 7:33* John the Baptist came neither eating bread nor *d'ing* wine

*Luke 10:7* eating and *d'ing* such things as they give

*Luke 22:18* I [Jesus] will not *d* of the fruit...until the kingdom of God shall come

*John 4:7* Jesus saith unto her [the Samaritan woman], Give me to *d*

*John 4:14* *d'eth* of the water that I [Jesus] shall give him shall never thirst

*John 6:53* Except ye...*d* his [Jesus'] blood, ye have no life in you

*Acts 23:12* saying that they would neither eat nor *d* till they had killed Paul

*Rom 12:20* if he [your enemy] thirst, give him *d*

*Rom 14:17* the kingdom of God is not meat and *d*

*1 Cor 10:31* Whether therefore ye eat, or *d*...do all to the glory of God

*1 Cor 11:25* as oft as ye *d* it, in remembrance of me [Jesus]

*1 Cor 11:29* eateth and *d'eth* damnation to himself

*1 Tim 5:23* *D* no longer water, but use a little wine

*Rev 16:6* thou hast given them blood to *d*

## DRY BONES, EZEKIEL'S VISION OF. Ezek 37:1–14.

## DUMB

*Isa 53:7* as a sheep before her shearers is *d*

*Mark 7:37* he [Jesus] maketh... the *d* to speak

*Luke 1:20* thou [Zacharias] shalt be *d,* and not able to speak

*1 Cor 12:2* Ye know that ye were Gentiles, carried away unto these *d* idols

## DURA (a plain where an image of the Babylonian king was set up). Dan 3:1.

## DYING

*2 Cor 4:10* in the body the *d* of the Lord Jesus

*Heb 11:21* Jacob, when he was a *d,* blessed both the sons of Joseph

# -E-

## EARTH [LY]

*Gen 1:1* God created the heaven and the *e*

*Gen 6:6* it repented the LORD ... he had made man on the *e*

*Gen 9:1* Be fruitful, and multiply, and replenish the *e*

*Gen 12:3* and in thee [Abraham] shall all families of the *e* be blessed

*Deut 30:19* call heaven and *e* to record this day against you

*1 Kgs 10:23* Solomon exceeded all the kings of the *e* ... for wisdom

*Job 1:8* there is none like him [Job] in the *e*

*Job 19:25* he shall stand at the latter day upon the *e*

*Job 38:4* Where wast thou [Job] when I [God] laid the foundations of the *e*

*Ps 8:1* how excellent is thy [God's] name in all the *e*

*Ps 24:1* The *e* is the LORD'S, and the fulness thereof

*Ps 37:11* But the meek shall inherit the *e*

*Ps 67:2* thy [God's] way may be known upon *e*

*Ps 82:8* Arise, O God, judge the *e* ... inherit all nations

*Ps 96:1* O sing ... a new song: sing unto the LORD, all the *e*

*Ps 108:5* Be thou exalted, O God ... and thy glory above all the *e*

*Isa 6:3* the whole *e* is full of his [God's] glory

*Isa 45:22* be ye saved, all the ends of the *e*

*Isa 55:9* higher than the *e,* so are my [God's] ways higher than your ways

*Isa 66:1* heaven is my [God's] throne ... *e* is my footstool

*Joel 3:16* and the heavens and the *e* shall shake

*Hab 2:20* let all the *e* keep silence before him [God]

*Matt 5:13* Ye are ... salt of the *e*

*Matt 6:10* Thy [God's] will be done in *e,* as it is in heaven

*Matt 12:40* shall the Son of man be ... three nights in the heart of the *e*

*Matt 16:19* whatsoever thou shalt loose on *e* shall be loosed in heaven

*Matt 24:35* Heaven and *e* shall pass away, but my [Jesus'] words shall not pass away

*Matt 28:18* All power is given unto me [Jesus] in heaven and in *e*

*Luke 2:14* on *e* peace, good will toward men

*Luke 23:44* darkness over all the *e* until the ninth hour

*John 3:12* I [Jesus] have told you *e'ly* things, and ye believe not

*John 12:32* if I [Jesus] be lifted up from the *e*

*Acts 1:8* ye shall be witnesses ... the uttermost part of the *e*

*2 Cor 5:1* our *e'ly* house of this tabernacle were dissolved

*Col 3:2* Set your affection on things above, not on things on the *e*

*Rev 7:1* four angels standing on the four corners of the *e*

*Rev 21:1* I [John] saw a new heaven and a new *e*

**EAST SEA.** See *Salt Sea.*

**EAT [EN, ER, ETH, ING]**

*Gen 2:17* the tree of...good and evil, thou shalt not *e*

*Gen 3:11* Hast thou *e'en* of the tree...thou shouldest not *e*

*Ex 16:35* the children of Israel did *e* manna

*Lev 11:41* every creeping thing...shall not be *e'en*

*Judg 14:14* Out of the *e'er* came forth meat

*Ps 102:9* For I have *e'en* ashes like bread

*Eccl 2:24* nothing better for a man, than that he should *e* and drink

*Jer 31:29* fathers have *e'en* a sour grape

*Ezek 3:1* *e* that thou [Ezekiel] findest; *e* this roll

*Ezek 12:18* *e* thy [Ezekiel's] bread with quaking

*Matt 6:25* Take no thought for your life, what ye shall *e*

*Matt 9:11* Why *e'eth* your [disciples'] Master with publicans

*Matt 15:20* to *e* with unwashen hands defileth not a man

*Matt 26:26* they were *e'ing,* Jesus took bread...blessed it

*Mark 7:28* dogs under the table *e* of the children's crumbs

*Mark 14:18* One of you which *e'eth* with me [Jesus] shall betray me

*Luke 5:30* Why do ye *e* and drink with...sinners

*Luke 7:33* John the Baptist came neither *e'ing* bread nor drinking wine

*Luke 15:23* bring...the fatted calf...let us *e,* and be merry

*John 4:32* I [Jesus] have meat to *e* that ye know not of

*John 6:50* This is...bread... from heaven, that a man may *e*...and not die

*Acts 10:13* there came a voice... Rise, Peter; kill, and *e*

*1 Cor 10:31* ye *e,* or drink...do all to the glory of God

*1 Cor 11:26* as often as ye *e* this bread, and drink this cup

*1 Cor 11:29* he that *e'eth*... unworthily, *e'eth*...damnation to himself

*2 Thes 3:10* if any would not work, neither should he *e*

*Rev 2:7* him that overcometh will I give to *e*...tree of life

**EBAL** (a mountain where Joshua built an altar after destroying the city of Ai). Deut 11:29; 27:4,13 • **Josh 8:30–35.**

**116**

**EBED-MELECH** (an Ethiopian eunuch who rescued Jeremiah from a dungeon). **Jer 38:7–13; 39:15–18.**

**EBENEZER** (a memorial site in Philistine territory that commemorated Israel's victory over the Philistines). 1 Sam 4:1–10; 5:1; **7:10–12.**

**EBER** (a great-grandson of Shem and ancestor of the Hebrew race). Gen 10:21–25; 11:14–17 • 1 Chr 1:18–23.

**ECCLESIASTES, BOOK OF.** A wisdom book in the Old Testament, probably written by King Solomon, which declares that life derives joy and meaning not from riches, fame, or work but from reverence for God and obedience to His commandments.

**EDEN, GARDEN OF** (the fruitful garden created specifically by the Lord as the home for Adam and Eve). **Gen 2:8–3:24;** 4:16 • Isa 51:3 • Ezek 28:13; 31:9,16–18; 36:35 • Joel 2:3.

**EDIFY [IETH, ING]**
*1 Cor 14:4* speaketh in an unknown tongue *e'ieth* himself
*Eph 4:12* for the *e'ing* of the body of Christ

*1 Thes 5:11* comfort…and *e* one another

**EDOM**
1. The name given to Esau, Jacob's brother, after he traded away his birthright. Gen 25:30.
2. The land where the descendants of Esau settled. Gen 36:21,31–32,43 • Num 20:14–23; 34:3 • Josh 15:1,21 • Judg 11:17–18 • 2 Sam 8:14 • 2 Kgs 3:8–26 • Jer 25:21; 27:3; 40:11; 49:7–22 • Ezek 25:12–14 • Amos 1:6–11 • Obad 1,8. *Idumea:* Mark 3:8.

**EGYPT** (an ancient nation along the Nile River which held the Hebrew people in slavery before their miraculous deliverance). Gen 12:10; 37:28–36 • **Ex 1:7–14; 12:29–36** • Isa 19:3–25; 30:1–7; 36:6 • Jer 46:8 • Ezek 30:25 • Matt 2:13–15.

**EHUD** (a judge of Israel who killed King Eglon of Moab). Judg 3:15–26.

**EKRON** (a major Philistine city captured by Israel). Josh 13:3; 15:11,45–46; 19:43 • **Judg 1:18** • 1 Sam 5:10; 6:16–17; 7:14; 17:52 • 2 Kgs 1:2–6,16 • Jer 25:20 • Amos 1:8 • Zeph 2:4 • Zech 9:5,7.

**ELAH**

1. A valley where David killed the Philistine giant Goliath. **1 Sam 17:2,49;** 21:9.

2. A king of Israel who was assassinated and succeeded by Zimri. 1 Kgs 16:6–10.

**ELAM** (a son of Shem and ancestor of the Elamites). **Gen 10:22** • 1 Chr 1:17.

**ELAMITES** (descendants of Elam who lived in Mesopotamia in the area later populated by the Medes and Persians). Gen 14:1,9 • Ezra 4:9 • Isa 11:11; 21:2; 22:6 • Jer 25:25; 49:34–39 • Ezek 32:24 • Dan 8:2 • Acts 2:9.

**EL-BETHEL.** See *Bethel.*

**ELDER [S]**

*Matt 15:2* Why do thy [Jesus'] disciples transgress the tradition of the *e's*

*Luke 15:25* his [father of prodigal son] *e* son was in the field

*Acts 14:23* they [Paul and Barnabas] had ordained them *e's*

*Acts 20:17* he [Paul] sent to Ephesus, and called the *e's*

*1 Tim 5:1* Rebuke not an *e,* but entreat him as a father

*1 Tim 5:17* Let the *e's* that rule well be counted worthy

*Jas 5:14* call for the *e's* ... and let them pray over him

*2 John 1* The *e* unto the elect lady and her children

*Rev 4:10* The four and twenty *e's* fall down before him

**ELEAZAR** (a son of Aaron who succeeded his father as high priest). Ex 6:23–25; 28:1 • Lev 10:6–7 • Num 3:32; **20:25–28** • Josh 14:1; 24:33.

**ELECT**

*Isa 42:1* mine [God's] *e,* in whom my soul delighteth

*Mark 13:27* he [Jesus] shall gather together his *e* from the four winds

*Col 3:12* Put on ... as the *e* of God ... bowels of mercies

*1 Pet 1:2* **E** according to the foreknowledge of God

**ELECTION**

*Rom 11:5* a remnant according to the *e* of grace

*2 Pet 1:10* give diligence to make your calling and *e* sure

**ELI** (a high priest of Israel with whom the prophet Samuel lived during his boyhood years). **1 Sam 1:9–3:17;** 4:15–18; 14:3 • 1 Kgs 2:27.

**ELIAKIM**

1. An aide to King Hezekiah of Judah who mediated

peace with the invading Assyrian army. **2 Kgs 18:18–19:2** • **Isa 22:20–25;** 36:3, 11,22; 37:2.

2. Another name for King Jehoiakim of Judah. See *Jehoiakim.*

**ELIAS.** See *Elijah.*

**ELIHU** (a man who criticized Job and his three friends). Job 32:2–6; 34:1; 35:1; 36:1.

**ELIJAH** (a courageous prophet who opposed King Ahab and his successor, Ahaziah, because of their encouragement of Baal worship throughout the Northern Kingdom). **1 Kgs 17–21** • **2 Kgs 1:1–18; 2:1–11;** 3:11; 9:36; 10:10,17 • 2 Chr 21:12 • Mal 4:5. *Elias:* Matt 17:3–4 • Mark 9:4–13 • Luke 9:30–54 • John 1:21,25 • Rom 11:2 • Jas 5:17.

**ELIPHAZ**
1. A son of Esau. Gen 36:10 • 1 Chr 1:35–36.
2. One of the three friends who comforted Job. His speeches appear in Job 4:1–5:27; 15:1–35; 22:1–30.

**ELISABETH** (mother of John the Baptist and a relative of Mary, earthly mother of Jesus). Luke 1:5–60.

**ELISEUS.** See *Elisha.*

**ELISHA** (a prophet selected and anointed by Elijah as his successor). 1 Kgs 19:16–19 • **2 Kgs 2:1–15;** 3:11–14; 4:1–38; 5:9–10,20,25; 6:1–32; 7:1; 8:1–14; 9:1; 13:14–21. *Eliseus:* Luke 4:27.

**ELON** (a minor judge of Israel). Judg 12:11–12.

**ELOTH** (a former Edomite city used as a port city by King Solomon). **1 Kgs 9:26** • 2 Chr 8:17; 26:2.

**ELYMAS.** See *Bar-jesus.*

**EMMAUS** (a village near Jerusalem where Jesus appeared to two of His followers after His resurrection). Luke 24:13–33.

**END [ED, S]**
*Gen 2:2* on the seventh day God *e'ed* his work
*Job 28:24* For he [God] looketh to the *e's* of the earth
*Job 42:12* the LORD blessed the latter *e* of Job
*Ps 22:27* the *e's* of the world shall…turn unto the LORD
*Ps 39:4* make me to know mine *e*…measure of my days
*Ps 102:27* thy [God's] years shall have no *e*

*Prov 14:12* the *e* thereof are the ways of death

*Eccl 7:8* Better is the *e* of a thing than the beginning

*Eccl 12:12* of making many books there is no *e*

*Isa 9:7* Of...his [the Messiah's] ... peace ... there shall be no *e*

*Jer 8:20* summer is *e'ed,* and we are not saved

*Dan 12:9* words are...sealed till the time of the *e*

*Matt 10:22* he that endureth to the *e* shall be saved

*Matt 24:6* all these things must come to pass...*e* is not yet

*Matt 28:20* I [Jesus] am with you alway, even unto the *e* of the world

*John 18:37* Jesus answered... To this *e* was I born

*Rom 10:4* Christ is the *e* of the law for righteousness

*1 Cor 15:24* Then cometh the *e*

*Eph 3:21* be glory in the church by Christ Jesus...world without *e*

*1 Pet 4:7* But the *e* of all things is at hand

*Rev 2:26* he that overcometh... keepeth my works unto the *e*

*Rev 22:13* Alpha and Omega, the beginning and the *e*

**END [S] OF THE EARTH**

*1 Sam 2:10* the LORD shall judge the *e's-o-t-e*

*Ps 48:10* so is thy [God's] praise unto the *e's-o-t-e*

*Ps 61:2* From the *e-o-t-e* will I cry unto thee [God]

*Ps 67:7* all the *e's-o-t-e* shall fear him [God]

*Isa 40:28* the Creator of the *e's-o-t-e,* fainteth not

*Isa 42:10* Sing...his [God's] praise from the *e-o-t-e*

*Isa 45:22* be ye saved, all the *e's-o-t-e*

*Acts 13:47* thou [Paul] shouldest be for salvation unto the *e's-o-t-e*

**EN-DOR** (a city where King Saul sought advice from a fortune teller). Josh 17:11 • **1 Sam 28:1–10** • Ps 83:9–10.

**ENDUED**

*Luke 24:49* tarry ye in... Jerusalem, until...*e* with power

*Jas 3:13* Who is...*e* with knowledge among you

**ENDURE [D, ING, TH]**

*Ex 18:23* then thou [Moses] shalt be able to *e*

*1 Chr 16:34* his [God's] mercy *e'th* for ever

*Esth 8:6* how can I [Esther] *e* to see the evil that shall come

*Job 8:15* he shall hold it fast, but it shall not *e*

*Ps 9:7* LORD shall *e* for ever

*Ps 19:9* The fear of the LORD is clean, *e'ing* for ever

*Ps 30:5* For his [God's] anger *e'th* but a moment

*Ps 89:36* His [David's] seed shall *e* for ever

*Ps 102:12* But thou, O LORD, shalt *e* for ever

*Ps 107:1* give thanks unto... LORD...his mercy *e'th* for ever

*Ps 145:13* thy [God's] dominion *e'th* throughout all generations

*Prov 27:24* doth the crown *e* to every generation

*Matt 10:22* he that *e'th* to the end shall be saved

*Mark 13:13* he that shall *e* unto the end...shall be saved

*1 Cor 13:7* [charity] hopeth all things, *e'th* all things

*2 Tim 2:3* *e* hardness, as a good soldier of Jesus Christ

*2 Tim 4:3* they will not *e* sound doctrine...having itching ears

*2 Tim 4:5* watch thou in all things, *e* afflictions

*Heb 6:15* after he [Abraham] had patiently *e'd*

*Heb 12:2* who [Jesus] for the joy...set before him *e'd* the cross

*Jas 1:12* Blessed is the man that *e'th* temptation

*Jas 5:11* Behold, we count them happy which *e*

**ENEMY [IES]**

*Deut 20:4* LORD...goeth...to fight...against your *e'ies*

*1 Sam 18:29* Saul became David's *e* continually

*Job 19:11* he [God] counteth me...as one of his *e'ies*

*Ps 6:7* Mine eye...waxeth old because of all mine *e'ies*

*Ps 9:3* *e'ies* are turned back, they shall fall

*Ps 18:17* He [God] delivered me from my strong *e*

*Ps 23:5* Thou [God] preparest a table...presence of mine *e'ies*

*Ps 27:11* lead me in a plain path, because of mine *e'ies*

*Ps 61:3* thou [God] hast been... a strong tower from the *e*

*Ps 97:3* A fire...burneth up his [God's] *e'ies* round about

*Ps 110:1* until I [God] make thine *e'ies* thy footstool

*Prov 25:21* If thine *e* be hungry, give him bread

*Matt 5:44* I [Jesus] say unto you, Love your *e'ies*

*Rom 12:20* Therefore if thine *e* hunger, feed him

*1 Cor 15:25* For he [Jesus] must reign, till he hath put all *e'ies* under his feet

*1 Cor 15:26* The last *e* that shall be destroyed is death

*Gal 4:16* Am I [Paul]...your *e,* because I tell you the truth

*2 Thes 3:15* count him not as an *e,* but admonish him

*Jas 4:4* a friend of the world is the *e* of God

**EN-GEDI** (an oasis near the Dead Sea where David hid from King Saul). Josh 15:62 • **1 Sam 23:29–24:1** • 2 Chr 20:2 • Song 1:14 • Ezek 47:10.

**ENMITY**

*Gen 3:15* I [God] will put *e* between thee [the serpent] and the woman

*Rom 8:7* Because the carnal mind is *e* against God

*Jas 4:4* the friendship of the world is *e* with God

**ENOCH**

1. The firstborn son of Cain and a city named for him. Gen 4:17–18.

2. The father of Methuselah, who was taken into God's presence without experiencing physical death. Gen 5:18–24 • Luke 3:37 • Heb 11:5 • Jude 14. *Henoch:* 1 Chr 1:3.

**ENTER [ED, ETH, ING]**

*Ps 100:4* **E** into his [God's] gates with thanksgiving

*Prov 17:10* A reproof *e'eth* more into a wise man than an hundred stripes into a fool

*Ezek 3:24* the spirit *e'ed* into me [Ezekiel]

*Matt 6:6* when thou prayest, *e* into thy closet

*Matt 7:21* Not every one that saith…Lord, Lord, shall *e* into the kingdom of heaven

*Mark 7:18* thing from without *e'eth* into the man, it cannot defile him

*Mark 14:38* pray, lest ye *e* into temptation

*Luke 11:52* them that were *e'ing* in ye hindered

*Luke 13:24* Strive to *e* in at the strait gate

*Luke 18:25* easier for a camel… than for a rich man to *e* into the kingdom

*Luke 22:3* Then *e'ed* Satan into Judas surnamed Iscariot

*John 3:4* can he *e* the second time into his mother's womb, and be born

*John 10:2* he that *e'eth* in by the door is the shepherd

*Acts 11:8* nothing…unclean hath at any time *e'ed* into my [Peter's] mouth

*Rom 5:12* by one man sin *e'ed* into the world

*1 Cor 2:9* *e'ed* into the heart of man, the things which God hath prepared

*Heb 9:12* he [Jesus] *e'ed* in once into the holy place

**ENVY [IETH, ING]**

*Prov 3:31* **E** thou not the oppressor

*Prov 27:4* but who is able to stand before *e*

*Mark 15:10* chief priests had delivered him [Jesus] for *e*

*Rom 13:13* Let us walk honestly…not in strife and *e'ing*

*1 Cor 13:4* charity *e'ieth* not ...
   vaunteth not itself
*Gal 5:26* not be desirous of ...
   glory, ... *e'ing* one another
*Phil 1:15* Some ... preach Christ
   even of *e* and strife
*Titus 3:3* living in malice and
   *e* ... hating one another
*Jas 3:16* where *e'ing* and strife
   is, there is confusion

**EPAPHRAS** (a church leader
who was called a "fellowpris-
oner" by the apostle Paul). Col
1:7–8; 4:12 • **Phlm 23.**

**EPAPHRODITUS** (a believer
who visited Paul while he was
imprisoned in Rome). Phil
2:25; **4:18.**

**EPHESIANS, EPISTLE TO
THE.** A letter of the apostle
Paul to the church at Ephesus
on the theme of the risen
Christ as Lord of creation and
head of His body, the church.

**EPHESUS** (a major city of
Asia Minor where Paul spent
two to three years and established a church). **Acts 18:19–21;
19:1–10;** 20:16–17 • 1 Cor 15:32;
16:8 • Eph 1:1 • 1 Tim 1:3 •
2 Tim 1:18; 4:12 • Rev 1:11; 2:1.

**EPHRAIM**
   1. A son of Joseph and
ancestor of one of the twelve
tribes of Israel. Gen 41:52;
48:1–20 • Num 26:28 • 1 Chr
7:20–22. The tribe of Ephraim
settled in central Canaan. Josh
16:1–10.
   2. A symbolic name for the
nation of Israel, meaning
"fruitful," used especially in the
books of Isaiah, Jeremiah, and
Hosea. Isa 7:2–17 • Jer 31:9–20
• Hos 5:3–14.
   3. A city in the wilderness
to which Jesus and His disciples retreated. John 11:54.
   4. A forest where Absalom's
forces were defeated by David's
army. 2 Sam 18:6–18.

**EPHRATAH.** See *Bethlehem.*

**EPHRATH.** See *Bethlehem.*

**EPHRON** (a Hittite who sold
a cave to Abraham). **Gen
23:8–20;** 25:9; 49:29–30; 50:13.

**EPICUREANS** (followers of
the Greek philosopher Epicu-
rus whom Paul addressed in
Athens). Acts 17:18.

**EQUAL**
*Prov 26:7* The legs of the lame
   are not *e*
*Ezek 18:25* Is not my [God's]
   way *e* ... your ways unequal
*John 5:18* he [Jesus] ... said
   also that God was his
   Father, making himself *e*
   with God

*Phil 2:6* Who [Jesus] ... thought it not robbery to be *e* with God

*Col 4:1* give unto your servants that which is just and *e*

**ERASTUS** (a believer whom Paul sent into Macedonia). Acts 19:22 • 2 Tim 4:20.

**ERR [ED]**

*Job 6:24* understand wherein I [Job] have *e'ed*

*Isa 9:16* leaders of this people cause them to *e*

*Isa 63:17* why hast thou [God] made us to *e* from thy ways

*Matt 22:29* Ye do *e*, not knowing the scriptures

*1 Tim 6:10* they have *e'ed* from the faith

*Jas 5:19* if any of you do *e* from the truth

**ERROR**

*2 Sam 6:7* God smote him [Uzzah] there for his *e*

*Matt 27:64* the last *e* shall be worse than the first

*2 Pet 3:17* being led away with the *e* of the wicked

**ESAIAS.** See *Isaiah.*

**ESAR-HADDON** (a king of Assyria who succeeded his father, Sennacherib). **2 Kgs 19:37** • Ezra 4:2 • Isa 37:38.

**ESAU** (the oldest son of Isaac who traded his birthright for a bowl of stew). Esau was the ancestor of the Edomites. **Gen 25:26–34;** 26:34; 27:1–42; 28:6–9; 32:3–19; 33:1–16; 35:1,29; 36:1–43 • Josh 24:4 • 1 Chr 1:34–35 • Mal 1:2–3 • Rom 9:13 • Heb 12:16. *Edom:* Gen 36:8.

**ESCAPE [D]**

*1 Sam 22:1* David ... *e'd* to the cave Adullam

*Job 19:20* I [Job] am *e'd* with the skin of my teeth

*Ps 71:2* cause me to *e:* incline thine [God's] ear unto me

*Isa 37:31* remnant that is *e'd* of the house of Judah

*Jer 25:35* no way to flee, nor the principal of the flock to *e*

*John 10:39* but he [Jesus] *e'd* out of their hand

*1 Cor 10:13* God ... will with the temptation also make a way to *e*

*Heb 2:3* How shall we *e*, if we neglect so great salvation

**ESEK** (a well that the servants of Isaac and Abimelech quarreled over). Gen 26:20.

**ESH-BAAL.** See *Ish-bosheth.*

**ESH-COL** (a brook explored by the spies sent into Canaan). **Num 13:22–27;** 32:9 • Deut 1:24.

**ESTABLISH [ED]**

*Gen 9:9* I [God] *e* my covenant with you [Noah]

*Ps 7:9* *e* the just: for the righteous God trieth the hearts

*Ps 78:5* he [God] *e'ed* a testimony in Jacob

*Ps 90:17* *e* thou [God] the work of our hands

*Prov 3:19* The LORD...by understanding hath...*e'ed* the heavens

*Prov 12:19* The lip of truth shall be *e'ed* for ever

*Prov 16:3* Commit...unto the LORD...thy thoughts shall be *e'ed*

*Ezek 16:62* I [God] will *e* my covenant with thee

*Matt 18:16* mouth of...witnesses every word...be *e'ed*

*Acts 16:5* so were the churches *e'ed* in the faith

*Rom 10:3* going about to *e* their own righteousness

*Heb 8:6* he [Jesus] is the mediator of a better covenant... *e'ed* upon better promises

**ESTHER** (a young Jewish woman who became queen under King Ahasuerus of Persia and used her influence to save her countrymen). Esth 2–9.

**ESTHER, BOOK OF.** A historical book of the Old Testament named for its major personality, Queen Esther of Persia. This book shows that God protects and sustains His people.

**ETERNAL**

*Deut 33:27* The *e* God is thy refuge

*Mark 3:29* he that shall blaspheme against the Holy Ghost...is in danger of *e* damnation

*John 17:3* life *e,* that they might know...God

*2 Cor 4:18* things which are not seen are *e*

*2 Cor 5:1* an house not made with hands, *e* in the heavens

*1 Tim 1:17* unto the King *e,* immortal, invisible

*Heb 5:9* he [Jesus] became the author of *e* salvation

*Heb 9:12* by his [Jesus'] own blood he...obtained *e* redemption for us

**ETERNAL LIFE**

*Mark 10:17* what shall I do that I may inherit *e-l*

*John 3:15* whosoever believeth in him [Jesus] should not perish, but have *e-l*

*John 6:54* Whoso eateth my [Jesus'] flesh...hath *e-l*

*John 6:68* thou [Jesus] hast the words of *e-l*

*John 10:28* I [Jesus] give unto them *e-l*

*Rom 6:23* the gift of God is *e-l* through Jesus Christ

*1 Tim 6:12* Fight the good fight of faith, lay hold on *e-l*

*1 John 2:25* promise that he [Jesus] hath promised...*e-l*

*1 John 3:15* no murderer hath *e-l* abiding in him

*1 John 5:11* God hath given to us *e-l*...in his Son

*Jude 21* mercy of our Lord Jesus Christ unto *e-l*

**ETHIOPIA** (an ancient nation south of Egypt). Gen 2:13 • 2 Chr 12:3 • Job 28:19 • Ps 68:31 • Isa 45:14 • Dan 11:43 • Amos 9:7 • Acts 8:27.

**EUNICE** (mother of Timothy who was commended for her faith by the apostle Paul). 2 Tim 1:5.

**EUPHRATES** (a major river in Mesopotamia). Gen 2:14; 15:18 • Josh 1:4 • 2 Sam 8:3 • 2 Kgs 23:29 • 2 Chr 35:20 • Jer 13:4–7 • Rev 9:14; 16:12.

**EUTYCHUS** (a young man who fell from a window during Paul's sermon at Troas). Acts 20:9–12.

**EVANGELIST [S]**
*Acts 21:8* entered into the house of Philip the *e*

*Eph 4:11* he [God] gave some... prophets; and some, *e's*

*2 Tim 4:5* do the work of an *e*

**EVE** (first woman and mother of the human race). Gen 3:20; 4:1 • 2 Cor 11:3 • 1 Tim 2:13.

**EVERLASTING**
*Deut 33:27* and underneath are the *e* arms

*Ps 24:7* and be ye lift up, ye *e* doors

*Ps 90:2* even from *e* to *e,* thou art God

*Ps 100:5* For the LORD is good; his mercy is *e*

*Ps 119:144* righteousness of thy [God's] testimonies is *e*

*Isa 9:6* his [Jesus'] name shall be called...The *e* Father

*Isa 26:4* in the LORD JEHO-VAH is *e* strength

*Isa 40:28* the *e* God...fainteth not, neither is weary

*Isa 60:19* the LORD shall be unto thee an *e* light

*Jer 31:3* I [God] have loved thee with an *e* love

*Dan 7:14* his [God's] dominion is an *e* dominion

*Matt 25:41* Depart from me [Jesus], ye cursed, into *e* fire

**EVERLASTING COVENANT**
*Gen 9:16* the *e-c* between God and every living creature

*Heb 13:20* Jesus, that great shepherd of the sheep, through the blood of the *e-c*

**EVERLASTING LIFE**

*John 3:16* whosoever believeth in him [Jesus] should not perish, but have *e-l*

*John 4:14* a well of water springing up into *e-l*

*John 5:24* He that...believeth on him [God] that sent me [Jesus], hath *e-l*

*John 6:47* He that believeth on me [Jesus] hath *e-l*

**EVIL [S]**

*Gen 50:20* ye thought *e* against me [Joseph]; but God meant it unto good

*Deut 30:15* I [Moses] have set before thee...death and *e*

*Josh 24:15* if it seem *e* unto you to serve the LORD

*1 Sam 16:14* an *e* spirit from the LORD troubled him [Saul]

*Job 2:10* shall we receive good at the hand of God, and... not receive *e*

*Job 28:28* to depart from *e* is understanding

*Ps 23:4* valley of the shadow of death, I will fear no *e*

*Ps 34:13* Keep thy tongue from *e,* and thy lips from...guile

*Ps 38:20* They...that render *e* for good are...adversaries

*Ps 51:4* Against thee [God]... have I...done this *e*

*Ps 119:101* I have refrained my feet from every *e* way

*Prov 3:7* fear the LORD, and depart from *e*

*Prov 15:3* eyes of the LORD are in every place, beholding the *e* and the good

*Prov 31:12* She will do him good and not *e*

*Isa 5:20* Woe unto them that call *e* good, and good *e*

*Jer 1:14* Out of the north an *e* shall break forth

*Jer 2:13* my [God's] people have committed two *e's*

*Matt 5:11* men...shall say all manner of *e* against you

*Matt 6:13* lead us not into temptation...deliver us from *e*

*Mark 3:4* lawful to do good on the sabbath...or to do *e*

*Luke 11:13* ye then, being *e,* know how to give good gifts

*John 3:19* men loved darkness... because their deeds were *e*

*Rom 7:19* the *e* which I [Paul] would not, that I do

*Rom 12:9* Abhor that which is *e;* cleave to...good

*Rom 12:21* Be not overcome of *e*...overcome *e* with good

*Eph 5:16* Redeeming the time, because the days are *e*

*Eph 6:13* ye may be able to withstand in the *e* day

*1 Thes 5:22* Abstain from all appearance of *e*

*1 Tim 6:10* love of money is the root of all *e*

*Heb 3:12* lest there be in any of you an *e* heart of unbelief

*Jas 3:8* the tongue...is an unruly *e,* full of deadly poison

*Jas 3:16* where envying... is, there is... every *e* work
*3 John 11* Beloved, follow not that which is *e*

## EVILDOER [S]

*Ps 26:5* I have hated the congregation of *e's*
*Ps 119:115* Depart from me, ye *e's*
*1 Pet 4:15* let none of you suffer... as an *e,* or... busybody

**EVIL-MERODACH** (a king of Babylonia who released King Jehoiachin of Judah from prison). **2 Kgs 25:27–30** • Jer 52:31.

## EXALT [ED, ETH]

*1 Chr 29:11* thou [God] art *e'ed* as head above all
*Ps 34:3* let us *e* his [God's] name together
*Ps 46:10* I [God] will be *e'ed* among the heathen
*Ps 57:11* Be thou *e'ed,* O God, above the heavens
*Ps 97:9* thou [God] art *e'ed* far above all gods
*Ps 99:5* *E* ye the LORD... and worship at his footstool
*Prov 14:34* Righteousness *e'eth* a nation
*Isa 25:1* O LORD, thou art my God; I will *e* thee
*Isa 40:4* Every valley shall be *e'ed*... hill... made low
*Luke 14:11* he that humbleth himself shall be *e'ed*

*Phil 2:9* God also hath highly *e'ed* him [Jesus]
*1 Pet 5:6* that he [God] may *e* you in due time

## EXAMPLE

*Matt 1:19* Then Joseph her [Mary's] husband... not willing to make her a publick *e*
*John 13:15* I [Jesus] have given you an *e*
*1 Tim 4:12* be thou an *e* of the believers, in word

## EXCEEDING [LY]

*Gen 17:2* I [God]... will multiply thee [Abraham] *e'ly*
*Ps 68:3* rejoice before God: yea, let them *e'ly* rejoice
*Jon 3:3* Now Nineveh was an *e* great city
*Jon 4:1* it displeased Jonah *e'ly,* and he was very angry
*Matt 2:10* they [the wise men] rejoiced with *e* great joy
*Matt 5:12* be *e* glad: for great is your reward in heaven
*Matt 26:38* My [Jesus'] soul is *e* sorrowful, even unto death
*Mark 15:14* cried out the more *e'ly,* Crucify him [Jesus]
*2 Cor 4:17* our light affliction... worketh for us a far more *e*... weight of glory
*Eph 2:7* he [God] might show the *e* riches of his grace
*Eph 3:20* unto him [Jesus] that is able to do *e* abundantly above all... we ask

*Jude 24* him [Jesus] that is able to...present you faultless before...his glory with *e* joy

**EXCELLENT**

*Ps 8:9* how *e* is thy [God's] name in all the earth

*Ps 150:2* praise him [God] according to his *e* greatness

*Isa 12:5* for he [God] hath done *e* things

*Dan 6:3* because an *e* spirit was in him [Daniel]

*1 Cor 12:31* yet show I [Paul] unto you a more *e* way

*Heb 8:6* hath he [Jesus] obtained a more *e* ministry

*Heb 11:4* Abel offered...a more *e* sacrifice than Cain

**EXCUSE**

*Luke 14:18* they all with one consent began to make *e*

*Rom 1:20* they are without *e*

**EXHORT [ED, ING]**

*1 Thes 2:11* we *e'ed* and comforted...every one of you

*2 Tim 4:2* *e* with all longsuffering and doctrine

*Titus 2:9* *E* servants to be obedient unto their own masters

*Heb 10:25* Not forsaking the assembling of ourselves... but *e'ing* one another

**EXODUS, BOOK OF.** An Old Testament book which recounts the release of the Hebrew peo-

ple from Egyptian enslavement and the early years of their history as a nation. It describes God's miraculous provision for His people in the wilderness (16:1–17:7); Moses' reception of the Ten Commandments (chap. 20); and the building of the tabernacle in the wilderness (chaps. 36–40).

**EXPEDIENT**

*John 11:50* *e*...that one man should die for the people

*John 16:7* *e* for you that I [Jesus] go away

*1 Cor 6:12* All things are lawful...but all things are not *e*

**EYE**

*Ex 21:24* *E* for *e,* tooth for tooth, hand for hand

*Deut 34:7* when he [Moses] died...*e* was not dim, nor... natural force abated

*Job 42:5* now mine [Job's] *e* seeth thee [God]

*Ps 6:7* Mine *e* is consumed because of grief

*Ps 17:8* Keep me as the apple of the *e*

*Prov 28:22* He that hasteth to be rich hath an evil *e*

*Matt 5:38* it hath been said...*e* for an *e*...tooth for a tooth

*Matt 6:23* if thine *e* be evil, thy whole body...full of darkness

*Mark 9:47* if thine *e* offend thee, pluck it out

**129**

*Luke 6:41* the mote that is in thy brother's *e*

*1 Cor 2:9 E* hath not seen, nor ear heard

*1 Cor 12:17* If the whole body were an *e,* where...hearing

*1 Cor 12:21* the *e* cannot say unto the hand

*1 Cor 15:52* in the twinkling of an *e,* at the last trump

*Rev 1:7* he [Jesus] cometh with clouds...every *e* shall see him

**EYE [S] OF THE LORD**

*Gen 6:8* Noah found grace in the *e's-o-t-L*

*1 Kgs 15:5* David did...right in the *e's-o-t-L*

*2 Chr 16:9 e's-o-t-L* run to and fro throughout the...earth

*Ps 33:18* the *e-o-t-L* is upon them that fear him

*Prov 15:3* The *e's-o-t-L* are in every place, beholding the evil and the good

*1 Pet 3:12* the *e's-o-t-L* are over the righteous

**EYEWITNESSES**

*Luke 1:2* which...were *e,* and ministers of the word

*2 Pet 1:16* we...were *e* of his [Jesus'] majesty

**EZEKIAS.** See *Hezekiah.*

**EZEKIEL** (a prophet of Judah carried into exile by the Babylonians and author of the book that bears his name). Ezek 1:3. He is not mentioned outside the Book of Ezekiel.

**EZEKIEL, BOOK OF.** A prophetic book of the Old Testament addressed to the Jewish captives in Babylon about 585 B.C., offering God's promise that His people would be restored to their homeland after their period of suffering and exile was over.

**EZION-GABER.** See *Ezion-geber.*

**EZION-GEBER** (a town with a harbor for King Solomon's trading ships). **1 Kgs 9:26–28;** 22:48 • 2 Chr 8:17–18. *Ezion-gaber:* Num 33:35–36 • Deut 2:8 • 2 Chr 20:36.

**EZRA** (a scribe and priest who led a reform movement among the Jews after the Exile and author of the book that bears his name). Ezra 7:1–25; 10:1–16 • Neh 8:1–13; 12:13–36.

**EZRA, BOOK OF.** A historical book of the Old Testament that describes events in Jerusalem after the Jewish captives began returning to their homeland about 500 B.C.

# -F-

## FABLES

*1 Tim 1:4* Neither give heed to *f* and endless genealogies
*1 Tim 4:7* refuse profane and old wives' *f*

## FACE OF THE LORD

*Ps 34:16* The *f-o-t-L* is against them that do evil
*Luke 1:76* go before the *f-o-t-L* to prepare his ways
*1 Pet 3:12* the *f-o-t-L* is against them that do evil

## FAIR HAVENS (a harbor on the island of Crete where Paul stopped during his voyage to Rome). Acts 27:8.

## FAITH

*Hab 2:4* but the just shall live by his *f*
*Matt 17:20* *f* as a grain of mustard seed
*Acts 6:8* Stephen, full of *f* and power, did great wonders
*Rom 1:17* righteousness of God revealed from *f* to *f*
*Rom 3:28* justified by *f* without the deeds of the law
*Rom 5:1* justified by *f,* we have peace with God
*Rom 10:17* So then *f* cometh by hearing
*1 Cor 13:13* abideth *f,* hope, charity, these three

*Gal 2:20* I [Paul] live by the *f* of the Son of God
*Gal 3:24* unto Christ, that we might be justified by *f*
*Gal 5:22* fruit of the Spirit is love … goodness, *f*
*Eph 2:8* by grace are ye saved through *f*
*Eph 6:16* Above all, taking the shield of *f*
*1 Tim 5:8* denied the *f,* and is worse than an infidel
*1 Tim 6:12* Fight the good fight of *f*
*2 Tim 4:7* finished my course, I [Paul] have kept the *f*
*Heb 10:23* hold fast the profession of our *f*
*Heb 11:1* Now *f* is the substance of things hoped for
*Heb 12:2* Jesus the author and finisher of our *f*
*Jas 2:17* *f,* if it hath not works, is dead, being alone
*1 John 5:4* victory that overcometh the world, even our *f*
*Jude 3* contend for the *f* … delivered unto the saints

## FAITH CHAPTER OF THE BIBLE. Heb 11.

## FAITHFUL [NESS]

*Ps 31:23* for the LORD preserveth the *f*
*Ps 119:90* Thy [God's] *f'ness* is unto all generations
*Prov 27:6* *F* are the wounds of a friend

*Lam 3:23* new every morning: great is thy [God's] *f'ness*

*Matt 25:21* Well done, thou good and *f* servant

*Luke 16:10* *f* in that which is least is *f* also in much

*1 Cor 4:2* required in stewards, that a man be found *f*

*1 Cor 10:13* God is *f,* who will not suffer you to be tempted

*2 Thes 3:3* the Lord is *f,* who shall stablish you

*1 John 1:9* he [Jesus] is *f* and just to forgive us our sins

*Rev 2:10* be thou *f* unto death

## FAITHLESS

*Luke 9:41* O *f* and perverse generation

*John 20:27* Thomas … be not *f*

## FALL [EN, ETH, ING]

*Ps 116:8* thou [God] hast delivered … my feet from *f'ing*

*Ps 145:14* The LORD upholdeth all that *f*

*Prov 16:18* Pride goeth before destruction … haughty spirit before a *f*

*Eccl 4:10* woe to him that is alone when he *f'eth*

*Dan 3:6* whoso *f'eth* not down and worshippeth shall … be cast into the … furnace

*Hos 14:1* thou [Israel] hast *f'en* by thine iniquity

*Luke 2:34* this child [Jesus] is set for the *f* … of many

*Luke 6:39* shall they not both *f* into the ditch

*John 12:24* corn of wheat *f* into the ground and die

*1 Cor 10:12* thinketh he standeth take heed lest he *f*

*Heb 10:31* It is a fearful thing to *f* into the hands of the living God

*Jas 1:2* joy when ye *f* into divers temptations

*Jude 24* Now unto him [Jesus] that is able to keep you from *f'ing*

*Rev 14:8* Babylon is *f'en,* is *f'en,* that great city

**FALL OF MAN.** Gen 3:1–24.

## FALSE [LY]

*Ex 20:16* shalt not bear *f* witness against thy neighbour

*Lev 19:11* Ye shall not steal, neither deal *f'ly*

*Prov 11:1* A *f* balance is abomination to the LORD

*Jer 29:9* prophesy *f'ly* unto you in my [God's] name

*Matt 5:11* say all manner of evil against you *f'ly,* for my [Jesus'] sake

## FALSE PROPHET [S]

*Matt 7:15* Beware of *f-p's* … in sheep's clothing

*Matt 24:11* many *f-p's* shall rise, and shall deceive many

*Mark 13:22* *f-p's* shall rise … show signs and wonders

*Acts 13:6* a *f-p,* a Jew, whose name was Bar-jesus

*2 Pet 2:1* there were **f-p's** also among the people

*1 John 4:1* many **f-p's** are gone out into the world

*Rev 19:20* the beast was taken, and with him the **f-p**

## FALSE WITNESS [ES]

*Deut 5:20* Neither shalt…bear **f-w** against thy neighbour

*Ps 35:11* **F-w'es**…laid to my charge things that I knew not

*Prov 6:19* A **f-w** that speaketh lies

*Prov 14:5* a **f-w** will utter lies

*Mark 14:56* many bare **f-w** against him [Jesus]

## FAST [ING]

*Ps 109:24* knees are weak through **f'ing**

*Matt 17:21* this kind goeth not out but by prayer and **f'ing**

*Mark 2:20* bridegroom [Jesus] shall be taken away…then shall they **f**

*1 Cor 16:13* Watch ye, stand **f** in the faith

*Gal 5:1* Stand **f**…wherewith Christ hath made us free

*1 Thes 5:21* Prove all things; hold **f** that which is good

*Heb 10:23* hold **f** the profession of our faith

## FATHER

*Gen 2:24* shall a man leave his **f** and his mother

*Gen 17:5* a **f** of many nations have I [God] made thee [Abraham]

*Ex 20:12* Honour thy **f** and thy mother

*Lev 20:9* one that curseth his **f**…shall be surely put to death

*Ps 27:10* When my **f**…forsake me…LORD will take me up

*Ps 103:13* Like as a **f** pitieth his children

*Prov 4:1* Hear…the instruction of a **f**

*Prov 15:20* A wise son maketh a glad **f**

*Isa 9:6* his [Jesus'] name shall be…The everlasting **F**

*Isa 64:8* LORD, thou art our **f**; we are the clay

*Ezek 18:20* neither shall the **f** bear the iniquity of the son

*Mal 2:10* Have we not all one **f**

*Matt 5:48* even as your **F**…in heaven is perfect

*Matt 6:9* Our **F**…in heaven

*Matt 10:37* loveth **f** or mother more than me [Jesus] is not worthy of me

*Matt 23:9* one is your **F**, which is in heaven

*Matt 28:19* baptizing them in the name of the **F**

*Mark 14:36* Abba, **F**, all things are possible unto thee

*Luke 9:59* suffer me first to go and bury my **f**

*Luke 15:22* the **f** said to his servants, Bring…the best robe

*Luke 23:34* **F,** forgive them ...
they know not what they do

*Luke 24:49* I [Jesus] send the
promise of my **F**

*John 6:44* No man can come to
me [Jesus], except the **F**
which ... sent me draw him

*John 10:30* I [Jesus] and my **F**
are one

*John 14:6* no man cometh unto
the **F,** but by me [Jesus]

*John 14:16* I [Jesus] will pray
the **F,** and he shall give you
another Comforter

*John 15:8* Herein is my [Jesus']
**F** glorified ... bear much fruit

*John 16:23* ask the **F** in my
[Jesus'] name, he will give it

*John 20:21* my **F** hath sent me
[Jesus], even so send I you

*Acts 1:7* not for you to know
the ... seasons, which the **F**
hath put in his own power

*Eph 4:6* One God and **F** of all

*Phil 2:11* confess that Jesus
Christ is Lord, to the glory
of God the **F**

*Col 1:19* For it pleased the **F**
that in him [Jesus] should
all fulness dwell

*Jas 1:17* good gift ... cometh
down from the **F** of lights

*Jas 2:21* Abraham our **f** justified by works

*1 John 1:3* our fellowship is
with the **F,** and with his Son

*1 John 2:1* we have an advocate with the **F,** Jesus Christ

*1 John 3:1* manner of love the
**F** hath bestowed upon us

## FAULT [LESS, S]

*Luke 23:4* I [Pilate] find no **f** in
this man [Jesus]

*Gal 6:1* Brethren, if a man be
overtaken in a **f**

*Jas 5:16* Confess your **f's** one to
another

*Jude 24* present you **f'less**
before ... presence of his
[Jesus'] glory

*Rev 14:5* without **f** before the
throne of God

## FEAR [ED, EST, ETH]

*Gen 22:12* I [God] know that
thou [Abraham] **f'est** God

*Deut 6:13* **f** the LORD thy God,
and serve him

*Josh 4:14* **f'ed** him [Joshua], as
they **f'ed** Moses

*1 Chr 16:25* he [God] also is to
be **f'ed** above all gods

*Job 1:1* Job ... was perfect ...
and one that **f'ed** God

*Job 1:9* Satan answered ...
Doth Job **f** God for nought

*Job 28:28* Behold, the **f** of the
Lord, that is wisdom

*Ps 19:9* **f** of the LORD is clean,
enduring for ever

*Ps 23:4* **f** no evil: for thou [God]
art with me

*Ps 27:1* The LORD is my ... salvation; whom shall I **f**

*Ps 34:11* I will teach you the **f**
of the LORD

*Ps 46:2* will not we **f,** though
the earth be removed

*Ps 103:13* the LORD pitieth
them that **f** him

*Ps 111:10* *f* of the LORD is the beginning of wisdom

*Ps 112:1* Blessed is the man that *f'eth* the LORD

*Ps 118:6* I will not *f:* what can man do unto me

*Prov 15:16* Better is little with the *f* of the LORD than great treasure and trouble

*Eccl 12:13* *F* God, and keep his commandments

*Mal 4:2* that *f* my name shall ... Sun of righteousness arise

*Matt 28:8* they [the women] departed quickly from the sepulchre with *f*

*Mark 4:41* *f'ed* exceedingly ... What manner of man is this

*Luke 22:2* they [chief priests and scribes] *f'ed* the people

*Acts 2:43* And *f* came upon every soul

*Phil 2:12* work out your own salvation with *f*

*2 Tim 1:7* God hath not given us the spirit of *f*

*Heb 13:6* I will not *f* what man shall do unto me

*1 John 4:18* perfect love casteth out *f*

*Rev 15:4* Who shall not *f* thee, O Lord ... glorify thy name

**FEAR NOT**

*Gen 15:1* *F-n,* Abram: I [God] am thy shield

*Gen 21:17* What aileth thee, Hagar? *f-n*

*Dan 10:12* *F-n,* Daniel ... thy words were heard

*Joel 2:21* *F-n,* O land; be glad and rejoice

*Matt 1:20* Joseph ... *f-n* to take unto thee Mary

*Matt 28:5* *F-n* ye [women at the tomb]: for I know that ye seek Jesus

*Luke 1:13* *F-n,* Zacharias: for thy prayer is heard

*Luke 1:30* *F-n,* Mary: for thou hast found favour with God

*Luke 2:10* *F-n* ... I bring you [shepherds] good tidings of great joy

*Luke 12:32* *F-n* ... it is your Father's good pleasure to give you the kingdom

*Acts 27:24* Saying, *F-n,* Paul; thou must be brought before Caesar

*Rev 1:17* *F-n;* I [Jesus] am the first and the last

**FEARFUL [LY, NESS]**

*Ps 55:5* *F'ness* and trembling are come upon me

*Ps 139:14* I am *f'ly* and wonderfully made

*Matt 8:26* Why are ye *f,* O ye of little faith

*Heb 10:31* a *f* thing to fall into the hands of the living God

**FEAST OF HARVEST OR INGATHERING.** See *Pentecost.*

**FEAST OF WEEKS.** See *Pentecost.*

135

**FELIX** (governor of Judea who heard Paul's defense at Caesarea). Acts 23:24–26; **24:3, 10–27;** 25:14.

## FELLOWSHIP
*Acts 2:42* continued stedfastly in the apostles' doctrine and *f*

*2 Cor 6:14* what *f* hath righteousness...unrighteousness

*Eph 5:11* have no *f* with the unfruitful works of darkness

*Phil 3:10* That I [Paul] may know him [Jesus]...and the *f* of his sufferings

*1 John 1:7* we have *f* one with another

**FESTUS** (successor of Felix as Roman governor of Judea before whom Paul made his defense). Acts 24:27; **25:1–24; 26:24–32.**

## FIERY SERPENTS IN THE WILDERNESS. Num 21:4–9.

## FILTHY
*Ps 14:3* they are all together become *f*

*Isa 64:6* all our righteousnesses are as *f* rags

*1 Tim 3:8* must the deacons be grave...not greedy of *f* lucre

## FINGER OF GOD
*Ex 8:19* the magicians said... This is the *f-o-G*

*Ex 31:18* gave unto Moses... two...tables of stone, written with the *f-o-G*

*Luke 11:20* if I [Jesus] with the *f-o-G* cast out devils

## FINISH [ED]
*Gen 2:1* heavens and the earth were *f'ed*

*Neh 6:15* wall was *f'ed* in the twenty and fifth day

*Luke 14:28* counteth the cost, whether...sufficient to *f* it

*John 4:34* My [Jesus'] meat is to...*f* his [God's] work

*John 17:4* *f'ed* the work which thou [God] gavest me [Jesus]

*John 19:30* It is *f'ed:* and he [Jesus]...gave up the ghost

*2 Tim 4:7* I [Paul] have *f'ed* my course...kept the faith

## FIRE AND BRIMSTONE
*Ps 11:6* Upon the wicked he [God] shall rain snares, *f-a-b*

*Luke 17:29* the same day that Lot went out of Sodom it rained *f-a-b*

*Rev 14:10* he [worshiper of beast] shall be tormented with *f-a-b*

## FIRSTFRUITS
*Ex 23:19* first of the *f*...bring into...house of...God

*Prov 3:9* Honour the LORD... with the *f* of...thine increase

*1 Cor 15:20* now is Christ risen...*f* of them that slept

## FLESH AND BLOOD

*Matt 16:17* **f-a-b** hath not revealed it unto thee [Peter]

*1 Cor 15:50* **f-a-b** cannot inherit the kingdom of God

*Eph 6:12* wrestle not against **f-a-b,** but...principalities

## FOOLISH [LY, NESS]

*Ps 5:5* The **f** shall not stand in thy [God's] sight

*Ps 69:5* O God, thou knowest my **f'ness**

*Prov 10:1* a **f** son is the heaviness of his mother

*Prov 12:23* the heart of fools proclaimeth **f'ness**

*Prov 14:17* He that is soon angry dealeth **f'ly**

*Prov 15:20* a **f** man despiseth his mother

*Eccl 4:13* Better is...a wise child than an old and **f** king

*Matt 7:26* likened unto a **f** man, which built his house upon the sand

*Matt 25:3* They that were **f**... took no oil with them

*1 Cor 1:23* Christ crucified... unto the Greeks **f'ness**

*1 Cor 1:27* chosen the **f** things... to confound the wise

*1 Cor 3:19* wisdom of this world is **f'ness** with God

*Gal 3:1* **f** Galatians, who hath bewitched you

*Titus 3:9* avoid **f** questions, and genealogies

## FORGIVE [ING, TH]

*Num 14:18* The LORD is long-suffering...**f'ing** iniquity

*2 Chr 7:14* then will I [God] hear...and will **f** their sin

*Ps 86:5* thou, Lord, art good, and ready to **f**

*Ps 103:3* Who [God] **f'th** all thine iniquities

*Matt 6:14* your heavenly Father will also **f** you

*Matt 18:21* how oft shall my brother sin...and I [Peter] **f**

*Mark 11:26* neither will your Father...**f** your trespasses

*Luke 5:21* Who can **f** sins, but God alone

*Luke 6:37* **f,** and ye shall be forgiven

*Luke 23:34* **f** them; for they know not what they do

*Eph 4:32* be ye kind...**f'ing** one another

*1 John 1:9* he [Jesus] is faithful and just to **f** us our sins

## FORGIVEN

*Ps 32:1* Blessed is he whose transgression is **f**

*Matt 12:31* blasphemy against the Holy Ghost shall not be **f**

*Luke 6:37* forgive, and ye shall be **f**

*Rom 4:7* Blessed are they whose iniquities are **f**

*1 John 2:12* your sins are **f** you for his [Jesus'] name's sake

137

## FORGIVENESS

*Acts 26:18* that they may receive *f* of sins

*Col 1:14* In [Jesus] we have redemption...the *f* of sins

## FORNICATION

*Matt 19:9* put away his wife, except it be for *f*

*1 Cor 5:1* reported...that there is *f* among you

*1 Cor 6:18* committeth *f* sinneth against his own body

*Gal 5:19* Now the works of the flesh are...Adultery, *f*

*1 Thes 4:3* this is the will of God...abstain from *f*

*Rev 17:4* a golden cup in her [woman on scarlet beast] hand full...of her *f*

## FOUNDATION [S]

*Job 38:4* Where wast thou [Job] when I [God] laid the *f's* of the earth

*Isa 28:16* I [God] lay in Zion for a *f* a stone

*Matt 25:34* inherit the kingdom prepared for you from the *f* of the world

*1 Cor 3:11* other *f* can no man lay than...Jesus Christ

*Eph 2:20* built upon the *f* of the apostles

*Heb 1:10* Thou, Lord...hast laid the *f* of the earth

*Heb 11:10* city which hath *f's*... builder and maker is God

*Rev 21:14* And the wall of the city had twelve *f's*

## FREE [LY]

*Gen 2:16* every tree of the garden thou mayest *f'ly* eat

*Ps 51:12* uphold me with thy [God's] *f* spirit

*Matt 10:8* *f'ly* ye have received, *f'ly* give

*John 8:32* and the truth shall make you *f*

*Rom 3:24* justified *f'ly* by his [God's] grace through... Christ Jesus

*Rom 6:18* *f* from sin, ye became the servants of righteousness

*Rom 8:2* Jesus hath made me *f* from the law of sin

*1 Cor 9:19* though I [Paul] be *f* from all men

*Gal 3:28* there is neither bond nor *f*

*Gal 5:1* in the liberty wherewith Christ hath made us *f*

*Col 3:11* neither Greek nor Jew...bond nor *f*

*Rev 22:17* let him take the water of life *f'ly*

## FRUIT OF THE SPIRIT. Gal 5:22–26.

# -G-

**GAASH, MOUNT** (a mountain where Joshua was buried). **Josh 24:29–30** • Judg 2:9 • 2 Sam 23:30 • 1 Chr 11:32.

**GABRIEL** (an archangel who appeared to Daniel, Zacharias, and the Virgin Mary). Dan 8:16; 9:21 • Luke 1:19,26.

**GAD** (a son of Jacob and ancestor of one of the twelve tribes of Israel). Gen 30:11; 35:26; 46:16; 49:19 • Ex 1:4 • 1 Chr 5:11. The tribe of Gad settled east of the Jordan River. **Num 32:1–33** • Josh 13:24,28; 22:9–34.

**GADARENES** (people from the area of Gadara in Perea where Jesus healed a demon-possessed man). Mark 5:1–20 • Luke 8:26,37. *Gergesenes:* Matt 8:28.

**GAIN [ED]**
*Matt 18:15* if he shall hear thee...hast *g'ed* thy brother
*Mark 8:36* profit a man, if he shall *g* the whole world
*Luke 19:16* thy pound hath *g'ed* ten pounds
*1 Cor 9:20* I [Paul] became as a Jew, that I might *g* the Jews
*Phil 1:21* to me [Paul] to live is Christ, and to die is *g*

*1 Tim 6:6* godliness with contentment is great *g*

**GALATIA** (a territory of central Asia Minor visited by Paul during the first missionary journey). **Acts 16:6; 18:23** • 1 Cor 16:1 • Gal 1:2 • 2 Tim 4:10 • 1 Pet 1:1.

**GALATIANS, EPISTLE TO THE.** A short epistle of the apostle Paul to the churches at Galatia on the themes of Christian liberty and justification by faith alone.

**GALILEE** (a Roman province in northern Palestine where Jesus spent most of His earthly ministry). Mark 1:9–28; 3:7 • Luke 23:6–55 • John 4:3–54.

**GALILEE, SEA OF.** A freshwater lake in northern Palestine associated with the ministry of Jesus. Mark 1:16–20; 4:35–41; 7:31. *Lake of Gennesaret:* Luke 5:1. *Sea of Chinneroth:* Josh 12:3. *Sea of Tiberias:* John 21:1.

**GALLIO** (a Roman ruler of Achaia who refused to get involved in the dispute between Paul and the Jewish leaders in Corinth). Acts 18:12–17.

**GAMALIEL** (a teacher of the law under whom Paul studied). Acts 5:33–39; **22:3.**

**GARDEN OF EDEN.** Gen 2:8–3:24.

**GASHMU** (a Samaritan leader who opposed the rebuilding of Jerusalem's walls under Nehemiah). Neh 6:6.

**GATH** (a major Philistine city captured by David). Josh 11:22 • 1 Sam 5:8; 6:17; 17:4; 21:10–15; 27:3–12 • 2 Kgs 12:17 • **1 Chr 18:1** • 2 Chr 11:5–8 • Amos 6:1–3 • Mic 1:10.

**GAZA** (a major Philistine city where Samson was killed). Josh 10:41; 11:22; 15:47 • **Judg 16:21–30** • Amos 1:6–7 • Acts 8:26. *Azzah:* Jer 25:20.

**GAZER.** See *Gezer.*

**GEDALIAH** (a friend and supporter of the prophet Jeremiah). 2 Kgs 25:22–25 • Jer 39:14; **40:5–16;** 41:1–18; 43:6.

**GEDEON.** See *Gideon.*

**GEHAZI** (Elisha's servant who was struck with leprosy because of his greed). 2 Kgs 4:12–36; **5:20–27;** 8:4–6.

**GENEALOGIES OF JESUS.** See *Jesus, Life and Ministry of.*

**GENERATION [S]**
*Gen 2:4* the *g's* of the heavens and of the earth
*Num 32:13* all the *g,* that had done evil…was consumed
*Ps 24:6* This is the *g* of them that seek him [God]
*Ps 33:11* thoughts of his [God's] heart to all *g's*
*Ps 71:18* I have showed thy [God's] strength unto this *g*
*Ps 85:5* draw out thine [God's] anger to all *g's*
*Ps 90:1* thou [God] hast been our dwelling place in all *g's*
*Ps 100:5* his [God's] truth endureth to all *g's*
*Prov 27:24* doth the crown endure to every *g*
*Eccl 1:4* One *g* passeth away, and another *g* cometh
*Dan 4:3* and his [God's] dominion is from *g* to *g*
*Matt 24:34* *g* shall not pass, till…these things be fulfilled
*Luke 3:7* *g* of vipers, who hath warned you
*Luke 16:8* in their *g* wiser than the children of light
*Col 1:26* mystery…hath been hid from ages and from *g's*
*1 Pet 2:9* But ye are a chosen *g,* a royal priesthood

**GENESIS, BOOK OF.** The first book of the Old Testament that describes the creation of the universe and recounts the early history of the people of Israel, including the patriarchs Abraham, Isaac, Jacob, and Joseph.

**GENNESARET, LAKE OF.**
See *Galilee, Sea of.*

**GENTILE [S]**
*Isa 42:6* a covenant of the people, for a light of the *G's*
*Isa 60:3* *G's* shall come to thy [God's] light
*Jer 16:19* *G's* shall come unto thee [God] from the ends of the earth
*Mal 1:11* my [God's] name shall be great among the *G's*
*Matt 12:18* Behold my [God's] servant ... he shall show judgment to the *G's*
*Mark 10:42* to rule over the *G's* exercise lordship
*Luke 2:32* A light to lighten the *G's* ... glory of ... Israel
*Acts 9:15* for he [Paul] is a chosen vessel ... to bear my [God's] name before the *G's*
*Acts 13:46* we [Paul and Barnabas] turn to the *G's*
*Acts 14:27* he [God] ... opened the door of faith unto the *G's*
*Acts 18:6* from henceforth I [Paul] will go unto the *G's*
*Rom 2:9* of the Jew first, and also of the *G*
*Rom 3:29* God of the Jews only ... not also of the *G's*

*1 Cor 12:13* baptized into one body, whether ... Jews or *G's*
*Eph 3:6* *G's* should be ... partakers of his [God's] promise

**GERGESENES.**
See *Gadarenes.*

**GERIZIM, MOUNT** (a mountain considered a sacred worship place by the Samaritans). Deut 11:29; 27:12 • Josh 8:33 • Judg 9:7 • **John 4:5,20–21.**

**GESHEM** (an Arabian who opposed the rebuilding of Jerusalem's walls under Nehemiah). Neh 2:19; 6:1–2.

**GETHSEMANE** (a garden outside Jerusalem where Jesus agonized in prayer on the night before He was arrested). Matt 26:30–56 • Mark 14:32.

**GEZER** (a major Canaanite city captured by Joshua and settled by the Levites). **Josh 10:33;** 12:12; 16:3,10; **21:21** • Judg 1:29 • 1 Kgs 9:15–17 • 1 Chr 6:67; 7:28; 20:4. *Gazer:* 2 Sam 5:25 • 1 Chr 14:16.

**GIBEAH** (hometown and capital city of King Saul). **1 Sam 10:26; 15:34** • Judg 19:12–16; 20:4–43 • Hos 9:9; 10:9. *Gibeath:* Josh 18:28.

**GIBEON** (a Canaanite city whose inhabitants surrendered to avoid destruction by Joshua). **Josh 9:3–21;** 10:1–41 • 2 Sam 21:1–9.

**GIDEON** (a judge of Israel who defeated the Midianite army with a force of only three hundred warriors). Judg 6–8. *Gedeon:* Heb 11:32. *Jerubbaal:* Judg 6:25–32.

**GIFT [S]**

*2 Chr 19:7* there is no iniquity… nor respect of persons, nor taking of *g's*

*Prov 19:6* every man is a friend to him that giveth *g's*

*Matt 2:11* they [wise men] presented…him [Jesus] *g's*

*Matt 5:24* reconciled to thy brother, and then come and offer thy *g*

*Luke 11:13* If ye then, being evil, know how to give good *g's* unto your children

*John 4:10* If thou knewest the *g* of God

*Rom 1:11* I [Paul] may impart unto you some spiritual *g*

*Rom 12:6* *g's* differing according to the grace that is given to us

*1 Cor 12:4* diversities of *g's,* but the same Spirit

*1 Cor 12:31* But covet earnestly the best *g's*

*1 Cor 13:2* though I [Paul] have the *g* of prophecy

*2 Cor 9:15* Thanks be unto God for his unspeakable *g*

*1 Tim 4:14* Neglect not the *g* that is in thee

*Jas 1:17* Every good *g* and every perfect *g* is from above

**GIFT OF GOD**

*Eccl 3:13* enjoy the good of all his labour, it is the *g-o-G*

*Acts 8:20* thou [Simon the magician] … thought … the *g-o-G* may be purchased

*Rom 6:23* *g-o-G* is eternal life through Jesus Christ

*Eph 2:8* saved through faith… not of yourselves: it is the *g-o-G*

*2 Tim 1:6* stir up the *g-o-G*

**GIHON**

1. One of the four rivers of the Garden of Eden, associated with Ethiopia. Gen 2:13.

2. A place near Jerusalem where Solomon was proclaimed king. 1 Kgs 1:33–45.

**GILBOA, MOUNT** (a mountain range where King Saul died). 1 Sam 31:1–8 • 2 Sam 1:6,21 • **1 Chr 10:1–8.**

**GILEAD**

1. A fertile, flat tableland east of the Jordan River settled by the tribes of Gad, Reuben, and Manasseh. **Deut 3:12–17** • 2 Sam 17:26 • 1 Kgs 17:1.

2. A hill where Gideon divided his army for battle against the Midianites. Judg 7:1–7.

**GILGAL** (a memorial site near the city of Jericho). **Josh 4:19–24;** 10:1–43 • 1 Sam 13:4–15 • Amos 4:4–5.

**GIRGASHITES.** See *Girgasites.*

**GIRGASITES** (an ancient tribe which inhabited Canaan). Gen 10:15–16. *Girgashites:* Deut 7:1.

**GIVE [TH]**
*Gen 12:7* Unto thy [Abraham's] seed will I [God] *g* this land
*Ex 20:12* that thy days may be long upon the land which the LORD…*g'th* thee
*Num 6:26* The LORD lift up his countenance…*g* thee peace
*Deut 16:17* Every man shall *g* as he is able
*Josh 21:43* the LORD gave…all the land which he sware to *g* unto their fathers
*1 Kgs 3:9* **G** therefore thy servant [Solomon] an understanding heart
*1 Chr 16:34* *g* thanks unto the LORD; for he is good
*Ps 5:1* **G** ear to my words, O LORD…my meditation
*Ps 29:2* **G** unto the LORD the glory due unto his name

*Ps 29:11* LORD will *g* strength unto his people
*Ps 37:4* he [God] shall *g* thee the desires of thine heart
*Ps 85:12* LORD shall *g* that which is good
*Ps 91:11* he [God] shall *g* his angels charge over thee
*Ps 107:1* *g* thanks unto the LORD, for he is good
*Ps 119:125* I am thy [God's] servant; *g* me understanding
*Ps 119:130* The entrance of thy [God's] words *g'th* light
*Prov 2:6* For the LORD *g'th* wisdom
*Prov 22:9* he *g'th* of his bread to the poor
*Prov 25:21* If thine enemy be hungry, *g* him bread
*Isa 7:14* the Lord…shall *g* you a sign…a virgin shall conceive…bear a son
*Isa 49:6* I [God] will also *g* thee for a light to the Gentiles
*Mic 6:7* shall I *g* my firstborn for my transgression
*Matt 5:15* a candle…*g'th* light unto all…in the house
*Matt 6:11* **G** us this day our daily bread
*Matt 10:8* freely ye have received, freely *g*
*Matt 11:28* Come unto me [Jesus]…I will *g* you rest
*Matt 16:19* *g* unto thee the keys of the kingdom
*Matt 20:28* Even as the Son of man came…to *g* his life a ransom for many

*Mark 8:37* what shall a man *g* in exchange for his soul

*Mark 10:40* sit on my [Jesus'] right hand ... is not mine to *g*

*Luke 12:32* for it is your Father's good pleasure to *g* you the kingdom

*Luke 15:12 g* me the portion of goods that falleth to me

*Luke 20:22* Is it lawful for us to *g* tribute unto Caesar

*John 4:14* water that I [Jesus] shall *g* him shall never thirst

*John 10:11* good shepherd *g'th* his life for the sheep

*John 13:34* new commandment I [Jesus] *g* unto you

*John 14:16* and he [God] shall *g* you another Comforter

*John 16:23* Whatsoever ye shall ask ... in my [Jesus'] name, he [God] will *g* it you

*Acts 6:4 g* ourselves continually to prayer

*Rom 14:12* every one ... shall *g* account ... to God

*1 Cor 3:7* neither he that watereth; but God that *g'th* the increase

*1 Cor 13:3* though I [Paul] *g* my body to be burned

*1 Cor 15:57* thanks be to God, which *g'th* us the victory

*2 Cor 3:6* the spirit *g'th* life

*2 Cor 9:7* let him *g;* not grudgingly, or of necessity

*1 Thes 5:18* In every thing *g* thanks ... this is ... will of God

*Jas 4:6* God ... *g'th* grace unto the humble

*1 Pet 3:15* be ready always to *g* an answer

*Rev 2:10* and I [Jesus] will *g* thee a crown of life

**GIVING, PRINCIPLES OF.**
2 Cor 8:1–24; 9:6–8.

**GLAD [LY, NESS]**
*1 Chr 16:31* heavens be *g,* and let the earth rejoice

*Ps 9:2* I will be *g* and rejoice in thee [God]

*Ps 30:11* Thou [God] hast ... girded me with *g'ness*

*Ps 46:4* the streams ... make *g* the city of God

*Ps 68:3* let the righteous be *g*

*Ps 100:2* Serve the LORD with *g'ness*

*Ps 118:24* the day ... the LORD hath made ... rejoice and be *g* in it

*Ps 122:1 g* when they said unto me, Let us go into the house of the LORD

*Prov 15:20* A wise son maketh a *g* father

*Joel 2:21* be *g* and rejoice: for the LORD will do great things

*Matt 5:12* be exceeding *g:* for great is your reward

*Mark 12:37* common people heard him [Jesus] *g'ly*

*Luke 15:32* meet that we should make merry, and be *g*

*John 20:20* were the disciples *g,* when they saw the Lord

*Acts 13:48* when the Gentiles heard this, they were *g*

*Rom 10:15* beautiful are the feet...that...bring *g* tidings

*2 Cor 12:15* I [Paul] will very *g'ly* spend and be spent

## GLORIFY [IED, ING]

*Ps 86:12 g* thy [God's] name for evermore

*Isa 49:3* art my [God's] servant...in whom I will be *g'ied*

*Matt 5:16* see your good works, and *g* your Father

*Matt 9:8* multitudes...marvelled, and *g'ied* God

*Luke 2:20* shepherds returned, *g'ing* and praising God

*Luke 7:16* came a fear on all: and they [crowd] *g'ied* God

*Luke 23:47* centurion saw what was done, he *g'ied* God

*John 12:23* hour is come...Son of man should be *g'ied*

*John 14:13* that the Father may be *g'ied* in the Son

*John 17:1* that thy Son also may *g* thee [God]

*John 17:4* I [Jesus] have *g'ied* thee [God] on the earth

*Rom 8:30* whom he [Jesus] justified, them he also *g'ied*

*Rom 15:6* may with one mind and one mouth *g* God

*1 Cor 6:20 g* God in your body

*2 Thes 1:12* name of our Lord... may be *g'ied* in you

*1 Pet 4:16* but let him *g* God on this behalf

## GLORY

*1 Sam 4:21* named the child I-chabod...The *g* is departed

*1 Chr 16:24* Declare his [God's] *g* among the heathen

*1 Chr 29:11* Thine, O LORD, is the greatness...and the *g*

*Ps 24:7* and the King of *g* shall come in

*Ps 29:2* Give unto the LORD the *g* due unto his name

*Ps 57:5* let thy [God's] *g* be above all the earth

*Ps 72:19* let the whole earth be filled with his [God's] *g*

*Ps 84:11* the LORD will give grace and *g*

*Ps 96:3* Declare his [God's] *g* among the heathen

*Ps 113:4* LORD is high above all nations, and his *g* above the heavens

*Prov 17:6* the *g* of children are their fathers

*Isa 6:3* the whole earth is full of his [God's] *g*

*Isa 66:18* all nations and tongues...shall come, and see my [God's] *g*

*Jer 13:16* Give *g* to the LORD your God

*Hag 2:9 g* of this latter house shall be greater

*Matt 6:13* kingdom, and the power, and the *g*

*Matt 6:29* Solomon in all his *g* was not arrayed

*Mark 10:37* sit, one on thy [Jesus'] right hand...in thy *g*

*Luke 21:27* the Son of man coming in a cloud with power and great **g**

*John 1:14* we beheld his [Jesus'] **g** ... full of grace

*Rom 5:3* we **g** in tribulations

*Rom 8:18* sufferings ... are not worthy to be compared with the **g** ... revealed

*2 Cor 10:17* he that glorieth, let him **g** in the Lord

*Gal 5:26* Let us not be desirous of vain **g**

*Gal 6:14* forbid that I [Paul] should **g,** save in the cross

*1 Tim 1:17* unto the King eternal ... be ... **g** for ever

*Heb 2:7* thou [God] crownedst him [Jesus] with **g** ... honour

*1 Pet 4:13* when his [Jesus'] **g** shall be revealed

*1 Pet 5:4* ye shall receive a crown of **g** that fadeth not

*Rev 4:11* Thou art worthy, O Lord, to receive **g**

## GLORY OF GOD

*Ps 19:1* The heavens declare the **g-o-G**

*John 11:4* sickness is not unto death, but for the **g-o-G**

*Rom 3:23* all have sinned ... come short of the **g-o-G**

*1 Cor 10:31* whatsoever ye do, do all to the **g-o-G**

*Phil 2:11* Jesus Christ is Lord, to the **g-o-G** the Father

## GLORY OF THE LORD

*Ex 24:16* the **g-o-t-L** abode upon mount Sinai

*Ps 104:31* The **g-o-t-L** shall endure for ever

*Isa 40:5* the **g-o-t-L** shall be revealed ... all flesh ... see it

*Isa 60:1* the **g-o-t-L** is risen upon thee

*Ezek 11:23* the **g-o-t-L** went up from the midst of the city

*Hab 2:14* knowledge of the **g-o-t-L**, as the waters cover the sea

*Luke 2:9* **g-o-t-L** shone round about them [shepherds]

## GNASHING OF TEETH

*Matt 8:12* there shall be weeping and **g-o-t**

*Matt 22:13* cast him into outer darkness; there shall be weeping and **g-o-t**

*Luke 13:28* weeping and **g-o-t,** when ye shall see ... yourselves thrust out

## GODLY [INESS]

*2 Cor 7:10* **g** sorrow worketh repentance

*1 Tim 4:8* **g'iness** is profitable unto all things

*1 Tim 6:6* **g'iness** with contentment is great gain

*2 Tim 3:5* a form of **g'iness,** but denying the power

*2 Tim 3:12* all that will live **g** in Christ Jesus shall suffer persecution

*Titus 2:12* live soberly, right-eously, and *g*

**GOG, PRINCE OF MAGOG** (a tribal leader condemned by the prophet Ezekiel and a representative of the forces of evil which oppose God and His people). Ezek 38:2–18; 39:1–11 • Rev 20:8–15.

**GOLAN** (one of the six cities of refuge). Deut 4:43 • **Josh 20:8–9;** 21:27.

**GOLGOTHA.** See *Calvary.*

**GOLIATH** (a Philistine giant killed by David). **1 Sam 17:4–54;** 21:9; 22:10 • 2 Sam 21:19 • 1 Chr 20:5.

**GOMER** (unfaithful wife of the prophet Hosea). Hos 1:1–11; 3:1–5.

**GOMORRAH** (a city destroyed by God because of its wickedness). **Gen 19:23–29.** Referred to as an example of God's punishment in Deut 29:23; 32:32 • Isa 1:9–10; 13:19 • Jer 23:14; 49:18; 50:40 • Amos 4:11 • Zeph 2:9. *Gomorrha:* Matt 10:15 • 2 Pet 2:6.

**GOOD SHEPHERD, JESUS AS.** See *"I Am" Statements of Jesus.*

**GOOD WORKS**
*Matt 5:16* see your *g-w,* and glorify your Father
*Acts 9:36* Dorcas…was full of *g-w* and almsdeeds
*Eph 2:10* we are his [God's] workmanship…unto *g-w*
*2 Tim 3:17* man of God may be…furnished unto all *g-w*

**GOODNESS**
*Ps 23:6* Surely *g* and mercy shall follow me
*Ps 33:5* the earth is full of the *g* of the LORD
*Ps 107:8* that men would praise the LORD for his *g*
*Prov 20:6* Most men will proclaim every one his own *g*
*Gal 5:22* fruit of the Spirit is… gentleness, *g,* faith

**GOSHEN** (an Egyptian district where the Israelites lived). Gen 45:10; 46:28–29,34; 47:1–27; 50:8 • Ex 8:22; 9:26.

**GOSPEL**
*Matt 24:14 g* of the kingdom… preached in all the world
*Mark 16:15* preach the *g* to every creature
*Luke 4:18* he [God] hath anointed me [Jesus] to preach the *g* to the poor
*Rom 1:16* I [Paul] am not ashamed of the *g* of Christ
*Rom 10:15* beautiful are the feet…preach the *g* of peace

*1 Cor 9:14* they which preach the *g* should live of the *g*

*Gal 1:7* some that ... would pervert the *g* of Christ

*Gal 4:13* I [Paul] preached the *g* unto you at the first

*Eph 6:15* feet shod with the preparation of the *g* of peace

*Phil 1:12* things ... have fallen out rather unto the furtherance of the *g*

*Phil 1:27* conversation be as it becometh the *g* of Christ

*2 Tim 1:8* partaker of the afflictions of the *g*

*2 Tim 2:8* Jesus ... raised from the dead according to my *g*

*1 Pet 4:17* end be of them that obey not the *g* of God

**GOZAN** (a place to which the people of the Northern Kingdom were deported after their defeat by the Assyrians). 2 Kgs 18:11.

**GRACE**

*Gen 6:8* Noah found *g* in the eyes of the LORD

*Ps 84:11* the LORD will give *g* and glory

*John 1:14* beheld his [Jesus'] glory ... full of *g* and truth

*John 1:17* *g* and truth came by Jesus Christ

*Rom 3:24* justified freely by his [God's] *g*

*Rom 5:20* sin abounded, *g* did much more abound

*Rom 6:1* Shall we continue in sin, that *g* may abound

*2 Cor 8:9* ye know the *g* of our Lord Jesus Christ

*2 Cor 9:8* God is able to make all *g* abound

*2 Cor 12:9* My [God's] *g* is sufficient for thee

*Eph 1:7* forgiveness of sins, according to the riches of his [Jesus'] *g*

*Eph 2:8* by *g* are ye saved through faith

*Eph 4:7* *g* according to the measure of the gift of Christ

*Col 4:6* speech be alway with *g,* seasoned with salt

*1 Tim 1:14* *g* of our Lord was exceeding abundant

*Titus 3:7* being justified by his [Jesus'] *g,* we should be made heirs ... of eternal life

*Heb 4:16* Let us ... come boldly unto the throne of *g*

*Jas 4:6* God ... giveth *g* unto the humble

*2 Pet 3:18* grow in *g,* and in the knowledge of ... Jesus

*Rev 22:21* *g* of our Lord Jesus Christ be with you all

**GRACE OF GOD**

*Luke 2:40* child [Jesus] grew ... *g-o-G* was upon him

*1 Cor 15:10* by the *g-o-G* I [Paul] am what I am

*Eph 3:7* I [Paul] was made a minister, according to the gift of the *g-o-G*

*Titus 2:11* the *g-o-G* that bringeth salvation

*Heb 2:9* that he [Jesus] by the *g-o-G* should taste death for every man

*1 Pet 4:10* as good stewards of the manifold *g-o-G*

## GRACIOUS [LY]

*Num 6:25* The LORD...be *g* unto thee

*Ps 77:9* Hath God forgotten to be *g*

*Ps 103:8* LORD is merciful and *g,* slow to anger

*Ps 119:29* grant me thy [God's] law *g'ly*

*Isa 33:2* O LORD, be *g* unto us

*Amos 5:15* God...will be *g* unto the remnant of Joseph

*Luke 4:22* bare him [Jesus] witness, and wondered at the *g* words

## GRAVE [S]

*Job 17:1* the *g's* are ready for me [Job]

*Job 21:13* in a moment [the wicked] go down to the *g*

*Ps 30:3* thou [God] hast brought up my soul from the *g*

*Ps 88:3* my life draweth nigh unto the *g*

*Eccl 9:10* no work...nor wisdom, in the *g*

*Isa 53:9* he [God's servant] made his *g* with the wicked

*Matt 27:52* *g's* were opened... bodies of the saints...arose

*John 5:28* all that are in the *g's* shall hear his [Jesus'] voice

*John 11:17* he [Lazarus] had lain in the *g* four days

*1 Cor 15:55* O *g,* where is thy victory

*1 Tim 3:8* must the deacons be *g,* not doubletongued

## GREAT [ER]

*Gen 1:16* two *g* lights; the *g'er* light to rule the day

*Gen 12:2* I [God] will make of thee [Abraham] a *g* nation

*1 Sam 12:24* how *g* things he [God] hath done for you

*1 Chr 11:9* So David waxed *g'er* and *g'er*

*1 Chr 16:25* *g* is the LORD, and greatly to be praised

*Job 32:9* *G* men are not always wise

*Ps 31:19* Oh how *g* is thy [God's] goodness

*Ps 47:2* the LORD...is a *g* King over all the earth

*Ps 48:1* *G* is the LORD, and greatly to be praised

*Ps 77:13* who is so *g* a God as our God

*Ps 95:3* LORD is...a *g* King above all gods

*Ps 119:156* *G* are thy tender mercies, O LORD

*Ps 126:3* The LORD hath done *g* things for us

*Prov 22:1* good name is rather to be chosen than *g* riches

*Isa 9:2* people that walked in darkness have seen a *g* light

*Jer 10:6* thy [God's] name is *g* in might

*Jer 32:17* thou [God]…made the…earth by thy *g* power

*Dan 7:17* These *g* beasts, which are four, are four kings

*Joel 2:31* sun shall be turned into darkness…before the *g*…day of the LORD

*Jon 1:2* go to Nineveh, that *g* city, and cry against it

*Hag 2:9* The glory of this latter house shall be *g'er*

*Matt 4:16* people…in darkness saw *g* light

*Matt 5:12* Rejoice…for *g* is your reward in heaven

*Matt 11:11* least…is *g'er* than he [John the Baptist]

*Matt 19:22* he [rich young ruler] went away sorrowful: for he had *g* possessions

*Matt 20:26* *g* among you, let him be your minister

*Mark 12:31* none other commandment *g'er* than these

*Mark 13:26* Son of man coming…with *g* power

*Luke 1:32* He [Jesus] shall be *g*…the Son of the Highest

*Luke 2:5* Mary his [Joseph's] espoused wife, being *g* with child

*Luke 10:2* harvest truly is *g*, but the labourers are few

*Luke 22:44* his [Jesus'] sweat was as…*g* drops of blood

*John 13:16* servant is not *g'er* than his lord

*John 15:13* *G'er* love hath no man than this

*Acts 16:26* a *g* earthquake… the foundations of the prison were shaken

*Eph 5:32* a *g* mystery…concerning Christ and the church

*Heb 2:3* escape, if we neglect so *g* salvation

*Heb 4:14* Seeing then…we have a *g* high priest [Jesus]

*Heb 12:1* compassed about…*g* a cloud of witnesses

*Jas 3:5* Even so the tongue… boasteth *g* things

*1 John 4:4* *g'er* is he…in you

*3 John 4* no *g'er* joy than to hear…my [John's] children walk in truth

*Rev 6:17* the *g* day of his [God's] wrath is come

**GREAT COMMISSION.** See *Jesus, Life and Ministry of.*

**GREAT FLOOD.** Gen 7:1–8:22.

**GREAT SEA** (the sea on Israel's western border, known today as the *Mediterranean Sea*). Josh 1:4; 9:1. *Sea of the Philistines:* Ex 23:31.

**GREECE.** See *Javan.*

**GRIEF**

*Job 2:13* they saw that his [Job's] *g* was very great

*Ps 6:7* Mine eye is consumed because of *g*

*Prov 17:25* A foolish son is a *g* to his father

*Isa 53:3* a man of sorrows [God's servant], and acquainted with *g*

*Jer 45:3* LORD hath added *g* to my [Jeremiah's] sorrow

**GRIEVE [D]**

*Gen 6:6* repented…he [God] had made man…it *g'd* him

*Ps 78:40* oft did they…*g* him [God] in the desert

*Ps 95:10* Forty years…was I [God] *g'd* with…generation

*Mark 3:5* he [Jesus]…*g'd* for the hardness of their hearts

*Mark 10:22* he [rich young ruler]…went away *g'd:* for he had great possessions

*John 21:17* Peter was *g'd* because he [Jesus] said…the third time, Lovest thou me

*Eph 4:30* *g* not the holy Spirit

**GROW [ETH]**

*Ps 104:14* He [God] causeth the grass to *g* for the cattle

*Matt 6:28* Consider the lilies of the field, how they *g*

*Eph 2:21* the building…*g'eth* unto an holy temple

*1 Pet 2:2* sincere milk of the word, that ye may *g* thereby

*2 Pet 3:18* *g* in grace, and in… our Lord and Saviour

**GUIDE [S]**

*Ps 48:14* this God…will be our *g* even unto death

*Isa 58:11* the LORD shall *g* thee continually

*Matt 23:24* Ye blind *g's,* which strain at a gnat

*John 16:13* he [Holy Spirit] will *g* you into all truth

*Acts 8:31* How can I [Ethiopian eunuch], except some man should *g* me

**GUILT [Y]**

*Deut 19:13* put away the *g* of innocent blood from Israel

*Matt 26:66* They…said, He [Jesus] is *g'y* of death

*1 Cor 11:27* eat…drink… unworthily, shall be *g'y* of the…blood of the Lord

*Jas 2:10* yet offend in one point, he is *g'y* of all

# -H-

**HABAKKUK** (a prophet of Judah and author of the book that bears his name). Hab 1:1; 3:1.

**HABAKKUK, BOOK OF.** A short prophetic book of the Old Testament that struggles with the problem of the suffering of God's people at the hands of the pagan Babylonians.

**HAGAR** (Sarah's Egyptian slave who became the mother of Ishmael by Abraham). **Gen 16:1–16; 21:9–17.** *Agar:* Gal 4:24.

**HAGGAI** (a prophet after the Exile and author of the book that bears his name). Ezra 5:1; 6:14 • Hag 1–2.

**HAGGAI, BOOK OF.** A short prophetic book of the Old Testament written to encourage the Jewish captives who had returned to their homeland after three generations under the Babylonians and Persians.

**HAI.** See *Ai.*

**HALAH** (a region in Assyria where captives from the Northern Kingdom were settled). 2 Kgs 17:6; 18:11 • 1 Chr 5:26.

**HALF TRIBE OF MANASSEH** (a phrase referring to two distinct settlements of the tribe of Manasseh—one in central Palestine and the other east of the Jordan River). Num 32:33 • Deut 29:8 • Josh 22:10 • 1 Chr 6:61,71.

**HAM** (youngest son of Noah and ancestor of the people of several nations). Gen 5:32; 6:10; 7:13; 9:18,22; 10:1–20; 14:5 • 1 Chr 1:4,8.

**HAMAN** (an aide to King Ahasuerus of Persia who plotted to kill the Jews). Esth 3:1–9:25.

**HAMATH-ZOBAH.** See *Zobah.*

**HANAMEEL** (a cousin of Jeremiah from whom the prophet bought a field). Jer 32:7–12.

**HANANI** (Nehemiah's brother who brought news about the suffering citizens of Jerusalem). **Neh 1:2–3; 7:2.**

**HAND OF GOD**
*Job 2:10* receive good at the **h-o-G,** and...not receive evil
*Eccl 9:1* the wise, and their works, are in the **h-o-G**
*Acts 7:56* I [Stephen] see...the Son of man standing on the right **h-o-G**

*Col 3:1* things which are above, where Christ sitteth on the right *h-o-G*

*1 Pet 3:22* Who [Jesus] is … on the right *h-o-G*

**HANDWRITING ON A WALL.** Dan 5:5–9.

**HANNAH** (mother of Samuel the prophet who prayed earnestly for Samuel to be born and devoted him to God's service). **1 Sam 1:5–28;** 2:1–10.

**HARAN** (a pagan city of Mesopotamia where Abraham lived for a time). **Gen 11:31–32; 12:4–5;** 27:43; 28:10; 29:4 • 2 Kgs 19:12 • Isa 37:12 • Ezek 27:23. *Charran:* Acts 7:2,4.

**HATE [D, ST, TH]**
*Lev 19:17* Thou shalt not *h* thy brother in thine heart

*Ps 5:5* thou [God] *h'st* all workers of iniquity

*Ps 41:7* All that *h* me whisper … against me

*Ps 69:4* They that *h* me without a cause are more than the hairs of mine head

*Ps 119:163* I *h* … lying: but thy [God's] law do I love

*Prov 8:13* The fear of the LORD is to *h* evil

*Prov 13:24* He that spareth his rod *h'th* his son

*Prov 14:20* poor is *h'd* even of his own neighbour

*Eccl 3:8* A time to love, and a time to *h*

*Isa 1:14* your appointed feasts my [God's] soul *h'th*

*Amos 5:21* I [God] *h,* I despise your feast days

*Matt 5:44* I [Jesus] say unto you … do good to them that *h* you

*Matt 6:24* he will *h* the one, and love the other

*Mark 13:13* *h'd* of all men for my [Jesus'] name's sake

*Luke 14:26* and *h* not his father, and mother

*John 12:25* he that *h'th* his life … shall keep it

*John 15:18* it [the world] *h'd* me [Jesus] before it *h'd* you

*John 15:23* He that *h'th* me [Jesus] *h'th* my Father also

*1 John 2:9* He that saith he is in the light, and *h'th* his brother, is in darkness

*1 John 4:20* If a man say, I love God, and *h'th* his brother, he is a liar

**HAZAEL** (a leader anointed king of Syria at God's command by the prophet Elijah). **1 Kgs 19:15–17** • 2 Kgs 8:8–29; 9:14–15; 10:32; 12:17–18; 13:3, 22–25 • 2 Chr 22:5–6 • Amos 1:4.

**HAZOR** (a royal Canaanite city destroyed by Joshua). **Josh 11:1–13;** 12:19; 19:36 • Judg

4:2,17 • 1 Sam 12:9 • 1 Kgs 9:15 • 2 Kgs 15:29.

## HEAD [S]

*Gen 3:15* it shall bruise thy [the serpent's] *h*

*1 Sam 17:51* David ... slew him [Goliath] ... cut off his *h*

*2 Sam 14:25* to the crown of his *h* there was no blemish in him [Absalom]

*1 Chr 29:11* thou [God] art exalted as *h* above all

*Job 1:20* Job arose ... and shaved his *h*

*Ps 3:3* thou, O LORD, art ... the lifter up of mine *h*

*Ps 23:5* thou [God] anointest my *h* with oil

*Ps 24:7* Lift up your *h's,* O ye gates

*Ps 118:22* The stone ... is become the *h* stone

*Ps 140:7* God ... hast covered my *h* in the day of battle

*Jer 9:1* Oh that my [Jeremiah's] *h* were waters

*Dan 7:6* beast had also four *h's*

*Matt 10:30* hairs of your *h* are all numbered

*Matt 21:42* The stone which the builders rejected ... is become the *h* of the corner

*Matt 27:39* they ... reviled him [Jesus], wagging their *h's*

*Mark 6:28* brought his [John the Baptist's] *h* in a charger

*Mark 14:3* a woman ... brake the box, and poured it [ointment] on his [Jesus'] *h*

*Mark 15:17* a crown of thorns, and put it about his [Jesus'] *h*

*Luke 9:58* Son of man hath not where to lay his *h*

*John 19:30* he [Jesus] bowed his *h,* and gave up the ghost

*Acts 18:6* Your blood be upon your own *h's*

*Rom 12:20* heap coals of fire on his [your enemy's] *h*

*1 Cor 11:3* and the *h* of the woman is the man

*1 Cor 12:21* eye cannot say ... nor ... the *h* to the feet, I have no need of you

*Col 1:18* he [Jesus] is the *h* of the body, the church

*Rev 1:14* His *h* and his hairs were white like wool

*Rev 17:3* I [John] saw a woman ... having seven *h's* and ten horns

## HEAL [ING]

*2 Chr 7:14* I [God will] hear from heaven ... forgive their sin ... *h* their land

*Ps 41:4* LORD, be merciful unto me: *h* my soul

*Eccl 3:3* A time to kill, and a time to *h*

*Jer 3:22* I [God] will *h* your backslidings

*Mal 4:2* Sun of righteousness arise with *h'ing* in his wings

*Matt 4:23* Jesus went about ... *h'ing* all manner of sickness

*Matt 10:8* *H* the sick, cleanse the lepers, raise the dead

*Luke 4:18* he [God] hath sent me [Jesus] to *h* the broken-hearted

*Luke 9:2* he [Jesus] sent them [disciples]...to *h* the sick

*1 Cor 12:30* Have all the gifts of *h'ing*...do all interpret

## HEAR [EST, ETH, ING]

*Deut 6:4* *H,* O Israel: The LORD our God is one

*1 Sam 3:9* Speak, LORD, for thy servant [Samuel] *h'eth*

*Job 35:13* Surely God will not *h* vanity

*Job 42:5* I [Job] have heard of thee by the *h'ing* of the ear

*Ps 4:3* the LORD will *h* when I call unto him

*Ps 17:6* incline thine [God's] ear...and *h* my speech

*Ps 55:17* and he [God] shall *h* my voice

*Ps 65:2* O thou [God] that *h'est* prayer

*Ps 69:33* For the LORD *h'eth* the poor

*Ps 86:1* Bow down thine ear, O LORD, *h* me

*Ps 115:6* They have ears, but they *h* not

*Prov 4:1* *H,* ye children, the instruction of a father

*Prov 13:1* wise son *h'eth* his father's instruction

*Prov 18:13* answereth a matter before he *h'eth* it, it is folly

*Prov 19:20* *H* counsel, and receive instruction

*Eccl 7:5* better to *h* the rebuke of the wise, than...to *h* the song of fools

*Isa 1:2* *H,* O heavens, and give ear, O earth

*Isa 59:1* LORD's hand is not shortened...neither his ear heavy, that it cannot *h*

*Isa 65:24* while they are yet speaking, I [God] will *h*

*Jer 22:29* O earth...*h* the word of the LORD

*Ezek 37:4* dry bones, *h* the word of the LORD

*Matt 7:24* *h'eth* these sayings of mine [Jesus]...doeth them

*Matt 13:9* Who hath ears to *h,* let him *h*

*Matt 13:13* *h'ing* they *h* not, neither do they understand

*Matt 13:16* blessed are your... ears, for they *h*

*Matt 17:5* This is my [God's] beloved Son...*h* ye him

*Mark 7:37* he [Jesus] maketh... the deaf to *h*

*Luke 2:46* found him [Jesus]... sitting in the midst of the doctors...*h'ing* them

*Luke 8:21* my [Jesus'] brethren are these which *h* the word of God, and do it

*Luke 11:28* Yea...blessed are they that *h* the word of God, and keep it

*John 3:8* wind bloweth...thou *h'est* the sound thereof

*John 10:27* My [Jesus'] sheep *h* my voice...I know them

*Acts 2:8* how *h* we every man in our own tongue

*Acts 9:7* the men ... stood speechless, *h'ing* a voice, but seeing no man

*Acts 17:21* Athenians ... spent their time ... but ... to *h* some new thing

*Acts 28:28* salvation ... is sent unto the Gentiles ... that they will *h* it

*Rom 10:14* how shall they *h* without a preacher

*1 Cor 12:17* whole body were an eye, where were the *h'ing*

*Jas 1:19* let every man be swift to *h,* slow to speak

*1 John 5:14* if we ask any thing according to his [God's] will, he *h'eth* us

*Rev 2:7* *h* what the Spirit saith unto the churches

*Rev 3:20* any man *h* my [Jesus'] voice ... open the door

*Rev 22:17* let him that *h'eth* say, Come

**HEARD [EST]**

*Gen 3:8* they [Adam and Eve] *h* the voice of the LORD God

*Ex 3:7* I [God] have surely ... *h* their [Israel's] cry

*Job 42:5* I [Job] have *h* ... by the hearing of the ear

*Ps 28:6* the LORD ... hath *h* the voice of my supplications

*Ps 34:4* I sought the LORD, and he *h* me ... delivered me

*Ps 40:1* he [God] inclined unto me, and *h* my cry

*Ps 116:1* I love the LORD, because he hath *h* my voice

*Ps 119:26* I have declared my ways ... thou [God] *h'est* me

*Isa 6:8* *h* the voice of the Lord, saying, Whom shall I send

*Isa 40:28* hast thou not *h* ... God ... fainteth not

*Isa 42:2* He [God's servant] shall not ... cause his voice to be *h* in the street

*Jer 31:15* A voice was *h* in Ramah ... bitter weeping

*Matt 6:7* the heathen ... think that they shall be *h* for their much speaking

*Mark 12:37* common people *h* him [Jesus] gladly

*Luke 2:20* shepherds returned ... praising God for all ... they had *h* and seen

*Luke 12:3* spoken in darkness shall be *h* in the light

*Acts 4:20* speak the things which we have seen and *h*

*Acts 9:4* *h* a voice saying ... Saul, Saul

*Acts 11:1* apostles ... *h* that the Gentiles had also received the word of God

*Acts 17:32* *h* of the resurrection ... some mocked

*Rom 10:14* how shall they believe in him [Jesus] of whom they have not *h*

*1 Cor 2:9* Eye hath not seen, nor ear *h*

*Phil 4:9* things, which ye have ... *h,* and seen ... do

*1 John 1:3* which we have seen and *h* declare we unto you

*1 John 3:11* the message that ye *h* from the beginning

*Rev 1:10* I [John] was in the Spirit on the Lord's day, and *h* behind me a great voice

**HEART [S]**

*Ex 7:14* the LORD said … Pharaoh's *h* is hardened

*Deut 6:5* love the LORD thy God with all thine *h*

*Deut 10:16* Circumcise therefore the foreskin of your *h*

*1 Sam 12:24* serve him [God] in truth with all your *h*

*Ps 7:10* God … saveth the upright in *h*

*Ps 13:5* my *h* shall rejoice in thy [God's] salvation

*Ps 19:8* statutes of the LORD are right, rejoicing the *h*

*Ps 19:14* Let the … meditation of my *h,* be acceptable

*Ps 24:4* He that hath clean hands, and a pure *h*

*Ps 37:4* he [God] shall give thee the desires of thine *h*

*Ps 40:8* thy [God's] law is within my *h*

*Ps 51:10* Create in me a clean *h,* O God

*Ps 53:1* fool hath said in his *h,* There is no God

*Ps 66:18* regard iniquity in my *h,* the Lord will not hear me

*Ps 90:12* teach us to number our days, that we may apply our *h's* unto wisdom

*Ps 119:11* Thy [God's] word have I hid in mine *h*

*Ps 139:23* Search me, O God, and know my *h*

*Ps 147:3* He [God] healeth the broken in *h*

*Prov 2:2* apply thine *h* to understanding

*Prov 3:5* Trust in the LORD with all thine *h*

*Prov 15:13* merry *h* maketh a cheerful countenance

*Prov 16:5* Every one that is proud in *h* is an abomination

*Prov 17:22* A merry *h* doeth good like a medicine

*Prov 21:2* but the LORD pondereth the *h's*

*Eccl 9:7* and drink thy wine with a merry *h*

*Jer 17:9* The *h* is deceitful above all things

*Jer 29:13* ye shall … find me [God], when ye shall search … with all your *h*

*Jer 31:33* I [God] will … write it [God's law] in their *h's*

*Ezek 11:19* one *h,* and I will put a new spirit within you

*Ezek 36:26* new *h* also will I [God] give you

*Matt 5:8* Blessed are the pure in *h* … they shall see God

*Matt 6:21* where your treasure is, there will your *h* be also

*Matt 11:29* I [Jesus] am meek and lowly in *h*

*Matt 15:8* honoureth me [Jesus] with their lips; but their *h* is far from me

*Mark 12:30* love the Lord thy God with all thy *h*

*Luke 2:19* Mary kept all these things…pondered…in her *h*

*John 14:1* Let not your *h* be troubled

*Acts 4:32* them that believed were of one *h*

*Rom 1:24* God also gave them up…through the lusts of their own *h's*

*Rom 5:5* love of God is shed abroad in our *h's*

*Rom 10:9* believe in thine *h* that God hath raised him [Jesus] from the dead

*2 Cor 3:2* Ye are our epistle written in our *h's*

*2 Cor 4:6* God…hath shined in our *h's*

*2 Cor 9:7* as he purposeth in his *h,* so let him give

*Phil 4:7* peace of God…shall keep your *h's* and minds through Christ

*2 Thes 3:5* Lord direct your *h's* into the love of God

*Heb 3:12* lest there be in any of you an evil *h* of unbelief

*Heb 3:15* harden not your *h's,* as in the provocation

*Heb 4:12* word of God is quick… a discerner…of the *h*

*Jas 4:8* purify your *h's,* ye double minded

## HEAVEN [S]

*Gen 1:1* God created the *h* and the earth

*Deut 1:10* ye are this day as the stars of *h*

*Deut 4:39* that the LORD he is God in *h* above

*2 Sam 22:14* The LORD thundered from *h*

*1 Kgs 8:23* no God like thee, in *h* above, or on earth beneath

*2 Kgs 2:11* Elijah went up by a whirlwind into *h*

*1 Chr 16:26* gods of the people are idols…LORD made the *h's*

*2 Chr 7:14* will I [God] hear from *h*…forgive their sin

*Job 28:24* For he [God]…seeth under the whole *h*

*Ps 8:3* consider thy [God's] *h's,* the work of thy fingers

*Ps 11:4* LORD's throne is in *h*

*Ps 19:1* The *h's* declare the glory of God

*Ps 57:5* Be thou exalted, O God, above the *h's*

*Ps 89:6* who in the *h* can be compared unto the LORD

*Ps 103:11* For as the *h* is high above the earth, so great is his [God's] mercy

*Ps 108:5* Be thou exalted, O God, above the *h's*

*Ps 121:2* help cometh from the LORD…made *h* and earth

*Ps 136:26* thanks unto the God of *h*…mercy endureth for ever

*Ps 139:8* If I ascend up into *h,* thou [God] art there

*Eccl 3:1* a time to every purpose under the *h*

*Isa 55:9* *h's* are higher than the earth, so are my [God's] ways higher than your ways

*Jer 23:24* Do not I fill *h* and earth? saith the LORD

*Jer 32:17* thou [God] hast made the *h* and the earth by thy great power

*Jer 51:15* He [God]…hath stretched out the *h* by his understanding

*Mal 3:10* prove me…if I [God] will not open you the windows of *h*

*Matt 4:17* Jesus began to preach…Repent: for the kingdom of *h* is at hand

*Matt 5:3* poor in spirit: for theirs is the kingdom of *h*

*Matt 5:12* great is your reward in *h:* for so persecuted they the prophets…before you

*Matt 5:34* Swear not at all; neither by *h*

*Matt 5:48* even as your Father which is in *h* is perfect

*Matt 6:9* Father which art in *h,* Hallowed be thy name

*Matt 6:20* lay up for yourselves treasures in *h*

*Matt 7:21* Not every one… shall enter…kingdom of *h*

*Matt 16:19* give unto thee [Peter] the keys of the kingdom of *h*

*Matt 18:3* become as little children, ye shall not enter into the kingdom of *h*

*Matt 19:14* of such [little children] is the kingdom of *h*

*Matt 26:64* shall ye see the Son of man…coming in the clouds of *h*

*Matt 28:18* All power is given unto me [Jesus] in *h* and in earth

*Mark 1:10* he [Jesus] saw the *h's* opened, and the Spirit… descending upon him

*Mark 13:32* But of that hour knoweth no man, no, not the angels which are in *h*

*Luke 3:22* voice came from *h,* which said…in thee [Jesus] I [God] am well pleased

*Luke 16:17* easier for *h* and earth to pass, than one tittle of the law to fail

*Luke 24:51* he [Jesus] was parted…carried up into *h*

*John 3:27* receive nothing, except it be given him from *h*

*John 6:38* I [Jesus] came down from *h,* not to do mine own will, but…him that sent me

*Acts 1:11* men of Galilee, why stand ye gazing up into *h*

*Acts 4:12* none other name under *h* given among men, whereby we must be saved

*2 Cor 5:1* house not made with hands, eternal in the *h's*

*Phil 2:10* every knee should bow, of things in *h*

*1 Thes 4:16* Lord himself shall descend from *h* with a shout

*Jas 5:12* swear not, neither by *h*…let your yea be yea

*2 Pet 3:13* we…look for new *h's* and a new earth

*Rev 5:3* no man in *h*…was able to open the book

*Rev 20:1* angel come down from *h,* having the key of the bottomless pit

*Rev 21:1* And I [John] saw a new *h* and a new earth

## HEAVEN AND EARTH

*Gen 14:19* Blessed be Abram… possessor of *h-a-e*

*Ex 20:11* in six days the LORD made *h-a-e*

*Ps 69:34* Let the *h-a-e* praise him [God], the seas

*Ps 124:8* Our help is in…the LORD, who made *h-a-e*

*Matt 5:18* Till *h-a-e* pass, one jot…shall in no wise pass

*Matt 24:35* **H-a-e** shall pass away, but my [Jesus'] words shall not pass away

*Acts 17:24* Lord of *h-a-e*, dwelleth not in temples made with hands

## HEAVENLY

*Matt 6:14* your *h* Father will also forgive you

*Luke 2:13* with the angel a multitude of the *h* host

*John 3:12* how shall ye believe, if I [Jesus] tell you of *h* things

*Acts 26:19* I [Paul] was not disobedient unto the *h* vision

## HEBREWS, EPISTLE TO THE.

An epistle, author unknown, written to believers of Jewish background to show that Jesus had replaced the Old Testament ceremonial law and sacrificial system.

## HEBRON

(an ancient town in Canaan where Sarah died and that later became one of the six cities of refuge). Gen 13:18; **23:2–20;** 35:27; 37:14 • Josh 10:3–39 • Judg 1:10,20 • 2 Sam 3:2–32; 5:1–13 • 1 Chr 11:1–3 • 2 Chr 11:10. *Kirjath-arba:* Gen 23:2 • Josh 14:15.

## HEED

*Josh 23:11* Take good *h*…that ye love the LORD

*Prov 17:4* A wicked doer giveth *h* to false lips

*Matt 6:1* Take *h* that ye do not your alms before men

*Mark 8:15* Take *h,* beware of the…Pharisees

*Luke 12:15* Take *h,* and beware of covetousness

*Luke 21:8* Take *h*…be not deceived: for many shall come in my [Jesus'] name

*1 Cor 3:10* every man take *h* how he buildeth thereupon

*1 Cor 10:12* thinketh he standeth take *h* lest he fall

*Heb 3:12* Take *h*…lest there be in…you an evil heart

**HEIR [S]**
*Mark 12:7* This is the *h;* come, let us kill him
*Gal 3:29* Abraham's seed, and *h's* according to the promise
*Gal 4:7* if a son, then an *h* of God through Christ
*Titus 3:7* justified by his [Jesus'] grace…be made *h's*
*Heb 1:2* whom he [God] hath appointed *h* [Jesus] of all things
*Heb 11:9* Isaac and Jacob, the *h's* with him [Abraham] of the same promise

**HELL**
*Job 26:6* *H* is naked before him, and destruction hath no covering
*Ps 18:5* sorrows of *h* compassed me about
*Ps 139:8* make my bed in *h,* behold, thou [God] art there
*Prov 27:20* *H* and destruction are never full
*Jon 2:2* out of the belly of *h* cried I [Jonah]
*Matt 5:22* say, Thou fool, shall be in danger of *h* fire
*Matt 10:28* fear him…able to destroy…soul and body in *h*
*Matt 16:18* gates of *h* shall not prevail against it [the church]
*Luke 10:15* Capernaum…shalt be thrust down to *h*
*Rev 1:18* I [Jesus]…have the keys of *h* and of death

*Rev 20:14* death and *h* were cast into the lake of fire

**HENOCH.** See *Enoch,* No. 2.

**HERMOGENES** (a believer who deserted Paul). 2 Tim 1:15.

**HERMON, MOUNT** (a mountain in Syria that marked the northern limit of Joshua's conquest). **Josh 11:3,17; 12:1,5** • Pss 89:12; 133:3. *Senir:* Ezek 27:5. *Shenir, Sirion:* Deut 3:9.

**HEROD** (the name of several Roman rulers in Palestine during New Testament times).

1. Herod the Great, who ordered the slaughter of innocent children after Jesus was born. **Matt 2:1–22** • Luke 1:5.

2. Herod Archelaus, son and successor of Herod the Great. Matt 2:22.

3. Herod Philip, ruler in northern Galilee when Jesus began His public ministry. Luke 3:1,19–20.

4. Herod Antipas, who executed John the Baptist. **Matt 14:1–12** • Mark 6:14–22; 8:15 • Luke 3:1,19; 9:7,9; 13:31; 23:7–12 • Acts 4:27; 13:1.

5. Herod Agrippa I, who executed James, leader of the Jerusalem church. Acts 12:1–19.

6. Herod Agrippa II, before whom Paul made his defense at Caesarea. Acts 25:13–26:32.

**HERODIANS** (an influential Jewish group that joined forces with the Pharisees against Jesus). Matt 22:16 • **Mark 3:6; 12:13.**

**HERODIAS** (wife of Herod Antipas who had John the Baptist executed). **Matt 14:1–11** • Mark 6:17.

**HEZEKIAH** (a godly king of Judah who implemented religious reforms). 2 Kgs 18:1–8; 19:1–37; 20:1–21 • **2 Chr 29:1–36; 31:1–21** • Isa 38:9–22. *Ezekias:* Matt 1:9.

**HID [DEN]**

*Gen 3:8* Adam and his wife *h* themselves from … the LORD

*Ex 3:6* Moses *h* his face; for he was afraid to look upon God

*Ps 38:9* my groaning is not *h* from thee [God]

*Ps 51:6* in the *h'den* part thou [God] shalt make me to know wisdom

*Ps 119:11* Thy [God's] word have I *h* in mine heart

*Isa 53:3* we *h* … our faces from him [God's servant]

*Matt 5:14* A city that is set on an hill cannot be *h*

*Matt 11:25* thou [God] hast *h* these things from the wise

*Luke 13:21* It [kingdom of God] is like leaven, which a woman took and *h*

*1 Cor 2:7* the *h'den* wisdom, which God ordained before the world unto our glory

*Heb 11:23* Moses … was *h* three months of his parents

**HIDE [ING, ST, TH]**

*Job 14:13* thou [God] wouldest *h* me in the grave

*Ps 10:1* why *h'st* thou [God] thyself in times of trouble

*Ps 13:1* how long wilt thou [God] *h* thy face from me

*Ps 17:8 h* me under the shadow of thy [God's] wings

*Ps 51:9 H* thy [God's] face from my sins

*Ps 69:17 h* not thy [God's] face from thy servant

*Ps 119:114* Thou [God] art my *h'ing* place and my shield

*Prov 19:24* A slothful man *h'th* his hand in his bosom

*Isa 45:15* thou art a God that *h'st* thyself

*Jer 23:24* Can any *h* himself in secret places that I [God] shall not see him

*Rev 6:16 h* us from the face of him that sitteth on the throne

**HIERAPOLIS** (a city in Asia Minor mentioned by Paul). Col 4:13.

**HIGH [ER, EST, LY]**

*Gen 14:18* Melchizedek … was the priest of the most *h* God

*Deut 28:1* God will set thee on *h* above all nations

*Job 41:34* He [God] beholdeth all *h* things

*Ps 7:17* I will...sing praise to the name of the LORD most *h*

*Ps 47:2* the LORD most *h* is terrible...a great King

*Ps 61:2* lead me to the rock that is *h'er* than I

*Ps 69:29* let thy salvation, O God, set me up on *h*

*Ps 91:1* He that dwelleth in the secret place of the most *H*

*Ps 93:4* LORD on *h* is mightier than...many waters

*Ps 97:9* thou, LORD, art *h* above all the earth

*Ps 99:2* The LORD ...is *h* above all the people

*Ps 103:11* as the heaven is *h* above the earth, so great is his [God's] mercy

*Ps 113:4* The LORD is *h* above all nations

*Isa 6:1* I [Isaiah] saw also the Lord...*h* and lifted up

*Isa 33:5* The LORD is exalted; for he dwelleth on *h*

*Isa 52:13* my [God's] servant shall be exalted...be very *h*

*Isa 55:9* heavens are *h'er* than the earth, so are my [God's] ways *h'er* than your ways

*Matt 4:8* the devil taketh him [Jesus] up into an exceeding *h* mountain

*Luke 1:28* Hail, thou [Mary] that art *h'ly* favoured

*Luke 1:32* He [Jesus]...shall be called the Son of the *H'est*

*Luke 2:14* Glory to God in the *h'est*...on earth peace

*Luke 20:46* Beware of the scribes, which...love...the *h'est* seats in the synagogues

*Luke 24:49* tarry...until... endued with power from on *h*

*Rom 13:1* be subject unto the *h'er* powers

*Eph 4:8* ascended up on *h,* he [Jesus] led captivity captive

*Eph 6:12* wrestle...against spiritual wickedness in *h* places

*Phil 2:9* God also hath *h'ly* exalted him [Jesus]

*Phil 3:14* the prize of the *h* calling of God in Christ Jesus

**HIGH PRIEST [S]**

*Matt 26:65* *h-p* rent his clothes, saying, He [Jesus] hath spoken blasphemy

*John 18:19* *h-p* then asked Jesus of his...doctrine

*Heb 3:1* Apostle and *H-P* of our profession, Christ Jesus

*Heb 4:15* we have not an *h-p* which cannot be touched with...our infirmities

*Heb 6:20* even Jesus, made an *h-p* for ever

*Heb 7:27* Who [Jesus] needeth not daily, as those *h-p's,* to offer up sacrifice

**HIGH PRIESTLY PRAYER OF JESUS.** John 17:1–26.

**HILKIAH** (a high priest during King Josiah's reign who found the lost book of the Law). **2 Kgs 22:4–23:4** • 2 Chr 34:9–22.

**HINNOM, VALLEY OF** (a narrow ravine outside Jerusalem where pagan worship involving child sacrifice was conducted). Josh 15:8; 18:16 • 2 Kgs 23:10 • **2 Chr 28:3;** 33:6 • Neh 11:30 • Jer 7:31–32; **19:2–6.**

**HIRAM** (a king of Tyre who assisted David and Solomon with their building projects in Jerusalem). **2 Sam 5:11 • 1 Kgs 5:1–12;** 9:11–27; 10:11,22 • 1 Chr 14:1. *Huram:* 2 Chr 2:3–12.

**HITTITES** (an ancient people who lived in Canaan). Gen 23:10–20 • 2 Sam 11:15–17 • 1 Kgs 15:5.

**HOBAB.** See *Jethro.*

**HOLD [ING]**
*Ex 20:7* the LORD will not *h* him guiltless that taketh his name in vain
*Job 6:24* Teach me, and I will *h* my tongue
*Ps 83:1* Keep not thou silence, O God: *h* not thy peace
*Ps 139:10* thy [God's] right hand shall *h* me

*Jer 2:13* they have … hewed them out … cisterns, that can *h* no water
*Luke 16:13* he will *h* to the one, and despise the other
*Phil 2:16* **H'ing** forth the word of life … I [Paul] may rejoice
*1 Thes 5:21* Prove all things; *h* fast that which is good
*1 Tim 3:9* **H'ing** the mystery of the faith
*Heb 4:14* we have a great high priest … Jesus … let us *h* fast our profession
*Heb 10:23* *h* fast the profession of our faith
*Rev 3:11* *h* that fast … that no man take thy crown

**HOLY [INESS]**
*Ex 3:5* place whereon thou [Moses] standest is *h* ground
*Ex 15:11* who is like thee [God], glorious in *h'iness*
*Ex 20:8* Remember the sabbath day, to keep it *h*
*Lev 11:44* ye shall be *h;* for I [God] am *h*
*Lev 20:7* be ye *h:* for I am the LORD your God
*Ps 11:4* The LORD is in his *h* temple
*Ps 24:3* who shall stand in his [God's] *h* place
*Ps 29:2* worship the LORD in the beauty of *h'iness*
*Ps 51:11* take not thy [God's] *h* spirit from me

*Ps 89:18* and the *H* One of Israel is our king

*Ps 96:9* worship the LORD in the beauty of *h'iness*

*Ps 99:5* worship at his [God's] footstool; for he is *h*

*Ps 103:1* all that is within me, bless his [God's] *h* name

*Ps 145:21* let all flesh bless his [God's] *h* name for ever

*Isa 6:3* one [seraphim] cried … *H, h, h,* is the LORD of hosts

*Hab 2:20* the LORD is in his *h* temple … earth keep silence

*Rom 12:1* bodies a living sacrifice, *h,* acceptable unto God

*Rom 16:16* Salute one another with an *h* kiss

*1 Cor 3:17* temple of God is *h,* which temple ye are

*Eph 5:27* it [the church] should be *h* and without blemish

*1 Thes 4:7* God hath … called us unto … *h'iness*

*1 Tim 2:8* men pray every where, lifting up *h* hands

*2 Tim 3:15* And that from a child thou [Timothy] hast known the *h* scriptures

*1 Pet 1:16* it is written, Be ye *h;* for I [God] am *h*

*1 Pet 2:5* Ye also … are built up … an *h* priesthood

*1 Pet 2:9* ye are a chosen generation … an *h* nation

*Rev 21:2* I John saw the *h* city, new Jerusalem

## HOLY GHOST

*Matt 1:18* she [Mary] was found with child of the *H-G*

*Matt 3:11* he [Jesus] shall baptize you with the *H-G*

*Matt 12:31* blasphemy against the *H-G* shall not be forgiven

*Matt 28:19* baptizing them in the name of the … *H-G*

*Luke 1:35* The *H-G* shall come upon thee [Mary]

*Luke 1:67* Zacharias was filled with the *H-G*

*Luke 2:25* the *H-G* was upon him [Simeon]

*Luke 3:22* *H-G* descended … like a dove upon him [Jesus]

*John 14:26* the *H-G* … shall teach you all things

*Acts 1:8* receive power, after that … *H-G* is come upon you

*Acts 6:3* look ye out … seven men … full of the *H-G*

*Acts 13:2* *H-G* said, Separate me Barnabas and Saul

*Rom 14:17* kingdom of God is … joy in the *H-G*

*1 Cor 12:3* and that no man can say that Jesus is the Lord, but by the *H-G*

*2 Pet 1:21* holy men of God spake … by the *H-G*

## HONEST [LY, Y]

*Acts 6:3* seven men of *h* report

*Rom 13:13* Let us walk *h'ly* … not in rioting

*Phil 4:8* things are *h,* whatsoever things are just

*1 Tim 2:2* lead a quiet…life in all godliness and *h'y*

**HONOUR [ED, ETH]**

*Ex 20:12* **H** thy father and thy mother

*1 Chr 16:27* Glory and *h* are in his [God's] presence

*Ps 8:5* thou [God]…hast crowned him [man] with glory and *h*

*Prov 3:9* **H** the LORD with thy substance…and…firstfruits

*Prov 22:4* By…the fear of the LORD are riches, and *h*

*Matt 13:57* Jesus said…A prophet is not without *h*, save in his own country

*Mark 7:6* people *h'eth* me [Jesus] with their lips, but their heart is far from me

*John 5:23* *h'eth* not the Son *h'eth* not the Father

*John 12:26* if any man serve me [Jesus], him will my Father *h*

*Rom 12:10* Be kindly affectioned one to another…in *h* preferring one another

*1 Cor 12:26* one member be *h'ed*, all the members rejoice

*Rev 4:11* Thou art worthy, O Lord, to receive glory and *h*

**HOPE [D]**

*Job 7:6* My [Job's] days…are spent without *h*

*Ps 38:15* in thee, O LORD, do I *h*…thou wilt hear

*Ps 71:5* thou art my *h*, O Lord

*Ps 119:114* Thou [God] art my… shield: I *h* in thy word

*Ps 146:5* Happy is he…whose *h* is in the LORD

*Jer 17:7* Blessed is the man… whose *h* the LORD is

*Lam 3:24* LORD is my portion… therefore…I *h* in him

*Rom 12:12* Rejoicing in *h;* patient in tribulation

*Rom 15:13* the God of *h* fill you with all joy

*1 Cor 13:13* now abideth faith, *h*, charity, these three

*Col 1:27* which is Christ in you, the *h* of glory

*1 Thes 4:13* that ye sorrow not… as others which have no *h*

*Heb 11:1* faith is the substance of things *h'd* for

*1 Pet 3:15* every man that asketh you a reason of the *h* that is in you

**HOPHNI** (an immoral son of Eli the high priest who was killed by the Philistines). 1 Sam 1:3; 2:12–17; **4:1–11.**

**HOR, MOUNT** (a mountain in Moab where Aaron died). **Num 20:22–29;** 21:4; 33:37–41 • Deut 32:50.

**HOSEA** (a prophet to the Northern Kingdom and author of the book that bears his name). Hos 1:1–2. *Osee:* Rom 9:25.

**HOSEA, BOOK OF.** A prophetic book of the Old Testament that compares the idolatry of God's people with the physical adultery of the prophet's wife, Gomer (1:2–5; 2:2–5). Just as Hosea redeemed her from slavery and restored her as his mate, God promised that He would eventually restore His people after a period of punishment by their enemies (4:1–14:9).

### HOSHEA

1. The last king of Israel who was taken to Assyria as a captive. 2 Kgs 15:30; **17:1–6;** 18:1–10.

2. Another name for Joshua. See *Joshua.*

### HOSPITALITY

*1 Tim 3:2* A bishop then must be … given to *h,* apt to teach
*1 Pet 4:9* Use *h* one to another without grudging

### HOUR [S]

*Matt 10:19* given you in that same *h* what ye shall speak
*Matt 24:42* know not what *h* your Lord doth come
*Matt 26:40* ye [Peter] not watch with me [Jesus] one *h*
*Mark 13:32* of that day and that *h* knoweth no man
*Luke 12:40* Son of man cometh at an *h* when ye think not

*John 11:9* Are there not twelve *h's* in the day
*John 12:23 h* is come … Son of man should be glorified

### HOUSE [S]

*Gen 12:1* Get thee [Abraham] … from thy father's *h*
*Gen 28:17* he [Jacob] … said … this is none other but the *h* of God
*Gen 39:4* he [Potiphar] made him [Joseph] overseer over his *h*
*Ex 12:7* blood … strike it … on the upper door post of the *h's*
*Ex 20:2* I am … God, which have brought thee … out of the *h* of bondage
*Ex 20:17* Thou shalt not covet thy neighbour's *h*
*Deut 6:7* talk of them when thou sittest in thine *h*
*Deut 25:14* not have in thine *h* divers measures
*Josh 24:15* but as for me [Joshua] and my *h,* we will serve the LORD
*2 Sam 12:10* sword shall never depart from thine [David's] *h*
*1 Kgs 12:19* Israel rebelled against the *h* of David
*1 Chr 17:1* I [David] dwell in an *h* of cedars
*1 Chr 22:6* Then he [David] … charged him [Solomon] to build an *h* for the LORD
*2 Chr 2:1* Solomon determined to build an *h* for the … LORD

*2 Chr 7:16* sanctified this *h,* that my [God's] name may be there for ever

*2 Chr 21:7* LORD would not destroy the *h* of David

*Job 17:13* If I [Job] wait, the grave is mine *h*

*Job 22:18* Yet he [God] filled their *h's* with good things

*Ps 66:13* I will go into thy [God's] *h* with ... offerings

*Ps 69:9* the zeal of thine *h* hath eaten me up

*Ps 84:4* Blessed are they that dwell in thy [God's] *h*

*Ps 84:10* rather be a doorkeeper in the *h* of my God

*Ps 127:1* Except the LORD build the *h*

*Prov 12:7* the *h* of the righteous shall stand

*Prov 15:25* The LORD will destroy the *h* of the proud

*Isa 2:5* *h* of Jacob ... let us walk in the light of the LORD

*Jer 18:3* Then I [Jeremiah] went down to the potter's *h*

*Jer 29:28* build ye *h's,* and dwell in them

*Ezek 43:5* the glory of the LORD filled the *h*

*Amos 3:15* great *h's* shall have an end, saith the LORD

*Hag 2:9* glory of this latter *h* ... greater than of the former

*Mal 3:10* that there may be meat in mine [God's] *h*

*Matt 2:11* they [wise men] were come into the *h,* they saw the young child [Jesus]

*Matt 7:24* a wise man, which built his *h* upon a rock

*Matt 10:6* go rather to the lost sheep of the *h* of Israel

*Matt 13:57* Jesus said ... A prophet is not without honour, save ... in his own *h*

*Matt 15:24* I [Jesus] am not sent but unto the lost sheep of the *h* of Israel

*Matt 23:14* ye [scribes and Pharisees] devour widows' *h's*

*Mark 3:25* if a *h* be divided against itself

*Mark 11:17* My [God's] *h* shall be called ... the *h* of prayer

*Luke 14:23* compel them to come in ... my *h* may be filled

*Luke 19:9* This day is salvation come to this *h*

*John 14:2* In my Father's *h* are many mansions

*Acts 16:31* and thou shalt be saved, and thy *h*

*Acts 28:30* Paul dwelt two ... years in his own hired *h*

*1 Cor 16:19* Aquila and Priscilla salute you ... with the church ... in their *h*

*2 Cor 5:1* a building of God, an *h* not made with hands

*1 Tim 3:5* if a man know not how to rule his own *h*

*1 Tim 3:12* deacons ... ruling ... their own *h's* well

*1 Tim 5:8* for those of his own *h,* he hath denied the faith

*1 Pet 2:5* Ye also ... are built up a spiritual *h*

*1 Pet 4:17* judgment must begin at the *h* of God

## HOUSE OF THE LORD
*Deut 23:18* Thou shalt not bring…the price of a dog, into the *h-o-t-L*

*1 Sam 3:15* Samuel…opened the doors of the *h-o-t-L*

*1 Kgs 6:1* he [Solomon] began to build the *h-o-t-L*

*1 Kgs 8:11* glory of the LORD had filled the *h-o-t-L*

*1 Kgs 8:63* the king [Solomon] and all the children of Israel dedicated the *h-o-t-L*

*1 Kgs 14:26* And he [Shishak] took away the treasures of the *h-o-t-L*

*2 Kgs 22:8* I [Hilkiah] have found the book of the law in the *h-o-t-L*

*2 Kgs 25:9* he [Nebuzar-adan] burnt the *h-o-t-L*

*2 Chr 36:7* Nebuchadnezzar also carried of the vessels of the *h-o-t-L* to Babylon

*Ps 23:6* I will dwell in the *h-o-t-L* for ever

*Ps 27:4* I may dwell in the *h-o-t-L* all the days

*Ps 122:1* glad when they said… Let us go into the *h-o-t-L*

## HOUSEHOLD
*Matt 10:36* a man's foes shall be they of his own *h*

*Gal 6:10* do good unto…them who are of the *h* of faith

*Eph 2:19* fellowcitizens with the saints, and of the *h* of God

## HULDAH (a prophetess who foretold the collapse of Jerusalem). 2 Kgs 22:14–20 • 2 Chr 34:22–28.

## HUMBLE [D, TH]
*Ps 10:12* O God, lift up thine hand: forget not the *h*

*Ps 35:13* clothing was sackcloth: I *h'd* my soul

*Isa 5:15* and the mighty man shall be *h'd*

*Matt 18:4* shall *h* himself as this little child…is greatest

*Luke 18:14* he that *h'th* himself shall be exalted

*Phil 2:8* he [Jesus] *h'd* himself… became obedient unto death

*Jas 4:10* *H* yourselves…and he [God] shall lift you up

## HUMILITY
*Acts 20:19* Serving the Lord with all *h* of mind

*1 Pet 5:5* be clothed with *h:* for God resisteth the proud

## HUR (a man who held up the arms of Moses to give the Israelites victory over the Amalekites). **Ex 17:8–13;** 24:14.

## HURAM. See *Hiram*.

## HUSBAND [S]
*Gen 3:16* thy [Eve's] desire shall be to thy *h*

*Prov 12:4* A virtuous woman is a crown to her *h*

*Isa 54:5* For thy Maker is thine *h;* the LORD of hosts is his name

*Matt 1:19* Joseph her [Mary's] *h,* being a just man

*Mark 10:12* if a woman shall put away her *h*...she committeth adultery

*1 Cor 7:3* the *h* render unto the wife due benevolence

*1 Cor 7:14* unbelieving *h* is sanctified by the wife

*Eph 5:25* **H's,** love your wives... as Christ...loved the church

*Col 3:19* **H's,** love your wives, and be not bitter against them

*1 Tim 3:2* A bishop...must be blameless, the *h* of one wife

*1 Tim 3:12* let the deacons be the *h's* of one wife

*1 Pet 3:1* wives, be in subjection to your own *h's*

*Rev 21:2* I John saw...new Jerusalem...prepared as a bride adorned for her *h*

**HUSHAI** (a friend of King David who remained loyal to the king during Absalom's rebellion). 2 Sam 15:32–37; 16:16–18; 17:5–15 • 1 Kgs 4:16 • 1 Chr 27:33.

**HYMENAEUS** (an early believer who denied the faith and was excommunicated by Paul). 1 Tim 1:19–20 • 2 Tim 2:16–18.

**HYPOCRISY**

*Matt 23:28* within ye [Pharisees] are full of *h*

*Mark 12:15* But he [Jesus], knowing their [Pharisees'] *h,* said...bring me a penny

**HYPOCRITE [S]**

*Job 20:5* and the joy of the *h* but for a moment

*Matt 6:2* do not sound a trumpet...as the *h's* do

*Matt 6:16* be not, as the *h's,* of a sad countenance

*Matt 7:5* *h,* first cast out the beam out of thine own eye

*Matt 23:13* woe unto you, scribes and Pharisees, *h's*

*Luke 13:15* *h,* doth not...you on the sabbath...lead him [ox] away to watering

# -I-

## I AM GOD
*Ps 46:10* Be still, and know that *I-a-G*
*Isa 45:22* be ye saved, all the ends of the earth: for *I-a-G*
*Hos 11:9* *I-a-G,* and not man

## "I AM" STATEMENTS OF JESUS IN JOHN'S GOSPEL
1. Bread of life (John 6:35)
2. Light of the world (John 8:12)
3. Door of the sheep (John 10:7)
4. Good shepherd (John 10:11,14)
5. Resurrection and the life (John 11:25)
6. Way, the truth, and the life (John 14:6)
7. True vine (John 15:1)

**IBZAN** (a minor judge of Israel). Judg 12:8–10.

**ICHABOD** (a grandson of Eli who was given this symbolic name, meaning "inglorious," when his mother learned that Eli and Phinehas were dead). 1 Sam 4:19–22.

**ICONIUM** (a city in Asia Minor visited by Paul and Barnabas). **Acts 13:51; 14:1, 19–22;** 16:1–7 • 2 Tim 3:11.

## IDLE [NESS]
*Prov 19:15* and an *i* soul shall suffer hunger
*Prov 31:27* She…eateth not the bread of *i'ness*
*Eccl 10:18* and through *i'ness* of the hands the house droppeth through
*Matt 12:36* every *i* word that men shall speak, they shall give account
*Luke 24:11* words seemed to them [the disciples] as *i* tales

## IDOL [S]
*Lev 19:4* Turn ye not unto *i's*
*1 Chr 16:26* all the gods of the people are *i's*
*Ps 135:15* The *i's* of the heathen are silver and gold
*Ezek 14:6* Repent, and turn… from your *i's*
*Acts 7:41* they made a calf… offered sacrifice unto the *i*
*1 Cor 8:4* we know that an *i* is nothing in the world
*2 Cor 6:16* what agreement hath…temple of God with *i's*
*1 John 5:21* Little children, keep yourselves from *i's*

**IDUMEA.** See *Edom,* No. 2.

## IGNORANCE
*Num 15:27* And if any soul sin through *i*
*Acts 17:30* And the times of this *i* God winked at
*1 Pet 2:15* ye may put to silence the *i* of foolish men

## IGNORANT [LY]

*Acts 4:13* they [the Sanhedrin]... perceived that they [Peter and John] were...*i* men

*Acts 17:23* Whom...ye *i'ly* worship, him [Jesus] declare I [Paul] unto you

*1 Cor 12:1* concerning spiritual gifts...I [Paul] would not have you *i*

*1 Thes 4:13* not have you to be *i*, brethren, concerning them which are asleep

*2 Pet 3:8* be not *i* of this...one day is with the Lord as a thousand years

## IMAGE [S]

*Gen 31:19* Rachel had stolen the *i's* that were her father's

*Ex 20:4* Thou shalt not make unto thee any graven *i*

*Deut 7:25* graven *i's* of their gods shall ye burn with fire

*2 Kgs 17:10* they set them up *i's* and groves

*Ps 97:7* Confounded be all they that serve graven *i's*

*Ps 106:19* They made a calf... and worshipped the molten *i*

*Isa 21:9* all the graven *i's* of her [Babylon's] gods he [God] hath broken

*Isa 42:8* my glory will I [God] not give...neither my praise to graven *i's*

*Dan 3:18* we [Daniel's three friends] will not...worship the golden *i*

*Mic 1:7* all the graven *i's*... shall be beaten to pieces

*Mark 12:16* And he [Jesus] saith...Whose is this *i* and superscription

*Rom 1:23* changed the glory of...God into an *i* made like to corruptible man

*Rom 8:29* to be conformed to the *i* of his [God's] Son

*1 Cor 15:49* we shall also bear the *i* of the heavenly

*2 Cor 3:18* But we all...are changed into the same *i* from glory to glory

*Col 1:15* Who [Jesus] is the *i* of the invisible God

## IMAGE OF GOD

*Gen 1:27* God created man...in the *i-o-G*

*Gen 9:6* for in the *i-o-G* made he [God] man

*2 Cor 4:4* the glorious gospel of Christ, who is the *i-o-G*

## IMAGINATION [S]

*Gen 6:5* God saw that...every *i* of the thoughts of his [man's] heart was only evil

*Jer 16:12* ye walk every one after the *i* of his evil heart

*Lam 3:61* Thou [God] hast heard...their *i's* against me

*Luke 1:51* he [God]...scattered the proud in the *i* of their hearts

*Rom 1:21* they glorified him not as God...but became vain in their *i's*

**IMMORTALITY**

*1 Cor 15:53* For … this mortal must put on *i*

*2 Tim 1:10* Jesus … hath brought life and *i* to light through the gospel

**IMPOSSIBLE**

*Matt 17:20* and nothing shall be *i* unto you

*Mark 10:27* With men it is *i*, but not with God

*Luke 18:27* things … *i* with men are possible with God

*Heb 11:6* without faith it is *i* to please him [God]

**IMPUTE [D, ING, TH]**

*Ps 32:2* Blessed is the man unto whom the LORD *i'th* not iniquity

*Rom 4:8* Blessed is the man to whom the Lord will not *i* sin

*Rom 4:22* it was *i'd* to him [Abraham] for righteousness

*2 Cor 5:19* To wit … God was in Christ … not *i'ing* their trespasses unto them

*Jas 2:23* it was *i'd* unto him [Abraham] for righteousness

**IN CHRIST**

*Rom 8:1* no condemnation to them which are *i-C*

*Rom 12:5* we, being many, are one body *i-C*

*1 Cor 4:10* fools for Christ's sake, but ye are wise *i-C*

*1 Cor 15:19* in this life only we have hope *i-C*

*1 Cor 15:22* as in Adam all die, even so *i-C* shall all be made alive

*2 Cor 2:14* unto God, which … causeth us to triumph *i-C*

*2 Cor 5:17* if any man be *i-C*, he is a new creature

*2 Cor 5:19* To wit, that God was *i-C*, reconciling the world unto himself

*Eph 1:10* he [God] might gather … in one all things *i-C*

*Phil 2:1* If there be therefore any consolation *i-C*

*Phil 2:5* Let this mind be in you, which was also *i-C*

*Phil 3:14* the prize of the high calling of God *i-C*

*1 Thes 4:16* the dead *i-C* shall rise first

**IN THE BEGINNING**

*Gen 1:1* *I-t-b* God created the heaven and the earth

*John 1:1* *I-t-b* was the Word, and the Word was with God

*Heb 1:10* Thou, Lord, *i-t-b* hast laid the foundation of the earth

**IN THE SIGHT OF GOD**

*Prov 3:4* find favour and good understanding *i-t-s-o-G*

*Luke 16:15* that which is highly esteemed among men is abomination *i-t-s-o-G*

*Gal 3:11* no man is justified by the law *i-t-s-o-G*

175

## IN THE SPIRIT

*Ezek 37:1* The hand of the LORD...carried me [Ezekiel] out *i-t-s* of the LORD

*John 11:33* When Jesus...saw her [Mary] weeping...he groaned *i-t-s*

*Acts 19:21* Paul purposed *i-t-s*... to go to Jerusalem

*Acts 20:22* I [Paul] go bound *i-t-s* unto Jerusalem

*Rom 8:9* But ye are not in the flesh, but *i-t-S*

*Gal 5:16* Walk *i-t-S*...not fulfil the lust of the flesh

*Gal 5:25* If we live *i-t-S,* let us also walk *i-t-S*

*Rev 1:10* I [John] was *i-t-S* on the Lord's day

*Rev 21:10* he [an angel] carried me [John] away *i-t-s* to a great...mountain

## INCLINE [D, TH]

*Ps 17:6* *i* thine [God's] ear unto me...hear my speech

*Ps 40:1* I waited patiently... and he [God] *i'd* unto me, and heard my cry

*Prov 2:18* her [the strange woman's] house *i'th* unto death

*Prov 4:20* My son...*i* thine ear unto my sayings

## INCORRUPTIBLE

*1 Cor 9:25* they do it to obtain a corruptible crown...we an *i*

*1 Cor 15:52* dead shall be raised *i,* and we shall all be changed

## INCREASE [D, ING, TH]

*Gen 7:18* the waters...were *i'd* greatly upon the earth

*Ex 1:7* the children of Israel... *i'd* abundantly

*Lev 26:4* and the land shall yield her *i*

*Job 1:10* his [Job's] substance is *i'd* in the land

*Ps 3:1* how are they *i'd* that trouble me [David]

*Ps 67:6* Then shall the earth yield her *i*

*Ps 73:12* these are the ungodly...they *i* in riches

*Ps 105:24* And he [God] *i'd* his people greatly

*Prov 1:5* A wise man will hear, and will *i* learning

*Prov 24:5* a man of knowledge *i'th* strength

*Eccl 1:18* he that *i'th* knowledge *i'th* sorrow

*Eccl 5:10* not be satisfied with silver; nor he that loveth abundance with *i*

*Isa 9:7* Of the *i* of his [Messiah's] government and peace there shall be no end

*Luke 2:52* Jesus *i'd* in wisdom and stature

*Luke 17:5* apostles said unto the Lord, *I* our faith

*John 3:30* He [Jesus] must *i,* but I [John the Baptist] must decrease

*Acts 6:7* word of God *i'd;* and the...disciples multiplied

*1 Cor 3:7* neither is he that planteth any thing…but God that giveth the *i*

*Col 1:10* being fruitful in every good work, and *i'ing* in the knowledge of God

*1 Thes 3:12* the Lord make you to *i* and abound in love

**INDIA** (a region that served as the eastern limit of the Persian Empire). Esth 1:1; 8:9.

**INFIRMITY [IES]**

*Ps 77:10* my *i:* but I will remember…the most High

*Prov 18:14* The spirit of a man will sustain his *i*

*Matt 8:17* might be fulfilled… Himself [Jesus] took our *i'ies*…bare our sicknesses

*Rom 8:26* the Spirit also helpeth our *i'ies*

*Rom 15:1* We…strong ought to bear the *i'ies* of the weak

*2 Cor 12:9* gladly…will I [Paul]…glory in my *i'ies*

*Gal 4:13* through *i* of the flesh I [Paul] preached the gospel

*Heb 4:15* not an high priest [Jesus] which cannot be touched with…our *i'ies*

**INHERIT [ED]**

*Josh 14:1* countries which the children of Israel *i'ed*

*Ps 37:9* those that wait upon the LORD…shall *i* the earth

*Ps 37:29* The righteous shall *i* the land

*Prov 11:29* He that troubleth his own house…*i* the wind

*Matt 5:5* Blessed are the meek: for they shall *i* the earth

*Matt 25:34* Come…*i* the kingdom prepared for you

*Luke 18:18* Good Master, what shall I [rich young ruler] do to *i* eternal life

*1 Cor 6:10* nor extortioners, shall *i* the kingdom of God

*Gal 5:21* they which do such things shall not *i* the kingdom of God

*Rev 21:7* He that overcometh shall *i* all things

**INHERITANCE**

*Num 18:23* among…Israel they [Levites] have no *i*

*Num 27:8* a man die, and have no son…cause his *i* to pass unto his daughter

*Deut 32:9* Jacob is the lot of his [God's] *i*

*Josh 11:23* Joshua gave it [Canaan] for an *i* unto Israel

*Ps 2:8* I [God] shall give thee the heathen for thine *i*

*Ps 33:12* Blessed is…the people whom he [God] hath chosen for his own *i*

*Ps 94:14* neither will he [God] forsake his *i*

*Prov 20:21* An *i* may be gotten hastily at the beginning

*Mark 12:7* kill him [the heir], and the *i* shall be ours

*Eph 1:11* In whom [Jesus] also we have obtained an *i*

*Eph 5:5* no…idolater, hath…*i* in the kingdom of Christ

*Heb 11:8* Abraham…called… into a place which he should after receive for an *i,* obeyed

## INIQUITY [IES]

*Ex 20:5* I the LORD…am a jealous God, visiting the *i* of the fathers upon the children

*Num 14:18* The LORD is long-suffering…forgiving *i*

*Job 13:23* How many are mine *i'ies* and sins

*Job 15:16* filthy is man, which drinketh *i* like water

*Job 34:22* There is no darkness…where the workers of *i* may hide

*Ps 5:5* thou [God] hatest all workers of *i*

*Ps 25:11* O LORD, pardon mine *i;* for it is great

*Ps 31:10* my strength faileth because of mine *i*

*Ps 51:2* Wash me throughly from mine *i*

*Ps 51:5* I was shapen in *i;* and in sin did my mother conceive me

*Ps 51:9* blot out all mine *i'ies*

*Ps 85:2* Thou [God] hast forgiven the *i* of thy people

*Ps 103:10* He [God] hath not dealt with us…nor rewarded us according to our *i'ies*

*Prov 10:29* destruction shall be to the workers of *i*

*Isa 6:7* thine [Isaiah's] *i* is taken away

*Isa 40:2* her [Israel's] *i* is pardoned: for she hath received…double for all her sins

*Isa 53:5* he [God's servant] was bruised for our *i'ies*

*Isa 53:6* LORD…laid on him [God's servant]…*i* of us all

*Isa 59:2* *i'ies* have separated… you and your God

*Isa 64:6* our *i'ies,* like the wind, have taken us away

*Jer 14:20* We acknowledge, O LORD…the *i* of our fathers

*Jer 31:30* every one shall die for his own *i*

*Lam 5:7* we have borne their [our fathers'] *i'ies*

*Matt 23:28* ye [Pharisees] are full of hypocrisy and *i*

*Luke 13:27* depart from me [Jesus], all ye workers of *i*

*Rom 4:7* Blessed are they whose *i'ies* are forgiven

*1 Cor 13:6* [charity] rejoiceth not in *i,* but…in the truth

*2 Tim 2:19* every one that nameth the name of Christ depart from *i*

*Heb 10:17* sins and *i'ies* will I [God] remember no more

*Jas 3:6* the tongue is a fire, a world of *i*

## INSTRUCT [ED]

*Job 40:2* Shall he that contendeth with the Almighty *i* him

*Ps 32:8* I [God] will *i* thee and teach thee…guide thee

*Prov 21:11* when the wise is *i'ed,* he receiveth knowledge

*Luke 1:4* certainty of those things, wherein thou hast been *i'ed*

*1 Cor 2:16* who hath known the mind of the Lord, that he may *i* him

*Phil 4:12* I [Paul] am *i'ed* both to be full and to be hungry

## INTEGRITY

*Job 2:9* Dost thou [Job] still retain thine *i*

*Job 31:6* Let me [Job] be weighed...that God may know mine *i*

*Ps 25:21* Let *i* and uprightness preserve me

*Prov 19:1* Better is the poor that walketh in his *i,* than he that is perverse

*Prov 20:7* The just man walketh in his *i*

## INTERCESSION [S]

*Rom 8:26* the Spirit itself maketh *i*...with groanings

*Rom 8:34* who [Jesus]... maketh *i* for us

*1 Tim 2:1* that...prayers, *i's,* and giving of thanks, be made for all men

*Heb 7:25* he [Jesus] ever liveth to make *i* for them

## INVISIBLE

*Rom 1:20* *i* things of him [God]...are clearly seen

*Col 1:15* Who [Jesus] is the image of the *i* God

*1 Tim 1:17* unto the King eternal, immortal, *i*...be honour and glory

**ISAAC** (a son born to Abraham and Sarah in their old age and father of Jacob and Esau). Gen 17:19,21; **21:3–12;** 22:2–14; 24:4–67; **25:5–28;** 26:1–35; 27:1–46 • Heb 11:9,20.

**ISAIAH** (a major prophet of Judah and author of the book that bears his name; he warned that the nation would be destroyed by Assyria, but a righteous remnant would be saved). 2 Kgs 19:2–20; 20:1–19 • 2 Chr 26:22; 32:20,32 • **Isa 1:2–9; 11:11.** *Esaias:* Matt 4:14.

**ISAIAH, BOOK OF.** A major Old Testament prophetic book noted for its prediction of the coming Messiah (7:14; 9:7) and particularly its emphasis on the Messiah as God's "suffering servant" (42:1–9; 49:1–6; 50:4–9; 52:13–53:12). Many Bible students call Isaiah the "fifth Gospel" because it echoes the New Testament themes of salvation and redemption.

**ISCARIOT, JUDAS** (the disciple who betrayed Jesus). Matt 10:4; 26:14,25,47; 27:3 • Mark 3:19; 14:10,43 • Luke 22:3,

47–48 • John 6:71; 12:4; 13:2, 26,29; 18:2–5 • Acts 1:16,25.

**ISH-BOSHETH** (a son of King Saul who succeeded his father as king of Israel and served briefly until defeated by David). 2 Sam 2:8–15; 3:7–15; 4:5–12. *Esh-baal:* 1 Chr 8:33.

**ISHMAEL** (Abraham's son born to Sarah's maid Hagar; known as the father of the Arab peoples). **Gen 16:1–16;** 17:25; 21:8–21; 25:9–18 • 1 Chr 1:28–31.

**ISRAEL**
1. Another name for Jacob. Gen 32:28; 35:10. See *Jacob.*
2. The Northern Kingdom, formed when the ten northern tribes rebelled against the two southern tribes and established its own kingship under Rehoboam. 1 Kgs 12:1–33.

3. A general name for the entire nation of the Jewish people. Num 1:2.

**ISSACHAR** (a son of Jacob and ancestor of one of the twelve tribes of Israel). Gen 30:17–18; 35:23; 46:13; 49:14 • Ex 1:3 • Num 1:8,28–29 • Josh 17:10–11 • Judg 5:15 • 1 Chr 2:1; 7:1; 12:32,40 • Ezek 48:25–26,33. The tribe of Issachar settled in northern Canaan. Josh 19:17–23.

**ITHAMAR** (youngest son of Aaron who oversaw the tabernacle during the wilderness wanderings). Ex 6:23; 28:1; **38:21** • Lev 10:6–16 • 1 Chr 24:1–6.

**ITUREA** (a small province ruled by Herod Philip when John the Baptist began his ministry). Luke 3:1.

# -J-

**JABBOK** (a small stream beside which Jacob wrestled with an angel). **Gen 32:22–31** • Num 21:24 • Deut 2:37; 3:16 • Josh 12:2 • Judg 11:13,22.

**JACHIN AND BOAZ** (two bronze pillars which stood in front of Solomon's temple at Jerusalem). 1 Kgs 7:13–22 • 2 Chr 3:17.

**JACOB** (father of several sons who became the ancestors of the twelve tribes of Israel). See **Gen 25:19–34; 27:1–35:29; 48:1–49:33** for a sketch of Jacob.

1. Born with twin brother Esau (Gen 25:21–26)
2. Secured Esau's birthright (Gen 25:28–34)
3. Secured his father's blessing (Gen 27:1–41)
4. Fled to Haran (Gen 27:42–28:10)
5. Saw vision of angels at Bethel (Gen 28:11–22)
6. Worked seven years for Leah (Gen 29:16–25)
7. Worked seven years for Rachel (Gen 29:26–30)
8. Birth of his sons (Gen 29:31–30:24)
9. Wrestled with an angel at Peniel (Gen 32:24–30)
10. Name changed from Jacob to *Israel* (Gen 32:28; 35:10)
11. Reconciled with Esau (Gen 33:1–16)
12. Blessed Joseph and Joseph's sons (Gen 48:1–22)
13. Blessed his other sons (Gen 49:1–28)
14. Died in Egypt (Gen 49:29–33)
15. Buried in Canaan (Gen 50:1–14)

Jacob is also mentioned in Ex 1:1,5 • Lev 26:42 • Josh 24:4 • 1 Sam 12:8 • Mal 1:2 • Matt 1:2; 8:11 • Luke 1:33; 13:28 • John 4:5,12 • Acts 3:13; 7:8–46 • Rom 9:13; 11:26 • Heb 11:9,20–21.

**JAEL** (a woman who killed Sisera, a commander of the forces of King Jabin of Hazor). **Judg 4:17–22;** 5:6,24.

**JAH.** See *Jehovah.*

**JAIR** (a minor judge of Israel). Judg 10:3–5.

**JAIRUS** (a ruler of a synagogue whose daughter was raised from the dead by Jesus). Mark 5:22–23,36–43 • Luke 8:41–42,49–56.

**JAMBRES** (an Egyptian magician who opposed Moses). 2 Tim 3:8.

## JAMES

1. A son of Zebedee and a disciple of Jesus. Matt 4:21; 10:2; 17:1 • Mark 1:19,29; 3:17; 5:37; 9:2; 10:35,41; 13:3; 14:33 • Luke 5:10; 6:14; 8:51; 9:28,54 • Acts 1:13; 12:2.

2. A son of Alphaeus and a disciple of Jesus. Matt 10:3 • Mark 3:18 • Luke 6:15 • Acts 1:13.

3. A half brother of Jesus who became a leader in the church at Jerusalem and probable author of the New Testament book that bears his name. Matt 13:55; 27:56 • Mark 6:3; 15:40; 16:1 • Acts 12:17; 15:13; 21:18 • 1 Cor 15:7 • Gal 1:19; 2:9,12 • Jas 1:1 • Jude 1.

**JAMES, EPISTLE OF.** A short epistle written probably by James, the half brother of Jesus, and known for its plain language and practical application of the gospel to the believer's daily life.

**JANNES** (an Egyptian magician who opposed Moses). 2 Tim 3:8.

**JAPHETH** (a son of Noah considered the father of the Indo-European races). Gen 5:32; 6:10; 7:13; **9:18–27; 10:1–5** • 1 Chr 1:4–5.

**JAPHO.** See *Joppa.*

**JASHOBEAM** (chief of David's mighty men, or brave warriors). 1 Chr 11:10–11; 27:2.

**JASON** (a citizen of Thessalonica who provided lodging for Paul and Silas). Acts 17:5–9.

**JAVAN** (a son of Japheth considered the father of the Ionians, or Greeks). Gen 10:2,4 • 1 Chr 1:5–7 • Isa 66:19.

**JEBUS.** See *Jerusalem.*

**JEBUSITES** (tribal enemies of the Israelites from whom David took the city of Jebus, or Jerusalem). Gen 15:21 • Josh 15:63 • Judg 1:21; 3:5; 19:11 • **2 Sam 5:6–9** • 1 Kgs 9:20 • 1 Chr 11:4–6 • 2 Chr 8:7 • Ezra 9:1 • Neh 9:8.

**JECONIAH.** See *Jehoiachin.*

## JEHOAHAZ

1. A king of the Northern Kingdom who led the nation into sin and idolatry. 2 Kgs 10:35; **13:1–8** • 2 Chr 25:17,25.

2. Son and successor of Josiah as king of Judah. Jehoahaz reigned only three months. 2 Kgs 23:31–34 • 2 Chr 36:2,4. *Shallum:* 1 Chr 3:15.

**JEHOASH.** See *Joash,* No. 1.

**JEHOIACHIN** (son and successor of Jehoiakim as king of Judah. Jehoiachin reigned only three months). **2 Kgs 24:8–16;** 25:27 • 2 Chr 36:8–9 • Jer 52:31. *Coniah:* Jer 22:24. *Jeconiah:* 1 Chr 3:16–17.

**JEHOIAKIM** (a king of Judah who was defeated and carried away as a captive by the Babylonians). 2 Kgs 24:1–6 • 1 Chr 3:15–16 • **2 Chr 36:4–8** • Jer 26:1–23; 36:1–32 • Dan 1:1–2. *Eliakim:* 2 Kgs 23:34.

**JEHORAM**
1. A king of Judah who murdered his own brothers in order to succeed his father Jehoshaphat. 1 Kgs 22:50 • **2 Chr 21:1–20.** *Joram:* 2 Kgs 8:21.
2. A king of Israel who was assassinated by Jehu. 2 Kgs 1:17; 3:1,6; **9:24.** *Joram:* 2 Kgs 8:16.

**JEHOSHAPHAT** (a king of Judah who implemented religious reforms). 1 Kgs 22:2–50 • **2 Chr 17:1–12;** 18:1–21:1. *Josaphat:* Matt 1:8.

**JEHOSHUAH.** See *Joshua.*

**JEHOVAH** (a name for God, rendered "Lord" in most translations of the Bible, which comes from a Hebrew verb meaning "to be," indicating His eternity and self-existence). Ex 6:3 • Ps 83:18 • Isa 12:2; 26:4. *JAH:* Ps 68:4.

**JEHOVAH-JIREH** (a name for God meaning "the Lord will provide"). Gen 22:14.

**JEHOVAH-NISSI** (a name for God meaning "the Lord is my banner"). Ex 17:15–16.

**JEHOVAH-SHALOM** (name of an altar built by Gideon, meaning "the Lord is peace"). Judg 6:24.

**JEHU** (a king of Israel who gained the throne by killing King Ahab's descendants). 2 Kgs 9:2–10:36.

**JEMIMA** (a daughter of Job born after his recovery from affliction). Job 42:14.

**JEPHTHAE.** See *Jephthah.*

**JEPHTHAH** (a judge of Israel who made a rash vow to sacrifice his only child as an offering to God). **Judg 11:1–40;** 12:1–7. *Jephthae:* Heb 11:32.

**JEREMIAH** (a major prophet who preached God's message of doom to the nation of Judah before it fell to the Babylonians and author of the book that bears his name). He is mentioned outside the Book of Jeremiah in 2 Chr 35:25; 36:12, 21–22 • Ezra 1:1 • Dan 9:2. *Jeremias:* Matt 16:14. *Jeremy:* Matt 2:17; 27:9.

**JEREMIAH, BOOK OF.** A major Old Testament prophetic book noted for its warnings that the nation of Judah would fall to the Babylonians unless the people repented and turned back to God. Jeremiah also expounded the concept of a new covenant (Jer 31). This new agreement between God and His people, based on grace and forgiveness, was needed because the old covenant of law had failed to keep the people on the path of righteousness.

**JEREMIAS.** See *Jeremiah.*

**JEREMY.** See *Jeremiah.*

**JERICHO** (a Canaanite city captured by Joshua and regarded as one of the world's oldest cities). Num 22:1; 31:12 • Deut 34:3 • **Josh 6:1–27** • 2 Kgs 2:4–18. The Jericho of the New Testament was built on a site near Old Testament Jericho. Matt 20:29 • Mark 10:46 • Luke 19:1.

**JEROBOAM**

1. Jeroboam I, first king of the Northern Kingdom after the kingdom of Solomon split into two separate nations following the death of Solomon. 1 Kgs 12:17–30 • 2 Chr 13:19–20.

2. Jeroboam II, king of Israel who was denounced for his encouragement of idol worship. 2 Kgs 14:16–29 • **Amos 7:7–9.**

**JERUBBAAL.** See *Gideon.*

**JERUSALEM** (the religious and political capital of the Jewish people and the city where Jesus was crucified).

1. Called *Salem* in Abraham's time (Gen 14:18)

2. Then known as *Jebus,* captured by David and made his capital (2 Sam 5:6–8 • 1 Chr 11:4)

3. Site of first temple built by Solomon (1 Kgs 5:5–8)

4. Captured by Babylonia (Jer 39:1–8)

5. Temple rebuilt under Zerubbabel (Ezra 1:1–4)

6. Walls rebuilt under Nehemiah (Neh 12:27–47)

7. Jesus predicted its destruction (Luke 19:41–44)

8. Jesus enters as the triumphant Messiah (Matt 21:9–10)

9. Jesus crucified outside the city (Luke 9:31; 23:33)

10. Church begins at Jerusalem (Acts 2:1–47)

11. Future heavenly city described as "new Jerusalem" (Rev 21:1–3)

**JESHUA.** See *Joshua.*

**JESSE** (father of David and an ancestor of Christ). **Ruth 4:17,22** • 1 Sam 16:1–22 • 1 Chr 2:13–15 • Isa 11:1–10 • **Matt 1:5–6** • Luke 3:32 • Acts 13:22 • Rom 15:12.

## JESUS, APPEARANCES OF, AFTER HIS RESURRECTION

1. To Mary Magdalene at the empty tomb (Mark 16:9 • John 20:11–18)

2. To other women at the empty tomb (Matt 28:1–10)

3. To two followers on their way to Emmaus (Mark 16:12–13 • Luke 24:13–32)

4. To Peter, apparently in Jerusalem (Luke 24:33–35)

5. To ten of His disciples in Jerusalem, Thomas absent (Luke 24:36–43 • John 20:19–25)

6. To the eleven disciples in Jerusalem, Thomas present (John 20:26–29)

7. To His disciples at the Sea of Galilee (John 21:1–14)

8. To His disciples at His ascension near Jerusalem (Mark 16:19–20 • Luke 24:44–53)

9. To five hundred followers (1 Cor 15:6)

10. To James and all the apostles (1 Cor 15:7)

11. To the apostle Paul (1 Cor 15:8)

## JESUS, LIFE AND MINISTRY OF

1. Genealogies of (Matt 1:1–17 • Luke 3:23–38)

2. Birth in Bethlehem (Luke 2:1–20)

3. Flight into Egypt and settlement in Nazareth (Matt 2:13–23 • Luke 2:39–40)

4. Found among esteemed teachers in Jerusalem (Luke 2:41–52)

5. Baptized by John the Baptist (Matt 3:13–17 • Mark 1:9–11)

6. Tempted in the wilderness (Matt 4:1–11 • Mark 1:12–13 • Luke 4:1–13)

7. Centered His early ministry around Capernaum in Galilee (Matt 4:13–16 • Luke 4:22–31)

8. Selected twelve disciples for special training (Matt 10:2–4 • Mark 3:13–19 • Luke 6:12–16)

9. Sermon on the Mount (Matt 5:1–7:29 • Luke 6:17–49)

10. Sent disciples out to preach and heal (Matt 10:1, 5–42 • Mark 6:7–13 • Luke 9:1–6)

11. Predicted His death, resurrection, and return (Luke 12:35–59)

12. Transfiguration (Matt 17:1–8 • Mark 9:2–8 • Luke 9:28–36)

13. Triumphal entry into Jerusalem (Matt 21:1–11 • Mark 11:1–11 • Luke 19:28–40 • John 12:12–19)

14. Instituted the Memorial Supper (Matt 26:26–30 • Mark 14:22–26 • Luke 22:14–20)

15. Agonized in prayer in Gethsemane (Matt 26:36–46 • Mark 14:26,32–42 • Luke 22:39–46)

16. Betrayed by Judas and arrested (Matt 26:47–56 • Mark 14:43–52 • Luke 22:47–53 • John 18:1–12)

17. Trial before the Jewish authorities (Matt 26:57–68; 27:1–2 • Mark 14:53–65; 15:1 • Luke 22:54–23:1 • John 18:24)

18. Trial before Pilate (Matt 27:2–26 • Mark 15:1–15 • Luke 23:2–25 • John 18:28–19:16)

19. Crucifixion by Roman soldiers (Matt 27:33–37 • Mark 15:22–26 • Luke 23:32–34 • John 19:17–24)

20. Death (Matt 27:45–54 • Mark 15:33–39 • Luke 23:44–48 • John 19:28–30)

21. Burial in Joseph's tomb (Matt 27:57–60 • Mark 15:42–46 • Luke 23:50–54 • John 19:38–42)

22. Resurrection (Matt 28:2–4 • 1 Cor 15:1–19)

23. Appearances to His followers. See *Jesus, Appearances of, After His Resurrection.*

24. Great Commission to His followers (Matt 28:16–20 • Mark 16:15–18 • Acts 1:7–8)

25. Ascension to His Father (Mark 16:19 • Luke 24:50–51 • Acts 1:9–11)

## JESUS, MIRACLES OF

1. Blind Bartimaeus healed (Matt 20:29–34 • Mark 10:46–52 • Luke 18:35–43)

2. Blind man at Bethsaida healed (Mark 8:22–26)

3. Centurion's servant healed (Matt 8:5–13 • Luke 7:1–10)

4. Daughter of a Canaanite woman healed (Matt 15:21–28 • Mark 7:24–30)

5. Deaf man healed (Mark 7:31–37)

6. Demon-possessed blind man healed (Matt 12:22–24)

7. Demon-possessed boy healed (Matt 17:14–21 • Mark 9:14–29 • Luke 9:37–42)

8. Demon-possessed deaf man healed (Matt 9:32–34)

9. Demon-possessed man healed at Capernaum (Mark 1:21–26 • Luke 4:31–35)

10. Ear of Malchus healed (Luke 22:50–51 • John 18:10)

11. Feeding of the five thousand (Matt 14:13–23 • Mark 6:30–44 • Luke 9:10–17 • John 6:1–15)

12. Feeding of the four thousand (Matt 15:29–38 • Mark 8:1–10)

13. First miraculous catch of fish on the Sea of Galilee (Luke 5:4–10)

14. Jairus's daughter healed (Matt 9:23–26 • Mark 5:35–42 • Luke 8:49–56)

15. Lame man healed on the sabbath (John 5:1–15)

16. Lazarus raised from the dead (John 11:1–44)

17. A leper healed (Matt 8:1–4 • Mark 1:40–45 • Luke 5:12–16)

18. Man blind from birth healed (John 9:1–41)

19. Man with a paralyzed hand healed on the Sabbath (Matt 12:9–14 • Mark 3:1–6 • Luke 6:6–11)

20. Man with the dropsy healed (Luke 14:1–6)

21. Paralyzed man healed (Matt 9:1–8 • Mark 2:1–12 • Luke 5:17–26)

22. Peter's mother-in-law healed (Matt 8:14–15 • Mark 1:29–31 • Luke 4:38–39)

23. Production of a coin to pay the temple tax (Matt 17:24–27)

24. Royal official's son healed (John 4:46–54)

25. Second miraculous catch of fish at the Sea of Galilee (John 21:1–14)

26. Stilling of the storm (Matt 8:18,23–27 • Mark 4:35–41 • Luke 8:22–25)

27. Ten lepers healed (Luke 17:11–19)

28. Transfiguration before His disciples (Matt 17:1–8 • Mark 9:2–8 • Luke 9:28–36)

29. Two blind men healed (Matt 9:27–31)

30. Walking on the water (Matt 14:24–36 • Mark 6:45–56 • John 6:16–21)

31. Water turned into wine (John 2:1–11)

32. Widow's son raised from the dead (Luke 7:11–17)

33. Wild man among the tombs healed (Matt 8:28–34 • Mark 5:1–20 • Luke 8:26–39)

34. Withering of a fig tree (Matt 21:19–22 • Mark 11:20–26)

35. Woman with a crooked back healed (Luke 13:10–17)

36. Woman with a hemorrhage healed (Matt 9:20–22 • Mark 5:24–34 • Luke 8:43–48)

## JESUS, PARABLES OF

1. The barren fig tree (Luke 13:1–9)

2. Building on sand and rock (Matt 7:24–27)

3. The dishonest manager (Luke 16:1–8)

4. The dragnet (Matt 13:47–51)

5. The good Samaritan (Luke 10:25–37)

6. The hidden treasure (Matt 13:44)

7. The lamp on a lampstand (Mark 4:21–25 • Luke 8:16–18)

8. The landowner (Matt 13:52)

9. The large banquet (Luke 14:15–24)

10. The lost coin (Luke 15:8–10)

11. The lost sheep (Matt 18:12–14 • Luke 15:1–7)

12. The minas (Luke 19:11–27)

13. The mustard seed (Matt 13:31–32 • Mark 4:30–32 • Luke 13:18–19)

14. The pearl of great price (Matt 13:45–46)

15. The persistent widow (Luke 18:1–8)

16. The prodigal son (Luke 15:11–32)

17. The proud Pharisee (Luke 18:9–14)

18. The rich fool (Luke 12:13–21)

19. The rich man and Lazarus (Luke 16:19–31)

20. The sower and the soils (Matt 13:1–9 • Mark 4:1–9 • Luke 8:4–8)

21. The talents (Matt 25:14–30)

22. The ten virgins (Matt 25:1–13)

23. The two vineyard workers (Matt 21:28–32)

24. The unforgiving servant (Matt 18:23–35)

25. The vineyard owner (Matt 21:33–46 • Mark 12:1–12 • Luke 20:9–19)

26. The vineyard workers (Matt 20:1–16)

27. The wedding banquet (Matt 22:1–14)

28. The wheat and the tares (Matt 13:24–30)

29. The yeast (Matt 13:33–35 • Luke 13:20–21)

**JESUS, PROPHECIES ABOUT.** See *Messianic Prophecies.*

**JETHRO** (Moses' father-in-law who advised Moses to delegate some of his leadership responsibilities). Ex 3:1; 4:18; **18:1–27.** *Hobab:* Num 10:29. *Reuel:* Ex 2:18.

**JEZEBEL** (a wife of King Ahab who promoted Baal worship in Israel). 1 Kgs 16:31; 18:4,13; 19:1–2; 21:5–25 • 2 Kgs 9:7–37 • Rev 2:20.

**JEZREEL** (a symbolic name, meaning "God scatters," given by the prophet Hosea to his son to show that King Jehu and his family would be punished). Hos 1:3–5.

**JOAB** (commander of King David's army during most of David's reign). 1 Sam 26:6 • 2 Sam 2:13–32; 3:22–31; 11:1–25; 14:1–33; 18:2–29; 20:9–23 • 1 Kgs 2:5–33 • 1 Chr 11:6–39; 19:8–15; 21:2–6; 27:7, 24,34.

**JOANNA** (a woman who prepared spices for Jesus' burial and proclaimed His resurrection). Luke 8:1–3; 23:55–56; **24:1–10.**

**JOASH**
1. A king of Judah who brought religious reforms to the nation but then turned to idol worship. 2 Kgs 12:4–20 • 2 Chr 24:1–22. *Jehoash:* 2 Kgs 11:21.
2. A king of Israel who led the nation into sin through his idolatry. 2 Kgs 13:10–25.

**JOATHAM.** See *Jotham.*

**JOB** (a godly man whose faith sustained him through fierce trials and sufferings). **Job 1:1–22; 42:1–17** • Ezek 14:14,20 • Jas 5:11.

**JOB, BOOK OF.** A wisdom book of the Old Testament that addresses the issue of human suffering. The book is written in the form of a poetic drama revolving around the discussion of this problem by Job and his three friends: Eliphaz, Bildad, and Zophar.

**JOEL** (a prophet of Judah in the days of King Uzziah and author of the book that bears his name). Joel 1:1 • Acts 2:16.

**JOEL, BOOK OF.** A brief prophetic book of the Old Testament that uses a devastating swarm of locusts (1:1–20) as an early warning sign of God's judgment in order to call His people to repentance. The prophet predicted the outpouring of God's spirit (2:28–32), an event that happened on the day of Pentecost (Acts 2:16–21).

**JOHANAN** (a supporter of Gedaliah, governor of Judah, who took a remnant of the Jews to Egypt). **2 Kgs 25:22–23** • Jer 40:8–16; **41:11–18**; 42:1,8; 43:2–6.

**JOHN, FIRST, SECOND, AND THIRD EPISTLES OF.** Three short epistles written by John, one of the twelve disciples of Jesus. First John focuses on such themes as the incarnation of Christ (1:1–5) and the meaning of love and fellowship

(2:15–5:3). Second John calls on believers to abide in the commandments of God (vv. 1–10). Third John commends two believers and condemns a third.

**JOHN, GOSPEL OF.** One of the four Gospels, written by the apostle John to show that "Jesus is the Christ, the Son of God" (20:31). John is unique among the Gospels in that it majors on the theological meaning of the events in Jesus' life rather than the events themselves. Also unique to John's Gospel are the "I am" sayings of Jesus, in which Jesus reveals characteristics of His divine nature.

**JOHN THE APOSTLE** (a fisherman from Galilee who became one of the twelve apostles of Jesus and author of the Gospel that bears his name as well as the books of 1, 2, 3 John and Revelation). Matt 4:21; 10:2; 17:1 • Mark 1:19,29; 3:17; 5:37; 9:2,38; 10:35,41; 13:3; 14:33 • Luke 5:10; 6:14; 8:51; 9:28,49,54; 22:8 • Acts 1:13; 3:1–11; 4:13,19; 8:14; 12:2 • Gal 2:9 • Rev 1:1,4,9; 21:2.

**JOHN THE BAPTIST** (a prophet who prepared the way for Christ). Matt 3:1–14; 4:12; 9:14; 11:2–18; 14:2–10; 16:14; 17:13; 21:25–32 • Mark 1:4–14;

2:18; 6:14–29; 8:28; 11:30–32 • Luke 1:13–63; 3:2–20; 5:33; 7:18–33; 9:7–9; 11:1; 16:16; 20:4,6 • John 1:6–40; 3:23–27; 4:1; 5:33–36; 10:40–41 • Acts 1:5,22; 10:37; 11:16; 13:24–25; 19:4.

**JONAH** (a prophet swallowed by a "great fish" while fleeing from God's call to preach at Nineveh in Assyria). 2 Kgs 14:25 • Jon 1:17. *Jonas:* Luke 11:30.

**JONAH, BOOK OF.** A short prophetic book of the Old Testament that emphasizes God's universal love. Through his experience of preaching to the pagan citizens of Nineveh, Jonah learned that God is concerned for all people, not just the citizens of his native land (4:1–11).

**JONAS.** See *Jonah.*

**JONATHAN** (a loyal friend of David). 1 Sam 13:2–22; 14:1–49; 18:1–4; 19:1–7; 20:1–42; 23:16–18; 31:2 • 2 Sam 1:4–26; 4:4; 9:3–7; 21:7–14 • 1 Chr 8:33–34; 9:39–40; 10:2.

**JOPPA** (a city where Peter had his vision on full acceptance of the Gentiles). 2 Chr 2:16 • Ezra 3:7 • Jon 1:3 • Acts

9:36–43; **10:5–32;** 11:5,13. *Japho:* Josh 19:46.

**JORAM.** See *Jehoram.*

**JORDAN RIVER** (the major river of Palestine in which Jesus was baptized). Gen 13:8–13; 32:10 • Num 34:12 • Deut 3:27 • Josh 3:17; 4:1–24 • 2 Sam 17:22–24 • 2 Kgs 2:5–14; 5:10–14 • **Matt 3:6–15.**

**JOSAPHAT.** See *Jehoshaphat.*

**JOSEPH**
1. A son of Jacob, sold into slavery by his brothers, who became a high official in the Egyptian government. See **Gen 37–50** for a sketch of Joseph. Ex 1:5–8; 13:19 • Num 27:1; 32:33; 34:23; 36:12 • Deut 27:12 • Josh 14:4; 16:1,4; 17:1–16; 24:32 • Ps 105:17 • John 4:5 • Acts 7:9–18 • Heb 11:21–22.
2. The husband of Mary, Jesus' mother. Matt 1:16–24; 2:13–23 • Luke 1:27; 2:4–43; 3:23 • John 1:45; 6:42.
3. A secret disciple of Jesus who buried Jesus in his own tomb. Matt 27:57–60 • **Mark 15:43–46** • **Luke 23:50–53** • John 19:38.

**JOSES.** See *Barnabas.*

**JOSHUA** (Moses' successor who led the Israelites into the Promised Land and rallied the people to victory over the Canaanites). Ex 17:9–14; 24:13; 32:17; 33:11 • Num 11:28; 14:6–38; 26:65; 27:18–23; 32:12,28; 34:17 • Deut 1:38; 3:21,28; 31:3–23; 34:9 • **Josh 1:1–24:31** • Judg 2:6–23 • 1 Kgs 16:34. *Hoshea:* Deut 32:44. *Jehoshuah:* 1 Chr 7:27. *Jeshua:* Neh 8:17. *Oshea:* Num 13:8.

**JOSHUA, BOOK OF.** An Old Testament book that details the conquest and settlement of the land of Canaan by the Israelites under the leadership of Joshua.

**JOSIAH** (a king of Judah who led a reform movement to reestablish God's Law and abolish idolatry). 2 Kgs 22:3–9; **23:3–25.** *Josias:* Matt 1:10–11.

**JOTHAM** (a king of Judah who failed to destroy places of pagan worship). **2 Kgs 15:5–38;** 16:1 • 1 Chr 3:12; 5:17 • 2 Chr 26:21,23; 27:1–9 • Isa 1:1; 7:1 • Hos 1:1 • Mic 1:1. *Joatham:* Matt 1:9.

**JOURNEY [ED, ING, INGS]**
*Gen 12:9* Abram *j'ed,* going on still toward the south
*Ex 3:18* let us [Israelites] go … three days' *j* … that we may sacrifice to the LORD

191

*Jon 3:3* Nineveh was…great city of three days' *j*

*Luke 9:3* Take nothing for your *j,* neither staves

*Luke 10:33* Samaritan, as he *j'ed,* came where he [the wounded traveler] was

*Luke 13:22* he [Jesus] went through the cities…teaching, and *j'ing* toward Jerusalem

*Luke 15:13* younger son…took his *j* into a far country

*Acts 9:3* as he [Paul] *j'ed,* he came near Damascus

*2 Cor 11:26* In *j'ings* often, in perils of waters

## JOY

*Ps 16:11* in thy [God's] presence is fulness of *j*

*Ps 30:5* weeping may endure for a night, but *j* cometh in the morning

*Ps 43:4* Then will I go…unto God my exceeding *j*

*Ps 51:12* Restore…the *j* of thy [God's] salvation

*Ps 126:5* They that sow in tears shall reap in *j*

*Prov 15:21* Folly is *j* to him that is destitute of wisdom

*Isa 12:3* with *j*…draw water out of the wells of salvation

*Isa 52:9* Break forth into *j*…ye waste places of Jerusalem

*Lam 5:15* *j* of our heart is ceased; our dance is turned into mourning

*Hab 3:18* I will *j* in the God of my salvation

*Matt 2:10* they [wise men]…rejoiced with…great *j*

*Matt 28:8* And they [the women] departed quickly…with fear and great *j*

*Luke 2:10* bring you [shepherds] good tidings of great *j*

*Luke 15:10* *j*…over one sinner that repenteth

*John 16:20* your sorrow shall be turned into *j*

*Acts 20:24* I [Paul] might finish my course with *j*

*Rom 14:17* kingdom of God is…peace, and *j*

*Gal 5:22* fruit of the Spirit is love, *j,* peace

*Heb 12:2* who [Jesus] for the *j* that was set before him endured the cross

*Jas 1:2* count it all *j* when ye fall into divers temptations

*3 John 4* no greater *j*…children walk in truth

## JOYFUL [LY, NESS]

*Ps 35:9* my soul shall be *j* in the LORD

*Ps 66:1* Make a *j* noise unto God, all ye lands

*Ps 95:1* make a *j* noise to the rock of our salvation

*Ps 149:5* Let the saints be *j* in glory…sing aloud

*Eccl 9:9* Live *j'ly* with the wife whom thou lovest

*Isa 49:13* Sing, O heavens; and be *j,* O earth

*Luke 19:6* he [Zacchaeus]…received him [Jesus] *j'ly*

*Col 1:11* Strengthened…unto all patience…with *j'ness*

**JUBAL** (a musician regarded as the ancestor of those who play the harp and the flute). Gen 4:21.

**JUDAEA** (a district in southern Palestine in New Testament times). Matt 2:1,5,22 • Mark 1:5; 3:7 • Luke 6:17 • John 4:3,47,54 • Acts 10:37 • Rom 15:31 • 2 Cor 1:16 • Gal 1:22 • 1 Thes 2:14.

**JUDAH**
1. A son of Jacob and ancestor of one of the twelve tribes of Israel. Gen 29:35; 38:1–26; 43:3,8; 44:14–18; 46:12,28; 49:8–9 • Ex 1:2 • Num 26:19 • Ruth 4:12 • 1 Chr 2:1–10; 4:1,21,27; 5:2; 9:4 • Neh 11:24. The tribe of Judah settled in southern Canaan. Josh 15:1–12.
2. The Southern Kingdom, or nation of Judah, with Jerusalem as its capital that was overrun and taken into exile by the Babylonians. 2 Chr 36:4–20.

**JUDAS** (one of the twelve disciples of Jesus, called "brother of James" to set him apart from the disciple Judas [Iscariot] who betrayed Jesus). Luke 6:16 • John 14:22 • Acts 1:13.

*Lebbaeus:* Matt 10:3. Thaddaeus: Mark 3:18.

**JUDAS ISCARIOT.** See *Iscariot, Judas.*

**JUDE** (half brother of Jesus and author of the New Testament epistle that bears his name). Jude 1. *Judas:* Matt 13:55.

**JUDE, EPISTLE OF.** A short letter written like a brief essay or tract and addressed to the problem of false teachings in the early church.

**JUDGE [S, ST, TH]**
*Gen 18:25* Shall not the *J* of all the earth do right
*Ex 18:13* on the morrow… Moses sat to *j* the people
*Judg 2:16* LORD raised up *j's*
*1 Sam 2:10* the LORD shall *j* the ends of the earth
*1 Sam 8:6* they [the people] said, Give us a king to *j* us
*1 Kgs 3:9* Give…thy [God's] servant [Solomon] an understanding heart to *j* thy people
*Job 22:13* can he [God] *j* through the dark cloud
*Ps 7:8 j* me, O LORD, according to my righteousness
*Ps 7:11* God *j'th* the righteous
*Ps 43:1 J* me, O God, and plead my cause

*Ps 72:2* He [God] shall *j* thy people with righteousness

*Ps 75:7* God is the *j*...putteth down one...setteth up another

*Prov 31:9 j* righteously, and plead the cause of the poor

*Lam 3:59* thou [God] hast seen my wrong:*j* thou my cause

*Matt 7:1 J* not, that ye be not judged

*John 7:24 J* not according to the appearance

*John 12:48* word that I [Jesus] have spoken...shall *j* him in the last day

*Rom 14:10* But why dost thou *j* thy brother

*2 Tim 4:1* Jesus Christ, who shall *j* the quick and the dead

*2 Tim 4:8* the righteous *j,* shall give me [Paul] at that day [a crown of righteousness]

*Jas 2:4* ye...are become *j's* of evil thoughts

*Jas 4:12* one lawgiver [God]... who art thou that *j'st* another

*Rev 19:11* in righteousness he [Jesus] doth *j*

**JUDGES, BOOK OF.** A historical book of the Old Testament that records the exploits of several different judges, or military deliverers, in Israel's history.

**JUDGES OF ISRAEL** (popular military leaders or deliverers who led Israel between the time of Joshua's death and the beginning of the kingship). The judges of Israel were: Othniel (Judg 3:9–11), Ehud (Judg 3:15–30), Shamgar (Judg 3:31), Deborah and Barak (Judg 4:4–24), Gideon (Judg 6:11–8:32), Abimelech (Judg 9:1–54), Tola (Judg 10:1–2), Jair (Judg 10:3–5), Jephthah (Judg 11:1–12:7), Ibzan (Judg 12:8–10), Elon (Judg 12:11–12), Abdon (Judg 12:13–15), Samson (Judg 14:1–16:31), Eli (1 Sam 4:15–18), Samuel (1 Sam 7:15), and Samuel's sons (1 Sam 8:1–3).

**JUDGMENT**

*Ex 12:12* against all the gods of Egypt I [God]...execute *j*

*1 Chr 18:14* David reigned... and executed *j*

*Job 8:3* Doth God pervert *j*

*Job 32:9* neither do the aged understand *j*

*Ps 1:5* the ungodly shall not stand in the *j*

*Ps 72:2* He [God] shall judge... thy poor with *j*

*Ps 101:1* I will sing of mercy and *j:* unto thee [God]

*Ps 119:66* Teach me good *j* and knowledge

*Prov 21:3* To do justice and *j* is more acceptable to the LORD than sacrifice

*Prov 29:26* every man's *j* cometh from the LORD

*Eccl 12:14* God shall bring every work into *j*

*Isa 42:1* he [God's servant] shall bring forth *j* to the Gentiles

*Jer 9:24* I am the LORD which exercise … *j*

*Jer 33:15* he [Messiah] shall execute *j* and righteousness

*Amos 5:24* But let *j* run down as waters

*Matt 5:22* whosoever is angry with his brother … shall be in danger of the *j*

*John 5:30* as I [Jesus] hear, I judge: and my *j* is just

*John 9:39* For *j* I [Jesus] am come into this world

*Rom 14:10* we shall all stand before the *j* seat of Christ

*2 Cor 5:10* we must all appear before the *j* seat of Christ

*Heb 9:27* appointed unto men once to die, but after this the *j*

*1 Pet 4:17* *j* must begin at the house of God

*1 John 4:17* we may have boldness in the day of *j*

*Rev 14:7* Fear God … for the hour of his *j* is come

## JUDGMENT OF GOD

*Rom 2:3* thinkest thou … that thou shalt escape the *j-o-G*

*2 Thes 1:5* a manifest token of the righteous *j-o-G*

**JUPITER** (chief god of Roman mythology and a name applied to Barnabas by the citizens of Lystra). Acts 14:12.

## JUST [LY]

*Gen 6:9* Noah was a *j* man

*Job 4:17* Shall mortal man be more *j* than God

*Ps 37:12* The wicked plotteth against the *j*

*Prov 4:18* path of the *j* is as the shining light

*Prov 11:1* a *j* weight is his [God's] delight

*Prov 20:7* The *j* man walketh in his integrity

*Eccl 7:20* not a *j* man upon earth, that … sinneth not

*Isa 45:21* no God … beside me; a *j* God and a Saviour

*Mic 6:8* what doth the LORD require … but to do *j'ly*

*Hab 2:4* but the *j* shall live by his faith

*Matt 1:19* Joseph her [Mary's] husband, being a *j* man

*Luke 2:25* Simeon … was *j* and devout

*Rom 1:17* as it is written, The *j* shall live by faith

*Col 4:1* give unto your servants that which is *j*

*1 Pet 3:18* For Christ also hath once suffered for sins, the *j* for the unjust

*1 John 1:9* he [Jesus] is faithful and *j* to forgive us our sins

## JUSTICE

*Job 8:3* or doth the Almighty pervert *j*

*Ps 82:3* do *j* to the afflicted and needy

*Prov 21:3* To do *j*...is more acceptable...than sacrifice

*Jer 23:5* a King [Jesus] shall... execute judgment and *j*

## JUSTIFICATION

*Rom 4:25* Who [Jesus]...was raised again for our *j*

*Rom 5:18* by the righteousness of one [Jesus] the free gift came...unto *j* of life

## JUSTIFY [IED, IETH]

*Job 9:20* If I *j* myself, mine own mouth...condemn me

*Job 25:4* How then can man be *j'ied* with God

*Matt 12:37* by thy words thou shalt be *j'ied*

*Rom 3:24* *j'ied* freely by his [God's] grace through... Christ Jesus

*Rom 3:28* *j'ied* by faith without the deeds of the law

*Rom 5:1* being *j'ied* by faith, we have peace with God

*Rom 8:33* It is God that *j'ieth*

*1 Cor 6:11* ye are *j'ied* in the name of the Lord

*Gal 2:16* a man is not *j'ied* by the works of the law

*Titus 3:7* *j'ied* by his [God's] grace, we should be made heirs...of eternal life

*Jas 2:21* Was not Abraham our father *j'ied* by works

# -K-

**KADESH** (a wilderness region where the Israelites camped before entering Canaan). Gen 14:7; 16:14; 20:1 • Num 20:1,14, 16–22; **33:36–37** • Deut 1:46 • Judg 11:16–17 • Ps 29:8. *Kadesh-barnea:* **Num 32:8** • Josh 14:7.

**KEDAR** (a son of Ishmael and founder of an Arabic tribe). Gen 25:12–13 • Isa 21:17 • Jer 49:28–29.

**KEDESH** (one of the six cities of refuge, situated in the territory of Naphtali). Josh 20:1–7 • Judg 4:10–11 • 1 Chr 6:76.

## KEEP [ETH, ING]

*Gen 2:15* God…put him [Adam] into the garden of Eden…to *k* it

*Ex 12:14 k* it [the Passover] a feast to the LORD

*Ex 19:5 k* my [God's] covenant, then ye shall be a peculiar treasure

*Ex 20:8* Remember the sabbath day, to *k* it holy

*Ex 31:14 k* the sabbath…it is holy unto you

*Deut 5:10* showing mercy unto…them that…*k* my [God's] commandments

*Ps 17:8 K* me as the apple of the eye…hide me

*Ps 34:13 K* thy tongue from evil…thy lips from…guile

*Ps 91:11* he [God] shall…*k* thee in all thy ways

*Ps 119:4* Thou [God] hast commanded us to *k* thy precepts

*Ps 119:34* Give me understanding, and I shall *k* thy [God's] law

*Ps 119:146* save me…I shall *k* thy [God's] testimonies

*Ps 121:4* he [God] that *k'eth* Israel…neither slumber nor sleep

*Ps 127:1* except the LORD *k* the city, the watchman waketh but in vain

*Ps 141:3* Set a watch, O LORD… *k* the door of my lips

*Prov 3:1* let thine heart *k* my [God's] commandments

*Prov 4:23 K* thy heart with all diligence

*Prov 13:3* He that *k'eth* his mouth *k'eth* his life

*Prov 21:23 k'eth* his…tongue *k'eth* his soul from troubles

*Prov 29:11* fool uttereth all his mind…wise man *k'eth* it in

*Eccl 3:7* time to *k* silence, and a time to speak

*Isa 26:3* wilt *k* him…whose mind is stayed on thee [God]

*Ezek 20:19* walk in my [God's] statutes, and *k* my judgments

*Hab 2:20* let all the earth *k* silence before him [God]

*Mark 7:9* reject the command-ment...that ye [Pharisees] may *k* your own tradition

*Luke 2:8* shepherds...*k'ing* watch over their flock

*Luke 11:28* Yea rather, blessed are they that hear the word of God, and *k* it

*John 9:16* This man [Jesus] is not of God, because he *k'eth* not the sabbath

*John 14:15* If ye love me [Jesus], *k* my commandments

*John 15:10* If ye *k* my [Jesus'] commandments, ye shall abide in my love

*1 Cor 7:19* Circumcision is nothing...but the *k'ing* of the commandments

*1 Cor 9:27* But I [Paul] *k* under my body, and bring it into subjection

*1 Cor 14:28* no interpreter, let him *k* silence in the church

*Eph 4:3* *k* the unity of the Spirit in the bond of peace

*Phil 4:7* peace of God...*k* your hearts...through Christ

*2 Thes 3:3* Lord...shall stab-lish you...*k* you from evil

*2 Tim 1:12* he [Jesus] is able to *k* that...I have committed

*Jas 1:27* Pure religion...is this...to *k* himself unspotted

*Jas 2:10* *k* the whole law, and yet offend in one point, he is guilty of all

*1 John 5:3* this is the love of God...*k* his commandments

*1 John 5:21* Little children, *k* yourselves from idols

*Jude 24* unto him [Jesus] that is able to *k* you from falling

*Rev 2:26* he that...*k'eth* my [Jesus'] works...to him will I give power

## KEEP HIS COMMANDMENTS

*Deut 13:4* Ye shall walk after the LORD...and *k-h-c*

*Ps 78:7* That they might...not forget the works of God, but *k-h-c*

*Eccl 12:13* *k-h-c:* for this is the whole duty of man

*1 John 2:3* we do know that we know him, if we *k-h-c*

**KENAN** (a son of Enoch and great-grandson of Adam). 1 Chr 1:1–2. *Cainan:* Gen 5:9.

**KENITES** (a nomadic Midian-ite tribe that was friendly toward the Israelites). Gen 15:19 • Num 24:20–22 • Judg 4:11,17–22 • 1 Sam 15:6; 30:29 • 1 Chr 2:55.

**KENIZZITES** (a Canaanite tribe whose land was promised to Abraham's descendants). Gen 15:18–19.

## KEPT

*Ex 3:1* Moses *k* the flock of Jethro

*Ps 18:21* For I have *k* the ways of the LORD

*Ps 32:3* When I *k* silence, my bones waxed old

*Ps 78:56* they ... provoked ... God ... *k* not his testimonies

*Ps 119:55* I have remembered thy [God's] name ... and have *k* thy law

*Matt 19:20* these things have I *k* from my youth

*Luke 2:19* But Mary *k* all these things ... in her heart

*John 17:12* I [Jesus] *k* them [the disciples] in thy [God's] name ... none ... is lost

*Gal 3:23* before faith came, we were *k* under the law

*2 Tim 4:7* I [Paul] ... have fought a good fight ... *k* the faith

*1 Pet 1:5* *k* by the power of God through faith

**KETURAH** (a wife of Abraham whose sons were ancestors of Arabian tribes). Gen 25:1,4 • 1 Chr 1:32–33.

**KEY [S]**

*Matt 16:19* give unto thee the *k's* of the kingdom

*Rev 9:1* to him [angel] was given ... *k* of ... bottomless pit

**KIDRON** (a valley or ravine that David crossed while fleeing from his son Absalom). **2 Sam 15:23–30** • 2 Kgs 23:4–6,12 •

2 Chr 15:16; 29:16; 30:14 • Jer 31:40. *Cedron:* John 18:1.

**KILL [ED, EDST, EST, ETH]**

*Gen 37:31* they [Joseph's brothers] ... *k'ed* a kid of the goats

*Ex 2:14* intendest thou [Moses] to *k* me [Hebrew slave], as thou *k'est* the Egyptian

*Ex 20:13* Thou shalt not *k*

*Num 35:15* every one that *k'eth* any person unawares may flee

*Deut 5:17* Thou shalt not *k*

*1 Sam 2:6* The LORD *k'eth,* and maketh alive

*2 Sam 12:9* thou [David] hast *k'ed* Uriah the Hittite

*Ps 44:22* for thy [God's] sake are we *k'ed* all the day long

*Prov 21:25* The desire of the slothful *k'eth* him

*Eccl 3:3* A time to *k,* and a time to heal

*Matt 5:21* whosoever shall *k* ... in danger of the judgment

*Matt 23:37* O Jerusalem ... thou that *k'est* the prophets

*Mark 3:4* Is it lawful ... on the sabbath ... save life, or to *k*

*Mark 8:31* Son of man must suffer ... and be *k'ed*

*Mark 9:31* after ... he [Jesus] is *k'ed,* he shall rise

*Mark 12:7* *k* him [the heir] ... inheritance shall be ours

*Luke 12:4* Be not afraid of them that *k* the body

*Luke 12:5* after he hath *k'ed* hath power to cast into hell

*Luke 15:23* bring hither the fatted calf, and *k* it

*Luke 22:2* chief priests and scribes sought how they might *k* him [Jesus]

*John 10:10* thief cometh ... to *k,* and to destroy

*John 16:2* whosoever *k'eth* you will think that he doeth God service

*Acts 10:13* Peter; *k,* and eat

*Acts 12:2* he [Herod] *k'ed* James the brother of John

*Rom 8:36* For thy sake we are *k'ed* all the day long

*2 Cor 3:6* letter *k'eth,* but the spirit giveth life

*Jas 4:2* ye *k,* and desire to have, and cannot obtain

*Rev 11:7* beast ... shall overcome them [two witnesses], and *k* them

### KINGDOM [S]

*Ex 19:6* unto me [God] a *k* of priests, and an holy nation

*1 Sam 15:28* The LORD hath rent the *k* of Israel from thee [Saul] this day

*2 Sam 7:16* thine [David's] house and thy *k* shall be established for ever

*1 Kgs 4:21* And Solomon reigned over all *k's*

*1 Chr 29:11* thine is the *k,* O LORD ... thou art exalted

*Ps 22:28* the *k* is the LORD's

*Ps 68:32* Sing unto God, ye *k's* of the earth

*Ps 145:13* Thy [God's] *k* is an everlasting *k*

*Dan 2:39* after thee [Nebuchadnezzar] shall arise another *k*

*Dan 4:3* his [God's] *k* is an everlasting kingdom

*Dan 4:31* The *k* is departed from thee [Nebuchadnezzar]

*Dan 5:28* Thy [Belshazzar's] *k* is divided ... given to ... Medes

*Matt 6:10* Thy [God's] *k* come. Thy will be done

*Matt 8:12* children of the *k* ... cast ... into outer darkness

*Matt 24:7* nation shall rise against nation ... *k* against *k*

*Mark 3:24* *k* be divided against itself, that *k* cannot stand

*Luke 1:33* of his [Jesus'] *k* there shall be no end

*Luke 4:5* the devil ... showed unto him [Jesus] all the *k's* of the world

*Luke 12:32* your Father's good pleasure to give you the *k*

*Luke 23:42* remember me [thief] when thou [Jesus] comest into thy *k*

*John 18:36* My [Jesus'] *k* is not of this world

*1 Thes 2:12* God, who hath called you unto his *k*

*Rev 11:15* *k's* of this world are become the *k's* of our Lord

### KINGDOM OF GOD

*Matt 6:33* seek ye first the *k-o-G,* and his righteousness

*Mark 1:15* time is fulfilled, and the *k-o-G* is at hand

*Mark 9:47* better ... to enter into the *k-o-G* with one eye

*Mark 10:14* forbid them [children] not ... such is the *k-o-G*

*Mark 10:25* eye of a needle, than for a rich man to enter into the *k-o-G*

*Luke 9:2* he [Jesus] sent them [the disciples] ... to preach ... *k-o-G*

*Luke 9:62* No man ... looking back, is fit for the *k-o-G*

*John 3:3* Except a man be born again ... cannot see the *k-o-G*

*Rom 14:17* *k-o-G* is not meat and drink; but righteousness

*1 Cor 6:9* the unrighteous shall not inherit the *k-o-G*

*1 Cor 15:50* flesh and blood cannot inherit the *k-o-G*

**KINGDOM OF HEAVEN**

*Matt 5:10* Blessed are they which are persecuted ... their's is the *k-o-h*

*Matt 5:20* ye shall in no case enter into the *k-o-h*

*Matt 7:21* Not every one that saith unto me, Lord, Lord, shall enter into the *k-o-h*

*Matt 16:19* I [Jesus] will give ... thee ... keys of the *k-o-h*

*Matt 18:4* humble himself as this little child, the same is greatest in the *k-o-h*

*Matt 23:13* ye [scribes and Pharisees] shut up the *k-o-h* against men

**KINGS, BOOKS OF FIRST AND SECOND.** Two historical books of the Old Testament that cover a period of roughly four centuries in Jewish history— from about 970 to 587 B.C. First Kings begins with the reign of Solomon as successor to David (1 Kgs 1:1–11:43). The closing chapters of 2 Kings cover the final years of the nation of Judah before it fell to the Babylonians.

**KING'S HIGHWAY** (an important road linking Damascus and Egypt that ran through Israel). Num 20:17–21.

**KIRJATH-ARBA.** See *Hebron*.

**KIRJATH-JEARIM** (a fortified city of the Gibeonites where the ark of the covenant was kept for a time). Josh 9:17; 15:60; 18:28 • **1 Chr 13–16.** *Baalah:* Josh 15:9.

**KISHON** (a river in northern Palestine where Elijah killed the prophets of Baal). Judg 4:13 • **1 Kgs 18:40.** *Kison:* Ps 83:9.

**KISON.** See *Kishon*.

**KISS [ED]**

*Gen 50:1* Joseph ... wept upon him [Jacob], and *k'ed* him

*Ps 85:10* righteousness and peace have *k'ed* each other

*Matt 26:49* he [Judas]...said, Hail...and *k'ed* him [Jesus]

*Luke 15:20* his [prodigal son's] father...fell on his neck, and *k'ed* him

*Luke 22:48* Judas, betrayest thou the Son of man with a *k*

*2 Cor 13:12* Greet one another with an holy *k*

*1 Pet 5:14* Greet ye one another with a *k* of charity

**KITTIM.** See *Cyprus.*

**KNOCK [ED]**

*Luke 11:9 k,* and it shall be opened unto you

*Acts 12:13* as Peter *k'ed* at the door...a damsel came

*Rev 3:20* I [Jesus] stand at the door, and *k*

**KNOW THAT I AM THE LORD**

*Ex 7:5* Egyptians shall *k-t-I-a-t-L,* when I stretch forth mine hand upon Egypt

*Ezek 6:7* slain shall fall...and ye shall *k-t-I-a-t-L*

*Ezek 16:62* will establish my covenant with thee; and thou shalt *k-t-I-a-t-L*

*Ezek 30:19* will I execute judgments in Egypt: and they shall *k-t-I-a-t-L*

**KNOW THE LORD**

*Jer 31:34* they shall teach no more...*K-t-L:* for they shall all know me

*Heb 8:11* not teach...his brother, saying, *K-t-L:* for all shall know me

**KNOWLEDGE**

*Gen 2:17* tree of the *k* of good and evil, thou shalt not eat

*1 Sam 2:3* for the LORD is a God of *k,* and by him actions are weighed

*Job 21:22* Shall any teach God *k?* seeing he judgeth

*Job 35:16* he [Job] multiplieth words without *k*

*Ps 19:2* night unto night showeth *k*

*Ps 139:6* Such *k* is too wonderful for me

*Ps 144:3* what is man, that thou [God] takest *k* of him

*Prov 1:7* fear of the LORD is the beginning of *k*

*Prov 10:14* Wise men lay up *k:* but the mouth of the foolish is near destruction

*Prov 20:15* the lips of *k* are a precious jewel

*Prov 24:5* a man of *k* increaseth strength

*Eccl 1:18* he that increaseth *k* increaseth sorrow

*Hos 6:6* I [God] desired...*k* of God more than...offerings

*Hab 2:14* earth...filled with the *k* of the glory of the LORD

*Rom 11:33* depth of the riches... wisdom and *k* of God

*1 Cor 12:8* to one is given... word of wisdom: to another... word of *k*

*1 Cor 13:2* though I [Paul]…
understand…all *k*

*Eph 3:19* know the love of
Christ, which passeth *k*

*Phil 1:9* love may abound…in
*k* and in all judgment

*1 Tim 2:4* all men…to come
unto the *k* of the truth

*2 Tim 3:7* never able to come to
the *k* of the truth

*2 Pet 1:5* add to your faith
virtue; and to virtue *k*

*2 Pet 3:18* grow in grace, and in
the *k* of our Lord

**KOHATH** (a son of Levi and
founder of the Kohathites,
priests who cared for the tabernacle accessories). Gen 46:11 •
Ex 6:18–19 • Num 3:30–31.

**KORAH** (leader of a rebellion
against Moses in the wilderness). Ex 6:21,24 • Num
16:30–33. *Core:* Jude 11.

# -L-

**LABAN** (father of Leah and Rachel, who were given in marriage to Jacob). Gen 24:29, 50; 29:5–29; 30:25–40; 31:2–55.

## LABOUR [ED, ETH, S]
*Ex 20:9* Six days shalt thou *l*, and do all thy work

*Ps 104:23* Man goeth forth…to his *l* until the evening

*Ps 127:1* Except the LORD build the house, they *l* in vain that build it

*Prov 23:4* *L* not to be rich

*Eccl 3:9* What profit hath he… wherein he *l'eth*

*Eccl 3:13* man should…enjoy the good of all his *l*

*Matt 11:28* Come unto me [Jesus], all ye that *l* and are heavy laden

*1 Cor 3:8* his own reward according to his own *l*

*1 Cor 15:58* your *l* is not in vain in the Lord

*2 Cor 11:23* in *l's*…abundant, in stripes above measure

*Phil 2:16* I [Paul] have not… *l'ed* in vain

*Heb 4:11* Let us *l* therefore to enter into that rest

## LABOURER [S]
*Matt 9:37* The harvest…is plenteous, but the *l's* are few

*Luke 10:7* for the *l* is worthy of his hire

*1 Cor 3:9* For we are *l's* together with God

**LACHISH** (an Amorite city captured by Joshua). **Josh 10:3–35;** 12:11; 15:39 • 2 Kgs 14:19; 18:14–17 • 2 Chr 25:27 • Neh 11:30 • Isa 36:1–2 • Jer 34:1,7.

## LACK [ED, EST]
*Gen 18:28* wilt thou [God] destroy all the city for *l* of five

*Hos 4:6* people are destroyed for *l* of knowledge

*Matt 19:20* these things have I kept…what *l* I yet

*Luke 18:22* *l'est* thou one thing: sell all…distribute unto the poor

*Luke 22:35* When I [Jesus] sent you [the disciples] without purse…*l'ed* ye any thing

*Jas 1:5* any of you *l* wisdom, let him ask of God

**LAISH.** See *Dan,* No. 2.

## LAMB OF GOD
*John 1:29* the *L-o-G*…taketh away the sin of the world

*John 1:36* he [John the Baptist] saith, Behold the *L-o-G*

## LAME
*Prov 26:7* The legs of the *l* are not equal

*Luke 7:22* tell John…how that the blind see, the *l* walk

*Luke 14:13* call the poor...the *l,* the blind

**LAMECH** (father of Noah). **Gen 5:25–31** • 1 Chr 1:3 • Luke 3:36.

**LAMENTATIONS, BOOK OF.** A short book of the Old Testament that expresses the prophet Jeremiah's grief at the destruction of Jerusalem and the temple by the pagan Babylonians.

**LAMP [S]**

*Judg 7:20* brake the pitchers... held the *l's* in their...hands
*2 Sam 22:29* For thou art my *l,* O LORD
*Job 41:19* Out of his [God's] mouth go burning *l's*
*Ps 119:105* Thy [God's] word is a *l* unto my feet
*Matt 25:3* foolish took their *l's,* and took no oil

**LAODICEA** (a major city in Asia Minor where one of the seven churches addressed in the Book of Revelation was located). Col 2:1; 4:13–16 • **Rev 3:14–18.**

**LASCIVIOUSNESS**

*Gal 5:19* works of the flesh are...Adultery...*l*
*Jude 4* certain men...turning the grace of our God into *l*

**LAST**

*Prov 23:32* At the *l* it [wine] biteth like a serpent
*Isa 2:2* in the *l* days...LORD'S house shall be established
*Isa 44:6* I [God] am the first, and I am the *l*
*Matt 20:8* give them [the laborers] their hire...from the *l* unto the first
*Mark 9:35* desire to be first, the same shall be *l*
*Mark 10:31* many that are first shall be *l*
*1 Cor 15:26* The *l* enemy... destroyed is death
*1 Cor 15:45* the *l* Adam was made a quickening spirit
*2 Tim 3:1* in the *l* days perilous times shall come
*Heb 1:2* Hath in these *l* days spoken...by his [God's] Son
*Rev 1:11* I [Jesus] am Alpha and Omega, the first and the *l*
*Rev 22:13* I [Jesus] am...the first and the *l*

**LAWFUL [LY]**

*Matt 12:2* thy [Jesus'] disciples do that which is not *l*... upon the sabbath day
*Matt 19:3* Is it *l* for a man to put away his wife
*Mark 3:4* Is it *l* to do good on the sabbath...or...evil
*Mark 12:14* Is it *l* to give tribute to Caesar
*1 Cor 6:12* All things are *l* unto me [Paul], but all things are not expedient

*1 Tim 1:8* the law is good, if a man use it *l'ly*

**LAWLESS**
*1 Tim 1:9* law is…made…for the *l* and disobedient

**LAY [ETH, ING]**
*Ps 71:10* they that *l* wait for my soul take counsel
*Prov 10:14* Wise men *l* up knowledge
*Isa 28:16* I [God] *l* in Zion for a foundation…a tried stone
*Jer 6:21* Behold, I [God] will *l* stumblingblocks before this people
*Ezek 25:17* know that I am the LORD, when I shall *l* my vengeance upon them
*Matt 6:20* *l* up for yourselves treasures in heaven
*Matt 28:6* Come, see the place where the Lord *l*
*Luke 9:58* Son of man hath not where to *l* his head
*Luke 12:21* he that *l'eth* up treasure…not rich toward God
*Luke 21:12* *l* their hands on you [the disciples], and persecute you
*John 10:15* I [Jesus] *l* down my life for the sheep
*John 13:37* Peter said…Lord… I will *l* down my life for thy [Jesus'] sake
*John 15:13* that a man *l* down his life for his friends

*1 Cor 3:11* can no man *l* than that is laid…Jesus Christ
*1 Cor 16:2* *l* by him in store, as God hath prospered
*1 Tim 4:14* with the *l'ing* on of the hands of the presbytery
*1 Tim 5:22* *L* hands suddenly on no man
*Heb 12:1* *l* aside…the sin which doth…beset us
*1 Pet 2:1* *l'ing* aside all malice, and all guile

**LAZARUS** (the brother of Mary and Martha whom Jesus raised from the dead). **John 11:1–44; 12:1–11.**

**LEAD [ETH]**
*Ex 13:21* LORD went before them [Israelites]…to *l* them
*Ps 23:2* he [God] *l'eth* me beside the still waters
*Ps 25:5* *L* me in thy [God's] truth, and teach me
*Ps 61:2* *l* me to the rock that is higher than I
*Ps 139:10* Even there shall thy [God's] hand *l* me
*Isa 11:6* and a little child shall *l* them
*Isa 40:11* He [God]…shall gently *l* those…with young
*Matt 6:13* *l* us not into temptation…deliver us from evil
*Matt 7:14* narrow is the way, which *l'eth* unto life
*Luke 6:39* he [Jesus] spake a parable…Can…blind *l*… blind

207

*Rev 7:17* Lamb...shall *l* them unto living...waters

**LEAH** (a wife of Jacob who gave birth to several of his children). **Gen 29:16–35; 30:9–20;** 31:4,14; 33:1–7; 34:1; 35:23; 46:15,18; 49:31.

**LEARN [ED, ING]**

*Ps 119:73* understanding, that I may *l* thy [God's] commandments

*Prov 1:5* A wise man...will increase *l'ing*

*Isa 1:17* **L** to do well...relieve the oppressed

*Jer 10:2* Thus saith the LORD, **L** not the way of the heathen

*Dan 1:17* God gave them [Daniel and his friends]...skill in all *l'ing* and wisdom

*Matt 11:29* Take my [Jesus'] yoke...and *l* of me

*Phil 4:11* I [Paul] have *l'ed,* in whatsoever state I am, therewith to be content

*2 Tim 3:7* *l'ing,* and never able to come to the...truth

*Heb 5:8* Though he [Jesus] were a Son, yet *l'ed* he obedience

**LEAST**

*Matt 2:6* Bethlehem, in the land of Juda, art not the *l* among the princes of Juda

*Matt 25:40* as ye have done it unto one of the *l* of these my [Jesus'] brethren

*Luke 7:28* he that is *l* in the kingdom...is greater than he [John the Baptist]

*Luke 9:48* *l* among you all, the same shall be great

*Eph 3:8* Unto me [Paul], who am less than the *l* of all saints

**LEAVEN**

*Matt 13:33* kingdom of heaven is like unto *l*

*Luke 12:1* Beware ye of the *l* of the Pharisees

*1 Cor 5:6* a little *l* leaveneth the whole lump

**LEBANON** (a rugged mountainous region in northern Palestine). Deut 1:7; 3:25 • Josh 11:16–17; 12:7; 13:5–7 • Judg 3:1–3 • 1 Kgs 5:5–18 • Isa 29:17; 37:24 • Ezek 17:3 • Hos 14:5–7.

**LEBBAEUS.** See *Judas.*

**LED**

*Ps 68:18* Thou hast ascended on high...*l* captivity captive

*Prov 4:11* I have taught thee... *l* thee in right paths

*Isa 55:12* go out with joy, and be *l* forth with peace

*Luke 4:1* Jesus...was *l* by the Spirit into the wilderness

*Luke 24:50* he [Jesus] *l* them out as far as to Bethany

*Acts 8:32* He [Jesus] was *l* as a sheep to the slaughter

*Acts 9:8 l* him [Paul] by the hand…into Damascus

*Rom 8:14 l* by the Spirit of God…are the sons of God

*Gal 5:18* if ye be *l* of the Spirit… not under the law

*2 Pet 3:17* lest ye also, being *l* away with the error of the wicked, fall

**LEHI** (a site where Samson killed one thousand Philistines). Judg 15:9–15.

**LEMUEL** (an unknown king mentioned in the Book of Proverbs). Prov 31:1–31.

**LEPER [S]**

*2 Kgs 5:1* Naaman…was also a mighty man…but he was a *l*

*2 Kgs 15:5* the king [Azariah]… was a *l* unto…his death

*Matt 8:2* there came a *l* and worshipped him [Jesus]

*Matt 11:5 l's* are cleansed, and the deaf hear

*Mark 14:3* in…house of Simon the *l,* as he [Jesus] sat at meat

*Luke 17:12* there met him [Jesus] ten men that were *l's*

**LEVI**

1. A son of Jacob and ancestor of the Levites. Gen 29:34; 34:25,30; 35:23; 49:5 • Ex 1:2; 6:16 • Num 3:17; 16:1; 26:59 • 1 Chr 6:38,43,47 • Ezra 8:18.

The tribe of Levi, known as the Levites, were responsible for taking care of the tabernacle and temple and assisting the priests in their ceremonial duties. Num 3:5–8.

2. Another name for Matthew. See *Matthew.*

**LEVITICUS, BOOK OF.** An Old Testament book filled with instructions about sanctification of the priests, regulations for worship and ceremonial offerings, and personal purification and dietary laws. The theme of the book is holiness.

**LIAR [S]**

*Ps 116:11* I said in my haste, All men are *l's*

*Prov 19:22* a poor man is better than a *l*

*Rom 3:4* let God be true, but every man a *l*

*Titus 1:12* The Cretians are alway *l's,* evil beasts

*1 John 1:10* that we have not sinned…make him [God] a *l*

*1 John 4:20* say, I love God… hateth his brother, he is a *l*

**LIBERTY**

*Lev 25:10* hallow the fiftieth year, and proclaim *l*

*Ps 119:45* walk at *l:* for I seek thy [God's] precepts

*Isa 61:1* sent me [God's servant]…to proclaim *l* to the captives

*Luke 4:18* to set at *l* them that are bruised

*Acts 26:32* This man [Paul] might have been set at *l*

*1 Cor 8:9* lest…this *l* of your's become a stumblingblock

*2 Cor 3:17* where the Spirit of the Lord is, there is *l*

*Gal 5:1* Stand fast therefore in the *l* wherewith Christ hath made us free

*2 Pet 2:19* While they promise them *l,* they…are the servants of corruption

**LIBYA** (Greek name for Africa). Jer 46:9 • Ezek 30:5; 38:5 • Dan 11:43 • Acts 2:10. *Lubim:* Nah 3:9. *Phut:* Ezek 27:10.

**LIE [S, ST, TH]**

*Lev 19:11* not steal…neither *l* one to another

*Num 23:19* God is not a man, that he should *l*

*Job 13:4* forgers of *l's*…physicians of no value

*Ps 23:2* He [God] maketh me to *l* down in green pastures

*Ps 58:3* the wicked…go astray…speaking *l's*

*Ps 62:9* men of high degree are a *l:* to be laid in the balance

*Prov 3:24* When thou *l'st* down, thou shalt not be afraid… sleep shall be sweet

*Prov 14:5* A faithful witness will not *l*

*Prov 14:25* but a deceitful witness speaketh *l's*

*Isa 11:6* and the leopard shall *l* down with the kid

*Ezek 34:15* I [God] will feed my flock, and I will cause them to *l* down

*Nah 3:1* Woe to the bloody city…full of *l's* and robbery

*Zeph 3:13* remnant of Israel shall not…speak *l's*

*Mark 5:23* My [Jairus's]… daughter *l'th* at the point of death

*Acts 5:3* Ananias, why hath Satan filled thine heart to *l*

*Rom 1:25* changed the truth of God into a *l*

*Rom 12:18* as much as *l'th* in you, live peaceably

*1 John 1:6* say that we have fellowship with him [God], and walk in darkness, we *l*

**LIFE**

*Gen 2:7* And the LORD God… breathed into his [man's] nostrils the breath of *l*

*Deut 19:21* *l* shall go for *l,* eye for eye, tooth for tooth

*Josh 1:5* not any man…stand before thee [Joshua] all the days of thy *l*

*Job 2:6* he [Job] is in thine [Satan's] hand; but save his *l*

*Job 36:6* He [God] preserveth not the *l* of the wicked

*Ps 23:6* mercy shall follow me all the days of my *l*

*Ps 27:1* L\ORD\ is the strength of my *l;* of whom ... be afraid

*Ps 31:10* *l* is spent with grief, and my years with sighing

*Ps 38:12* They ... that seek after my *l* lay snares for me

*Prov 4:23* Keep thy heart ... for out of it are the issues of *l*

*Prov 8:35* For whoso findeth me findeth *l*

*Prov 18:21* Death and *l* are in the ... tongue

*Jer 21:8* I [God] set before you ... *l,* and ... death

*Matt 6:25* no thought for your *l,* what ye shall eat

*Matt 19:16* what good thing shall I do ... have eternal *l*

*Matt 20:28* Even as the Son of man came ... to give his *l* a ransom for many

*Mark 8:35* whosoever will save his *l* shall lose it

*Luke 12:15* man's *l* consisteth not in the abundance of the things ... he possesseth

*John 1:4* In him [Jesus] was *l* ... the light of men

*John 3:15* whosoever believeth ... have eternal *l*

*John 3:36* He that believeth on the Son hath everlasting *l*

*John 6:35* I [Jesus] am the bread of *l*

*John 6:47* He that believeth on me [Jesus] hath everlasting *l*

*John 10:10* I [Jesus] am come that they might have *l*

*John 10:15* and I [Jesus] lay down my *l* for the sheep

*John 11:25* I [Jesus] am the resurrection, and the *l*

*John 14:6* I [Jesus] am the way, the truth, and the *l*

*John 15:13* that a man lay down his *l* for his friends

*Rom 6:23* gift of God is eternal *l* through Jesus Christ

*Rom 8:38* death, nor *l,* nor angels, nor principalities

*1 Cor 15:19* in this *l* only we have hope in Christ, we are ... most miserable

*Phil 2:16* Holding forth the word of *l*

*Jas 4:14* what is your *l?* It is even a vapour, that ... vanisheth away

*1 John 2:25* this is the promise ... even eternal *l*

*1 John 3:14* passed from death unto *l* ... we love the brethren

*1 John 5:12* He that hath the Son hath *l*

*Rev 20:15* not found written in the book of *l* was cast into the lake of fire

*Rev 22:17* let him take the water of *l* freely

## LIGHT [S]

*Gen 1:3* God said, Let there be *l:* and there was *l*

*Gen 1:16* two great *l's;* the greater *l* to rule the day

*Ps 27:1* The L\ORD\ is my *l* and my salvation

*Ps 119:105* Thy [God's] word is ... a *l* unto my path

*Prov 4:18* path of the just is as the shining *l*

*Isa 2:5* come ye, and let us walk in the *l* of the LORD

*Isa 9:2* people…in darkness have seen a great *l*

*Isa 60:1* Arise, shine; for thy *l* is come

*Isa 60:3* Gentiles shall come to thy [God's] *l*

*Amos 5:18* day of the LORD is darkness, and not *l*

*Matt 5:14* Ye are the *l* of the world

*Matt 11:30* my [Jesus'] yoke is easy, and my burden is *l*

*Luke 2:32* A *l* to lighten the Gentiles…glory of…Israel

*Luke 16:8* children of this world are…wiser than the children of *l*

*John 1:4* In him [Jesus] was life…life was the *l* of men

*John 1:9* That was the true *L* [Jesus]

*John 8:12* I [Jesus] am the *l* of the world

*Acts 9:3* shined round about him [Paul] a *l* from heaven

*Acts 13:47* set thee [Paul] to be a *l* of the Gentiles

*Acts 26:18* turn them from darkness to *l*

*Rom 13:12* and let us put on the armour of *l*

*Phil 2:15* midst of…perverse nation…ye shine as *l's*

*Jas 1:17* Every good gift…is… from the Father of *l's*

*1 Pet 2:9* who [Jesus] hath called you…into his marvellous *l*

*1 John 1:5* God is *l,* and in him is no darkness

*1 John 2:10* He that loveth his brother abideth in the *l*

## LIGHT OF THE WORLD, JESUS AS. See *"I Am" Statements of Jesus.*

## LIKENESS

*Gen 1:26* make man in our image, after our *l*

*Ezek 10:10* four had one *l,* as if a wheel had been in the midst of a wheel

*Phil 2:7* took upon him [Jesus]…form of a servant… made in the *l* of men

## LIVE [ING, S, TH]

*Gen 2:7* and man became a *l'ing* soul

*Gen 45:7* God sent me [Joseph]…to save your *l's*

*Deut 8:3* that man doth not *l* by bread only

*Job 14:14* If a man die, shall he *l* again

*Job 19:25* I [Job] know that my redeemer *l'th*

*Ps 63:4* Thus will I bless thee [God] while I *l*

*Ps 142:5* Thou [God] art my refuge and my portion in the land of the *l'ing*

*Jer 2:13* forsaken me [God] the fountain of *l'ing* waters

*Ezek 37:3* Son of man, can these bones *l*

*Dan 6:26* men tremble and fear before the God of Daniel... the *l'ing* God

*Jon 4:3* better for me [Jonah] to die than to *l*

*Hab 2:4* but the just shall *l* by his faith

*Matt 4:4* Man shall not *l* by bread alone

*Mark 12:27* not the God of the dead, but... of the *l'ing*

*Mark 12:44* she [a widow]... cast in... all her *l'ing*

*Luke 9:56* Son of man is not come to destroy men's *l's,* but to save them

*Luke 15:13* younger son... wasted his substance with riotous *l'ing*

*Luke 24:5* Why seek... the *l'ing* among the dead

*John 4:10* he [Jesus] would have given... *l'ing* water

*John 6:51* I [Jesus] am the *l'ing* bread

*John 11:25* believeth in me [Jesus], though he were dead, yet shall he *l*

*John 11:26* *l'th* ... in me [Jesus] shall never die

*Acts 17:28* in him [Jesus] we *l,* and move... have our being

*Rom 12:1* present your bodies a *l'ing* sacrifice

*Rom 12:18* If it be possible... *l* peaceably with all men

*Rom 14:7* none... *l'th* to himself... no man dieth to himself

*Rom 14:8* whether we *l*... or die, we are the Lord's

*1 Cor 9:14* preach the gospel should *l* of the gospel

*Gal 2:14* why compellest thou [Peter] the Gentiles to *l* as do the Jews

*Gal 2:19* I [Paul]... am dead to the law... might *l* unto God

*Gal 2:20* I [Paul] *l;* yet not I, but Christ *l'th* in me

*Gal 5:25* *l* in the Spirit, let us also walk in the Spirit

*Phil 1:21* to me [Paul] to *l* is Christ, and to die is gain

*1 John 3:16* we ought to lay down our *l's* for the brethren

*1 John 4:9* God sent his... Son... we might *l* through him

*Rev 1:18* I am he [Jesus] that *l'th,* and was dead

## LIVELY

*Ps 38:19* mine enemies are *l,* and they are strong

*1 Pet 1:3* a *l* hope by the resurrection of Jesus Christ

*1 Pet 2:5* Ye also, as *l* stones, are built up a spiritual house

## LIVING GOD

*Josh 3:10* ye shall know that the *l-G* is among you

*Ps 42:2* My soul thirsteth for God, for the *l-G*

*Jer 10:10* he [God] is the *l-G,* and an everlasting king

*Dan 6:20* O Daniel, servant of the *l-G*

213

*Matt 16:16* Peter...said, Thou art the Christ...Son of the *l-G*

*John 6:69* we [the disciples] believe and are sure...thou art...the Son of the *l-G*

*2 Cor 6:16* for ye are the temple of the *l-G*

*1 Tim 3:15* church of the *l-G,* the...ground of the truth

*Heb 10:31* a fearful thing to fall into the hands of the *l-G*

**LO-AMMI** (a symbolic name for Hosea's son, meaning "not my people," and signifying God's rejection of Israel). Hos 1:8–9.

**LOD.** See *Lydda.*

**LONGSUFFERING**

*Ps 86:15* But thou, O Lord, art...gracious, *l*

*Gal 5:22* fruit of the Spirit is love...*l,* gentleness

*2 Pet 3:9* Lord is...*l* to us-ward, not willing that any should perish

**LORD IS GOOD**

*Ps 34:8* O taste and see that the *L-i-g*

*Ps 100:5* the *L-i-g;* his mercy is everlasting

*Lam 3:25* The *L-i-g* unto them that wait for him

*Nah 1:7* The *L-i-g,* a strong hold in the day of trouble

**LORD WAS WITH HIM**

*Gen 39:3* his [Joseph's] master saw that the *L-w-w-h*

*1 Sam 3:19* Samuel grew, and the *L-w-w-h*

*1 Sam 18:12* Saul was afraid of David, because the *L-w-w-h*

*1 Sam 18:14* David behaved himself wisely...the *L-w-w-h*

*2 Kgs 18:7* the *L-w-w-h;* and he [Hezekiah] prospered

*1 Chr 9:20* Phinehas...was the ruler...and the *L-w-w-h*

*Luke 1:66* hand of the *L-w-w-h* [John the Baptist]

**LORD'S PRAYER.** Matt 6:9–13 • Luke 11:1–4.

**LORD'S SUPPER.** Matt 26:26–30 • Mark 14:22–26 • Luke 22:14–20 • 1 Cor 11:17–34.

**LO-RUHAMAH** (a symbolic name for Hosea's daughter, meaning "unloved," and expressing God's displeasure with Israel). Hos 1:6.

**LOSE [TH]**

*Eccl 3:6* A time to get, and a time to *l*

*Matt 10:39* *l'th* his life for my [Jesus'] sake shall find it

*Mark 8:36* gain the whole world, and *l* his own soul

*Luke 17:33* Whosoever shall... save his life shall *l* it

## LOSS

*Acts 27:22* no *l* of any man's life … but of the ship

*1 Cor 3:15* man's work shall be burned, he shall suffer *l*

*Phil 3:7* what things were gain to me [Paul] … I counted *l*

## LOST

*Ps 119:176* I have gone astray like a *l* sheep

*Matt 15:24* I [Jesus] am not sent but unto the *l* sheep of the house of Israel

*Luke 15:6* I have found my sheep which was *l*

*Luke 19:10* For the Son of man is come to seek and to save that which was *l*

*John 17:12* I [Jesus] have kept, and none of them [the disciples] is *l*

## LOT (Abraham's nephew who escaped the destruction of Sodom). Gen 11:27,31; 12:4–5; 13:1–14; 14:12–16; **19:1–29** • Deut 2:9,19 • Ps 83:8 • Luke 17:28–29 • 2 Pet 2:7.

## LOT'S WIFE TURNED INTO A PILLAR OF SALT. Gen 19:26.

## LOVE [D, ING, LY, ST, TH]

*Gen 29:20* unto him [Jacob] but a few days, for the *l* he had to her [Rachel]

*Gen 37:3* Israel *l'd* Joseph more than all his children

*Lev 19:18* *l* thy neighbour as thyself: I am the LORD

*Deut 6:5* *l* the LORD thy God with all thine heart

*Josh 23:11* Take good heed … that ye *l* the LORD your God

*Job 19:19* they whom I [Job] *l'd* are turned against me

*Ps 87:2* The LORD *l'th* the gates of Zion

*Ps 116:1* I *l* the LORD, because he hath heard my voice

*Ps 119:97* O how *l* I thy [God's] law

*Prov 3:12* whom the LORD *l'th* he correcteth

*Prov 7:18* take our fill of *l* until the morning

*Prov 10:12* Hatred stirreth up strifes: but *l* covereth all sins

*Prov 17:17* A friend *l'th* at all times

*Prov 22:1* good name … to be chosen than great riches … *l'ing* favour rather than silver

*Eccl 3:8* A time to *l,* and a time to hate

*Eccl 9:9* Live joyfully with the wife whom thou *l'st*

*Song 2:4* his [God's] banner over me was *l*

*Song 8:7* Many waters cannot quench *l*

*Jer 31:3* I [God] have *l'd* thee with an everlasting *l*

*Hos 11:4* I [God] drew them with … bands of *l*

*Mic 6:8* what doth the LORD require … but to … *l* mercy

*Matt 5:44* **L** your enemies, bless them that curse you

*Matt 10:37* **l'th** father or mother more than me [Jesus] is not worthy of me

*Matt 22:39* Thou shalt *l* thy neighbour as thyself

*Luke 16:13* he will hate the one, and *l* the other

*John 3:16* God so *l'd* the world...gave his only...Son

*John 13:34* *l* one another; as I [Jesus] have *l'd* you

*John 14:15* If ye *l* me [Jesus], keep my commandments

*John 15:9* Father hath *l'd* me [Jesus], so have I *l'd* you

*John 21:15* Simon...*l'st* thou me [Jesus] more than these

*Rom 5:8* God commendeth his *l* toward us

*Rom 8:28* we know that all things work together for good to them that *l* God

*Rom 8:37* we are more than conquerors through him [Jesus] that *l'd* us

*1 Cor 2:9* the things which God hath prepared for them that *l* him

*2 Cor 5:14* the *l* of Christ constraineth us

*2 Cor 9:7* for God *l'th* a cheerful giver

*Gal 2:20* live by...faith of...Son of God, who *l'd* me [Paul]

*Gal 5:22* But the fruit of the Spirit is *l,* joy, peace

*Eph 3:19* *l* of Christ, which passeth knowledge

*Eph 4:15* speaking the truth in *l*...grow up into him [Jesus]

*Eph 5:2* walk in *l,* as Christ also hath *l'd* us

*Eph 5:25* Husbands, *l* your wives, even as Christ also *l'd* the church

*Phil 1:9* that your *l* may abound yet more and more

*Phil 4:8* whatsoever things are *l'ly*...of good report

*1 Tim 6:10* *l* of money is the root of all evil

*2 Tim 1:7* God hath not given us the spirit of fear; but ... *l*

*Heb 12:6* whom the Lord *l'th* he chasteneth

*Jas 1:12* receive the crown of life...promised to them that *l* him [Jesus]

*1 John 2:10* He that *l'th* his brother abideth in the light

*1 John 2:15* any man *l* the world, the *l* of the Father is not in him

*1 John 3:14* He that *l'th* not his brother abideth in death

*1 John 4:7* every one that *l'th* is born of God

*1 John 4:10* not that we *l'd* God, but that he *l'd* us

*1 John 4:16* he that dwelleth in *l* dwelleth in God

*1 John 4:19* We *l* him [Jesus], because he first *l'd* us

*1 John 4:20* how can he *l* God whom he hath not seen

*1 John 5:3* this is the *l* of God...
keep his commandments

*Rev 2:4* thou [the church at
Ephesus] hast left thy first *l*

## LOVE CHAPTER OF THE BIBLE. 1 Cor 13.

## LOVE OF GOD

*Rom 5:5* the *l-o-G* is shed
abroad in our hearts

*Rom 8:39* height, nor depth...
shall...separate us from
the *l-o-G*...in Christ

*1 John 3:16* perceive we the
*l-o-G*, because he [Jesus]
laid down his life for us

*1 John 4:9* In this [God's Son]
was manifested the *l-o-G*
toward us

## LOVE ONE ANOTHER

*John 13:34* That ye *l-o-a;* as I
[Jesus] have loved you

*Rom 13:8* Owe no man any
thing, but to *l-o-a*

*1 John 3:11* the message...ye
heard...we should *l-o-a*

*1 John 4:7* Beloved, let us *l-o-a:*
for love is of God

## LOVE THY NEIGHBOUR

*Matt 5:43* it hath been said,
Thou shalt *l-t-n,* and hate
thine enemy

*Matt 19:19* Thou shalt *l-t-n* as
thyself

*Matt 22:39* second is like unto
it, Thou shalt *l-t-n* as thyself

*Mark 12:31* *l-t-n* as thyself.
There is none other com-
mandment greater

*Rom 13:9* any other commandment...namely, Thou shalt
*l-t-n* as thyself

*Gal 5:14* all the law is fulfilled
in one word... *l-t-n* as thyself

*Jas 2:8* fulfil the royal law...
Thou shalt *l-t-n* as thyself

## LOVINGKINDNESS

*Ps 36:7* How excellent is thy *l,*
O God

*Ps 63:3* thy [God's] *l* is better
than life, my lips...praise
thee

*Ps 92:2* To show forth thy
[God's] *l* in the morning

*Jer 9:24* I am the LORD which
exercise *l,* judgment

**LUBIM.** See *Libya.*

**LUCAS.** See *Luke.*

**LUCIFER.** See *Satan.*

**LUDIM** (a people descended
from Mizraim, a son of Ham).
Gen 10:13 • 1 Chr 1:11.

**LUKE** (a believer of Gentile
descent, apparently a physician, who accompanied Paul on
some of his missionary jour-
neys and author of the Gospel
that bears his name, as well as
the Book of Acts). Col 4:14 •
2 Tim 4:11. *Lucas:* Phlm 24.

**LUKE, GOSPEL OF.** One of the four Gospels which portrays Jesus as the Savior of all people, Gentiles as well as Jews. Luke shows that Jesus associated with all types of people, including sinners (5:30; 15:2), the poor and outcasts (6:20–23; 16:19–31), and the Samaritans (17:11–19).

**LUST [S]**

*Matt 5:28* whosoever looketh on a woman to *l* after her

*Mark 4:19* the *l's*...entering in, choke the word

*Rom 1:24* God...gave them up to uncleanness through the *l's* of their own hearts

*Gal 5:16* Walk in the Spirit... not fulfil the *l* of the flesh

*Jas 4:3* that ye may consume it upon your *l's*

*1 John 2:16* the *l* of the eyes, and the pride of life

**LUZ.** See *Bethel*.

**LYCAONIA** (a Roman province of Asia Minor visited by Paul). Acts 14:1–6,11.

**LYCIA** (a province of Asia Minor visited by Paul). Acts 27:5.

**LYDDA** (a town where Peter healed a lame man). Acts 9:32–35. *Lod:* 1 Chr 8:12 • Ezra 2:33 • Neh 7:37; 11:35.

**LYDIA** (a businesswoman converted under Paul's ministry at Philippi). Acts 16:14–15,40.

**LYSANIAS** (governor of Abilene, a region in Syria, when John the Baptist began his ministry). Luke 3:1.

**LYSTRA** (a city in Asia Minor where Paul was stoned by unbelieving Jews). **Acts 14:6–20;** 16:1–2 • 2 Tim 3:11.

# -M-

**MACEDONIA** (a mountainous country north of Greece and the first European territory visited by the apostle Paul). **Acts 16:9–12;** 18:5; 19:21–29; 20:1–3; 27:2 • Rom 15:26 • 1 Cor 16:5 • 2 Cor 1:16; 2:13; 7:5; 8:1; 9:2–4; 11:9 • Phil 4:15 • 1 Thes 1:7–8; 4:10 • 1 Tim 1:3.

**MACHIR** (son of Manasseh and ancestor of the Machirites). Gen 50:23 • Num 26:29; 32:39–40 • Judg 5:14.

**MACHPELAH** (a field with a cave that Abraham bought as a burial ground). **Gen 23:7–19;** 25:9; 49:29–31; 50:13.

**MAD [NESS]**
*1 Sam 21:13* he [David] … feigned himself *m* in their hands
*Luke 6:11* they [scribes and Pharisees] were filled with *m'ness* … what they might do to Jesus
*John 10:20* He [Jesus] hath a devil, and is *m*
*Acts 26:24* Paul … much learning doth make thee *m*

**MADIAN.** See *Midian,* No. 2.

**MAGDALA** (a city near the Sea of Galilee and probably the home of Mary Magdalene). Matt 15:39; 27:56.

**MAGNIFY [IED]**
*Josh 4:14* LORD *m'ied* Joshua in the sight of all Israel
*Job 7:17* What is man, that thou [God] shouldest *m* him
*Ps 34:3 m* the LORD with me
*Ps 40:16* The LORD be *m'ied*
*Ps 69:30* I will … *m* him [God] with thanksgiving
*Luke 1:46* Mary said, My soul doth *m* the Lord
*Phil 1:20* Christ shall be *m'ied* in my [Paul's] body

**MAHANAIM** (a sacred site where Jacob was visited by angels). **Gen 32:1–2** • Josh 13:26–30; 21:38 • 2 Sam 2:8–29; 17:24,27 • 1 Kgs 4:14 • 1 Chr 6:80.

**MAHER-SHALAL-HASH-BAZ** (a symbolic name for Isaiah's son, meaning "hasten the booty," signifying that Assyria would conquer Israel and Syria). Isa 8:1–4.

**MALACHI** (a prophet after the Exile and author of the book that bears his name). Mal 1:1.

**MALACHI, BOOK OF.** A short prophetic book of the Old Testament written after the Exile and directed against the shallow worship practices of the Jewish people.

**MALCHI-SHUA** (a son of King Saul who was killed by the Philistines at Gilboa). 1 Chr 10:2. *Melchi-shua:* 1 Sam 14:49.

**MALCHUS** (a servant whose ear was cut off by Peter). John 18:10–11.

**MALE**

*Gen 1:27 m* and female created he [God] them
*Mark 10:6* from the beginning of the creation God made them *m* and female
*Luke 2:23* Every *m* ... shall be called holy to the Lord
*Gal 3:28* neither *m* nor female ... all one in Christ Jesus

**MALICE**

*Eph 4:31* Let all bitterness, and wrath, and anger ... be put away from you, with all *m*
*Titus 3:3* living in *m* and envy
*1 Pet 2:1* Wherefore laying aside all *m,* and all guile

**MAMRE**

1. A town or district near Hebron where Abraham lived. Gen 13:18; 18:1–4; 23:17–19; 25:9; 35:27; 49:30; 50:13.

2. An Amorite supporter of Abraham. Gen 14:13,24.

**MANASSEH**

1. A son of Joseph and ancestor of one of the twelve tribes of Israel. Gen 41:51; 46:20; 48:1–20; 50:23 • Num 26:28–29; 27:1; 32:39–41; 36:1 • Deut 3:12–15 • Josh 13:31; 17:1–3 • 1 Kgs 4:13 • 1 Chr 7:14,17. *Manasses:* Rev 7:6. The tribe of Manasseh settled in central and northern Canaan on both sides of the Jordan River. Josh 17:1–17.

2. A king of Judah who encouraged pagan worship among the people. **2 Kgs 21:1–16** • 2 Chr 33:1–20.

**MANASSES.** See *Manasseh.*

**MANIFEST [ED]**

*Mark 4:22* nothing hid, which shall not be *m'ed*
*Luke 8:17* nothing is secret, that shall not be made *m*
*John 9:3* that the works of God should be made *m* in him
*1 Cor 3:13* Every man's work shall be made *m*
*2 Cor 4:10* life also of Jesus might be made *m* in our body
*1 Tim 3:16* God was *m* in the flesh, justified in the Spirit
*1 John 3:8* For this purpose the Son of God was *m'ed*
*1 John 4:9* In this [Jesus' death] ... *m'ed* the love of God
*Rev 15:4* thy [God's] judgments are made *m*

**MANKIND**

*1 Cor 6:9* unrighteous shall not inherit ... nor abusers of themselves with *m*

*Jas 3:7* every kind of beasts ... hath been tamed of *m*

**MANNA PROVIDED FOR ISRAEL IN THE WILDERNESS.** Ex 16:13–31.

**MARA** (a name, meaning "bitter," which signified Naomi's sorrow). Ruth 1:3–21.

**MARAN-ATHA** (an Aramaic phrase, meaning "come, O Lord," which expresses hope for the second coming of Jesus). 1 Cor 16:22.

**MARCUS.** See *Mark.*

**MARK** (a believer and author of the Gospel that bears his name who accompanied Paul and Barnabas on the first missionary journey as far as Perga and then returned to Jerusalem). Acts 12:12; **13:13;** 15:36–41 • 2 Tim 4:11. *Marcus:* 1 Pet 5:13.

**MARK, GOSPEL OF.** One of the four Gospels and probably the first to be written. Mark portrays Jesus as a person of action. He also emphasizes the humanity of Jesus, including incidents which reveal His dis-

appointment (8:12), anger (11:15–17), sorrow (14:34), and fatigue (4:38).

**MARRIAGE**

*Matt 22:2* a certain king, which made a *m* for his son

*Mark 12:25* neither marry, nor are given in *m*

*John 2:1* there was a *m* in Cana of Galilee

*Heb 13:4* **M** is honourable in all ... the bed undefiled

*Rev 19:9* called unto the *m* supper of the Lamb

**MARRY [IED, IETH]**

*Jer 3:14* Turn ... for I [God] am *m'ied* unto you

*Matt 5:32* shall *m* her that is divorced committeth adultery

*Mark 10:11* Whosoever ... put away his wife, and *m* another, committeth adultery

*Luke 14:20* *m'ied* a wife, and therefore I cannot come

*Luke 16:18* putteth away his wife, and *m'ieth* another, committeth adultery

*1 Cor 7:9* let them *m* ... it is better to *m* than to burn

*1 Cor 7:33* he that is *m'ied* careth for ... things ... of ... world

*1 Tim 5:14* that the younger women *m*, bear children, guide the house

**MARTHA** (the sister of Mary and Lazarus whom Jesus

rebuked because of her excessive worry about domestic duties). **Luke 10:38–42** • John 11:1–39; 12:2.

## MARVEL [LED]

*Matt 8:10* he [Jesus] *m'led*...I have not found so great faith

*Matt 8:27 m'led,* saying, What manner of man [Jesus] is this

*Matt 21:20* they [the disciples] *m'led,* saying, How soon is the fig tree withered

*Mark 6:6* he [Jesus] *m'led* because of their unbelief

*Mark 15:44* Pilate *m'led* if he [Jesus] were already dead

*Luke 2:33* Joseph and his mother *m'led* at those things...spoken of him [Jesus]

*John 3:7 M* not that I [Jesus] said...Ye [Nicodemus] must be born again

*John 7:15* Jews *m'led*...How knoweth this man [Jesus] letters

*Acts 4:13* they [religious leaders] *m'led*...they [Peter and John] had been with Jesus

*Gal 1:6* I [Paul] *m* that ye are...removed from him [Jesus] that called you

*1 John 3:13 M* not, my brethren, if the world hate you

## MARVELLOUS

*1 Chr 16:24* Declare his [God's] glory...his *m* works among all nations

*Ps 31:21* he [God] hath showed me his *m* kindness

*Ps 98:1* for he [God] hath done *m* things

*Ps 139:14* I will praise thee [God]...*m* are thy works

*1 Pet 2:9* him [Jesus] who hath called you out of darkness into his *m* light

*Rev 15:3* Great and *m* are thy works, Lord...Almighty

## MARY

1. Earthly mother of Jesus. Matt 1:16,18,20; 2:11 • Mark 6:3 • **Luke 1:26–56;** 2:5,16,19, 34 • Acts 1:14.

2. A woman, called Mary Magdalene, who witnessed the crucifixion of Jesus and visited the empty tomb. **Matt 27:56,61;** 28:1 • Mark 15:40,47; 16:9 • Luke 8:2; 24:10 • John 19:25; **20:1–18.**

3. Sister of Martha and Lazarus. Luke 10:39,42 • John 11:1–45; 12:3.

**MATHUSALA.** See *Methuselah.*

**MATTANIAH.** See *Zedekiah.*

**MATTHEW** (a tax collector who became a disciple of Jesus and author of the Gospel that bears his name). Matt 9:9; 10:3 • Mark 3:18 • Luke 6:15 • Acts 1:13. *Levi:* Mark 2:13–17 • Luke 5:27–32.

## MATTHEW, GOSPEL OF.

One of the four Gospels written to show the Jewish people that Jesus was the Messiah promised in the Old Testament. Matthew's Gospel also emphasizes the teaching ministry of Jesus, particularly His instructions to His disciples in the Sermon on the Mount (5:1–7:29).

## MATTHIAS (the person who replaced Judas as an apostle). Acts 1:15–26.

## MEASURE [D, ING, S]

*Deut 25:14* not have…divers *m's,* a great and a small

*Deut 25:15* a perfect and just *m* shalt thou have

*Job 38:5* Who hath laid the *m's* thereof, if thou knowest

*Ps 39:4* LORD, make me to know…the *m* of my days

*Isa 40:12* Who [God]…*m'd* the waters…hollow of his hand

*Ezek 40:3* a man…with a line of flax…and a *m'ing* reed

*Hos 1:10* Israel shall be as the sand of the sea…cannot be *m'd*

*Mark 4:24* with what *m* ye mete, it shall be *m'd* to you

*Luke 13:21* like leaven, which a woman took and hid in three *m's* of meal

*2 Cor 11:23* in stripes above *m,* in prisons more frequent

*Gal 1:13* beyond *m* I [Paul] persecuted the church

*Eph 4:7* grace according to the *m* of the gift of Christ

*Eph 4:13* all come…unto the *m*…of the fulness of Christ

*Rev 6:6* I [John] heard a voice… *m* of wheat for a penny

## MEDES (descendants of Japheth who founded an ancient kingdom between the Tigris River and the Caspian Sea). Gen 10:2 • 2 Kgs 17:6 • Esth 1:3,19 • Isa 13:17 • Dan 5:30–31; 6:1–28 • Acts 2:9.

## MEDIATOR

*1 Tim 2:5* one God, and one *m* between God and men

*Heb 8:6* he [Jesus] is the *m* of a better covenant

*Heb 9:15* he [Jesus] is the *m* of the new testament

## MEDITATE

*Ps 1:2* in his [God's] law doth he *m* day and night

*Ps 119:15* I will *m* in thy [God's] precepts

*Ps 143:5* I *m* on all thy [God's] works

*Luke 21:14* not to *m* before what ye shall answer

*1 Tim 4:15* *M* upon these things; give thyself…to them

## MEDITERRANEAN SEA.

See *Great Sea.*

**MEEK [NESS]**

*Num 12:3* the man Moses was very *m,* above all the men

*Ps 37:11* But the *m* shall inherit the earth

*Ps 147:6* LORD lifteth up the *m* ... casteth ... wicked down

*Isa 61:1* to preach good tidings unto the *m*

*Matt 5:5* Blessed are the *m* ... they shall inherit the earth

*Matt 11:29* I [Jesus] am *m* and lowly in heart

*Gal 5:23* *M'ness,* temperance: against such there is no law

*Gal 6:1* restore ... spirit of *m'ness* ... lest thou ... be tempted

*Col 3:12* Put on ... kindness ... *m'ness,* longsuffering

*1 Pet 3:15* be ready always to give an answer ... with *m'ness* and fear

**MEGIDDO** (a fortified city in the plain of Jezreel associated with the great battle in the end-time). Josh 12:21; 17:11 • Judg 1:27–28; 5:19–21 • 1 Kgs 4:12; 9:15–27 • 2 Kgs 23:29–30 • Rev 16:16. *Megiddon:* Zech 12:11.

**MEGIDDON.** See *Megiddo.*

**MELCHISEDEC.** See *Melchizedek.*

**MELCHI-SHUA.** See *Malchi-shua.*

**MELCHIZEDEK** (king of Salem who received tithes from Abraham). **Gen 14:18–20** • Ps 110:4. *Melchisedec:* Heb 7:11.

**MELITA** (an island where Paul was shipwrecked while sailing to Rome). Acts 28:1–8.

**MEMBER [S]**

*Job 17:7* eye ... is dim ... all my *m's* are as a shadow

*Rom 12:5* So we ... are one body in Christ, and every one *m's* one of another

*1 Cor 6:15* your bodies are the *m's* of Christ

*1 Cor 12:19* all one *m,* where were the body

*1 Cor 12:26* one *m* suffer, all the *m's* suffer

*Jas 3:5* tongue is a little *m,* and boasteth great things

**MEMORIAL SUPPER.** See *Jesus, Life and Ministry of; Lord's Supper.*

**MENAHEM** (a king of Israel who killed Shallum to assume the throne). 2 Kgs 15:14–22.

**MEPHIBOSHETH** (a son of Jonathan who was honored by King David). 2 Sam 4:4; **9:1–13;** 16:1–4; 19:24–30; 21:7. *Merib-baal:* 1 Chr 8:34.

**MERCIFUL**

*Deut 21:8* Be *m,* O LORD, unto thy people Israel

*Ps 41:4* I said, LORD, be *m* unto me: heal my soul

*Ps 67:1* God be *m* unto us, and bless us

*Ps 103:8* LORD is *m* and gracious, slow to anger

*Matt 5:7* Blessed are the *m:* for they shall obtain mercy

**MERCURIUS** (Roman name for the pagan god Mercury and the name applied to Paul by the people of Lystra). Acts 14:12.

**MERCY [IES]**

*Gen 39:21* LORD was with Joseph, and showed him *m*

*Ex 20:6* showing *m* unto ... them that love me [God]

*1 Chr 16:34* he [God] is good; for his *m* endureth for ever

*Ps 6:2* Have *m* upon me, O LORD; for I am weak

*Ps 13:5* But I have trusted in thy [God's] *m*

*Ps 23:6* *m* shall follow me all the days of my life

*Ps 25:6* Remember, O LORD, thy tender *m'ies*

*Ps 40:11* Withhold not thou thy [God's] tender *m'ies*

*Ps 85:7* Show us thy *m,* O LORD ... grant us thy salvation

*Ps 94:18* My foot slippeth; thy *m,* O LORD, held me up

*Ps 103:8* LORD is ... slow to anger, and plenteous in *m*

*Ps 103:17* *m* of the LORD is from everlasting

*Ps 119:77* Let thy [God's] tender *m'ies* come unto me

*Ps 136:1* give thanks unto the LORD ... *m* endureth for ever

*Isa 49:13* the LORD ... will have *m* upon his afflicted

*Hos 6:6* For I [God] desired *m,* and not sacrifice

*Mic 6:8* LORD require of thee, but to ... love *m*

*Matt 23:23* you [Pharisees] ... have omitted the weightier matters of the law ... *m,* and faith

*Luke 16:24* Abraham, have *m* ... and send Lazarus

*Rom 12:1* *m'ies* of God ... present your bodies a living sacrifice

*2 Cor 1:3* Father of *m'ies,* and the God of all comfort

*Eph 2:4* God, who is rich in *m* ... loved us

*Col 3:12* Put on ... bowels of *m'ies,* kindness

*Titus 3:5* according to his [God's] *m* he saved us

*Heb 4:16* obtain *m,* and find grace to help

*1 Pet 2:10* had not obtained *m,* but now have obtained *m*

*Jude 21* *m* of our Lord Jesus Christ unto eternal life

**MERIB-BAAL.** See *Mephibosheth.*

**MERODACH** (a pagan Babylonian god of war). Jer 50:2.

**MERODACH-BALADAN.** See *Berodach-baladan.*

**MERRY**

*Prov 15:13* A *m* heart maketh a cheerful countenance

*Prov 17:22* A *m* heart doeth good like a medicine

*Luke 15:23* bring...the fatted calf...let us eat, and be *m*

*Jas 5:13* Is any *m?* let him sing psalms

**MESHACH** (Daniel's friend who was thrown into the fiery furnace for refusing to worship an idol). Dan 1:7; 2:49; **3:13–30.**

**MESOPOTAMIA** (the territory between the Tigris and Euphrates rivers). Gen 24:10 • Deut 23:4 • Judg 3:8,10 • 1 Chr 19:6 • Acts 2:9; 7:2. *Padan-aram:* Gen 25:20.

**MESSENGER**

*Prov 13:17* A wicked *m* falleth into mischief

*Mal 3:1* I [God] will send my *m*...he shall prepare the way

*Luke 7:27* I send my [God's] *m* before thy face

**MESSIANIC PROPHECIES OF THE OLD TESTAMENT AND THEIR FULFILLMENT IN JESUS CHRIST**

1. Star out of Jacob (Num 24:17 • Luke 3:34)

2. Of the house of David (Isa 11:1–10 • Matt 1:1)

3. Son of man (Dan 7:13 • Mark 8:38)

4. Named Immanuel (Isa 7:14 • Matt 1:22–23)

5. Chief cornerstone (Ps 118:22 • 1 Pet 2:4,7)

6. A prophet like Moses (Deut 18:15–19 • Mark 6:14–15)

7. Bring in the new covenant (Jer 31:31–34 • Heb 12:24)

8. Call the Gentiles (Isa 11:10 • Rom 15:9–12)

9. Die for mankind's sin (Isa 53:4–6 • 1 Pet 1:18–20)

10. Born of a virgin (Isa 7:14 • Matt 1:18–25)

11. Born at Bethlehem (Mic 5:2 • Luke 2:4–7)

12. Flight into Egypt (Hos 11:1 • Matt 2:13–15)

13. Preceeded by a forerunner (Mal 3:1–2 • Mark 1:1–8)

14. Ministry of miracles (Isa 35:5–6 • Matt 11:4–5)

15. Meek and gentle (Isa 42:1–4 • Matt 12:15–21)

16. Full of wisdom and power (Isa 11:2 • Matt 3:16–17)

17. Anointed to preach God's good news (Isa 61:2–3 • Luke 4:43)

18. Triumphal entry into Jerusalem (Zech 9:9–10 • Matt 21:1–11)

19. Betrayed for thirty pieces of silver (Zech 11:12–13 • Matt 26:14–15)

20. Rejected by his own people (Isa 53:3 • John 1:11)

21. Crucified with criminals (Isa 53:12 • Matt 27:38)

22. Silent before his accusers (Isa 53:7 • Mark 15:4–5)

23. Mocked on the cross (Ps 22:6–8 • Matt 27:39–44)

24. No bones broken (Ps 34:20 • John 19:32–33,36)

25. Died for others (Isa 53:1–12 • 1 Pet 3:18)

26. Buried with the rich (Isa 53:9 • Matt 27:57–60)

27. Ascended to his Father (Ps 68:18 • Eph 4:8–10)

28. Makes intercession for believers (Zech 6:13 • Rom 8:34)

29. Serves as a heavenly high priest (Zech 6:12–13 • Heb 8:1–2)

30. Exalted above all (Ps 2:6–12 • Phil 2:9–11)

**METHUSELAH** (a son of Enoch who lived to the age of 969, the oldest recorded age in the Bible). **Gen 5:21–27** • 1 Chr 1:3. *Mathusala:* Luke 3:37.

**MICAH** (a prophet who denounced social injustices and author of the book that bears his name). Jer 26:18 • Mic 1:1.

**MICAH, BOOK OF.** A short prophetic book of the Old Testament known for its prediction that the Messiah would be born in Bethlehem (5:2).

**MICAIAH** (a prophet who predicted that King Ahab would be killed). **1 Kgs 22:8–28** • 2 Chr 18:7–27.

**MICHAEL** (an archangel who was thought to serve as a guardian over Israel). Dan 10:13,21; 12:1 • Jude 9 • Rev 12:7.

**MICHAL** (a daughter of King Saul and a wife of David). 1 Sam 14:49; 18:20–28; 19:9–17; 25:44 • 2 Sam 3:13–16; 6:16–23.

**MIDIAN**

1. A son of Abraham and founder of the Midianites. Gen 25:1–4 • 1 Chr 1:32–33.

2. A region in the Arabian desert occupied by the Midianites. Ex 2:15 • Judg 7:8–25; 8:3–28. *Madian:* Acts 7:29.

**MIDIANITES** (nomadic traders who occupied the land of Midian). Gen 37:28,36 • Num 31:2–7 • Judg 6:2–33; 7:1–25 • Ps 83:9.

**MIDNIGHT**

*Ps 119:62* At *m* I will rise to give thanks unto thee [God]

*Mark 13:35* know not when the master...cometh, at even, or at *m*

*Acts 16:25* at *m* Paul and Silas prayed, and sang praises

## MIGHT

*Gen 43:32* *m* not eat bread with the Hebrews...abomination unto the Egyptians

*Deut 6:5* love the LORD thy God...with all thy *m*

*Judg 6:14* Go in this thy [Gideon's] *m,* and thou shalt save Israel

*2 Sam 6:14* David danced... with all his *m*

*2 Chr 20:6* in thine [God's] hand is...power and *m*

*Job 23:3* Oh that I knew where I *m* find him [God]

*Ps 119:11* Thy [God's] word have I hid in mine heart, that I *m* not sin against thee

*Ps 145:6* the *m* of thy [God's] terrible acts

*Eccl 9:10* hand findeth to do, do it with thy *m*

*Jer 9:1* I [Jeremiah] *m* weep day and night for...my people

*Jer 9:23* neither let the mighty man glory in his *m*

*Zech 4:6* Not by *m*...but by my [God's] spirit

*Mark 14:35* if...possible, the hour *m* pass from him [Jesus]

*John 3:17* the world through him [Jesus] *m* be saved

*John 10:10* I [Jesus] am come that they *m* have life

*John 20:31* that ye *m* believe that Jesus is the Christ

*Rom 10:1* my [Paul's]... prayer...for Israel is, that they *m* be saved

*1 Cor 9:22* all things to all men...I [Paul] *m*...save some

*2 Cor 4:10* life...of Jesus *m* be...manifest in our body

*2 Cor 8:9* he [Jesus] became poor, that ye through his poverty *m* be rich

*Gal 4:5* we *m* receive the adoption of sons

*Eph 6:10* be strong in the Lord, and in the power of his *m*

*1 John 4:9* God sent his...Son... that we *m* live through him

## MIGHTY

*Ex 1:7* children of Israel... waxed exceeding *m*

*Deut 6:21* LORD brought us [Israelites] out...*m* hand

*2 Sam 1:27* How are the *m* fallen

*1 Chr 11:11* number of the *m* men whom David had

*Job 12:19* He [God]...overthroweth the *m*

*Job 34:24* He [God] shall break in pieces *m* men

*Job 36:5* Behold, God...is *m* in strength and wisdom

*Ps 24:8* LORD strong and *m,* the LORD *m* in battle

*Ps 50:1* The *m* God, even the Lord, hath spoken

*Ps 89:6* who among the…*m* can be likened unto the Lord

*Ps 150:2* Praise him [God] for his *m* acts…his…greatness

*Isa 9:6* his [Jesus'] name shall be called…The *m* God

*Ezek 20:34* I [God]…will gather you…with a *m* hand

*Amos 5:24* let judgment run down as waters, and righteousness as a *m* stream

*Matt 13:58* And he [Jesus] did not many *m* works… because of their unbelief

*Acts 2:2* a sound from heaven as of a rushing *m* wind

*1 Cor 1:26* not many *m,* not many noble, are called

*1 Cor 1:27* weak things of the world to confound the…*m*

*1 Pet 5:6* Humble yourselves… under the *m* hand of God

**MILCOM** (supreme god of the Ammonites). 1 Kgs 11:5,33 • 2 Kgs 23:13. *Molech:* Lev 20:2. *Moloch:* Acts 7:43.

**MILETUS** (a city where Paul met the leaders of the Ephesian church). Acts 20:15–38. *Miletum:* 2 Tim 4:20.

**MILLO**

1. A fortress at Shechem whose occupants proclaimed Abimelech as their king. Judg 9:6,20.

2. A defensive fortress tower built by David near Jerusalem and improved by Solomon. **2 Sam 5:9 • 1 Kgs 9:15,24;** 11:27 • 2 Kgs 12:20 • 1 Chr 11:8 • 2 Chr 32:5.

**MIND [S]**

*Neh 4:6* the people had a *m* to work

*Prov 29:11* A fool uttereth all his *m*

*Isa 26:3* keep him in perfect peace…*m* is stayed on thee

*Mark 12:30* love the Lord… with all thy *m*

*Luke 8:35* the man [demoniac]… clothed…in his right *m*

*Rom 1:28* God gave them over to a reprobate *m*

*Rom 8:5* they…after the flesh do *m* the things of the flesh

*Rom 11:34* who hath known the *m* of the Lord

*Rom 12:2* transformed by the renewing of your *m*

*Eph 4:17* walk not as other Gentiles…vanity of their *m*

*Phil 2:2* the same love, being of one accord, of one *m*

*Phil 2:3* but in lowliness of *m* let each esteem other better than themselves

*Phil 2:5* this *m* be in you, which was also in Christ

*Phil 4:7* peace of God…shall keep your hearts and *m's*

*2 Tim 1:7* God hath not given us the spirit of fear; but…of a sound *m*

*Heb 8:10* I [God] will put my laws into their *m*

*1 Pet 1:13* Wherefore gird up the loins of your *m*

## MINDFUL

*1 Chr 16:15* Be ye *m*...of his [God's] covenant

*Ps 8:4* What is man, that thou [God] art *m* of him

*Ps 115:12* LORD hath been *m* of us: he will bless us

## MINISTER [ED, S]

*Ps 9:8* he [God] shall *m* judgment to the people

*Ps 103:21* Bless ye the LORD... ye *m's* of his

*Matt 20:28* Son of man came not to be *m'ed* unto, but to *m*

*Mark 10:43* great among you, shall be your *m*

*Rom 15:16* I [Paul] should be... *m* of Jesus...to the Gentiles

*1 Cor 3:5* Who then is Paul... Apollos, but *m's* by whom ye believed

*2 Cor 11:23* Are they *m's* of Christ...I [Paul] am more

*Eph 3:7* I [Paul] was made a *m,* according to...grace

*1 Pet 4:10* even so *m* the same one to another

## MINISTRY

*Acts 6:4* we [the apostles] will give ourselves continually ... to the *m* of the word

*2 Cor 5:18* God...hath given to us the *m* of reconciliation

*Eph 4:12* perfecting of the saints, for the work of the *m*

*2 Tim 4:5* work of an evangelist, make full proof of thy *m*

*Heb 8:6* now hath he [Jesus] obtained a more excellent *m*

## MIRACLE [S]

*Mark 6:52* they [the disciples] considered not the *m* of the loaves

*John 2:11* This beginning of *m's* did Jesus in Cana

*John 3:2* no man can do these *m's* that thou [Jesus] doest, except God be with him

*John 9:16* How can a man that is a sinner do such *m's*

*John 12:37* though he [Jesus] had done so many *m's*...yet they believed not

*Acts 6:8* Stephen...did great wonders and *m's*

*1 Cor 12:10* To another the working of *m's*

## MIRACLES OF JESUS. See *Jesus, Miracles of.*

**MIRIAM** (a sister of Moses who arranged for their mother Jochebed to care for him). **Ex 2:4–10;** 15:20–21 • Num 12:1–16; 20:1; 26:59 • Deut 24:9 • 1 Chr 6:3 • Mic 6:4.

**MIZPAH** (a place where Jacob and Laban made a covenant

and agreed to a friendly separation). Gen 31:44–53.

**MIZRAIM** (a son of Ham whose descendants settled in Egypt). Gen 10:6,13 • 1 Chr 1:8,11.

**MNASON** (a believer who accompanied Paul on his last visit to Jerusalem). Acts 21:16.

**MOAB** (a son of Lot and the name of the land inhabited by him and his descendants). Gen 19:33–37 • Num 21:11–29 • Judg 11:15–25 • Ruth 1:1–22 • Jer 48:1–47.

**MOABITES** (inhabitants of Moab who were pagan worshipers and enemies of the Israelites). Gen 19:37 • Num 22:4 • Deut 2:9,11,29 • Judg 3:28 • 2 Sam 8:2 • 1 Kgs 11:1, 33 • 2 Kgs 3:18,21–24; 23:13; 24:2 • 1 Chr 18:2 • Ezra 9:1.

**MOCK [ED, ETH, ING]**
*1 Kgs 18:27* Elijah *m'ed* them [prophets of Baal] ... Cry aloud ... he is a god
*Job 12:4* I [Job] am as one *m'ed* of his neighbour
*Prov 14:9* Fools ... *m* at sin
*Prov 17:5* Whoso *m'eth* the poor reproacheth his Maker
*Jer 20:7* I am in derision daily, every one *m'eth* me

*Mark 10:34* they shall *m* him [Jesus] ... scourge him
*Mark 15:31* chief priests *m'ing* said ... himself he [Jesus] cannot save
*Luke 18:32* he [Jesus] shall be delivered unto the Gentiles, and shall be *m'ed*
*Luke 23:36* the soldiers also *m'ed* him [Jesus]
*Acts 2:13* *m'ing* said, These men [converts at Pentecost] are full of new wine
*Gal 6:7* Be not deceived; God is not *m'ed*

**MODEL PRAYER OF JESUS.** See *Lord's Prayer.*

**MOLECH.** See *Milcom.*

**MOLOCH.** See *Milcom.*

**MORDECAI** (a Jewish exile in Persia and a kinsman of Esther). Esth 2:5–23; 3:2–6; 4:1–17; 5:9–14; 6:2–13; 7:9–10; 8:1–15; 9:3–31; 10:2–3.

**MOREH** (a place near Shechem where Abraham built an altar after entering Canaan). **Gen 12:6–7** • Deut 11:30.

**MORESHETH-GATH** (birthplace of the prophet Micah). Mic 1:14.

**MORIAH** (a mountainous area near Jerusalem where Abraham was directed to sacrifice his son Isaac). **Gen 22:1–13** • 2 Chr 3:1.

**MOSES** (the great lawgiver and prophet who led the Israelites out of Egypt and guided their formative years as a nation). Moses is the central personality in the books of Exodus, Leviticus, Numbers, and Deuteronomy.

    1. Hidden on the Nile River as a baby (Ex 2:1–5)

    2. Reared in the house of Pharaoh (Ex 2:6–10)

    3. Fled to the land of Midian (Ex 2:11–22)

    4. Called to deliver the Hebrews from slavery (Ex 2:23–4:17)

    5. Led Israelites out of Egypt (Ex 13:17–22)

    6. Brought water out of a rock (Ex 17:3–6)

    7. Received the Ten Commandments (Ex 19:3; 20:1–17)

    8. Struck a rock in sin (Num 20:11–12)

    9. Raised up a brass serpent (Num 21:8–9)

    10. Joshua chosen as his successor (Num 27:18–23)

    11. Death of Moses (Deut 34:1–8)

Moses is also mentioned in Josh 1:1–17; 8:31–35; 11:12–23; 13:8–33; 14:2–11; 22:4–9 • 2 Kgs 18:4–12 • 1 Chr 23:13–15 • Ps 106:16–32 • Isa 63:11–12 • Dan 9:11,13 • Matt 17:3–4 • Mark 9:4–5 • Luke 16:29–31 • John 7:19–23 • Acts 7:20–44 • Rom 10:5,19 • Heb 3:2–16; 11:23–24 • Rev 15:3.

**MOURN [ETH, ING]**

*Job 2:11* Job's three friends ... came ... to *m* with him

*Ps 38:6* I am troubled ... I go *m'ing* all the day long

*Ps 88:9* Mine eye *m'eth* by reason of affliction

*Eccl 3:4* a time to *m,* and a time to dance

*Isa 60:20* the days of thy *m'ing* shall be ended

*Isa 61:2* to comfort all that *m*

*Amos 8:10* And I [God] will turn your feasts into *m'ing*

*Matt 5:4* Blessed are they that *m* ... shall be comforted

*Matt 9:15* children ... *m,* as long as the bridegroom [Jesus] is with them

*Jas 4:9* Be afflicted, and *m*

**MOVE [D, ING, TH]**

*Gen 1:2* Spirit of God *m'd* upon the ... waters

*Gen 9:3* Every *m'ing* thing that liveth shall be meat

*Ps 16:8* he [God] is at my right hand, I shall not be *m'd*

*Ps 46:5* God is in the midst of her [Jerusalem] ... not be *m'd*

*Ps 62:2* he [God] is my defence; I shall not be greatly *m'd*

*Ps 69:34* praise him [God], the seas, and every thing that *m'th* therein

*Ps 96:10* the LORD reigneth: the world...shall not be *m'd*

*Isa 6:4* posts of the door *m'd* at the voice of him [God]

*Mark 6:34* Jesus...was *m'd* with compassion toward them [the crowds]

*John 5:3* multitude...waiting for the *m'ing* of the water

*Acts 17:28* in him [God] we live...*m*...have our being

*Heb 12:28* a kingdom which cannot be *m'd*

*2 Pet 1:21* holy men...spake as...*m'd* by the Holy Ghost

## MULTITUDE [S]

*Gen 32:12* thy [Jacob's] seed as the sand...which cannot be numbered for *m*

*Ex 12:38* mixed *m* went up... with them [Israelites]

*Ps 69:13* O God, in the *m* of thy mercy hear me

*Ps 109:30* I will praise him [God] among the *m*

*Joel 3:14* *M's, m's* in the valley of decision

*Matt 5:1* seeing...*m's,* he [Jesus] went...into a mountain

*Matt 15:33* should we have... bread...fill so great a *m*

*Matt 22:33* *m* heard this, they were astonished

*Mark 4:1* whole *m* was by the sea on the land

*Mark 5:31* seest the *m* thronging thee [Jesus], and sayest... Who touched me

*Luke 2:13* with the angel a *m* of the heavenly host

*Luke 23:1* *m*...arose, and led him [Jesus] unto Pilate

*John 6:2* great *m* followed him [Jesus]...they saw his miracles

*1 Pet 4:8* charity shall cover the *m* of sins

*Rev 7:9* a great *m,* which no man could number

## MURMUR [ED, ING, INGS]

*Ex 15:24* the people *m'ed* against Moses

*Num 14:27* I [God]...heard... *m'ings* of the children of Israel

*Luke 5:30* Pharisees *m'ed* against his [Jesus'] disciples

*John 6:41* *m'ed*...because he [Jesus] said, I am the bread...from heaven

*John 7:12* there was much *m'ing* among the people concerning him [Jesus]

*Phil 2:14* Do all things without *m'ings* and disputings

## MYSTERY [IES]

*Mark 4:11* Unto you [the disciples] it is given to know the *m* of the kingdom

*Luke 8:10* it is given to know the *m'ies* of the kingdom... but to others in parables

*1 Cor 2:7* we speak the wisdom of God in a *m*

*1 Cor 4:1* ministers of Christ... stewards of the *m'ies* of God

*1 Cor 13:2* though I [Paul]... understand all *m'ies,* and all knowledge

*1 Cor 15:51* I show you a *m;* We shall not all sleep

*Eph 5:32* a great *m*...I [Paul] speak concerning Christ

*1 Tim 3:9* Holding the *m* of the faith in a pure conscience

# -N-

**NAAMAN** (a captain in the Syrian army who was healed of leprosy by the prophet Elisha). **2 Kgs 5:1–14** • Luke 4:27.

**NABAL** (a wealthy herdsman who refused to provide food for David and his army). **1 Sam 25:2–42** • 2 Sam 3:3.

**NABOTH** (an Israelite who was framed and killed by Jezebel so Ahab could take possession of his vineyard). **1 Kgs 21:1–23** • 2 Kgs 9:21–26.

**NADAB**
1. Aaron's son who was destroyed for offering "strange fire" to God. Ex 24:1,9–12; 28:1 • **Lev 10:1–7.**
2. A king of Israel who was assassinated and succeeded by Baasha. 1 Kgs 14:20; **15:25–31.**

**NAHASH** (a king of Ammon who befriended David). 2 Sam 10:1–2.

**NAHUM** (a prophet of Judah and author of the book that bears his name). Nah 1:1. *Naum:* Luke 3:25.

**NAHUM, BOOK OF.** A short prophetic book of the Old Testament that predicted the downfall of the pagan nation of Assyria because of the atrocities which it committed against God's people (3:7–19).

**NAIN** (a village near the Sea of Galilee where Jesus raised a widow's son from the dead). Luke 7:11–17.

**NAIOTH** (a place where David fled to escape from King Saul). 1 Sam 19:18–23; 20:1.

**NAOMI** (mother-in-law of Ruth). Ruth 1–4.

**NAPHTALI** (a son of Jacob and ancestor of one of the twelve tribes of Israel). Gen 30:8; 35:25; 46:24; 49:21 • Ex 1:4 • 1 Chr 2:2; 7:13 • Ezek 48:34. The tribe of Naphtali settled in northern Canaan. Josh 19:32–39.

**NAPHTUHIM** (inhabitants of central Egypt who were descendants of Mizraim, son of Ham). Gen 10:13.

**NATHAN** (a prophet who rebuked King David for his sin with Bath-sheba). 2 Sam 7:2–17; **12:1–25** • 1 Kgs 1:8–45 • 1 Chr 17:1–15; 29:29 • 2 Chr 9:29; 29:25 • Ps 51:1.

**NATHANAEL.**
See *Bartholomew*.

## NATION [S]

*Gen 12:2* make of thee [Abraham] a great *n*

*Gen 17:5* a father of many *n's* have I [God] made thee [Abraham]

*Gen 25:23* Two *n's* are in thy [Rebekah's] womb

*Ex 19:6* ye [Israel] shall be unto me [God]...an holy *n*

*Deut 9:1* possess *n's* greater and mightier than thyself

*Deut 28:1* God will set thee... above all *n's* of the earth

*1 Sam 8:5* make us a king to judge us like all the *n's*

*2 Sam 7:23* what one *n*...is like thy [God's] people

*1 Chr 16:24* Declare...his [God's] marvellous works among all *n's*

*Ps 22:28* and he [God] is the governor among the *n's*

*Ps 33:12* Blessed is the *n* whose God is the LORD

*Ps 67:2* thy [God's] way may be known...thy saving health among all *n's*

*Ps 72:11* all kings...all *n's* shall serve him [God]

*Ps 82:8* judge the earth...thou [God]...inherit all *n's*

*Ps 96:5* For all the gods of the *n's* are idols

*Ps 113:4* The LORD is high above all *n's*

*Prov 14:34* Righteousness exalteth a *n*

*Isa 2:4* *n* shall not lift up sword against *n*

*Isa 40:15* Behold, the *n's* are as a drop of a bucket

*Isa 52:10* LORD hath made bare his...arm in...all the *n's*

*Isa 60:12* *n*...that will not serve thee [God] shall perish

*Jer 1:5* ordained thee [Jeremiah] a prophet unto the *n's*

*Jer 2:11* Hath a *n* changed their gods

*Jer 50:41* a people shall come from the north, and a great *n*

*Ezek 12:15* I [God] shall scatter them among the *n's*

*Mic 4:3* *n* shall not lift up a sword against *n*

*Zeph 3:6* I [God] have cut off the *n's*...towers are desolate

*Hag 2:7* and the desire of all *n's* shall come

*Zech 8:22* strong *n's* shall come to seek the LORD

*Mal 3:9* ye have robbed me [God], even this whole *n*

*Matt 24:7* *n* shall rise against *n*...kingdom against kingdom

*Matt 24:14* gospel of the kingdom...preached...unto all *n's*

*Matt 25:32* before him [Jesus] shall be gathered all *n's*

*Matt 28:19* teach all *n's,* baptizing them

*Luke 24:47* repentance... preached...among all *n's*

*John 11:50* one man should die...that the whole *n* perish not

*Acts 2:5* devout men, out of every *n* under heaven

*Acts 10:35* in every *n* he that feareth him [God]…is accepted with him

*Acts 17:26* And [God] hath made of one blood all *n's*

*Phil 2:15* in the midst of a crooked and perverse *n*

*1 Pet 2:9* ye are a chosen generation…an holy *n*

*Rev 7:9* multitude, which no man could number, of all *n's*

**NATURAL**

*Deut 34:7* his [Moses'] eye…not dim, nor…*n* force abated

*1 Cor 2:14 n* man receiveth not the things of the Spirit

*1 Cor 15:44* It is sown a *n* body… raised a spiritual body

**NATURE**

*Rom 1:26* women did change the natural use into that… against *n*

*Rom 2:14* Gentiles…do by *n*… things contained in the law

*2 Pet 1:4* ye might be partakers of the divine *n*

**NAUM.** See *Nahum.*

**NAZARETH** (hometown of Jesus in the province of Galilee). Matt 2:20–23 • Luke 4:16–30.

**NAZARITE** (a person especially consecrated to God whose vows included abstaining from strong drink and not cutting his hair). Num 6:2–21 • Judg 13:5–7 • Lam 4:7 • Amos 2:11–12.

**NEAPOLIS** (a seaport where Paul landed during the second missionary journey). Acts 16:11.

**NEBO**
1. The highest point of Mount Pisgah where Moses died. Deut 32:49; 34:5–6.
2. Babylonian god of science and knowledge. Isa 46:1.

**NEBUCHADNEZZAR** (a king of Babylonia who captured Jerusalem and carried Judah into exile). **2 Kgs 25:1–26** • 2 Chr 36:7–13 • Jer 28:11–14 • Dan 1–4. *Nebuchadrezzar:* Jer 51:34.

**NEBUCHADREZZAR.** See *Nebuchadnezzar.*

**NEBUZAR-ADAN** (an officer in Nebuchadnezzar's army during the Babylonian siege of Jerusalem). 2 Kgs 25:8–20 • Jer 39:11–14.

**NECHO, NECHOH.** See *Pharaoh.*

**NEED [ED, ETH, S]**
*Matt 3:14* I [John the Baptist] have *n* to be baptized of thee [Jesus]…comest…to me

*Matt 6:8* Father knoweth what things ye have **n** of

*Luke 5:31* They that are whole **n** not a physician

*Luke 15:7* joy…over one sinner…than over…just persons, which **n** no repentance

*John 4:4* he [Jesus] must **n's** go through Samaria

*Acts 2:45* sold…and parted them [possessions] to all men, as every man had **n**

*Acts 17:25* though he [God] **n'ed** any thing, seeing he… giveth…life

*1 Cor 12:21* eye cannot say unto the hand…no **n** of thee

*Phil 4:19* But my God shall supply all your **n**

*2 Tim 2:15* a workman that **n'eth** not to be ashamed

*Heb 4:16* and find grace to help in time of **n**

*Heb 7:27* Who [Jesus] **n'eth** not daily…to offer up sacrifice, first for his own sins

**NEEDY**

*Deut 15:11* open thine hand… to thy **n,** in thy land

*Job 24:14* The murderer…killeth the poor and **n**

*Ps 37:14* The wicked have… bent their bow, to cast down the poor and **n**

*Ps 40:17* I am poor and **n;** yet the Lord thinketh upon me

*Ps 82:3* do justice to the afflicted and **n**

*Ps 86:1* O LORD, hear me: for I am poor and **n**

*Prov 31:9* and plead the cause of the poor and **n**

*Amos 8:6* buy the poor for silver…**n** for a pair of shoes

**NEGLECT [ED]**

*Matt 18:17* if he shall **n** to hear them, tell it unto the church

*Acts 6:1* widows were **n'ed** in the daily ministration

*1 Tim 4:14* **N** not the gift that is in thee [Timothy]

*Heb 2:3* How shall we escape, if we **n** so great salvation

**NEHEMIAH** (governor of Jerusalem who helped rebuild the city wall after the Exile and author of the book that bears his name). Neh 1:11; 2:1–6; 8:1–13.

**NEHEMIAH, BOOK OF.** An Old Testament historical book that records the rebuilding of Jerusalem's defensive wall after the Exile under the leadership of Nehemiah (1:1–7:73). The book also recounts the religious reforms undertaken by Nehemiah and Ezra.

**NEIGHBOUR [S]**

*Ex 20:16* not bear false witness against thy **n**

*Lev 19:13* not defraud thy **n,** neither rob him

*Lev 19:18* but thou shalt love thy *n* as thyself

*Ps 79:4* We are become a reproach to our *n's*

*Prov 11:12* He that is void of wisdom despiseth his *n*

*Prov 14:20* The poor is hated even of his own *n:* but the rich hath many friends

*Prov 24:28* Be not a witness against thy *n* without cause

*Prov 27:10* better is a *n* that is near than a brother far off

*Jer 31:34* they shall teach no more every man his *n*

*Zech 8:17* let none of you imagine evil … against his *n*

*Matt 22:39* Thou shalt love thy *n* as thyself

*Luke 10:36* Which … of these three … was *n* unto him that fell among the thieves

*Luke 15:6* he calleth … *n's,* saying … Rejoice with me … I have found my sheep

*Rom 13:10* Love worketh no ill to his *n*

*Gal 5:14* Thou shalt love thy *n* as thyself

*Eph 4:25* speak every man truth with his *n*

*Jas 2:8* fulfil the royal law … love thy *n* as thyself

**NERGAL** (a Babylonian god of war). 2 Kgs 17:30.

**NERGAL-SHAREZER** (a Babylonian prince who

released Jeremiah from prison). Jer 39:3–14.

**NEW**

*Ex 1:8* there arose up a *n* king … which knew not Joseph

*Ps 40:3* And he [God] hath put a *n* song in my mouth

*Ps 96:1* sing unto the LORD a *n* song … all the earth

*Eccl 1:9* there is no *n* thing under the sun

*Isa 1:14* Your *n* moons … my [God's] soul hateth

*Isa 42:10* Sing unto the LORD a *n* song

*Isa 65:17* I [God] create *n* heavens and a new earth

*Lam 3:23* they [God's mercies] are *n* every morning: great is thy faithfulness

*Ezek 36:26* a *n* spirit will I [God] put within you

*Amos 8:5* *n* moon be gone, that we may sell corn

*Matt 27:60* laid it [Jesus' body] in his [Joseph's] own *n* tomb

*Mark 2:22* no man putteth *n* wine into old bottles

*Luke 22:20* cup is the *n* testament in my [Jesus'] blood

*John 13:34* A *n* commandment I [Jesus] give unto you

*Acts 2:13* men [converts at Pentecost] are full of *n* wine

*1 Cor 5:7* Purge out … the old leaven … may be a *n* lump

*2 Cor 3:6* Who [Jesus] … made us able ministers of the *n* testament … of the spirit

*2 Cor 5:17* any man be in Christ, he is a *n* creature

*Eph 4:24* put on the *n* man

*2 Pet 3:13* we ... look for *n* heavens and a *n* earth

*Rev 21:1* I [John] saw a *n* heaven and a *n* earth

*Rev 21:5* Behold, I [Jesus] make all things *n*

## NEW BIRTH DISCUSSION OF JESUS WITH NICODEMUS. John 3:1–21.

## NEW COVENANT

*Jer 31:31* I [God] will make a *n-c* with the house of Israel

*Heb 8:8* I [God] will make a *n-c* with the house of Israel

*Heb 8:13* he [God] saith, A *n-c,* he hath made the first old

*Heb 12:24* And to Jesus the mediator of the *n-c*

## NEW JERUSALEM

*Rev 3:12* the city of my God, which is *n-J*

*Rev 21:2* I John saw the ... *n-J,* coming down from God

## NEWNESS

*Rom 6:4* even so we also should walk in *n* of life

*Rom 7:6* serve in *n* of spirit ... not in ... oldness of the letter

**NIBHAZ** (an idol worshiped by the Avites, who settled in Samaria). 2 Kgs 17:31.

**NICANOR** (one of the seven men chosen as "deacons" in the church at Jerusalem). Acts 6:1–5.

**NICODEMUS** (a Pharisee who talked with Jesus about the new birth and helped prepare Jesus' body for burial). **John 3:1–21;** 7:50–52; **19:39–40.**

**NICOLAITANES** (an early Christian sect condemned for its false beliefs). Rev 2:6,15.

**NICOLAS** (one of the seven men chosen as "deacons" in the church at Jerusalem). Acts 6:1–5.

**NIMROD** (a son of Cush who became a powerful king and empire builder in Babylonia, or Shinar). Gen 10:8–12 • 1 Chr 1:8–10 • Mic 5:6.

**NINEVE.** See *Nineveh.*

**NINEVEH** (capital of Assyria where the prophet Jonah preached God's message of judgment). Gen 10:11–12 • 2 Kgs 19:36 • Isa 37:37 • **Jon 1–4** • Nah 1:1; 2:8; 3:7 • Zeph 2:13 • Matt 12:41. *Nineve:* Luke 11:32.

**NISROCH** (a false god worshiped by King Sennacherib of Assyria). **2 Kgs 19:36–37** • Isa 37:38.

**NO** (capital of upper Egypt). Jer 46:25 • Ezek 30:14–16 • Nah 3:8.

**NOAH** (a righteous man who was chosen by God to preserve life on earth by building an ark to escape the great flood). Gen 5:29–32; 6:8–22; **7:1–8:22;** 9:1–29; 10:1,32 • 1 Chr 1:4 • Isa 54:9 • Ezek 14:14,20 • Heb 11:7 • 1 Pet 3:20 • 2 Pet 2:5. *Noe:* Luke 17:26.

**NOB** (a city where David fled to escape King Saul's wrath). **1 Sam 21:1–9;** 22:9–23 • Neh 11:32 • Isa 10:32.

**NOD** (a region where Cain lived after murdering his brother Abel). Gen 4:16–17.

**NOE.** See *Noah.*

**NOPH** (an ancient royal city of the Egyptians). Isa 19:13 • Jer 2:16; 44:1; 46:14,19 • Ezek 30:13,16.

**NORTHERN KINGDOM (ISRAEL) FALLS TO ASSYRIA.** 2 Kgs 17.

**NORTHERN TRIBES OF ISRAEL REVOLT.** 1 Kgs 12:6–24.

**NOTHING**

*Deut 2:7* forty years … God hath been with thee; thou hast lacked *n*

*Josh 11:15* he [Joshua] left *n* undone of all that the LORD commanded Moses

*2 Sam 12:3* poor man had *n,* save one little ewe lamb

*Job 8:9* we … know *n,* because our days … are a shadow

*Ps 49:17* when he dieth he shall carry *n* away

*Prov 13:7* There is that maketh himself rich, yet hath *n*

*Eccl 2:24 n* better for a man, than that … his soul enjoy good in his labour

*Isa 40:17* All nations before him [God] are as *n*

*Isa 44:10* a graven image that is profitable for *n*

*Jer 32:17* there is *n* too hard for thee [God]

*Dan 4:35* inhabitants of the earth are reputed as *n*

*Matt 5:13* salt … is … good for *n,* but to be cast out

*Matt 17:20 n* shall be impossible unto you

*Mark 6:8* they [the disciples'] … take *n* for their journey

*Mark 7:15 n* from without a man … can defile him

*Mark 9:29* This kind can come forth by *n,* but by prayer

*Luke 5:5* toiled all the night, and have taken *n*

*Luke 23:9* but he [Jesus] answered him [Pilate] *n*

*John 3:27* receive *n,* except it be given him from heaven

*John 5:19* The Son [Jesus] can do *n* of himself

*John 15:5* for without me [Jesus] ye can do *n*

*Acts 11:8 n*…unclean…entered into my [Peter's] mouth

*Rom 14:14* I [Peter] know… there is *n* unclean of itself

*1 Cor 1:19* I [God]…will bring to *n* the understanding of the prudent

*1 Cor 7:19* Circumcision is *n,* and uncircumcision is *n*

*1 Cor 13:2* though I [Paul]… have not charity, I am *n*

*Phil 2:3* Let *n* be done through strife or vainglory

*1 Tim 6:7* For we brought *n* into this world

*Heb 7:19* For the law made *n* perfect

**NUMBERS, BOOK OF.** An Old Testament book that focuses on the Israelites in the wilderness of Sinai—a period of more than forty years between their departure from Egypt and their occupation of Canaan.

# -O-

## OATH [S]

*Matt 5:33* perform unto the Lord thine *o's*

*Matt 26:72* And again he [Peter] denied with an *o*, I do not know the man [Jesus]

*Heb 7:20* not without an *o* he [Jesus] was made priest

*Jas 5:12* neither by any other *o:* but let your yea be yea

## OBADIAH (a prophet of Judah and author of the book that bears his name). Obad 1.

## OBADIAH, BOOK OF. A short prophetic book of the Old Testament that pronounces judgment against the Edomites because of their mistreatment of God's people, the Israelites.

## OBED-EDOM (a Philistine in whose house the ark of the covenant was kept before its removal to Jerusalem). 2 Sam 6:10–12 • **1 Chr 13:13–14; 15:24–25.**

## OBEDIENCE

*Rom 5:19* so by the *o* of one [Jesus] shall many be made righteous

*2 Cor 10:5* bringing into captivity every thought to the *o* of Christ

*Heb 5:8* Though he [Jesus] were a Son, yet learned he *o*

## OBEDIENT

*Isa 1:19* willing and *o,* ye shall eat the good of the land

*Acts 6:7* company of the priests were *o* to the faith

*Phil 2:8* he [Jesus] humbled himself…became *o* unto death

*1 Pet 1:14* As *o* children, not… according to the former lusts

## OBEY [ED, ETH, ING]

*Gen 22:18* thou [Abraham] hast *o'ed* my [God's] voice

*Ex 5:2* Who is the LORD, that I [Pharaoh] should *o* his voice

*Deut 27:10* Thou shalt…*o* the voice of the LORD

*Josh 24:24* our God will we serve…his voice will we *o*

*1 Sam 15:22* Behold, to *o* is better than sacrifice

*Jer 11:3* Cursed be the man… *o'eth* not…this covenant

*Jer 26:13* amend your ways… and *o* the voice of the LORD

*Mark 4:41* even the wind and the sea *o* him [Jesus]

*Acts 5:29* We [the apostles]…*o* God rather than men

*Gal 3:1* bewitched you [Galatians]…not *o* the truth

*Eph 6:1* Children, *o* your parents in the Lord

*Col 3:20* Children, *o* your parents in all things

*Heb 5:9* he [Jesus] became the author of...salvation unto all them that *o* him

*Heb 11:8* he [Abraham]... *o'ed*...not knowing whither he went

*Jas 3:3* bits in the horses' mouths, that they may *o* us

*1 Pet 1:22* purified your souls in *o'ing* the truth

## OFFER [ED, ETH, ING, INGS]

*Gen 4:4* LORD had respect unto Abel and to his *o'ing*

*Gen 22:2* *o* him [Isaac] there for a burnt *o'ing*

*Lev 10:1* And Nadab and Abihu...*o'ed* strange fire before the LORD

*Ps 50:23* Whoso *o'eth* praise glorifieth me [God]

*Ps 51:16* thou [God] delightest not in burnt *o'ing*

*Ps 96:8* bring an *o'ing,* and come into his [God's] courts

*Ps 119:108* Accept...the freewill *o'ings* of my mouth

*Hos 6:6* I [God] desired...the knowledge of God more than burnt *o'ings*

*Amos 5:22* neither will I [God] regard the peace *o'ings*

*Mal 3:8* have we robbed thee [God]? In tithes and *o'ings*

*Matt 5:24* be reconciled to thy brother, and then...*o* thy gift

*Mark 12:33* to love him [God] with all the heart...is more than...*o'ings* and sacrifices

*Luke 6:29* smiteth thee on the one cheek *o* also the other

*Luke 11:12* if he shall ask an egg, will he *o* him a scorpion

*Luke 21:4* all these have of their abundance cast in unto the *o'ings* of God

*Luke 23:36* the soldiers also mocked him [Jesus]...*o'ing* him vinegar

*1 Cor 8:1* Now as touching things *o'ed* unto idols

*Eph 5:2* Christ...hath given himself for us an *o'ing*

*2 Tim 4:6* I [Paul] am now ready to be *o'ed*

*Heb 7:27* he [Jesus] did once, when he *o'ed* up himself

*Heb 9:28* Christ was once *o'ed* to bear the sins of many

*Heb 10:10* sanctified through the *o'ing*...of Jesus Christ

*Heb 10:12* he [Jesus] had *o'ed* one sacrifice for sins for ever

*Heb 11:4* Abel *o'ed* unto God a more excellent sacrifice

*Heb 11:17* Abraham, when he was tried, *o'ed* up Isaac

*Heb 13:15* let us *o* the sacrifice of praise to God

*Jas 2:21* Was not Abraham our father justified...when he had *o'ed* Isaac his son

## OFFSPRING

*Job 5:25* seed...great, and thine [Job's] *o* as the grass

*Acts 17:28* For we are also his [God's] *o*

*Acts 17:29* we are the *o* of God

*Rev 22:16* I [Jesus] am the root and the *o* of David

**OG** (an Amorite king defeated by the Israelites at Edrei). **Num 21:32–35** • Deut 3:1,8, 10–13 • Josh 12:4 • Ps 135:11.

**OLD MAN / NEW MAN.** Eph 4:17–29.

**OLIVES, MOUNT OF** (a hill near Jerusalem where Jesus was betrayed on the night before His crucifixion). Zech 14:4 • Matt 21:1; 24:3; **26:30** • Mark 11:1; 13:3; 14:26 • Luke 19:29,37; 21:37; 22:39 • John 8:1. *Mount Olivet:* 2 Sam 15:30 • Acts 1:12.

**OLIVET, MOUNT.** See *Olives, Mount of.*

**OMRI** (a king of Israel who built Samaria as the capital city of the Northern Kingdom). **1 Kgs 16:23–28** • 2 Kgs 8:26 • 2 Chr 22:2 • Mic 6:16.

**ON**
    1. A leader who rebelled against Moses in the wilderness. Num 16:1–35.
    2. A city of lower Egypt noted as a center of sun worship. Gen 41:45,50. *Aven:* Amos 1:5.

**ONAN** (a son of Judah who failed to consummate a marriage union with Tamar). **Gen 38:8–10; 46:12** • Num 26:19 • 1 Chr 2:3.

**ONESIMUS** (a slave who was converted under Paul's ministry). Col 4:7–9 • Phlm 10.

**ONESIPHORUS** (a believer who befriended Paul when he was a prisoner in Rome). 2 Tim 1:16–18; 4:19.

**OPEN [ED, EST, ETH]**
*Gen 3:7* eyes of them [Adam and Eve] both were *o'ed*
*Job 11:5* that God would…*o* his lips against thee
*Ps 51:15* O Lord, *o* thou my lips
*Ps 119:131* I *o'ed* my mouth, and…longed for thy [God's] commandments
*Ps 145:16* Thou [God] *o'est* thine hand, and satisfiest the desire of every living thing
*Ps 146:8* The LORD *o'eth* the eyes of the blind
*Prov 13:3* he that *o'eth* wide his lips shall have destruction
*Prov 27:5* *O* rebuke is better than secret love
*Isa 35:5* Then the eyes of the blind shall be *o'ed*
*Isa 42:7* To *o* the blind eyes, to bring out the prisoners
*Isa 53:7* he [God's servant]… *o'ed* not his mouth

245

*Lam 3:46* enemies have *o'ed* their mouths against us

*Ezek 3:2* I [Ezekiel] *o'ed* my mouth, and he [God] caused me to eat that roll

*Mal 3:10* prove me [God]... herewith...if I will not *o* you the windows of heaven

*Matt 3:16* heavens were *o'ed* unto him [Jesus]

*Matt 7:7* knock, and it shall be *o'ed* unto you

*Matt 27:52* graves were *o'ed;* and many bodies...arose

*Mark 7:34* he [Jesus]...saith... Ephphatha, that is, Be *o'ed*

*Luke 24:31* eyes were *o'ed,* and they [Emmaus travelers] knew him [Jesus]

*John 9:30* know not from whence he [Jesus] is, and yet he hath *o'ed* mine eyes

*John 10:21* Can a devil *o* the eyes of the blind

*Acts 9:8* when his [Saul's] eyes were *o'ed,* he saw no man

*Acts 14:27* he [God] had *o'ed* the door of faith unto...Gentiles

*Acts 26:18* To *o* their eyes, and to turn them from darkness

*Rom 3:13* Their throat is an *o* sepulchre

*1 Cor 16:9* a great door...is *o'ed* unto me [Paul]

*1 Pet 3:12* the eyes of the Lord are over the righteous, and his ears are *o*

*Rev 3:7* write...he that *o'eth,* and no man shutteth

*Rev 3:8* I [Jesus] have set before thee an *o* door

*Rev 3:20* any man...*o* the door, I [Jesus] will come in

*Rev 4:1* door...*o'ed* in heaven

*Rev 5:9* worthy to take the book, and to *o* the seals

**OPENLY**

*Matt 6:4* Father which seeth in secret...shall reward thee *o*

*Mark 8:32* he [Jesus] spake that saying [about his death] *o*

*John 11:54* Jesus...walked no more *o* among the Jews

**OPHIR** (a gold-producing region visited by the ships of Solomon and the Phoenicians). **1 Kgs 9:26–28; 10:11; 22:48 •** 1 Chr 29:4 • 2 Chr 8:18; 9:10 • Job 22:24; 28:16 • Ps 45:9 • Isa 13:12.

**OPHRAH** (Gideon's hometown where an angel assured him of God's guidance and protection). **Judg 6:11–14,24;** 8:27,32; 9:5.

**ORDAIN [ED]**

*1 Chr 17:9* I [God] will *o* a place for my people Israel

*Ps 8:3* moon and the stars, which thou [God] hast *o'ed*

*Jer 1:5* I [God] *o'ed* thee [Jeremiah] a prophet unto the nations

*Mark 3:14* he [Jesus] *o'ed* twelve…they should be with him

*John 15:16* I [Jesus] have chosen you, and *o'ed* you

*Rom 13:1* the powers that be are *o'ed* of God

*1 Cor 9:14* the Lord *o'ed*… they…should live of the gospel

## ORDINANCE [S]

*Ex 12:43* LORD said…This is the *o* of the passover

*Lev 18:4* Ye shall…keep mine [God's] *o's*

*1 Pet 2:13* Submit yourselves to every *o* of man

**ORNAN.** See *Araunah.*

**OSEE.** See *Hosea.*

**OSHEA.** See *Joshua.*

**OTHNIEL** (the first judge of Israel who defeated the king of Mesopotamia). Judg 3:9–11.

## OUGHT

*Matt 5:23* rememberest…thy brother hath *o* against thee

*Luke 11:42* these *o* ye [Pharisees] to have done

*Luke 12:12* Holy Ghost shall teach you…what ye *o* to say

*Luke 18:1* men *o* always to pray, and not to faint

*John 13:14* ye also *o* to wash one another's feet

*John 19:7* and by our law he [Jesus] *o* to die

*Acts 5:29* We [the apostles] *o* to obey God rather than men

*Rom 12:3* think of himself more highly…he *o* to think

*Rom 15:1* strong *o* to bear the infirmities of the weak

*Eph 5:28* So *o* men to love… wives as their own bodies

*Col 4:6* ye may know how ye *o* to answer every man

*Heb 2:1* *o* to give…heed to… things…we have heard

*Jas 3:10* My brethren, these things *o* not so to be

*2 Pet 3:11* what manner of persons *o* ye to be

*1 John 4:11* Beloved…we *o* also to love one another

## OVERCOME [TH]

*Num 13:30* for we are well able to *o* it [Canaan]

*John 16:33* be of good cheer; I [Jesus] have *o* the world

*Rom 12:21* Be not *o* of evil, but *o* evil with good

*1 John 2:13* young men…ye have *o* the wicked one

*1 John 5:4* and this is the victory that *o'th* the world

*Rev 17:14* Lamb shall *o* them: for he is Lord of lords

*Rev 21:7* He that *o'th* shall inherit all things

**OWE [ST, TH]**
*Matt 18:28* he [servant] laid hands on him...saying, Pay me that thou *o'st*
*Luke 16:5* How much *o'st* thou unto my lord

*Rom 13:8* **O** no man any thing, but to love one another
*Phlm 18* he [Onesimus]...*o'th* thee ought, put that on mine [Paul's] account

**OZIAS.** See *Uzziah.*

# -P-

**PADAN-ARAM.**
See *Mesopotamia.*

**PALESTINE** (the territory of the Canaanites that became known as the land of the people of Israel). Joel 3:4. *Palestina:* Ex 15:14 • Isa 14:29,31.

**PAMPHYLIA** (a coastal region in Asia Minor visited by Paul). Acts 2:10; **13:13; 14: 24–25;** 15:38; 27:5.

**PAPHOS** (a city on the island of Cyprus where Paul blinded the magician Elymas). Acts 13:6–12.

**PARABLES OF JESUS.** See *Jesus, Parables of.*

**PARDON [ED, ETH]**
*1 Sam 15:25* **p** my [Saul's] sin, and turn again with me
*Neh 9:17* a God ready to **p,** gracious and merciful
*Ps 25:11* O LORD, **p** mine iniquity; for it is great
*Isa 40:2* her [Jerusalem's] iniquity is **p'ed**
*Jer 33:8* I [God] will **p** all their iniquities
*Mic 7:18* Who is a God like unto thee, that **p'eth** iniquity

**PARMENAS** (one of the seven men chosen as "deacons" in the church at Jerusalem). Acts 6:1–5.

**PARTHIANS** (inhabitants of Parthia, a country north of Media and Persia). Acts 2:1,9.

**PASHUR** (a priest who had the prophet Jeremiah imprisoned). **Jer 20:3–6;** 38:1.

**PASSOVER** (a festival that commemorated the Exodus of Israel from Egypt). **Ex 12:11–48** • Num 9:2–14 • 2 Chr 30:1–18; 35:1–19 • Matt 26:2–19 • Mark 14:1–16 • Luke 22:1–15 • 1 Cor 5:7 • Heb 11:28.

**PASTOR [S]**
*Jer 3:15* I [God] will give you **p's** according to mine heart
*Jer 17:16* I [Jeremiah] have not hastened from being a **p**
*Jer 23:1* Woe be unto the **p's** that … scatter the sheep
*Eph 4:11* he [God] gave some, apostles … and some, **p's**

**PATHROS** (a name for upper Egypt). Isa 11:11 • Jer 44:1,15 • Ezek 29:14; 30:14.

**PATIENCE**
*Rom 5:3* tribulation worketh **p**
*Rom 15:5* the God of **p** … grant you to be likeminded
*1 Thes 1:3* Remembering… your work of faith … and **p** of hope

*1 Tim 6:11* follow after … faith, love, *p,* meekness

*Heb 12:1* run with *p* the race that is set before us

*Jas 1:3* that the trying of your faith worketh *p*

*Jas 5:7* husbandman waiteth for the … fruit of the earth, and hath long *p* for it

**PATIENT [LY]**

*Ps 40:1* I waited *p'ly* for the LORD; and he inclined unto me

*Eccl 7:8* the *p* in spirit is better than the proud in spirit

*Rom 12:12* Rejoicing in hope; *p* in tribulation

*1 Thes 5:14* support the weak, be *p* toward all men

*Heb 6:15* And so, after he [Abraham] had *p'ly* endured, he obtained the promise

*Jas 5:7* *p* therefore, brethren, unto the coming of the Lord

**PATMOS** (a desolate island where the apostle John was exiled and where he wrote the Book of Revelation). Rev 1:9.

**PAUL** (an apostle to the Gentiles who was converted from persecuting the Christian faith to proclaiming its truths). Also known as *Saul* (Acts 8:1), Paul is the central personality of the second half of the Book of Acts. Recognized as the author of thirteen epistles of the New Testament: Romans, 1 and 2 Corinthians, Galatians, Ephesians, Philippians, Colossians, 1 and 2 Thessalonians, 1 and 2 Timothy, Titus, and Philemon. See **Acts 13–28** for a sketch of Paul's life.

1. Consented to Stephen's death (Acts 7:59–8:1)

2. Converted on road to Damascus (Acts 9:1–9)

3. Ministered with Barnabas at Antioch (Acts 11:25–26)

4. First missionary journey (Acts 13:1–14:28)

5. Second missionary journey (Acts 15:36–18:23)

6. Third missionary journey (Acts 19:1–21:16)

7. Arrested in Jerusalem and detained in Caesarea (Acts 21:27–26:32)

8. Journey to Rome and shipwrecked (Acts 27:1–28:10)

9. Preached while under house arrest at Rome (Acts 28:16–31)

**PAULUS, SERGIUS** (Roman proconsul of Cyprus who was converted under Paul's ministry). Acts 13:4–12.

**PAY [ED, ETH]**

*Ps 37:21* The wicked borroweth, and *p'eth* not again

*Ps 66:13* I will *p* thee [God] my vows

*Prov 7:14* this day have I *p'ed* my vows

*Eccl 5:4* thou vowest a vow unto God, defer not to *p* it

*Matt 18:34* his lord ... delivered him to the tormentors, till he should *p* all

*Matt 23:23* ye [scribes and Pharisees] *p* tithe of mint and anise and cummin

*Rom 13:6* for this cause *p* ye tribute ... are God's ministers

## PEACE

*Job 33:31* hold thy [Job's] *p,* and I [God] will speak

*Ps 4:8* I will both lay me down in *p,* and sleep

*Ps 34:14* seek *p,* and pursue it

*Ps 55:18* He [God] hath delivered my soul in *p*

*Ps 83:1* hold not thy *p,* and be not still, O God

*Ps 119:165* Great *p* have they which love thy [God's] law

*Ps 122:7* *P* be within thy walls

*Prov 17:28* a fool, when he holdeth his *p,* is counted wise

*Eccl 3:8* a time of war, and a time of *p*

*Isa 9:6* his [Messiah's] name shall be called ... Prince of *P*

*Isa 26:3* keep him in perfect *p* ... mind is stayed on thee [God]

*Isa 48:22* no *p,* saith the LORD, unto the wicked

*Isa 52:7* beautiful ... the feet of him ... that publisheth *p*

*Isa 53:5* chastisement of our *p* ... upon him [God's servant]

*Jer 29:7* And seek the *p* of the city ... for in the *p* thereof shall ye have *p*

*Matt 10:34* I [Jesus] came not to send *p,* but a sword

*Mark 4:39* he [Jesus] ... said unto the sea, *P,* be still

*Luke 2:14* Glory to God ... on earth *p,* good will toward men

*Luke 10:5* whatsoever house ye enter ... *P* be to this house

*John 14:27* my [Jesus'] *p* I give unto you

*John 16:33* that in me [Jesus] ye might have *p*

*Rom 2:10* honour, and *p,* to every man that worketh good

*Rom 5:1* we have *p* with God through ... Jesus Christ

*Rom 10:15* beautiful are the feet of them that preach the gospel of *p*

*Rom 14:19* follow after the things which make for *p*

*1 Cor 14:33* God is not the author of confusion, but of *p*

*Gal 5:22* fruit of the Spirit is love, joy, *p,* longsuffering

*Eph 2:14* he [Jesus] is our *p,* who hath made both one

*Eph 4:3* unity of the Spirit in the bond of *p*

*Phil 4:7* *p* of God, which passeth all understanding

*Col 3:15* let the *p* of God rule in your hearts

*2 Thes 3:16* Now the Lord of *p* himself give you *p*

## PECULIAR PEOPLE

*Deut 14:2* LORD hath chosen thee [Israel] to be a *p-p*

*Titus 2:14* he [Jesus] might... purify unto himself a *p-p*

*1 Pet 2:9* ye [Christians] are... an holy nation, a *p-p*

**PEKAH** (a king of Israel who assassinated Pekahiah to gain the throne). **2 Kgs 15:23–31** • 2 Chr 28:6 • Isa 7:1–9.

**PEKAHIAH** (a king of Israel who was assassinated and succeeded by Pekah, one of his military officers). 2 Kgs 15:23–26.

**PELETHITES** (a loyal unit of David's soldiers). 2 Sam 8:18; 15:14–18; 20:7,23 • 1 Kgs 1:38,44 • 1 Chr 18:17.

**PENIEL** (a place near the Jabbok River where Jacob wrestled with an angel). Gen 32:24–32. *Penuel:* Judg 8:8.

**PENTECOST** (a harvest festival being observed in Jerusalem when the Holy Spirit came in power upon the early believers). **Acts 2:1–47; 20:16** • 1 Cor 16:8. *Feast of Harvest* or *Ingathering:* Ex 23:16. *Feast of Weeks:* Ex 34:22.

**PENUEL.** See *Peniel.*

## PEOPLE OF GOD

*Heb 4:9* There remaineth...a rest to the *p-o-G*

*Heb 11:25* Choosing...to suffer affliction with the *p-o-G*

*1 Pet 2:10* in time past were not a people...now the *p-o-G*

**PEOR.** See *Baal-peor.*

## PERCEIVE [D, ING, ST, TH]

*Job 33:14* God speaketh... twice, yet man *p'th* it not

*Job 38:18* Hast thou [Job] *p'd* the breadth of the earth

*Isa 6:9* see ye indeed, but *p* not

*Mark 7:18* not *p,* that whatsoever...entereth into the man...cannot defile

*Luke 6:41* *p'st* not the beam that is in thine own eye

*Luke 8:46* I [Jesus] *p* that virtue is gone out of me

*Luke 9:47* Jesus, *p'ing*...their heart, took a child

*Acts 4:13* they [the Sanhedrin] ...*p'd* that they [Peter and John] were unlearned...men

*Acts 10:34* I [Peter] *p* that God is no respecter of persons

*1 John 3:16* *p* we the love of God, because he [Jesus] laid down his life

## PERFECT [ED, ING, LY]

*Gen 6:9* Noah was a just man and *p* in his generations

*Job 1:1* that man [Job] was *p* and upright

*Ps 18:30* his [God's] way is *p* ... word ... is tried

*Ps 18:32* It is God that ... maketh my way *p*

*Ps 19:7* law of the LORD is *p,* converting the soul

*Prov 4:18* path of the just ... shineth ... unto the *p* day

*Matt 5:48* even as your Father which is in heaven is *p*

*Rom 12:2* prove what is that good ... and *p,* will of God

*1 Cor 1:10* *p'ly* joined together in the same mind

*1 Cor 13:10* But when that which is *p* is come

*2 Cor 12:9* My [Jesus'] grace is sufficient ... strength is made *p* in weakness

*Eph 4:12* *p'ing* of the saints, for the work of the ministry

*2 Tim 3:17* That the man of God may be *p*

*Heb 5:9* And being made *p,* he [Jesus] became the author of eternal salvation

*Heb 10:14* he [Jesus] hath *p'ed* ... them that are sanctified

*Jas 1:17* good gift and every *p* gift is from above

*1 John 4:12* If we love one another ... his [God's] love is *p'ed* in us

*1 John 4:18* but *p* love casteth out fear

**PERFECTION**

*Ps 50:2* Out of Zion, the *p* of beauty, God hath shined

*2 Cor 13:9* this also we wish, even your *p*

*Heb 6:1* let us go on unto *p*

*Heb 7:11* If ... *p* were by the Levitical priesthood

**PERGA** (capital of Pamphylia and a city visited by the apostle Paul). Acts 13:13–14; 14:25.

**PERGAMOS** (a city where one of the seven churches addressed by John in the Book of Revelation was located). Rev 2:12–17.

**PERISH [ED, ETH, ING]**

*2 Sam 1:27* How are the mighty fallen, and the weapons of war *p'ed*

*Job 3:3* Let the day *p* wherein I [Job] was born

*Job 33:18* He keepeth ... his life from *p'ing* by the sword

*Job 34:15* All flesh shall *p* together ... man ... unto dust

*Ps 1:6* but the way of the ungodly shall *p*

*Ps 68:2* the wicked *p* at the presence of God

*Prov 19:9* and he that speaketh lies shall *p*

*Prov 29:18* Where there is no vision, the people *p*

*Matt 18:14* that one of these little ones should *p*

*Mark 4:38* Master [Jesus], carest thou not that we [the disciples] *p*

*Luke 15:17* father's [servants] have bread...and I [prodigal son] *p* with hunger

*John 3:16* whosoever believeth in him [Jesus] should not *p*

*John 6:27* Labour not for the meat which *p'eth*

*1 Cor 1:18* For the preaching of the cross is to them that *p* foolishness

*2 Cor 4:16* outward man *p,* yet the inward man is renewed

*2 Pet 3:9* The Lord...is longsuffering to us-ward, not willing that any should *p*

**PERIZZITES** (descendants of Perez who were conquered by Joshua's forces). Gen 15:20; 34:30 • Ex 3:8,17; 23:23 • Deut 7:1; 20:17 • **Josh 3:10;** 12:8; 17:15; 24:11 • Judg 1:4–5; 3:5 • 1 Kgs 9:20 • 2 Chr 8:7 • Ezra 9:1 • Neh 9:8.

**PERSECUTE [D, ING, ST]**

*Ps 7:1* O LORD...save me from all them that *p* me

*Ps 31:15* deliver me...from them that *p* me

*Ps 119:161* Princes have *p'd* me without a cause

*Matt 5:10* Blessed are they... *p'd* for righteousness' sake

*Matt 5:11* Blessed are ye, when men shall...*p* you

*Matt 5:44* Love...enemies... pray for them which...*p* you

*John 15:20* If they have *p'd* me [Jesus]...also *p* you

*Acts 9:4* Saul, Saul, why *p'st* thou me [Jesus]

*Rom 12:14* Bless them which *p* you: bless...curse not

*1 Cor 15:9* I [Paul] *p'd* the church of God

*2 Cor 4:9* *P'd,* but not forsaken; cast down, but not destroyed

*Phil 3:6* Concerning zeal, *p'ing* the church

**PERSECUTION**

*Lam 5:5* Our necks are under *p:* we...have no rest

*Acts 8:1* a great *p* against the church...at Jerusalem

*Rom 8:35* Who shall separate us from the love of Christ? shall...distress, or *p*

*2 Tim 3:12* all that will live... in Christ Jesus shall suffer *p*

**PERSIA** (a great empire that conquered Babylonia and allowed the Israelites to return to their native land). **2 Chr 36:20–23** • Ezra 1:1–8; 3:7; 4:3–24; 6:14; 7:1; 9:9 • Esth 1:3–18; 10:2 • Ezek 27:10; 38:5 • Dan 8:20; 10:1–20; 11:2.

**PERSUADE [D, ST, TH]**

*Luke 16:31* neither will they be *p'd,* though one rose from the dead

*Acts 18:13* This fellow [Paul] *p'th* men to worship God contrary to the law

*Acts 26:28* Almost thou [Paul] *p'st* me [Agrippa] to be a Christian

*Rom 8:38* I [Paul] am *p'd,* that neither death, nor life

*Rom 14:14* I [Paul] ... am *p'd* ... that there is nothing unclean of itself

*2 Cor 5:11* Knowing ... the terror of the Lord, we *p* men

*2 Tim 1:12* know whom I [Paul] have believed, and am *p'd* that he [Jesus] is able

**PETER.** See *Simon,* No. 1.

**PETER, FIRST AND SECOND EPISTLES OF.** Two short epistles, probably from the apostle Peter, written to encourage Christians who were experiencing persecution and discouragement (1 Peter) and to warn them against false teachers (2 Peter).

**PHARAOH** (title of the king of Egypt). The named pharaohs of the Bible are Shishak (1 Kgs 14:25–26), So (2 Kgs 17:4), Tirhakah (2 Kgs 19:9), Nechoh (2 Kgs 23:29; *Necho:* Jer 46:2) and Hophra (Jer 44:30).

**PHARISEES** (a Jewish sect whose traditional religious views brought them into conflict with Jesus and the apostles). Matt 12:14–34; 15:12–14; 16:1; 19:3; 22:15; 23:13–33 • Luke 7:36–50; 11:53–54 • Acts 5:34; 15:5; 23:5–8; 26:5 • Phil 3:5.

**PHARPAR** (a river of Damascus). 2 Kgs 5:9–12.

**PHEBE** (a believer commended by Paul for her support). Rom 16:1–2.

**PHENICE** (a Mediterranean coastal region north of Israel). Acts 11:19; 15:3. *Phenicia:* Acts 21:2.

**PHENICIA.** See *Phenice.*

**PHILADELPHIA** (a city where one of the seven churches addressed by John in the Book of Revelation was located). Rev 3:7–13.

**PHILEMON** (a believer to whom Paul wrote on behalf of Philemon's slave). Phlm 1,9–21.

**PHILEMON, EPISTLE TO.** A short book written by Paul to help Onesimus, a runaway slave. Paul encouraged Philemon to welcome Onesimus back as a Christian brother (v. 16).

**PHILIP**
1. One of the twelve apostles of Jesus. Matt 10:3 • Mark 3:18 • Luke 6:14 • John

1:43–48; 6:5–7; 12:20–22; 14:8–12 • Acts 1:13.

2. One of the seven men chosen as "deacons" in the church at Jerusalem and an evangelist in the early church. Acts 6:5; 8:5–40; 21:8.

3. A Roman ruler in northern Palestine. Luke 3:1. See also *Herod,* No. 4.

**PHILIPPI** (a city where Paul and Silas were miraculously released from prison). **Acts 16:12–34;** 20:6 • Phil 1:1 • 1 Thes 2:2.

**PHILIPPIANS, EPISTLE TO THE.** A short epistle written by Paul to the church at Philippi—a group for whom he expressed great appreciation and thanksgiving (1:1–11). Philippians has been called Paul's "epistle of joy" (4:4).

**PHILISTIA** (a coastal region beside the Mediterranean Sea that served as the land of the Philistines). Gen 21:32–34 • Ps 60:8; 87:4; 108:9.

**PHILISTIM.** See *Philistines.*

**PHILISTINES** (inhabitants of Philistia who were enemies of the Israelites, especially during the days of Saul and David). Gen 26:1–18 • Ex 13:17 • Josh 13:2–3 • Judg 14:1–4; 15:3–20;

16:5–31 • 1 Sam 17:8–57 • 2 Sam 21:15–19 • 1 Chr 10:1–12 • Jer 47:1–4 • Amos 6:2; 9:7. *Philistim:* Gen 10:14.

**PHILISTINES, SEA OF THE.** See *Great Sea.*

**PHINEHAS**

1. Aaron's grandson who became a high priest of Israel. 1 Chr 9:19–20.

2. A son of Levi and priest who corrupted his office through immoral behavior. 1 Sam 2:22–24.

**PHRYGIA** (a region of Asia Minor visited by Paul). Acts 2:10; **16:6.**

**PHUT.** See *Libya.*

**PHYSICIAN [S]**

*Jer 8:22* Is there no balm in Gilead … no *p* there

*Mark 5:26* [a certain woman] had suffered many things of many *p's*

*Luke 5:31* They that are whole need not a *p*

*Col 4:14* Luke, the beloved *p,* and Demas, greet you

**PIERCE [D, ING, INGS]**

*Job 30:17* My [Job's] bones are *p'd* … in the night

*Prov 12:18* There is that speaketh like the *p'ings* of a sword

*Zech 12:10* they shall look upon me [the Messiah] whom they have ***p'd***

*Luke 2:35* sword shall ***p*** through thy [Mary's]…soul

*John 19:34* one of the soldiers… ***p'd*** his [Jesus'] side

*Heb 4:12* word of God is… sharper…twoedged sword, ***p'ing***…soul and spirit

*Rev 1:7* he [Jesus] cometh… every eye shall see him, and they also which ***p'd*** him

**PILATE** (the Roman governor of Judea who presided at Jesus' trial). **Matt 27:2–65** • **Mark 15:1–44** • Luke 3:1; 13:1; **23:1–52** • **John 18:29–38; 19:1–38** • Acts 3:13; 4:27; 13:28 • 1 Tim 6:13.

**PILLAR OF CLOUD AND FIRE LEAD ISRAEL.** Ex 13:17–22.

**PISGAH, MOUNT** (a mountain peak in Moab from which Moses viewed Canaan before his death). Num 21:20; 23:14 • Deut 3:27; **34:1–6.**

**PISIDIA** (a mountainous district in Asia Minor visited by Paul). Acts 13:14; 14:24.

**PISON** (one of four rivers which flowed out of the Garden of Eden). Gen 2:10–14.

**PITHOM** (an Egyptian city built by Hebrew slaves). Ex 1:11.

**PLAGUES AGAINST EGYPT**

1. Water turned into blood (Ex 7:20–25)
2. Frogs (Ex 8:1–7)
3. Lice (Ex 8:16–19)
4. Flies (Ex 8:20–24)
5. Diseased livestock (Ex 9:3–7)
6. Boils (Ex 9:8–12)
7. Hail (Ex 9:13–25)
8. Locusts (Ex 10:1–15)
9. Darkness (Ex 10:21–23)
10. Death of Egyptian firstborn (Ex 12:1–36)

**PLAIN, SEA OF THE.** See *Salt Sea.*

**PLEASE [D, ING]**

*1 Sam 12:22* ***p'd*** the LORD to make you his people

*Ps 40:13* Be ***p'd,*** O LORD, to deliver me

*Ps 69:31* This also shall ***p*** the LORD better than an ox

*Isa 53:10* it ***p'ed*** the LORD to bruise him [God's servant]

*Mic 6:7* LORD be ***p'ed*** with thousands of rams

*Matt 17:5* my [God's] beloved Son, in whom I am well ***p'ed***

*Luke 3:22* my [God's] beloved Son; in thee I am well ***p'ed***

*John 8:29* I [Jesus] do always those things that ***p*** him [God]

*Rom 8:8* they that are in the flesh cannot *p* God

*1 Cor 1:21* it *p'ed* God by the foolishness of preaching

*Col 1:19* it *p'ed* the Father that in him [Jesus] should all fulness dwell

*Col 3:20* obey your parents... well *p'ing* unto the Lord

*Heb 11:6* without faith it is impossible to *p* him [God]

*1 John 3:22* do those things... *p'ing* in his [God's] sight

**PLEASURE [S]**

*Job 22:3* any *p* to the Almighty, that thou art righteous

*Job 36:11* If they obey...him [God], they shall spend their...years in *p's*

*Ps 147:11* The LORD taketh *p* in them that fear him

*Ps 149:4* For the LORD taketh *p* in his people

*Prov 21:17* He that loveth *p* shall be a poor man

*Isa 44:28* He [Cyrus]...shall perform all my [God's] *p*

*Ezek 33:11* I [God] have no *p* in the death of the wicked

*Mal 1:10* I have no *p* in you, saith the LORD of hosts

*Luke 12:32* your Father's good *p* to give you the kingdom

*Eph 1:9* his [Jesus'] good *p*... he hath purposed in himself

*2 Tim 3:4* lovers of *p's* more than lovers of God

*Heb 11:25* Choosing rather to suffer affliction...than to enjoy the *p's* of sin

*Rev 4:11* thou [God] hast created all things...for thy *p* they...were created

**PONTUS** (a coastal region along the Black Sea where Priscilla and Aquila settled). Acts 2:5,9; **18:2** • 1 Pet 1:1.

**POOR**

*Lev 19:10* thou shalt leave them [grapes] for the *p*

*Deut 15:11* the *p* shall never cease out of the land

*2 Sam 12:3* *p* man had nothing, save one little ewe lamb

*Job 5:15* He [God] saveth the *p* from the sword

*Job 30:25* was not my [Job's] soul grieved for the *p*

*Job 36:6* He [God]...giveth right to the *p*

*Ps 34:6* This *p* man cried, and the LORD heard him

*Ps 40:17* I am *p* and needy; yet the Lord thinketh upon me

*Ps 72:13* He [God] shall spare the *p* and needy

*Ps 109:22* I am *p* and needy, and my heart is wounded

*Prov 14:20* The *p* is hated even of his own neighbour

*Prov 21:17* He that loveth pleasure shall be a *p* man

*Prov 22:2* rich and *p*...LORD is the maker of them all

*Prov 22:22* Rob not the **p,** because he is **p**

*Eccl 4:13* Better is a **p** and a wise child than an old and foolish king

*Isa 25:4* thou [God] hast been a strength to the **p**

*Amos 2:6* they [Israel] sold... the **p** for a pair of shoes

*Matt 5:3* Blessed are the **p** in spirit

*Mark 10:21* sell whatsoever thou [rich young ruler] hast, and give to the **p**

*Mark 14:7* For ye have the **p** with you always

*Luke 4:18* anointed me [Jesus] to preach the gospel to the **p**

*Luke 14:13* makest a feast, call the **p,** the maimed

*Luke 19:8* Behold, Lord, the half of my [Zacchaeus's] goods I give to the **p**

*1 Cor 13:3* though I [Paul] bestow... goods to feed the **p**

*2 Cor 8:9* he [Jesus] was rich, yet... he became **p**

*Jas 2:5* God chosen the **p** of this world rich in faith

**POSSESSION [S]**

*Gen 17:8* I [God] will give... Canaan, for an everlasting **p**

*Gen 47:27* they [Israel] had **p's** therein [in Egypt], and grew, and multiplied

*Ps 2:8* I [God] shall give thee [his Son]... the uttermost parts of the earth for thy **p**

*Mark 10:22* he [rich young ruler]... went away grieved: for he had great **p's**

*Acts 5:1* Ananias, with Sapphira his wife, sold a **p**

**POSSIBLE**

*Matt 19:26* but with God all things are **p**

*Matt 26:39* if it be **p,** let this cup pass from me [Jesus]

*Mark 9:23* all things are **p** to him that believeth

*Luke 18:27* things... impossible with men are **p** with God

*Rom 12:18* If it be **p**... live peaceably with all men

*Heb 10:4* not **p**... blood of bulls... should take away sins

**POTIPHAR** (an Egyptian official who had Joseph imprisoned). Gen 37:36; **39:1–20.**

**POWER [S]**

*Ex 15:6* Thy right hand, O LORD, is... glorious in **p**

*1 Chr 29:11* Thine, O LORD, is the greatness, and the **p**

*Job 37:23* he [God] is excellent in **p,** and in judgment

*Ps 49:15* redeem my soul from the **p** of the grave

*Ps 68:35* he [God]... giveth strength and **p** unto his people

*Ps 111:6* He [God] hath showed... the **p** of his works

*Prov 18:21* Death and life are in the **p** of the tongue

*Jer 32:17* thou [God] hast made...the earth by thy great *p*

*Nah 1:3* LORD is slow to anger, and great in *p*

*Zech 4:6* Not by might, nor by *p,* but by my [God's] spirit

*Matt 6:13* thine [God's] is the kingdom, and the *p*

*Matt 24:30* Son of man coming in the clouds...with *p*

*Matt 28:18* All *p* is given unto me [Jesus]

*Mark 13:25* the *p's* that are in heaven shall be shaken

*Luke 4:32* his [Jesus'] word was with *p*

*Luke 9:1* he [Jesus]...gave them [disciples] *p*...over...devils

*Luke 24:49* tarry ye [the disciples]...until...endued with *p*

*John 1:12* gave he [Jesus] *p* to become the sons of God

*John 19:11* no *p* at all against me [Jesus], except it were given thee [Pilate] from above

*Acts 6:8* Stephen, full of faith and *p,* did great wonders

*Rom 8:38* neither death, nor life...nor *p's*

*Rom 13:1* every soul be subject unto the higher *p's*

*1 Cor 4:20* kingdom of God is not in word, but in *p*

*Eph 6:10* be strong in the Lord, and in the *p* of his might

*Eph 6:12* we wrestle...against principalities, against *p's*

*2 Tim 1:7* God hath not given us the spirit of fear; but of *p*

*Rev 4:11* Thou [God] art worthy...to receive glory...*p*

## POWER OF GOD

*Matt 22:29* not knowing the scriptures, nor the *p-o-G*

*Luke 22:69* Son of man sit on the right hand of the *p-o-G*

*Rom 1:16* it [the gospel] is the *p-o-G* unto salvation

*1 Cor 1:18* the preaching of the cross...is the *p-o-G*

*1 Cor 2:5* your faith should... stand...in the *p-o-G*

## POWERFUL

*Ps 29:4* voice of the LORD is *p*

*Heb 4:12* For the word of God is quick, and *p*

## PRAISE [D, ING, S]

*1 Chr 16:25* great is the LORD, and greatly to be *p'd*

*1 Chr 29:13* we thank thee [God]...*p* thy glorious name

*Ps 18:3* call upon the LORD, who is worthy to be *p'd*

*Ps 21:13* so will we sing and *p* thy [God's] power

*Ps 44:8* In God we boast...and *p* thy name for ever

*Ps 47:7* sing ye [God's] *p's* with understanding

*Ps 51:15* my mouth shall show forth thy [God's] *p*

*Ps 67:3* Let the people *p* thee, O God...all...*p* thee

*Ps 79:13* show forth thy [God's] *p* to all generations

*Ps 84:4* they will be still *p'ing* thee [God]

*Ps 92:1* a good thing...to sing *p's* unto thy [God's] name

*Ps 100:4* Enter into his [God's]...courts with *p*

*Ps 145:3* Great is the LORD, and greatly to be *p'd*

*Isa 42:10* Sing unto the LORD... his *p*...the end of the earth

*Luke 2:20* shepherds returned, glorifying and *p'ing* God

*John 12:43* loved the *p* of men more than the *p* of God

*Acts 16:25* Paul and Silas... sang *p's* unto God

*1 Pet 2:9* show forth the *p's* of him [God] who hath called you out of darkness

*Rev 19:5* *P* our God, all ye his servants...ye that fear him

## PRAISE THE LORD

*Ps 7:17* I will *p-t-L* according to his righteousness

*Ps 107:15* Oh that men would *p-t-L* for his goodness

*Ps 117:1* O *P-t-L,* all ye nations...all ye people

*Ps 150:6* Let every thing that hath breath *p-t-L*

## PRAY [EST, ETH, ING]

*2 Chr 7:14* my [God's] people... humble themselves, and *p*

*Ps 5:2* unto thee [God] will I *p*

*Ps 55:17* Evening, and morning, and at noon, will I *p*

*Jer 14:11* said the LORD unto me [Jeremiah], *P* not for this people for their good

*Dan 6:11* these men...found Daniel *p'ing*...before...God

*Matt 6:6* when thou *p'est,* enter into thy closet

*Matt 6:9* *p* ye: Our Father which art in heaven

*Mark 6:46* he [Jesus] departed into a mountain to *p*

*Mark 11:25* when ye stand *p'ing,* forgive

*Mark 13:33* watch and *p:* for ye know not when the time is

*Luke 6:28* *p* for them which despitefully use you

*Luke 11:1* Lord, teach us to *p*

*John 14:16* I [Jesus] will *p* the Father, and he shall give you another Comforter

*John 17:9* I [Jesus] *p*...for them [the disciples] which thou [God] hast given me

*Acts 10:9* Peter went up upon the housetop to *p*

*Rom 8:26* we know not what we should *p* for as we ought

*1 Cor 14:14* if I [Paul] *p*... unknown tongue...spirit *p'eth*

*2 Cor 5:20* we *p* you...be ye reconciled to God

*1 Thes 5:17* *P* without ceasing

*Jas 5:13* Is any among you afflicted? let him *p*

*Jas 5:16* *p* one for another, that ye may be healed

## PRAYER

*2 Chr 7:12* I [God] have heard thy [Solomon's] *p*

*Ps 6:9* LORD will receive my *p*

*Ps 66:20* God ... hath not turned away my *p*

*Ps 102:17* He [God] will regard the *p* of the destitute

*Prov 15:29* The LORD ... heareth the *p* of the righteous

*Matt 21:22* whatsoever ye shall ask in *p,* believing, ye shall receive

*Luke 19:46* My [God's] house is the house of *p*

*Acts 6:4* we [the apostles] will give ourselves ... to *p*

*Rom 10:1* my [Paul's] ... *p* to God for Israel ... they might be saved

*Jas 5:15* the *p* of faith shall save the sick

*Jas 5:16* fervent *p* of a righteous man availeth much

## PREACH [ED, ING]

*Isa 61:1* the LORD hath anointed me [God's servant] to *p* good tidings

*Matt 3:1* John the Baptist, *p'ing* in the wilderness

*Matt 4:17* Jesus began to *p,* and to say, Repent

*Matt 24:14* gospel ... shall be *p'ed* in all the world

*Mark 1:4* John did baptize ... and *p* ... repentance

*Mark 3:14* that he [Jesus] might send them [the disciples] forth to *p*

*Luke 24:47* remission of sins ... be *p'ed* in his [Jesus'] name

*Acts 5:42* they [the apostles] ceased not to ... *p* Jesus Christ

*Acts 8:4* they [believers] ... went every where *p'ing* the word

*Acts 8:5* Philip went down to ... Samaria, and *p'ed* Christ

*1 Cor 1:18* For the *p'ing* of the cross is to them that perish foolishness

*1 Cor 1:21* it pleased God by the foolishness of *p'ing* to save them that believe

*1 Cor 1:23* But we *p* Christ crucified

*1 Cor 9:27* lest ... when I [Paul] have *p'ed* to others, I myself should be a castaway

*1 Cor 15:14* if Christ be not risen, then is our *p'ing* vain

*2 Cor 4:5* we *p* not ourselves, but Christ Jesus

*Eph 3:8* I [Paul] should *p* among the Gentiles

*Phil 1:18* Christ is *p'ed;* and I [Paul] ... do rejoice

*2 Tim 4:2* *P* the word; be instant in season

*1 Pet 3:19* he [Jesus] went and *p'ed* unto the spirits in prison

## PREACH THE GOSPEL

*Mark 16:15* Go ye into all the world, and *p-t-g* to every creature

*Luke 4:18* he [God] ... anointed me [Jesus] to *p-t-g* to ... poor

*Rom 1:15* I [Paul] am ready to *p-t-g* to you that are at Rome

*Rom 10:15* beautiful are the feet of them that *p-t-g*

*1 Cor 1:17* For Christ sent me [Paul] not to baptize, but to *p-t-g*

*1 Cor 9:14* they which *p-t-g* should live of the gospel

## PREACHER

*Eccl 1:2* Vanity of vanities, saith the *P* ... all is vanity

*Rom 10:14* and how shall they hear without a *p*

*2 Tim 1:11* I [Paul] am appointed a *p* ... of the Gentiles

## PRECEPT [S]

*Ps 119:27* me to understand the way of thy [God's] *p's*

*Ps 119:100* I understand ... because I keep thy [God's] *p's*

*Isa 28:10* *p* upon *p;* line upon line ... here a little

*Dan 9:5* We have sinned ... rebelled, even by departing from thy [God's] *p's*

*Mark 10:5* Jesus ... said ... For the hardness of your heart he [Moses] wrote you this *p*

## PRECIOUS

*Ps 116:15* *P* in the sight of the LORD is ... death of his saints

*Ps 139:17* How *p* also are thy thoughts ... O God

*Prov 17:8* A gift is as a *p* stone in the eyes of him that hath it

*Eccl 7:1* A good name is better than *p* ointment

*Isa 28:16* a tried stone, a *p* corner stone

*Matt 26:7* came ... a woman having an alabaster box of very *p* ointment

*1 Cor 3:12* if any man build upon this foundation gold, silver, *p* stones

*Rev 21:19* foundations ... were garnished with ... *p* stones

## PREDESTINATE [D]

*Rom 8:29* whom he [God] did foreknow, he also did *p*

*Eph 1:5* Having *p'd* us unto the adoption of children by Jesus Christ

*Eph 1:11* *p'd* according to the purpose of him [God] who worketh all things

## PRESENCE OF THE LORD

*Gen 3:8* Adam and his wife hid ... from the *p-o-t-L*

*Ps 114:7* Tremble, thou earth, at the *p-o-t-L*

*Jon 1:3* Jonah rose up to flee ... from the *p-o-t-L*

*2 Thes 1:9* punished with ... destruction from the *p-o-t-L*

## PRICE

*1 Chr 21:24* I [David] will verily buy it [a threshingfloor] for the full *p*

*Job 28:18* the *p* of wisdom is above rubies

*Prov 31:10* find a virtuous woman...*p*...above rubies

*Isa 55:1* buy wine and milk without money and without *p*

*Matt 13:46* when he had found one pearl of great *p*

*Acts 5:2* [Ananias] kept back part of the *p*

*1 Cor 6:20* ye are bought with a *p:* therefore glorify God

**PRIDE**

*Lev 26:19* I [God] will break the *p* of your power

*Ps 10:2* wicked in his *p* doth persecute the poor

*Ps 73:6* *p* compasseth them about as a chain

*Prov 8:13* The fear of the LORD is to hate...*p*

*Prov 16:18* *P* goeth before destruction

*1 John 2:16* the lust of the eyes, and the *p* of life

**PRINCIPALITY [IES]**

*Rom 8:38* neither death, nor life, nor angels, nor *p'ies*

*Eph 1:21* Far above all *p,* and power, and might

*Eph 6:12* we wrestle...against *p'ies,* against powers

*Col 2:15* having spoiled *p'ies* and powers, he [Jesus] made a show of them openly

**PROCHORUS** (one of the seven men chosen as "deacons" in the church at Jerusalem). Acts 6:1–5.

**PROCLAIM [ED]**

*Lev 23:4* holy convocations, which ye shall *p*

*Prov 20:6* Most men will *p* every one his own goodness

*Isa 61:1* the LORD...hath sent me [God's servant]...to *p* liberty to the captives

*Jon 3:5* people of Nineveh believed God, and *p'ed* a fast

*Luke 12:3* spoken in the ear in closets shall be *p'ed* upon the housetops

**PROFANE [D]**

*Ezek 23:38* they have...*p'd* my [God's] sabbaths

*Ezek 44:23* teach...the difference between the holy and *p*

*Mal 2:11* Judah hath *p'd* the holiness of the LORD

*1 Tim 4:7* refuse *p* and old wives' fables

*2 Tim 2:16* But shun *p* and vain babblings

**PROFESS [ING]**

*Matt 7:23* will I [Jesus] *p*...I never knew you

*Rom 1:22* *P'ing* themselves... wise, they became fools

*Titus 1:16* *p* that they know God; but in works...deny him

**PROFESSION**

*1 Tim 6:12* thou...hast professed a good *p*

*Heb 3:1* consider the...High Priest of our *p,* Christ Jesus

*Heb 10:23* Let us hold fast the *p* of our faith

## PROFIT [ETH]

*Ps 30:9* *p* is there in my blood, when I go down to the pit

*Eccl 1:3* What *p* hath a man of all his labour

*Jer 2:11* changed their glory for that which doth not *p*

*Mark 8:36* *p* a man, if he... gain the whole world, and lose his own soul

*John 6:63* spirit that quickeneth; the flesh *p'eth* nothing

*Rom 3:1* or what *p* is there of circumcision

*1 Cor 13:3* have not charity, it *p'eth* me nothing

*Jas 2:14* doth it *p*...though a man...have not works

## PROMISE [D, S]

*Josh 23:10* he [God]...fighteth for you, as he hath *p'd*

*2 Chr 1:9* thy [God's] *p* unto David...be established

*Jer 33:14* I [God] will perform that...which I have *p'd*

*Luke 24:49* behold, I [Jesus] send the *p* of my Father

*Rom 15:8* Jesus Christ was a minister...truth of God, to confirm the *p's* made

*Gal 3:21* the law then against the *p's* of God

*Gal 3:29* Abraham's seed, and heirs according to the *p*

*Gal 4:28* we, brethren...are the children of *p*

*Eph 3:6* Gentiles should be... partakers of his [God's] *p*

*Eph 6:2* Honour thy father... first commandment with *p*

*Titus 1:2* eternal life, which God, that cannot lie, *p'd*

*Heb 11:9* he [Abraham] sojourned in the land of *p*

*Jas 1:12* crown of life, which the Lord hath *p'd*

*2 Pet 3:4* Where is the *p* of his [Jesus'] coming

*1 John 2:25* *p* that he [Jesus] hath *p'd* us, even eternal life

## PROPHECIES ABOUT JESUS. See *Messianic Prophecies.*

## PROPHECY [IES]

*1 Cor 12:10* to another *p;* to another discerning of spirits

*1 Cor 13:2* though I [Paul] have the gift of *p*

*1 Cor 13:8* whether there be *p'ies,* they shall fail

*2 Pet 1:20* no *p* of the scripture is of...private interpretation

## PROPHESY [IED, IETH]

*Ezek 37:4* he [God] said...*P* upon these bones...hear the word

*Joel 2:28* your sons and your daughters shall *p*

*Amos 7:15* LORD said...Go, *p* unto my people Israel

*Matt 7:22* have we not *p'ied* in thy [Jesus'] name

*Mark 7:6* Well hath Esaias *p'ied* of you hypocrites

*Acts 2:18* pour out … my [God's] Spirit … they shall *p*

*Rom 12:6* let us *p* according to the proportion of faith

*1 Cor 13:9* we know in part, and we *p* in part

*1 Cor 14:5* greater is he that *p'ieth* than he that speaketh with tongues

## PROPITIATION

*Rom 3:25* Whom [Jesus] God hath set forth … a *p* through faith

*1 John 2:2* he [Jesus] is the *p* for our sins … not for ours only

*1 John 4:10* God … sent his Son to be the *p* for our sins

## PROUD

*Job 40:12* Look on every one that is *p,* and bring him low

*Ps 94:2* thou [God] … render a reward to the *p*

*Ps 119:69* The *p* have forged a lie against me

*Prov 6:17* A *p* look, a lying tongue

*Prov 16:5* one that is *p* in heart is an abomination

*Eccl 7:8* the patient in spirit is better than the *p* in spirit

*2 Tim 3:2* men shall be … covetous, boasters, *p*

*Jas 4:6* God resisteth the *p,* but giveth grace unto the humble

## PROVE [D, TH]

*Deut 13:3* God *p'th* you … whether ye love the LORD

*Ps 26:2* Examine me, O LORD, and *p* me; try … my heart

*Mal 3:10* *p* me now … saith the LORD of hosts

*Rom 12:2* *p* what is that good, and … perfect, will of God

*Gal 6:4* But let every man *p* his own work

*1 Thes 5:21* *P* all things; hold fast that which is good

*1 Tim 3:10* be *p'd;* then let them use the office of a deacon

## PROVERBS, BOOK OF. A
wisdom book of the Old Testament filled with pithy sayings on how to live with maturity and integrity under the watchful eye of God—the source of all wisdom.

## PROVOKE [D, ING]

*Deut 32:16* They *p'd* him [God] … with strange gods

*Ps 78:17* sinned … against him [God] by *p'ing* … most High

*Ps 78:58* *p'd* him [God] to anger with their high places

*1 Cor 10:22* Do we *p* the Lord to jealousy

*1 Cor 13:5* [charity] is not easily *p'd,* thinketh no evil

*Gal 5:26* not be desirous of vain glory, *p'ing* one another

*Eph 6:4* fathers, *p* not your children to wrath

*Heb 10:24* consider one another to *p* ... to good works

**PSALMS, BOOK OF.** A poetic book of the Old Testament filled with hymns of praise and prayers that probably were meant to be sung to the accompaniment of a musical instrument. King David of Judah wrote many of these psalms (see, for example, Pss 54; 59; 65).

**PUBLIUS** (a Roman official who entertained Paul on the island of Miletus after a shipwreck). Acts 28:7–8.

**PUL.** See *Tiglath-Pileser III.*

**PUNISH [ED]**

*Isa 13:11* And I [God] will *p* the world for their evil

*Jer 21:14* I [God] will *p* you according to ... your doings

*Jer 50:18* Behold, I [God] will *p* the king of Babylon

*2 Thes 1:9* *p'ed* with everlasting destruction from the presence of the Lord

**PURIFY [IED, IETH]**

*Titus 2:14* that he [Jesus] might...*p*...a peculiar people

*Jas 4:8* and *p* your hearts, ye double minded

*1 Pet 1:22* *p'ied* your souls in obeying the truth

*1 John 3:3* every man that hath this hope...*p'ieth* himself

**PURPOSE [D, TH]**

*Eccl 3:1* a time to every *p* under the heaven

*Dan 1:8* Daniel *p'd*...that he would not defile himself

*Rom 8:28* to them who are the called according to his *p*

*2 Cor 9:7* as he *p'th* in his heart, so let him give

*Eph 3:11* eternal *p* which he *p'd* in Christ Jesus

*1 John 3:8* For this *p* the Son of God was manifested

# -Q-

## QUAIL PROVIDED FOR ISRAEL IN THE WILDERNESS. Ex 16:1–13.

## QUENCH [ED]

*2 Chr 34:25* my [God's] wrath... shall not be *q'ed*

*Song 8:7* Many waters cannot *q* love

*Jer 7:20* mine [God's] anger... shall not be *q'ed*

*Matt 12:20* A bruised reed shall he not break, and smoking flax shall he not *q*

*Mark 9:44* Where their worm dieth not...fire is not *q'ed*

*Eph 6:16* ye shall...*q* all the fiery darts of the wicked

*1 Thes 5:19* *Q* not the Spirit

## QUICK [EN, ENED, ENETH, ENING]

*Ps 71:20* Thou [God]...shalt *q'en* me

*Ps 80:18* *q'en* us, and we will call upon thy [God's] name

*Ps 119:88* *Q'en* me after thy [God's] lovingkindness

*Ps 143:11* *Q'en* me, O LORD, for thy name's sake

*Isa 11:3* make him [God's servant] of *q* understanding

*John 5:21* Son *q'eneth* whom he will

*John 6:63* the spirit that *q'eneth*...flesh profiteth nothing

*Acts 10:42* he [Jesus]...was ordained...Judge of *q* and dead

*1 Cor 15:45* the last Adam was made a *q'ening* spirit

*Eph 2:1* And you hath he *q'ened,* who were dead in trespasses and sins

*2 Tim 4:1* Jesus Christ...shall judge the *q* and the dead

*Heb 4:12* For the word of God is *q,* and powerful

# -R-

**RABBAH** (capital city of the Ammonites captured by David's army). Josh 13:25 • **2 Sam 12:26–31** • 1 Chr 20:1 • Jer 49:2–3 • Ezek 25:5 • Amos 1:14. *Rabbath:* Ezek 21:20.

**RABBATH.** See *Rabbah.*

**RACE**
*Eccl 9:11* I...saw...that the *r* is not to the swift
*1 Cor 9:24* in a *r* run all, but one receiveth the prize
*Heb 12:1* run with patience the *r*...set before us

**RACHAB.** See *Rahab.*

**RACHEL** (Jacob's wife who died giving birth to Benjamin). Gen 29:6–31; 30:1–25; 31:4–34; 33:1–7; **35:16–24;** 46:19–25; 48:7 • Ruth 4:11 • Matt 2:18. *Rahel:* Jer 31:15–17.

**RAHAB** (a harlot who hid the spies sent by Joshua to scout the city of Jericho). **Josh 2:1–24;** 6:17–25 • Heb 11:31 • Jas 2:25. *Rachab:* Matt 1:5.

**RAHEL.** See *Rachel.*

**RAINBOW AS GOD'S COVENANT SYMBOL.** Gen 9:11–17.

**RAISE [D, TH]**
*Judg 2:16* Nevertheless the LORD *r'd* up judges
*Ps 41:10* LORD, be merciful unto me, and *r* me up
*Ps 113:7* He [God] *r'th* up the poor out of the dust
*Jer 23:5* I [God] will *r* unto David a righteous Branch
*Amos 9:11* day will I [God] *r* up the tabernacle of David
*Hab 1:6* I [God] *r* up the Chaldeans...bitter...nation
*Matt 10:8* Heal the sick, cleanse the lepers, *r* the dead
*Matt 16:21* he [Jesus] must... be killed, and be *r'd* again
*John 2:19* Destroy this temple, and in three days I [Jesus] will *r* it up
*John 5:21* as the Father *r'th* up the dead, and quickeneth them
*Acts 10:40* Him [Jesus] God *r'd* up the third day
*Rom 6:4* as Christ was *r'd*... we...walk in newness of life
*Rom 10:9* believe...God hath *r'd* him [Jesus] from the dead
*1 Cor 6:14* God...will also *r* up us
*1 Cor 15:16* if the dead rise not, then is not Christ *r'd*
*2 Tim 2:8* Jesus Christ...was *r'd* from the dead
*Heb 11:19* God was able to *r* him [Jesus] up

**RAMAH.** See *Ramoth-gilead.*

**RAMESES** (a district of Egypt where Jacob and his descendants settled). **Gen 47:11** • Ex 12:37 • Num 33:3,5.

**RAMOTH.** See *Ramoth-gilead.*

**RAMOTH-GILEAD** (an Amorite city that became one of the six cities of refuge). Deut 4:43 • Josh 20:8 • 1 Chr 6:80. *Ramah:* 2 Kgs 8:29. *Ramoth:* 1 Kgs 22:3.

**RANSOM**
*Prov 13:8* The *r* of a man's life are his riches
*Hos 13:14* I [God] will *r* them from the power of the grave
*Mark 10:45* the Son of man came...to give his life a *r*
*1 Tim 2:6* Who [Jesus] gave himself a *r* for all

**READY**
*Ex 17:4* they be almost *r* to stone me [Moses]
*Job 17:1* My [Job's] days are extinct...graves are *r* for me
*Ps 86:5* thou, Lord, art good, and *r* to forgive
*Mark 14:38* The spirit truly is *r*, but the flesh is weak
*Luke 12:40* Be ye...*r*...the Son of man cometh...when ye think not
*Luke 22:33* Lord, I [Peter] am *r* to go with thee
*Rom 1:15* I [Paul] am *r* to preach...at Rome also

*2 Tim 4:6* For I [Paul] am now *r* to be offered
*1 Pet 3:15* be *r* always to give an answer to every man

**REAP [ETH, ING]**
*Lev 19:9* not wholly *r* the corners of thy field
*Job 4:8* they that...sow wickedness, *r* the same
*Ps 126:5* They that sow in tears shall *r* in joy
*Prov 22:8* He that soweth iniquity shall *r* vanity
*Hos 8:7* they have sown the wind...*r* the whirlwind
*Matt 25:24* an hard man, *r'ing* where thou hast not sown
*Luke 12:24* Consider...ravens: for they neither sow nor *r*
*John 4:37* One soweth, and another *r'eth*
*2 Cor 9:6* soweth bountifully shall *r* also bountifully
*Gal 6:7* whatsoever a man soweth, that shall he also *r*
*Gal 6:9* shall *r*, if we faint not

**REASON [ING]**
*Ps 90:10* if by *r* of strength they [days of our years] be fourscore years
*Isa 1:18* Come now, and let us *r* together, saith the LORD
*Luke 9:46* *r'ing* among them [the disciples], which... should be greatest
*Acts 6:2* not *r* that we [the apostles] should leave... word of God...serve tables

*1 Pet 3:15* asketh you a *r* of the hope that is in you

**REBECCA.** See *Rebekah.*

**REBEKAH** (wife of Isaac and mother of Jacob and Esau). Gen 22:23; 24:15–67; 26:7–8,35; 27:5–46; 28:5; 49:31. *Rebecca:* Rom 9:10.

**REBUKE [D, S, TH]**
*Ps 6:1* O LORD, *r* me not in thine anger
*Ps 119:21* Thou [God] hast *r'd* the proud that are cursed
*Prov 27:5* Open *r* is better than secret love
*Eccl 7:5* It is better to hear the *r* of the wise
*Ezek 25:17* I [God] will execute... vengeance...furious *r's*
*Nah 1:4* He [God] *r'th* the sea, and maketh it dry
*Matt 16:22* Peter took him [Jesus], and began to *r* him
*Mark 8:33* he [Jesus] *r'd* Peter... Get...behind me, Satan
*Luke 8:24* Then he [Jesus] arose, and *r'd* the wind
*Titus 2:15* These things speak... and *r* with all authority
*Rev 3:19* As many as I [Jesus] love, I *r* and chasten

**RECEIVE [D, ING, TH]**
*Job 2:10* *r* good at the hand of God, and...not *r* evil
*Prov 19:20* Hear counsel, and *r* instruction

*Isa 40:2* Jerusalem...hath *r'd* of the LORD'S hand double
*Mal 3:10* not be room enough to *r* it [God's blessing]
*Matt 7:8* For every one that asketh *r'th*
*Matt 10:8* freely ye have *r'd,* freely give
*Matt 11:5* blind *r* their sight, and the lame walk
*Matt 18:5* whoso...*r* one such little child...*r'th* me [Jesus]
*Matt 21:22* ask in prayer, believing, ye shall *r*
*Mark 10:15* Whosoever shall not *r* the kingdom of God as a little child
*Luke 23:41* we [two thieves] *r* the due reward of our deeds
*John 1:11* came unto his [Jesus'] own...own *r'd* him not
*John 3:27* *r* nothing, except it be given him from heaven
*John 14:3* come again, and *r* you unto myself [Jesus]
*John 20:22* he [Jesus] breathed on them [the disciples]...*R* ye the Holy Ghost
*Acts 1:8* But ye [the apostles] shall *r* power
*Acts 8:17* they [the Samaritans] *r'd* the Holy Ghost
*Acts 17:11* they [the Bereans] *r'd* the word with...readiness
*Acts 20:35* It is more blessed to give than to *r*
*Rom 8:15* ye have *r'd* the Spirit of adoption
*1 Cor 2:14* natural man *r'th* not the things of the Spirit

*1 Cor 3:14* If any man's work abide...he shall *r* a reward

*Heb 11:8* called to...a place which he [Abraham] should after *r* for an inheritance

*Heb 11:13* died in faith, not having *r'd* the promises

*Jas 1:12* man...endureth temptation...*r* the crown of life

*Jas 4:3* Ye ask, and *r* not, because ye ask amiss

*1 Pet 1:9* *R'ing* the end of your faith, even...salvation

*1 Pet 5:4* ye shall *r* a crown of glory that fadeth not

*Rev 4:11* Thou art worthy, O Lord, to *r* glory and honour

**RECHAB** (father of Jehonadab and ancestor of the Rechabites). 2 Kgs 10:15–23 • Jer 35:6–19.

**RECKON [ED, ETH]**

*Matt 25:19* lord of those servants...*r'eth* with them

*Luke 22:37* he [Jesus] was *r'ed* among the transgressors

*Rom 8:18* *r* that the sufferings... not worthy to be compared

**RECONCILE [D, ING]**

*Matt 5:24* be *r'ed* to thy brother...then...offer thy gift

*2 Cor 5:19* God was in Christ, *r'ing* the world unto himself

*2 Cor 5:20* in Christ's stead, be ye *r'ed* to God

*Eph 2:16* he [Jesus] might *r* both unto God...by the cross

**RECONCILIATION**

*2 Chr 29:24* priests...made *r* with their [animals'] blood

*2 Cor 5:18* God...hath given to us the ministry of *r*

*Heb 2:17* he [Jesus] might... make *r*...sins of the people

**RED SEA** (a body of water that the Israelites crossed miraculously to escape the Egyptian army). Ex 10:19; **14:16–29; 15:4,22** • Num 33:10–11.

**REDEEM [ED, ETH, ING]**

*Ps 26:11* *r* me, and be merciful unto me

*Ps 34:22* The Lord *r'eth* the soul of his servants

*Ps 49:15* But God will *r* my soul from...the grave

*Ps 77:15* Thou [God] hast... *r'ed* thy people

*Ps 107:2* Let the *r'ed* of the Lord say so

*Isa 43:1* Fear not: for I [God] have *r'ed* thee [Israel]

*Isa 50:2* Is my [God's] hand shortened...that it cannot *r*

*Isa 52:9* for the Lord...hath *r'ed* Jerusalem

*Luke 1:68* the Lord...hath visited and *r'ed* his people

*Gal 3:13* Christ hath *r'ed* us from the curse of the law

*Gal 4:5* To *r* them that were under the law

*Eph 5:16* **R'ing** the time, because the days are evil

*Col 4:5* Walk in wisdom...**r'ing** the time

*Titus 2:14* he [Jesus] might **r** us from all iniquity

## REDEMPTION

*Ps 130:7* for with the LORD there is...plenteous **r**

*Rom 3:24* justified...through the **r** that is in Christ Jesus

*Eph 1:7* we have **r** through his [Jesus'] blood

*Heb 9:12* by his [Jesus'] own blood he...obtained...**r**

## REGENERATION

*Matt 19:28* ye which...followed me [Jesus], in the **r**...sit upon twelve thrones

*Titus 3:5* he [Jesus] saved us, by the washing of **r**

**REHOBOAM** (son and successor of Solomon as king of Judah who refused to implement the reform measures called for by northern leaders). 1 Kgs 11:43; **12:1–24;** 14:21–31; 15:6 • 1 Chr 3:10 • 2 Chr 9:31; 10:1–18; 11:1–22; 12:1–16; 13:7. *Roboam:* Matt 1:7.

## REIGN [ED, ETH]

*Gen 37:8* Shalt thou [Joseph] indeed **r** over us

*Judg 9:8* The trees...said unto the olive tree, **R** thou over us

*2 Sam 5:4* David was thirty years old when he began to **r**

*1 Chr 29:26* David the son of Jesse **r'ed** over all Israel

*Ps 47:8* God **r'eth** over the heathen

*Ps 93:1* The LORD **r'eth,** he is clothed with majesty

*Ps 146:10* LORD shall **r** for ever

*Jer 23:5* a King shall **r** and prosper...execute judgment

*Luke 1:33* he [Jesus] shall **r** over the house of Jacob for ever

*Rom 5:14* death **r'ed** from Adam to Moses

*Rom 6:12* Let not sin...**r** in your mortal body

*1 Cor 15:25* he [Jesus] must **r,** till...all enemies under his feet

*Rev 11:15* Christ...shall **r** for ever and ever

*Rev 19:6* Alleluia...the Lord God omnipotent **r'eth**

## REJECT [ED]

*1 Sam 15:26* thou [Saul] hast **r'ed** the word of the LORD

*Isa 53:3* he [God's servant] is despised and **r'ed** of men

*Mark 7:9* ye [Pharisees] **r** the commandment of God

*Mark 12:10* The stone which the builders **r'ed**

*Luke 17:25* must he [Jesus] suffer many things, and be **r'ed** of this generation

## REJOICE [D, ING, TH]

*Deut 30:9* for the LORD will again *r* over thee

*1 Sam 2:1* My [Hannah's] heart *r'th* in the LORD

*1 Chr 16:10* let the heart of them *r* that seek the LORD

*Job 8:21* Till he [God] fill... thy lips with *r'ing*

*Ps 5:11* those that put their trust in thee [God] *r*

*Ps 19:8* statutes of the LORD are right, *r'ing* the heart

*Ps 32:11* Be glad in the LORD, and *r,* ye righteous

*Ps 40:16* Let all those that seek thee [God] *r* and be glad

*Ps 63:7* in the shadow of thy [God's] wings will I *r*

*Ps 97:1* The LORD reigneth; let the earth *r*

*Ps 108:7* God hath spoken in his holiness; I will *r*

*Ps 118:24* day... LORD hath made; we will *r* and be glad

*Ps 119:14* I have *r'd* in... thy [God's] testimonies

*Ps 126:6* come again with *r'ing,* bringing his sheaves

*Prov 5:18* and *r* with the wife of thy youth

*Prov 15:30* The light of the eyes *r'th* the heart

*Eccl 11:9* **R,** O young man, in thy youth

*Isa 29:19* poor... shall *r* in the Holy One of Israel

*Joel 2:21* be glad and *r:* for the LORD will do great things

*Matt 2:10* they [the wise men] *r'd* with... great joy

*Matt 5:12* **R** ... for great is your reward in heaven

*Luke 15:6* **R** with me; for I have found my sheep

*John 8:56* Abraham *r'd* to see my [Jesus'] day

*Rom 12:12* **R'ing** in hope; patient in tribulation

*Rom 12:15* **R** with them that do *r*... weep with them that weep

*Phil 1:18* Christ is preached; and I [Paul] therein do *r*

## REJOICE IN THE LORD

*Ps 33:1* **R-i-t-L,** O ye righteous

*Ps 97:12* **R-i-t-L**... and give thanks at... his holiness

*Hab 3:18* I will *r-i-t-L,* I will joy in... my salvation

*Phil 3:1* Finally, my brethren, *r-i-t-L*

*Phil 4:4* **R-i-t-L** alway: and again I say, Rejoice

## REMEMBER [ED, EST, ETH, ING]

*Gen 8:1* God *r'ed* Noah, and every living thing

*Gen 9:16* that I [God] may *r* the everlasting covenant

*Ex 2:24* God heard their [Israel's] groaning, and... *r'ed* his covenant

*Ex 20:8* **R** the sabbath day, to keep it holy

*Deut 8:18* thou shalt *r* the LORD thy God

*Deut 15:15 r* that thou [Israel] wast a bondman in…Egypt

*Ps 20:7* we will *r* the name of the LORD our God

*Ps 25:7 R* not the sins of my youth, nor my transgressions

*Ps 45:17* make thy [God's] name to be *r'ed*

*Ps 77:10 r* the years of the right hand of the most High

*Ps 78:39* he [God] *r'ed* that they were but flesh

*Ps 98:3* He [God] hath *r'ed* his mercy…toward…Israel

*Ps 103:14* For…he [God] *r'eth* that we are dust

*Ps 137:1* we [Israelites] wept, when we *r'ed* Zion

*Ps 137:7 R,* O LORD, the children of Edom

*Eccl 12:1 R* now thy Creator in the days of thy youth

*Jer 31:34* I [God] will *r* their sin no more

*Jon 2:7* my [Jonah's] soul fainted…I *r'ed* the LORD

*Matt 5:23* there [at the altar] *r'est* that thy brother hath ought against thee

*Luke 22:61* And Peter *r'ed* the word of the Lord

*Luke 23:42* Lord, *r* me [thief] when thou comest into thy kingdom

*Luke 24:8* they [the disciples] *r'ed* his [Jesus'] words

*John 16:21* as soon as she is delivered of the child, she *r'eth* no more the anguish

*1 Thes 1:3 R'ing* without ceasing your work of faith

*2 Tim 2:8 R* that Jesus Christ… was raised from the dead

*Heb 10:17* their sins…will I [God] *r* no more

## REMEMBRANCE

*Ps 30:4* give thanks at the *r* of his [God's] holiness

*Ps 102:12* endure for ever; and thy [God's] *r* unto all generations

*Luke 22:19* This is my [Jesus'] body…this do in *r* of me

*John 14:26* the Comforter… bring all things to your *r*

## REMISSION

*Heb 9:22* without shedding of blood is no *r*

*Heb 10:18* where *r*…is, there is no more offering for sin

## REMISSION OF SINS

*Matt 26:28* my [Jesus'] blood… is shed for many for the *r-o-s*

*Mark 1:4* John did baptize… preach the baptism of repentance for the *r-o-s*

*Luke 24:47* repentance and *r-o-s* should be preached…among all nations

*Acts 2:38* be baptized…in the name of Jesus…for the *r-o-s*

*Acts 10:43* whosoever believeth in him [Jesus] shall receive *r-o-s*

**REMPHAN** (a pagan Babylonian god worshiped by the Israelites). Acts 7:41–43.

## RENDER [ED, ING]

*Ps 38:20* They...that *r* evil for good are mine adversaries

*Ps 116:12* *r* unto the LORD for all his benefits

*Prov 12:14* and the recompence of a man's hands shall be *r'ed* unto him

*Luke 20:25* **R**...unto Caesar

*Rom 2:6* Who [God] will *r* to... man according to his deeds

*1 Cor 7:3* husband *r* unto the wife due benevolence

*1 Thes 5:15* See that none *r* evil for evil unto any man

*1 Pet 3:9* Not *r'ing* evil for evil...railing for railing

## RENEW [ED, EST, ING]

*Ps 51:10* clean heart, O God... *r* a right spirit within me

*Ps 104:30* thou [God] *r'est* the face of the earth

*Isa 40:31* they that wait upon the LORD...*r* their strength

*Rom 12:2* be ye transformed by the *r'ing* of your mind

*2 Cor 4:16* yet the inward man is *r'ed* day by day

## REPENT [ED, ETH]

*Gen 6:6* it *r'ed* the LORD that he had made man

*Job 42:6* I [Job] abhor myself... *r* in dust and ashes

*Matt 4:17* Jesus began to preach, and to say, **R**

*Luke 15:7* joy...in heaven over one sinner that *r'eth*

*Luke 17:3* if he [your brother] *r,* forgive him

*Acts 2:38* Peter said...**R,** and be baptized every one of you

*Rev 3:19* I [Jesus] rebuke... chasten: be zealous...and *r*

## REPENTANCE

*Matt 9:13* I [Jesus] am...come to call...sinners to *r*

*Luke 24:47* *r*...preached... among all nations

*2 Cor 7:10* godly sorrow worketh *r* to salvation

*2 Pet 3:9* all should come to *r*

**REPHAIM** (a valley near Jerusalem where David defeated the Philistines). **2 Sam 5:18–25; 23:13** • 1 Chr 11:15; 14:9 • Isa 17:5.

## REPROACH [ED, ETH]

*Ps 31:11* I was a *r* among all mine enemies

*Ps 55:12* For it was not an enemy that *r'ed* me

*Ps 102:8* Mine enemies *r* me all the day

*Prov 14:31* He that oppresseth the poor *r'eth* his Maker

*Prov 14:34* but sin is a *r* to any people

*Heb 11:26* Esteeming...*r* of Christ greater riches than... treasures in Egypt

*Heb 13:13* go ... unto him [Jesus] ... bearing his *r*

*1 Pet 4:14* ye be *r'ed* for the name of Christ, happy are ye

## REPROBATE [S]

*Rom 1:28* God gave them over to a *r* mind

*2 Cor 13:6* I [Paul] trust that ye ... know ... we are not *r's*

*2 Tim 3:8* men of corrupt minds, *r* concerning the faith

## REPROVE [D, TH]

*Ps 50:8* I [God] will not *r* thee for thy sacrifices

*Prov 9:7* He that *r'th* a scorner getteth ... shame

*John 16:8* he [the Holy Spirit] will *r* the world of sin

*Eph 5:13* all things that are *r'ed* are made manifest

*2 Tim 4:2* *r,* rebuke, exhort with all longsuffering

## REPUTATION

*Phil 2:7* made himself [Jesus] of no *r* ... took ... form of a servant

*Phil 2:29* Receive him [Epaphroditus] ... and hold such in *r*

## RESIST [ED, ETH]

*Matt 5:39* I [Jesus] say unto you, That ye *r* not evil

*Acts 7:51* ye do always *r* the Holy Ghost

*Heb 12:4* Ye have not yet *r'ed* unto blood

*Jas 4:6* God *r'eth* ... proud ... giveth grace unto the humble

*Jas 4:7* *R* the devil, and he will flee from you

## RESPECT [ETH]

*Gen 4:4* the LORD had *r* unto Abel and to his offering

*Ps 40:4* Blessed is that man that ... *r'eth* not the proud

*Ps 119:15* I will ... have *r* unto thy [God's] ways

## RESPECT OF PERSONS

*Prov 24:23* not good to have *r-o-p* in judgment

*Rom 2:11* For there is no *r-o-p* with God

*Eph 6:9* neither is there *r-o-p* with him [Jesus]

*1 Pet 1:17* who [God] without *r-o-p* judgeth ... every man's work

## RESTORE [TH]

*Ps 23:3* He [God] *r'th* my soul

*Ps 51:12* *R* unto me the joy of thy [God's] salvation

*Luke 19:8* Behold, Lord ... I [Zacchaeus] *r* him fourfold

*Acts 1:6* Lord, wilt thou ... *r* again the kingdom to Israel

*Gal 6:1* *r* such an one in the spirit of meekness

## RESURRECTION

*Matt 27:53* [the saints] came out of the graves after his [Jesus'] *r*

*Luke 20:33* Therefore in the *r* whose wife of them is she

*John 11:25* I [Jesus] am the *r,* and the life

*Acts 4:33* gave the apostles witness of the *r* of…Jesus

*Acts 17:32* they [philosophers] heard of the *r*…mocked

*1 Cor 15:13* no *r* of the dead, then is Christ not risen

*Phil 3:10* I [Paul] may know him [Jesus]…power of his *r*

*1 Pet 1:3* a lively hope by the *r* of Jesus Christ

*Rev 20:6* Blessed…is he that hath part in the first *r*

**RESURRECTION AND THE LIFE, JESUS AS.** See *"I Am" Statements of Jesus.*

**RESURRECTION OF JESUS.** See *Jesus, Life and Ministry of.*

**REUBEN** (a son of Jacob and ancestor of one of the twelve tribes of Israel). Gen 29:32; 37:21–29; 42:22,37; 46:8–9; 48:5; 49:3. The tribe of Reuben settled east of the Jordan River along the Dead Sea. Num 32:1–25.

**REUEL.** See *Jethro.*

**REVEAL [ED, ETH]**
*Job 20:27* heaven shall *r* his [man's] iniquity

*Isa 40:5* glory of the LORD shall be *r'ed*

*Dan 2:28* there is a God in heaven that *r'eth* secrets

*Matt 16:17* flesh and blood… not *r'ed* it unto thee [Peter]

*Luke 10:21* hid these things from the wise and…*r'ed* them unto babes

*Luke 10:22* no man knoweth… who the Father is…and he to whom the Son will *r* him

*Rom 1:17* righteousness of God *r'ed* from faith to faith

*1 Cor 3:13* it [man's work] shall be *r'ed* by fire

*Phil 3:15* God shall *r* even this

*1 Pet 1:5* kept by the power of God through faith…ready to be *r'ed* in the last time

*1 Pet 4:13* when his [Jesus'] glory shall be *r'ed*

**REVELATION**
*Gal 1:12* neither was I [Paul] taught it, but by the *r* of Jesus Christ

*Eph 3:3* by *r* he [God] made known…the mystery

*Rev 1:1* *R* of Jesus Christ, which God gave

**REVELATION OF JOHN, BOOK OF THE.** The last book of the New Testament that consists of a series of visions revealed by the Lord to the apostle John. These visions are considered by some interpreters to portray the end of the present age and the coming of God's kingdom.

## REVERENCE

*Lev 26:2* keep my [God's] sabbaths, and *r* my sanctuary

*Luke 20:13* it may be they will *r* him [vineyard owner's son]

*Heb 12:28* we may serve God ... with *r* and godly fear

## REVILE [D]

*Matt 5:11* Blessed are ye, when men shall *r* you

*Mark 15:32* And they [two thieves] that were crucified with him [Jesus] *r'd* him

*1 Pet 2:23* Who [Jesus], when he was *r'd, r'd* not again

## REWARD [ED, ETH]

*Gen 15:1* I [God] am thy [Abraham's] ... great *r*

*Ps 18:20* LORD *r'ed* me according to my righteousness

*Ps 31:23* the LORD ... plentifully *r'eth* the proud doer

*Ps 58:11* Verily there is a *r* for the righteous

*Ps 103:10* He [God] hath not ... *r'ed* us according to our iniquities

*Ps 127:3* and the fruit of the womb is his [God's] *r*

*Prov 17:13* Whoso *r'eth* evil for good, evil shall not depart from his house

*Matt 5:12* great is your *r* in heaven: for so persecuted they the prophets

*Matt 5:46* love them which love you, what *r* have ye

*Luke 23:41* we [two thieves] receive ... due *r* of our deeds

*1 Cor 3:8* every man shall receive his own *r*

*Col 3:24* ye shall receive the *r* of the inheritance

*1 Tim 5:18* The labourer is worthy of his *r*

**REZIN** (a king of Syria who was killed in the conquest by the Assyrians). **2 Kgs 15:37; 16:5–9** • Isa 7:4,8; 8:6; 9:11.

**RHODES** (a Greek island that Paul's ship passed). Acts 21:1.

## RIGHT HAND OF GOD

*Mark 16:19* he [Jesus] was received up ... and sat on the *r-h-o-G*

*Acts 7:55* he [Stephen] ... saw ... Jesus standing on the *r-h-o-G*

*Col 3:1* seek those things ... above, where Christ sitteth on the *r-h-o-G*

*Heb 10:12* this man [Jesus] ... sat down on the *r-h-o-G*

*1 Pet 3:22* Who [Jesus] is gone into heaven ... on the *r-h-o-G*

## RIGHTEOUS [LY, NESS]

*Gen 15:6* the LORD ... counted it ... for *r'ness*

*Gen 18:23* Wilt thou [God] ... destroy the *r* with the wicked

*Job 15:14* What is man…that he should be *r*

*Job 32:1* because he [Job] was *r* in his own eyes

*Ps 1:6* For the LORD knoweth the way of the *r*

*Ps 9:8* And he [God] shall judge the world in *r'ness*

*Ps 19:9* judgments of the LORD are true and *r*

*Ps 23:3* he [God] leadeth me in the paths of *r'ness*

*Ps 35:28* my tongue shall speak of thy [God's] *r'ness*

*Ps 37:16* A little that a *r* man hath is better than…riches

*Ps 37:29* The *r* shall inherit the land…dwell therein

*Ps 45:7* Thou [God] lovest *r'ness,* and hatest wickedness

*Ps 97:6* The heavens declare his [God's] *r'ness*

*Ps 119:137* ***R*** art thou, O LORD… upright…thy judgments

*Ps 129:4* LORD is *r:* he hath cut…the cords of the wicked

*Ps 145:17* The LORD is *r* in all his ways…holy in…works

*Prov 10:11* The mouth of a *r* man is a well of life

*Prov 14:34* ***R'ness*** exalteth a nation

*Prov 15:29* The LORD…heareth the prayer of the *r*

*Prov 16:8* Better is a little with *r'ness* than great revenues

*Prov 31:9* judge *r'ly,* and plead the cause of the poor

*Isa 62:2* the Gentiles shall see thy [God's] *r'ness*

*Jer 23:5* I [God] will raise unto David a *r* Branch

*Amos 5:24* let judgment run down as waters, and *r'ness* as a mighty stream

*Mal 4:2* Sun of *r'ness* arise with healing in his wings

*Matt 5:6* Blessed are they which…thirst after *r'ness*

*Matt 5:20* except your *r'ness*… exceed…*r'ness* of the scribes

*Matt 6:33* But seek ye first the kingdom of God, and his *r'ness*

*Luke 5:32* I [Jesus] came not to call the *r*…to repentance

*Luke 23:47* Certainly this [Jesus] was a *r* man

*Rom 1:17* *r'ness* of God revealed from faith to faith

*Rom 3:10* As it is written, There is none *r,* no, not one

*Rom 4:3* Abraham believed God…counted…for *r'ness*

Rom 5:19 by the obedience of one [Jesus]…many be made *r*

*Rom 10:10* with the heart man believeth unto *r'ness*

*2 Cor 5:21* might be made… *r'ness* of God in him [Jesus]

*2 Cor 6:14* what fellowship hath *r'ness* with unrighteousness

*Eph 6:14* having on the breastplate of *r'ness*

*2 Tim 4:8* laid up for me [Paul] a crown of *r'ness*

*Jas 5:16* fervent prayer of a *r* man availeth much

*1 Pet 3:12* For the eyes of the Lord are over the *r*

*1 Pet 3:14* if ye suffer for *r'ness'* sake, happy are ye

**RIMMON** (a pagan god worshiped by Naaman the leper). 2 Kgs 5:18.

**ROBOAM.** See *Rehoboam.*

**ROMANS, EPISTLE TO THE.** An epistle on the themes of righteousness and salvation, written by the apostle Paul to the Christians at Rome. The most systematic and theological of all of Paul's epistles, Romans expresses his conviction that the gospel is the power of salvation to all who believe (1:16–17).

**ROME** (capital city of the Roman Empire and the place where Paul was imprisoned during his final days). Acts 2:10; 18:2; 19:21; 23:11; **28:14–16** • Rom 1:7,15 • 2 Tim 1:17.

**RUHAMAH** (a symbolic name, meaning "having obtained favor," given by the prophet Hosea to his daughter to show that Israel would be forgiven). Hos 2:1.

**RULE [ING, TH]**

*Gen 1:16* two great lights; the greater light to *r* the day

*2 Sam 23:3* He that *r'th* over men must be just

*Matt 2:6* a Governor, that shall *r* my people Israel

*Col 3:15* let the peace of God *r* in your hearts

*1 Tim 3:5* if a man know not how to *r* his own house

*1 Tim 3:12* deacons…*r'ing*… their own houses well

**RUN [NETH, NING]**

*Ps 23:5* my cup *r'neth* over

*Eccl 1:7* All the rivers *r* into the sea…sea is not full

*Isa 40:31* they shall *r,* and not be weary

*Jer 5:1 R* ye [Jeremiah] to and fro through…streets of Jerusalem

*Amos 5:24* let judgment *r* down as waters

*Hab 2:2* Write the vision…that he may *r* that readeth it

*Matt 28:8* they [the women] departed…and did *r* to bring his [Jesus'] disciples word

*Luke 6:38* pressed down… shaken together, and *r'ning* over

*1 Cor 9:24 r* all, but one receiveth the prize

*Gal 5:7* Ye did *r* well; who did hinder you

*Heb 12:1* let us *r* with patience the race…before us

**RUTH** (a Moabite woman who remained loyal to her Jewish mother-in-law Naomi after the death of their husbands). Ruth 1–4.

**RUTH, BOOK OF.** A short Old Testament book on the power of love in dismal circumstances. Love bound Ruth and her mother-in-law Naomi together, even after their husbands died (1:1–2:23).

# -S-

## SACKCLOTH AND ASHES

*Esth 4:3* and many [Jews] lay in *s-a-a*

*Dan 9:3* seek [God] by prayer ... with fasting, and *s-a-a*

*Matt 11:21* they [Tyre and Sidon] would have repented long ago in *s-a-a*

## SACRIFICE [S]

*1 Sam 15:22* Behold, to obey is better than *s*

*Ps 4:5* Offer the *s's* of righteousness ... trust in the LORD

*Ps 51:17* The *s's* of God are a broken spirit

*Ps 116:17* offer to thee [God] the *s* of thanksgiving

*Prov 15:8* The *s* of the wicked is an abomination

*Prov 17:1* Better is a dry morsel ... than ... *s's* with strife

*Hos 6:6* For I [God] desired mercy, and not *s*

*Jon 2:9* I will *s* unto thee [God] with ... thanksgiving

*Rom 12:1* present your bodies a living *s*

*Heb 7:27* Who [Jesus] needeth not daily ... to offer up *s*

*Heb 11:4* Abel offered ... a more excellent *s* than Cain

*Heb 13:15* offer the *s* of praise to God continually

*1 Pet 2:5* offer up spiritual *s's*, acceptable to God

## SADDUCEES (a priestly aristocratic party of New Testament times that often opposed Jesus and His teachings). Matt 3:7; **16:1,6,11–12; 22:23–34** • **Mark 12:18** • **Luke 20:27** • Acts 4:1–3; 5:17–18; 23:6–8.

## SAINTS

*2 Chr 6:41* let thy [God's] *s* rejoice in goodness

*Ps 30:4* Sing unto the LORD, O ye *s* of his

*Ps 89:7* God is greatly to be feared in ... assembly of the *s*

*Ps 116:15* Precious in the sight of the LORD ... death of his *s*

*Matt 27:52* bodies of the *s* which slept arose

*Rom 12:13* Distributing to the necessity of *s*

*1 Cor 1:2* them ... sanctified in Christ Jesus, called to be *s*

*Eph 3:8* Unto me [Paul], who am less than the least of all *s*

*Eph 4:12* perfecting of the *s,* for the work of the ministry

*Rev 17:6* woman drunken with the blood of the *s*

## SAKE [S]

*Ps 23:3* paths of righteousness for his [God's] name's *s*

*Matt 5:10* Blessed are they which are persecuted for righteousness' *s*

*Mark 8:35* lose his life for my [Jesus'] *s* and the gospel's

*Luke 21:17* ye shall be hated ... for my [Jesus'] name's *s*

*Acts 9:16* he [Paul] must suffer for my [Jesus'] name's **s**

*Rom 8:36* For thy [God's] **s** we are killed all the day long

*1 Cor 4:10* We are fools for Christ's **s**

*2 Cor 8:9* for your **s's** he [Jesus] became poor

*1 Tim 5:23* use a little wine for thy stomach's **s**

*1 Pet 3:14* suffer for righteous-ness' **s,** happy are ye

**SALAMIS** (a town on the island of Cyprus where Paul and Barnabas preached during the first missionary journey). Acts 13:4–5.

**SALEM.** See *Jerusalem.*

**SALIM** (a place near the Jordan River where John the Baptist baptized). John 3:23.

**SALOME** (a woman who witnessed the crucifixion of Jesus and visited His tomb). Mark 15:40–41; 16:1.

**SALT**

*Job 6:6* Can that which is unsavoury be eaten without **s**

*Matt 5:13* Ye are the **s** of the earth

*Col 4:6* Let your speech be ... seasoned with **s**

**SALT SEA** (a salt-saturated body of water, referred to today as the *Dead Sea,* into which the Jordan River empties in southern Palestine). Gen 14:3 • Josh 3:16. *East Sea:* Joel 2:20. *Sea of the Plain:* Deut 3:17.

**SAMARIA** (capital city of Israel, or the Northern King-dom, that was captured by the Assyrians). 1 Kgs 16:24–29; 20:1–22 • **2 Kgs 17:3–24** • Amos 3:11–12.

**SAMARITANS** (inhabitants of the district of Samaria who were considered inferior by the Jews because of their mixed-blood ancestry). 2 Kgs 17:29 • Matt 10:5 • Luke 9:52; 10:33; 17:16 • John 4:9–40; 8:48 • Acts 8:25.

**SAMOS** (an island of Greece visited by the apostle Paul). Acts 20:15.

**SAMOTHRACIA** (an island in the Aegean Sea visited by the apostle Paul). Acts 16:11.

**SAMSON** (a judge of Israel with great physical strength who died when he destroyed a pagan Philistine temple). Judg 13:24; 14:1–20; 15:1–16; **16: 1–31** • Heb 11:32.

**SAMUEL** (a prophet and the last judge of Israel who anointed the first two kings of Judah—Saul and David). 1 Sam 1:20; 2:18–26; 3:1–21; 4:1; 7:3–15; 8:1–22; **9:14–27; 10:1–25;** 11:7–14; 12:1–25; 13:8–15; 15:1–35; **16:1–23;** 25:1; 28:3,11–20 • 1 Chr 6:28; 9:22; 11:3; 26:28; 29:29 • 2 Chr 35:18 • Ps 99:6 • Jer 15:1 • Acts 3:24; 13:20 • Heb 11:32. *Shemuel:* 1 Chr 6:33.

**SAMUEL, BOOKS OF FIRST AND SECOND.** Two historical books of the Old Testament named for the prophet Samuel, who anointed Saul and David as the first two kings of Israel. Their anointing marked the transition of the nation from a loose confederacy of tribes to a united kingdom under the leadership of a king.

**SANBALLAT** (a Samaritan who plotted to kill Nehemiah to stop his rebuilding projects). Neh 2:10,19; 4:1,7; 6:1–14; 13:28.

**SANCTIFICATION**
*1 Thes 4:3* this is the will of God, even your *s*
*2 Thes 2:13* God hath…chosen you to salvation through *s* of the Spirit

*1 Pet 1:2* Elect…through *s* of the Spirit

**SANCTIFY [IED]**
*Gen 2:3* God blessed the seventh day, and *s'ied* it
*Lev 20:7* **S** yourselves therefore, and be ye holy
*Deut 5:12* Keep the sabbath day to *s* it
*Josh 3:5* Joshua said unto the people, **S** yourselves
*1 Chr 15:14* priests…*s'ied* themselves to bring…the ark
*Joel 1:14* **S** ye a fast, call a solemn assembly
*John 17:17* **S** them [the disciples] through thy [God's] truth: thy word is truth
*1 Cor 6:11* ye are washed…ye are *s'ied*…ye are justified
*1 Tim 4:5* it is *s'ied* by the word of God and prayer
*1 Pet 3:15* But *s* the Lord God in your hearts

**SAPPHIRA** (a believer struck dead for lying and withholding money she had pledged to the church). Acts 5:1–11.

**SARAH** (wife of Abraham and mother of Isaac). Gen 17:15–21; 18:6–15; 20:2–18; 21:1–12; 23:1–19; 24:36; 25:10; 49:31 • Isa 51:2 • Rom 9:9 • *Sara:* Heb 11:11 • 1 Pet 3:6. *Sarai:* Gen 11:30; 12:5.

**SARDIS** (a city of Asia Minor and site of one of the seven churches addressed by John in the Book of Revelation). Rev 3:1–6.

**SAREPTA.** See *Zarephath.*

**SARGON** (a king of Assyria who captured Samaria and carried the Northern Kingdom into exile). Isa 20:1.

**SARON.** See *Sharon.*

**SATAN** (an evil being who opposes God; the devil). 1 Chr 21:1 • Job 1:6–12; 2:1–7 • Ps 109:6 • Zech 3:1–2 • Matt 4:10; 12:26; 16:23 • Mark 1:13; 3:23, 26; 4:15; 8:33 • Luke 4:8; 10:18; 11:18; 13:16; 22:3,31 • John 13:27 • Acts 5:3; 26:18 • Rom 16:20 • 1 Cor 5:5; 7:5 • 2 Cor 2:11; 11:14; 12:7 • 1 Thes 2:18 • 2 Thes 2:9 • 1 Tim 1:20; 5:15 • Rev 2:9,13,24; 3:9; 12:9; 20:2,7. *Belial:* 2 Cor 6:15. *Lucifer:* Isa 14:12.

**SAUL**
1. The first king of Israel who tried to kill David and was defeated by the Philistines. 1 Sam 9:1–31:12 • 1 Chr 10:2–13.
2. The original name of the apostle Paul. See *Paul.*

**SAVE [D, ING, TH]**
*Ex 14:30* LORD *s'd* Israel…out of…hand of…Egyptians
*Job 2:6* he [Job] is in thine [Satan's] hand; but *s* his life
*Ps 7:1 s* me from all them that persecute me
*Ps 7:10* My defence is of God, which *s'th* the upright
*Ps 44:6* not trust in my bow, neither shall my sword *s* me
*Ps 55:16* I will call upon God; and the LORD shall *s* me
*Ps 67:2* thy [God's] *s'ing* health among all nations
*Ps 80:19* cause thy [God's] face to shine…we shall be *s'd*
*Ps 107:13* he [God] *s'd* them out of their distresses
*Prov 20:22* wait on the LORD, and he shall *s* thee
*Isa 45:22* be ye *s'd,* all the ends of the earth
*Isa 59:1* LORD'S hand is not shortened, that it cannot *s*
*Jer 8:20* summer is ended, and we are not *s'd*
*Matt 1:21* he [Jesus] shall *s* his people from their sins
*Matt 10:22* he that endureth to the end shall be *s'd*
*Mark 8:35* whosoever will *s* his life shall lose it
*Mark 10:26* Who…can be *s'd*
*Luke 19:10* Son of man is come to seek and to *s* that which was lost
*Luke 23:35* He [Jesus] *s'd* others; let him save himself

*John 3:17* the world through him [Jesus] might be *s'd*

*John 12:47* I [Jesus] came not to judge... but to *s* the world

*Acts 2:21* whosoever shall call on... the Lord shall be *s'd*

*Acts 4:12* none other name... whereby we must be *s'd*

*Rom 5:10* we shall be *s'd* by his [Jesus'] life

*Rom 10:13* whosoever shall call upon the name of the Lord shall be *s'd*

*1 Cor 1:21* it pleased God by the foolishness of preaching to *s* them that believe

*1 Cor 9:22* I [Paul] am made all things to all men, that I might... *s* some

*Eph 2:8* by grace are ye *s'd* through faith

*1 Tim 1:15* Christ Jesus came into the world to *s* sinners

*2 Tim 1:9* Who [Jesus]... *s'd*... called us with an holy calling

*Heb 7:25* he [Jesus] is able also to *s* them to the uttermost

*Jas 2:14* though a man... have not works? can faith *s* him

**SAVIOUR**

*2 Sam 22:3* The God of my rock... is... my high tower... *s*

*Isa 43:11* beside me [God] there is no *s*

*Luke 2:11* unto you is born... in the city of David a *S*

*1 John 4:14* Father sent the Son to be the *S* of the world

**SCEVA** (a Jewish priest whose sons tried to cast out evil spirits as Paul did). Acts 19:11–16.

**SCRIPTURE [S]**

*Luke 4:21* This day is this *s* fulfilled in your ears

*Luke 24:45* they [the disciples] might understand the *s's*

*John 5:39* Search the *s's;* for in them... ye have eternal life

*John 20:9* as yet they [the disciples] knew not the *s,* that he [Jesus] must rise again

*Acts 17:11* These [the Bereans]... searched the *s's* daily

*Rom 4:3* what saith the *s?* Abraham believed God

*1 Cor 15:3* Christ died for our sins according to the *s's*

*2 Tim 3:16* All *s* is given by inspiration of God

*2 Pet 1:20* Knowing this... no prophecy of the *s* is of any private interpretation

**SECOND COMING OF JESUS.** Matt 25:32–46 • Luke 12:35–48 • John 14:3 • 1 Thes 4:13–18.

**SECRET [S]**

*Deut 29:29* *s* things belong unto the LORD

*Ps 44:21* God... knoweth the *s's* of the heart

*Ps 91:1* dwelleth in the *s* place of the most High

*Ezek 28:3* no *s* that they can hide from thee [God]

*Dan 2:28* a God in heaven that revealeth *s's*

*Matt 6:6* pray to thy Father which is in *s*

*Rom 2:16* God shall judge the *s's* of men by Jesus Christ

**SECUNDUS** (a believer who accompanied Paul on his third missionary journey). Acts 20:4.

## SEEK [ETH, ING]

*2 Chr 7:14* If my [God's] people ... pray, and *s* my face

*Ps 40:16* those that *s* thee [God] rejoice and be glad

*Ps 63:1* thou art my God; early will I *s* thee

*Ps 105:4* *S* the LORD, and his strength: seek his face

*Ps 119:2* Blessed are they ... that *s* him [God] with the whole heart

*Isa 55:6* *S* ye the LORD while he may be found

*Lam 3:25* LORD is good ... to the soul that *s'eth* him

*Matt 7:7* *s*, and ye shall find

*Matt 7:8* he that *s'eth* findeth

*Mark 8:12* Why doth this generation *s* after a sign

*Luke 12:31* But rather *s* ye the kingdom of God

*Luke 17:33* Whosoever shall *s* to save his life shall lose it

*Luke 19:10* Son of man is come to *s* and to save that which was lost

*John 5:30* because I [Jesus] *s* ... the will of the Father

*Rom 3:11* there is none that *s'eth* after God

*1 Cor 1:22* and the Greeks *s* after wisdom

*1 Cor 13:5* [charity] *s'eth* not her own

*Col 3:1* *s* those things ... above

*1 Pet 5:8* devil ... walketh ... *s'ing* whom he may devour

## SEEK THE LORD

*1 Chr 16:11* **S-t-L** and his strength ... continually

*Ps 34:10* they that *s-t-L* shall not want any good thing

*Prov 28:5* they that *s-t-L* understand all things

*Amos 5:6* **S-t-L,** and ye shall live

*Zech 8:22* nations shall come to *s-t-L* of hosts

**SEM.** See *Shem.*

**SENIR.** See *Hermon, Mount.*

**SENNACHERIB** (a king of Assyria who demanded tribute from King Hezekiah of Judah). **2 Kgs 18:13–16;** 19:16–36 • 2 Chr 32:1–22 • Isa 36:1; 37:17,21,37.

## SEPARATE [D]

*Prov 19:4* Wealth maketh ... friends; but the poor is *s'd* from his neighbour

*Isa 59:2* iniquities have *s'd* between you and your God

*Matt 25:32* he [Jesus] shall *s* them one from another

*Acts 13:2* **S** me Barnabas and Saul for the work

*Rom 8:39* Nor height … shall … **s** us from the love of God

*2 Cor 6:17* come out … and be ye **s,** saith the Lord

**SEPHARVAIM** (a city whose residents colonized the Northern Kingdom after Samaria fell to the Assyrians). 2 Kgs 17:24–31.

**SERAIAH** (a leader who carried Jeremiah's prophecy of doom for Judah to the city of Babylon). Jer 51:59–61.

**SERMON ON THE MOUNT.** Matt 5–7.

**SERVANT [S]**

*Gen 9:25* a **s** of **s's** shall he [Canaan] be

*Job 1:8* Hast thou [Satan] considered my [God's] **s** Job

*Ps 31:16* Make thy [God's] face to shine upon thy **s**

*Ps 34:22* The LORD redeemeth the soul of his **s's**

*Ps 113:1* Praise, O ye **s's** of the LORD

*Ps 116:16* I am thy [God's] **s** … son of thine handmaid

*Ps 119:125* I am thy [God's] **s;** give me understanding

*Prov 14:35* The king's favour is toward a wise **s**

*Isa 42:1* Behold my [God's] **s,** whom I uphold

*Isa 52:13* my [God's] **s** shall deal prudently

*Dan 9:17* hear the prayer of thy [God's] **s**

*Mal 1:6* A son honoureth his father, and a **s** his master

*Matt 10:24* disciple is not above his master, nor the **s** above his lord

*Matt 23:11* he that is greatest … shall be your **s**

*Matt 25:21* Well done, thou good and faithful **s**

*Mark 9:35* the same shall be last of all, and **s** of all

*Luke 12:37* Blessed are those **s's,** whom the lord … shall find watching

*Luke 15:19* make me [the prodigal son] as one of thy hired **s's**

*John 8:34* Whosoever committeth sin is the **s** of sin

*Rom 6:18* ye became the **s's** of righteousness

*1 Cor 9:19* I [Paul] made myself **s** unto all

*Gal 4:7* Wherefore thou art no more a **s,** but a son

*Phil 2:7* took upon him [Jesus] the form of a **s**

**SERVANT SONGS OF ISAIAH.** Isa 42:1–4; 49:1–6; 50:4–9; 52:13–53:12.

**SERVE [D, ING, ST]**

*Gen 27:29* Let people **s** thee [God] … nations bow down

*Gen 29:20* Jacob **s'd** seven years for Rachel

*Deut 6:13* Thou shalt fear the LORD thy God, and *s* him

*Ps 72:11* Yea … all nations shall *s* him [God]

*Dan 3:17* our [Daniel's three friends'] God whom we *s* is able to deliver us

*Dan 6:16* God whom thou [Daniel] *s'st* … deliver thee

*Matt 4:10* worship the LORD … him only shalt thou *s*

*Luke 16:13* No servant can *s* two masters

*John 12:26* any man *s* me [Jesus], let him follow me

*Acts 6:2* not reason that we [the apostles] should … *s* tables

*Rom 1:25* Who … worshipped and *s'd* the creature more than the Creator

*Rom 12:11* fervent in spirit; *s'ing* the Lord

*Gal 5:13* by love *s* one another

## SERVE THE LORD

*Josh 24:15* as for me [Joshua] and my house, we will *s-t-L*

*Ps 100:2* *S-t-L* with gladness

*Jer 30:9* they [Israel and Judah] shall *s-t-L* … and David their king

## SERVICE

*John 16:2* the time cometh … whosoever killeth you will think that he doeth God *s*

*Rom 12:1* present your bodies a living sacrifice … which is your reasonable *s*

*Rev 2:19* I know thy works … and *s,* and faith

## SEVEN CHURCHES, LETTERS TO

1. To Ephesus (Rev 2:1–7)
2. To Smyrna (Rev 2:8–11)
3. To Pergamos (Rev 2:12–17)
4. To Thyatira (Rev 2:18–29)
5. To Sardis (Rev 3:1–6)
6. To Philadelphia (Rev 3:7–13)
7. To Laodicea (Rev 3:14–22)

## SEVEN LAST WORDS OF JESUS FROM THE CROSS

1. "Father, forgive them; for they know not what they do" (Luke 23:34)
2. "Verily I say unto thee, to day shalt thou be with me in paradise" (Luke 23:43)
3. "Woman, behold they son! … Behold thy mother!" (John 19:26–27)
4. "My God, my God, why hast thou forsaken me" (Matt 27:46 • Mark 15:34)
5. "I thirst" (John 19:28)
6. "It is finished" (John 19:30)
7. "Father, into thy hands I commend my spirit" (Luke 23:46)

## SEVEN SIGNS OF JESUS IN JOHN'S GOSPEL

1. Turning of water into wine (John 2:1–11)

2. Healing of a nobleman's son (John 4:46–54)

3. Healing of a paralyzed man (John 5:1–9)

4. Feeding of the five thousand (John 6:5–14)

5. Walking on the water (John 6:15–21)

6. Healing of a man born blind (John 9:1–7)

7. Raising of Lazarus from the dead (John 11:38–44)

**SEVENTY WEEKS VISION OF DANIEL.** Dan 9:24–27.

**SHADRACH** (one of Daniel's friends who was miraculously delivered from the fiery furnace). Dan 1:7; 2:49; **3:1–28.**

**SHALLUM.** See *Jehoahaz, No. 2.*

**SHALMANESER** (an Assyrian king who defeated the Northern Kingdom and deported its people). **2 Kgs 17:3–6; 18:9.**

**SHAME [D]**

*Ps 4:2* how long will ye turn my [God's] glory into *s*

*Ps 14:6* Ye have *s'd* the counsel of the poor

*Ps 35:4* Let them be … put to *s* that seek after my soul

*Ps 83:16* Fill their faces with *s* … may seek thy [God's] name

*Ps 119:31* O LORD, put me not to *s*

*Prov 3:35* *s* shall be the promotion of fools

*Prov 13:18* *s* shall be to him that refuseth instruction

*Prov 29:15* a child left to himself bringeth his mother to *s*

*1 Cor 14:35* it is a *s* for women to speak in the church

*Phil 3:19* glory is in their *s*

*Heb 12:2* Jesus … endured the cross, despising the *s*

**SHAMEFULLY**

*Hos 2:5* she that conceived them hath done *s*

*Mark 12:4* and … they [husbandmen] … sent him [servant] away *s* handled

**SHAMGAR** (a judge who delivered Israel from the Philistines). **Judg 3:31;** 5:6.

**SHARON** (a fertile coastal plain along the Mediterranean Sea). 1 Chr 27:29 • Song 2:1 • Isa 33:9; 35:2; 65:10. *Saron:* Acts 9:35.

**SHEAR-JASHUB** (a symbolic name, meaning "a remnant shall return," given by Isaiah to his son to show God's promise to His people after their period of exile). Isa 7:3–4.

**SHECHEM**

1. A tribal leader killed by Simeon and Levi for seducing their sister Dinah. Gen 34:1–29.

2. A city of refuge in the territory of Ephraim. Josh 20:7 • Judg 9:1–57 • 1 Kgs 12:1,25. *Sichem:* Gen 12:6. *Sychem:* Acts 7:16.

## SHEEP

*1 Sam 15:14* What meaneth … this bleating of the *s*

*2 Sam 7:8* I [God] took thee [David] from the sheepcote, from following the *s*

*Ps 44:22* we are counted as *s* for the slaughter

*Ps 74:1* why doth thine [God's] anger smoke against the *s* of thy pasture

*Ps 95:7* people of his [God's] pasture, and the *s* of his hand

*Ps 119:176* I have gone astray like a lost *s*

*Isa 53:6* All we like *s* have gone astray

*Matt 10:16* send you forth as *s* in the midst of wolves

*Matt 15:24* I [Jesus] am not sent but unto the lost *s* of the house of Israel

*Mark 6:34* Jesus … saw … people … as *s* not having a shepherd

*Luke 15:6* I have found my *s* which was lost

*John 10:7* I [Jesus] am the door of the *s*

*John 10:11* good shepherd [Jesus] giveth his life for the *s*

*John 21:16* He [Jesus] saith unto him [Peter] … Feed my *s*

*1 Pet 2:25* For ye were as *s* going astray

**SHEM** (the oldest son of Noah who was preserved in the ark). Gen 5:32; 6:10; **7:13; 9:18–27;** 10:1–31; 11:10–11 • 1 Chr 1:4,17,24. *Sem:* Luke 3:36.

**SHEMAIAH** (a prophet of Judah who warned King Rehoboam not to attack Israel). **1 Kgs 12:22–24** • 2 Chr 11:2.

**SHEMER** (a man who sold King Omri of the Northern Kingdom a hill on which the city of Samaria was built). 1 Kgs 16:24.

**SHEMUEL.** See *Samuel.*

**SHENIR.** See *Hermon, Mount.*

## SHEPHERD [S]

*Gen 47:3* Thy servants [the Hebrews] are *s's*

*Ps 23:1* The LORD is my *s;* I shall not want

*Isa 40:11* He [God] shall feed his flock like a *s*

*Ezek 34:2* Son of man, prophesy against the *s's* of Israel

*Matt 9:36* were scattered abroad, as sheep having no *s*

*Luke 2:8* in the same country *s's* abiding in the field

*John 10:11* I [Jesus] am the good *s* … giveth his life

*Heb 13:20* that great *s* [Jesus] of the sheep

*1 Pet 5:4* when the chief *S* [Jesus] shall appear

**SHESHACH.** See *Babylonia.*

**SHESH-BAZZAR.** See *Zerubbabel.*

**SHIELD**

*Gen 15:1* Fear not, Abram: I [God] am thy *s*

*2 Sam 22:3* in him will I trust: he [God] is my *s*

*Ps 5:12* wilt thou [God] compass him as with a *s*

*Ps 33:20* the Lord…is…our *s*

*Ps 84:11* For the Lord God is a sun and *s*

*Ps 115:11* the Lord: he is their help and their *s*

*Prov 30:5* he [God] is a *s* unto them…put their trust in him

*Eph 6:16* Above all, taking the *s* of faith

**SHILOAH.** See *Siloam.*

**SHILOH**

1. A town in Ephraim where the Philistines captured the ark of the covenant. Josh 18:1–10 • Judg 21:12–23 • **1 Sam 4:3–11** • Jer 7:12,14.

2. A title of the coming Messiah that identified Him as a descendant of Judah. Gen 49:10.

**SHIMEI** (a man who insulted David when he was fleeing from Absalom). **2 Sam 16:5–13; 19:16–23** • 1 Kgs 2:8–44.

**SHINAR.** See *Babylonia.*

**SHINE [D, ING, TH]**

*Num 6:25* The Lord make his face *s* upon thee

*Ps 31:16* Make thy [God's] face to *s* upon thy servant

*Ps 67:1* God…bless us; and cause his face to *s* upon us

*Prov 4:18* But the path of the just is as the *s'ing* light

*Eccl 8:1* a man's wisdom maketh his face to *s*

*Isa 9:2* upon them [people in darkness] hath the light *s'd*

*Isa 60:1* Arise, *s;* for thy light is come

*Matt 5:16* Let your light so *s* before men

*Matt 17:2* and his [Jesus'] face did *s* as the sun

*John 1:5* light *s'th* in darkness

*John 5:35* He [Jesus] was a burning and a *s'ing* light

*Acts 9:3* there *s'd* round about him [Paul] a light

*2 Cor 4:6* For God…hath *s'd* in our hearts

*Rev 21:23* And the city had no need of the sun…to *s*

**SHUSHAN** (the wealthy and powerful capital city of Persia where Esther interceded for her people). Neh 1:1 • Esth

1:2,5; 2:3–8; 3:15; 4:8,16; 8:14–15; 9:6–19 • Dan 8:2.

**SICHEM.** See *Shechem,* No. 2.

**SICKNESS [ES]**

*Matt 4:23* Jesus went about... healing all manner of *s*

*Matt 8:17* spoken by Esaias... Himself [Jesus] took our infirmities, and bare our *s'es*

*John 11:4* Jesus... said, This *s* is not unto death

**SIDON** (a Phoenician city founded by Sidon, oldest son of Canaan). **Gen 10:15,19** • Matt 11:21–22; 15:21 • Mark 3:8; 7:24,31 • Luke 4:26; 6:17; 10:13–14 • Acts 12:20; 27:3. *Zidon:* Josh 11:8.

**SIGHT**

*Ex 3:3* I [Moses] will now turn aside, and see this great *s*

*Num 13:33* we were in our own *s* as grasshoppers

*Judg 2:11* children of Israel did evil in the *s* of the LORD

*1 Chr 29:25* the LORD magnified Solomon exceedingly in the *s* of all Israel

*Ps 9:19* let the heathen be judged in thy [God's] *s*

*Ps 19:14* Let the words of my mouth... be acceptable in thy [God's] *s,* O LORD

*Ps 78:12* Marvellous things did he [God] in the *s* of their fathers, in... Egypt

*Ps 90:4* a thousand years in thy [God's] *s* are... as yesterday

*Ps 116:15* Precious in the *s* of the LORD... death of his saints

*Eccl 6:9* Better is the *s* of the eyes than the wandering of the desire

*Matt 11:5* blind receive their *s,* and the lame walk

*Luke 1:15* he [John the Baptist] shall be great... *s* of the Lord

*Luke 15:21* I [prodigal son] have sinned... in thy *s*

*Acts 9:9* And he [Paul] was three days without *s*

*Jas 4:10* Humble yourselves in the *s* of the Lord

**SIGN [S]**

*Gen 1:14* let them [lights] be for *s's,* and for seasons

*Deut 6:8* bind them [Scriptures] for a *s* upon thine hand

*Isa 7:14* the Lord himself shall give you a *s*

*Dan 4:3* How great are his [God's] *s's*

*Matt 12:39* An evil... generation seeketh after a *s*

*Matt 24:3* what shall be the *s* of thy [Jesus'] coming

*Luke 2:12* this shall be a *s* unto you... babe wrapped in swaddling clothes

*1 Cor 1:22* the Jews require a *s*

*Rev 15:1* I [John] saw another *s* in heaven, great... marvellous

## SIGNS AND WONDERS

*Deut 6:22* LORD showed *s-a-w* ... upon Egypt

*Mark 13:22* false prophets shall rise ... show *s-a-w*

*John 4:48* Except ye see *s-a-w,* ye will not believe

*Acts 5:12* by the hands of the apostles were many *s-a-w* wrought among the people

**SIHON** (an Amorite king who refused to allow the Israelites to pass through his territory). Num 21:21–30.

**SILAS** (a church leader imprisoned with Paul at Philippi). Acts 15:40–41; 16:19,23. *Silvanus:* 2 Cor 1:19 • 2 Thes 1:1.

## SILENCE

*Ps 39:2* I was dumb with *s,* I held my peace

*Eccl 3:7* a time to keep *s,* and a time to speak

*Hab 2:20* let all the earth keep *s* before him [God]

*1 Cor 14:28* no interpreter, let him keep *s* in the church

*1 Cor 14:34* Let your women keep *s* in the churches

**SILOAH.** See *Siloam.*

**SILOAM** (a water reservoir supplied through King Hezekiah's underground tunnel from a spring outside Jerusalem). 2 Kgs 20:20 • Luke 13:4 • John 9:7–11. *Shiloah:* Isa 8:6. *Siloah:* Neh 3:15.

**SILVANUS.** See *Silas.*

## SIMEON

1. A son of Jacob and ancestor of one of the twelve tribes of Israel. Gen 29:33; 34:25,30; 35:23; 42:24,36; 43:23; 46:10; 48:5; 49:5 • Ex 1:2; 6:15. The tribe of Simeon settled in southern Canaan. Josh 19:1–9.

2. A righteous man who blessed the child Jesus in the temple at Jerusalem. Luke 2:25–35.

## SIMON

1. Simon Peter, one of the twelve apostles or disciples of Jesus and the leader of the church in Jerusalem after the resurrection and ascension of Jesus. Matt 4:18; 10:2; 16:16–17; 17:25 • Mark 1:16–36; 3:16; 14:37 • Luke 5:4–10; 6:14; 22:31; 24:34 • John 1:40–42; 6:8,68; 13:6,9,24,36; 18:10,15,25; 20:2,6; 21:2–17 • Acts 10:5,18,32 • 2 Pet 1:1.

(1) A fisherman and brother of Andrew (Matt 4:18)

(2) Called by Jesus (Matt 4:18–22)

(3) Included among Jesus' twelve apostles (Matt 10:2–4)

(4) Walked on the water to meet Jesus (Matt 14:28–33)

(5) Confessed Jesus as the Son of God (Matt 16:13–19)

(6) Condemned by Jesus for refusing to believe that Jesus would die (Matt 16:21–23)

(7) Witnessed the transfiguration of Jesus (Matt 17:1–8 • 2 Pet 1:16–18)

(8) With Jesus in the Garden of Gethsemane (Mark 14:32–42)

(9) Denied Jesus three times (Matt 26:69–75)

(10) Cut off the ear of a slave when Jesus was arrested (John 18:10–11)

(11) Ran to inspect the empty tomb after Jesus was resurrected (John 20:1–8)

(12) Reinstated by Jesus and challenged to continue His work (John 21:15–22)

(13) Preached sermon on the day of Pentecost when three thousand people believed on Jesus (Acts 2:38–41)

(14) Became the key leader in the early church at Jerusalem (Acts 3:12–26)

(15) Preached the gospel to Gentiles (Acts 10:24–48)

2. Simon Zelotes or Simon the Canaanite, another of the twelve apostles or disciples of Jesus. Matt 10:4 • Mark 3:18 • Luke 6:15 • Acts 1:13.

## SIMPLE

*Ps 19:7* testimony of the LORD is sure, making wise the *s*

*Prov 8:5* O ye *s,* understand wisdom

*Prov 22:3* but the *s* pass on, and are punished

## SIN [NED, NETH, S]

*Gen 4:7* if thou [Cain] doest not well, *s* lieth at the door

*Lev 16:34* make an atonement… for all their *s's* once a year

*1 Sam 15:24* Saul said…I have *s'ned*

*2 Chr 7:14* then will I [God] hear…forgive their *s*

*Job 1:22* In all this Job *s'ned* not, nor charged God

*Job 13:23* How many are mine iniquities and *s's*

*Ps 32:1* Blessed is he…whose *s* is covered

*Ps 41:4* for I have *s'ned* against thee [God]

*Ps 51:2* cleanse me from my *s*

*Ps 51:3* my *s* is ever before me

*Ps 51:4* Against thee [God], thee only, have I *s'ned*

*Ps 51:9* Hide thy [God's] face from my *s's*

*Ps 103:10* He [God] hath not dealt with us after our *s's*

*Ps 119:11* Thy [God's] word have I hid in mine heart, that I might not *s*

*Prov 14:34* but *s* is a reproach to any people

*Eccl 7:20* not a just man upon earth, that ... *s'neth* not

*Isa 1:18* though your *s's* be as scarlet ... white as snow

*Isa 6:7* touched thy [Isaiah's] lips ... iniquity is taken away ... *s* purged

*Isa 40:2* she [Jerusalem] ... received ... double for ... her *s's*

*Jer 14:20* we have *s'ned* against thee [God]

*Jer 31:34* I [God] will remember their *s* no more

*Ezek 18:20* The soul that *s'neth,* it shall die

*Mic 7:19* thou [God] wilt cast all their *s's* into the ... sea

*Matt 1:21* he [Jesus] shall save his people from their *s's*

*Matt 18:21* Lord, how oft shall my brother *s* against me, and I forgive him

*Matt 26:28* my [Jesus'] blood ... is shed for many for the remission of *s's*

*Luke 15:21* I [the prodigal son] have *s'ned* against heaven, and in thy [his father's] sight

*Luke 24:47* remission of *s's* ... preached in his [Jesus'] name

*John 1:29* Behold the Lamb of God, which taketh away the *s* of the world

*John 8:7* He that is without *s* ... let him first cast a stone

*John 9:2* who did *s,* this man, or his parents

*John 16:8* he [Jesus] will reprove the world of *s*

*Rom 3:9* Jews and Gentiles ... they are all under *s*

*Rom 3:23* all ... *s'ned,* and come short of the glory of God

Rom 4:7 Blessed are they ... whose *s's* are covered

*Rom 5:12* by one man [Adam] *s* entered into the world

*Rom 6:1* continue in *s,* that grace may abound

*Rom 6:12* Let not *s* ... reign in your mortal body

*Rom 6:23* wages of *s* is death

*Rom 7:17* no more I [Paul] that do it, but *s* ... in me

*1 Cor 6:18* he ... committeth fornication *s'neth* against his own body

*1 Cor 15:17* Christ be not raised ... yet in your *s's*

*2 Cor 5:21* he [God] hath made him [Jesus] to be *s* for us

*Heb 9:28* Christ was ... offered to bear the *s's* of many

*Heb 10:4* not possible that the blood of bulls ... should take away *s's*

*Heb 12:1* lay aside ... the *s* which doth so easily beset us

*Jas 4:17* knoweth to do good, and doeth it not, to him it is *s*

*1 John 1:7* blood of Jesus ... cleanseth us from all *s*

*1 John 1:8* say that we have no
*s,* we deceive ourselves

*1 John 1:9* he [Jesus] is faithful ... to forgive us our *s's*

*1 John 1:10* If we say that we
have not *s'ned,* we make
him [Jesus] a liar

*1 John 2:1* these things write I
unto you, that ye *s* not

*1 John 2:2* he [Jesus] is the pro-
pitiation for our *s's*

*1 John 4:10* he [God] ... sent his
Son [Jesus] to be the propi-
tiation for our *s's*

**SIN, WILDERNESS OF** (a
desert region where manna
and quail were miraculously
provided for the Israelites). Ex
16:1–8.

**SINAI** (a mountain peak
where Moses received the Ten
Commandments and other
parts of the Law from God). Ex
**19–23;** 24:16; 31:18; 34:2–32 •
Lev 7:38; 25:1; 26:46 • Num
1:1,19; 3:1–14; 9:1,5; 10:12;
26:64; 28:6; 33:15–16 • Deut
33:2 • Judg 5:5 • Neh 9:13 • Ps
68:8,17 • Gal 4:24–25. *Sina:*
Acts 7:30.

**SINCERITY**

*Josh 24:14* serve him [God] in *s*
and in truth

*1 Cor 5:8* keep the feast ... with
the ... bread of *s*

*2 Cor 8:8* I [Paul] speak ... to
prove the *s* of your love

**SING [ING]**

*Ex 15:21* **S** ye to the LORD, for
he hath triumphed

*Ps 59:17* Unto thee ... will I *s:*
for God is my defence

*Ps 67:4* let the nations be glad
and *s* for joy

*Ps 81:1* **S** aloud unto God our
strength: make a joyful noise

*Ps 92:1* It is a good thing ... to *s*
praises unto thy [God's] name

*Ps 100:2* come before his
[God's] presence with *s'ing*

*Ps 137:4* How shall we *s* the
LORD's song in a strange
land

*Song 2:12* the time of the *s'ing*
of birds is come

*Isa 49:13* break forth into *s'ing,*
O mountains

*Isa 52:9* *s* together, ye waste
places of Jerusalem

*Col 3:16* *s'ing* with grace in
your hearts to the Lord

*Jas 5:13* Is any merry? let him
*s* psalms

**SING UNTO THE LORD**

*1 Chr 16:23* **S-u-t-L,** all the earth

*Ps 13:6* I will *s-u-t-L* ... he ...
dealt bountifully with me

*Ps 95:1* let us *s-u-t-L* ... the
rock of our salvation

*Ps 96:1* *s-u-t-L,* all the earth

*Ps 98:1* O *s-u-t-L* a new song

*Ps 104:33* I will *s-u-t-L* as long
as I live

*Isa 12:5* **S-u-t-L;** for he hath
done excellent things

## SINNED AGAINST THE LORD

*Ex 10:16* I [Pharaoh] have **s-a-t-L** your God

*Josh 7:20* I [Achan] have **s-a-t-L** God of Israel

*2 Sam 12:13* I [David] have **s-a-t-L**

## SINNER [S]

*Ps 1:1* Blessed is the man that walketh not... nor standeth in the way of **s's**

*Eccl 9:18* but one **s** destroyeth much good

*Mark 2:17* I [Jesus] came... to call... **s's** to repentance

*Luke 5:30* Why do ye [Jesus] eat... with... **s's**

*Luke 15:10* joy... over one **s** that repenteth

*Luke 18:13* God be merciful to me [publican] a **s**

*Rom 5:8* while we were yet **s's,** Christ died for us

*1 Tim 1:15* Christ... came into the world to save **s's**

*Jas 4:8* Cleanse your hands, ye **s's**... purify your hearts

**SION.** See *Zion.*

**SIRION.** See *Hermon, Mount.*

**SISERA** (a Canaanite commander killed by Jael). Judg 4:2–22.

## SLEEP [EST, ETH, ING]

*Ps 13:3* lighten mine eyes, lest I **s** the **s** of death

*Ps 44:23* Awake, why **s'est** thou, O Lord

*Prov 6:9* How long wilt thou **s,** O sluggard

*Prov 20:13* Love not **s,** lest thou come to poverty

*Mark 5:39* the damsel is not dead, but **s'eth**

*Mark 13:36* coming suddenly he [Jesus] find you **s'ing**

*Mark 14:41* **S** on now, and take your [the disciples'] rest

*John 11:11* he [Jesus] saith... Our friend Lazarus **s'eth**

*1 Cor 15:51* shall not all **s,** but we shall all be changed

## SLEPT

*Ps 3:5* I laid me down and **s**

*Matt 28:13* Say ye, His [Jesus'] disciples... stole him away while we **s**

*1 Cor 15:20* now is Christ... the firstfruits of them that **s**

**SMYRNA** (a city north of Ephesus where one of the seven churches addressed by John in the Book of Revelation was located). Rev 2:8–11.

## SOBER [LY, NESS]

*Acts 26:25* I [Paul]... speak... words of truth and **s'ness**

*1 Thes 5:6* let us not sleep... but... watch and be **s**

*1 Tim 3:2* A bishop...must be blameless...vigilant, *s*

*Titus 2:12* we should live *s'ly,* righteously, and godly

*1 Pet 5:8* Be *s,* be vigilant...the devil...walketh about

**SODOM** (a city destroyed by God because of its wickedness and often mentioned as a symbol of evil and as a warning to sinners). **Gen 19:1–28** • Isa 1:9 • Jer 49:18 • Ezek 16:46–49 • Amos 4:11 • Zeph 2:9 • Matt 11:23–24 • 2 Pet 2:6 • Jude 7 • Rev 11:8. *Sodoma:* Rom 9:29.

**SODOMA.** See *Sodom.*

**SOLOMON** (David's son and successor as king of Israel, known for his wisdom, wealth, and lavish lifestyle, and probable author of the books of Ecclesiastes and Song of Solomon). See **1 Kgs 1–11 • 2 Chr 1–9** for a sketch of Solomon's life.

1. Prayed for wisdom and insight (1 Kgs 3:1–28)

2. Governed efficiently and became wealthy (1 Kgs 4:1–30)

3. Encouraged trade and commerce (1 Kgs 10:14–29)

4. Built the temple in Jerusalem (1 Kgs 5–8)

5. Married pagan wives (1 Kgs 11:1–8)

6. Burdened his subjects with excessive taxes (1 Kgs 12:4)

7. Northern tribes rebelled against his policies (1 Kgs 11:14–40)

8. Death of Solomon (1 Kgs 11:41–43).

**SON OF GOD**

*Matt 27:40* If thou [Jesus] be the *S-o-G,* come down from the cross

*Matt 27:54* Truly this [Jesus] was the *S-o-G*

*Luke 1:35* that holy thing... shall be called the *S-o-G*

*Luke 4:3* If thou be the *S-o-G,* command this stone...be made bread

*John 1:34* I [John the Baptist]... bare record that this [Jesus] is the *S-o-G*

*John 20:31* believe that Jesus is the Christ, the *S-o-G*

*1 John 4:15* Whosoever shall confess that Jesus is the *S-o-G,* God dwelleth in him

*1 John 5:12* he that hath not the *S-o-G* hath not life

**SON OF MAN**

*Ps 8:4* What is...the *s-o-m,* that thou [God] visitest him

*Ezek 2:1* *S-o-m* [Ezekiel], stand upon thy feet

*Matt 12:8* the *S-o-m* [Jesus] is Lord even of the sabbath day

*Matt 16:13* Whom do men say that I [Jesus] the *S-o-m* am

*Matt 24:44* an hour as ye think not...*S-o-m* [Jesus] cometh

*Mark 10:45* **S-o-m** [Jesus] came not to be ministered unto, but to minister

*Luke 9:58* **S-o-m** [Jesus] hath not where to lay his head

*Luke 22:48* But Jesus said… Judas, betrayest thou the **S-o-m** with a kiss

*John 3:14* even so must the **S-o-m** [Jesus] be lifted up

*John 12:23* The hour is come, that the **S-o-m** [Jesus] should be glorified

**SONG OF DEBORAH.** Judg 5:1–31.

**SONG OF MARY.** Luke 1:46–55.

**SONG OF MIRIAM.** Ex 15:20–21.

**SONG OF MOSES.** Deut 32:1–44.

**SONG OF SOLOMON, BOOK OF.** A short Old Testament book, probably written by Solomon, that is filled with expressions of affection between two lovers (1:13; 4:1–11; 7:2–10). Some interpreters insist the song symbolizes God's love for His people Israel, while others believe the book is a healthy affirmation of the joys of physical love between husband and wife.

**SONG OF ZACHARIAS.** Luke 1:67–79.

**SOPATER** (a believer who accompanied Paul on the third missionary journey). Acts 20:4.

**SORROW [FUL, S]**

*Ps 18:5* The **s's** of hell compassed me about

*Ps 38:17* my **s** is continually before me

*Eccl 1:18* he that increaseth knowledge increaseth **s**

*Isa 53:3* man of **s's**…acquainted with grief

*Jer 45:3* for the LORD hath added grief to my **s**

*Matt 19:22* he [rich young ruler] went away **s'ful**

*Matt 24:8* All these are the beginning of **s's**

*Matt 26:38* My [Jesus'] soul is exceeding **s'ful**

*John 16:20* your **s** shall be turned into joy

*2 Cor 7:10* godly **s** worketh repentance to salvation

*Rev 21:4* no more death, neither **s,** nor crying

**SOSIPATER** (a kinsman of Paul whose greetings were sent to the church at Rome). Rom 16:21.

**SOSTHENES** (a ruler of the synagogue at Corinth who was beaten by a mob). Acts 18:17.

## SOUL [S]

*Gen 2:7* man became a living *s*

*Deut 6:5* thou shalt love the LORD thy God...with all thy *s*

*1 Sam 18:1* *s* of Jonathan was knit with the *s* of David

*Job 19:2* How long will ye vex my [Job's] *s*

*Ps 19:7* law of the LORD is perfect, converting the *s*

*Ps 23:3* He [God] restoreth my *s*

*Ps 25:1* Unto thee, O LORD, do I lift up my *s*

*Ps 33:20* Our *s* waiteth for the LORD; he is our help

*Ps 35:9* And my *s* shall be joyful in the LORD

*Ps 42:2* My *s* thirsteth for God

*Ps 42:5* Why art thou cast down, O my *s*

*Ps 56:13* thou [God] hast delivered my *s* from death

*Ps 72:13* He [God]...shall save the *s's* of the needy

*Ps 84:2* My *s*...fainteth for the courts of the LORD

*Ps 103:1* Bless the LORD, O my *s*...bless his holy name

*Ps 142:4* refuge failed me; no man cared for my *s*

*Prov 11:30* and he that winneth *s's* is wise

*Prov 18:7* A fool's...lips are the snare of his *s*

*Lam 3:24* The LORD is my portion, saith my *s*

*Ezek 18:20* The *s* that sinneth, it shall die

*Mic 6:7* shall I give...fruit of my body for the sin of my *s*

*Matt 10:28* but rather fear him which is able to destroy...*s* and body

*Matt 11:29* ye shall find rest unto your *s's*

*Matt 16:26* what shall a man give in exchange for his *s*

*Mark 14:34* My [Jesus'] *s* is... sorrowful unto death

*John 12:27* Now is my [Jesus'] *s* troubled

*Rom 13:1* every *s* be subject unto the higher powers

*1 Pet 2:11* abstain from fleshly lusts, which war against the *s*

*1 Pet 2:25* returned unto the... Bishop of your *s's*

## SOUND [ING]

*John 3:8* The wind bloweth... thou hearest the *s*

*Acts 2:2* *s* from heaven as of a... mighty wind

*1 Cor 13:1* I [Paul] am become as *s'ing* brass

*1 Cor 14:8* if the trumpet give an uncertain *s*

*1 Cor 15:52* trumpet shall *s,* and the dead...raised

*2 Tim 4:3* when they will not endure *s* doctrine

## SOUTHERN KINGDOM (JUDAH) FALLS TO BABYLONIA. 2 Kgs 25.

## SOW [ED, ETH]

*Ps 126:5* They that *s* in tears shall reap in joy

*Prov 22:8* He that *s'eth* iniquity shall reap vanity

*Matt 13:24* kingdom...is likened unto a man which *s'ed* good seed

*Luke 8:5* as he [a sower] *s'ed,* some fell by the way side

*Luke 12:24* Consider the ravens...they neither *s* nor reap

*John 4:37* One *s'eth,* and another reapeth

*2 Cor 9:6* *s'eth* bountifully shall reap also bountifully

*Gal 6:7* whatsoever a man *s'eth,* that shall he also reap

## SOWN

*Hos 8:7* they have *s* the wind, and...reap the whirlwind

*Hag 1:6* Ye have *s* much, and bring in little

*Mark 4:18* these are they which are *s* among thorns

*1 Cor 15:42* It [the body] is *s* in corruption; it is raised in incorruption

**SPAIN** (a country in Europe that Paul expressed a desire to visit). Rom 15:24,28.

## SPEECH

*Gen 11:1* And the whole earth was...of one *s*

*Ex 4:10* I [Moses] am slow of *s*

*Prov 17:7* Excellent *s* becometh not a fool

*Isa 28:23* Give ye ear...hearken, and hear my [God's] *s*

*Mark 14:70* thou [Peter] art a Galilaean, and thy *s* agreeth

*1 Cor 2:1* I [Paul]...came not with excellency of *s*

*Col 4:6* Let your *s* be...seasoned with salt

**SPIES SENT INTO CANAAN.** Num 13:1–33.

## SPIRIT [S]

*1 Sam 28:7* Seek me [Saul] a woman that hath a familiar *s*

*2 Kgs 2:9* let a double portion of thy [Elijah's] *s* be upon me [Elisha]

*Job 32:8* there is a *s* in man

*Ps 31:5* Into thine hand I commit my *s*

*Ps 51:10* O God...renew a right *s* within me

*Prov 16:18* Pride goeth before destruction...haughty *s* before a fall

*Prov 25:28* He that hath no rule over his own *s*

*Isa 32:15* Until the *s* be poured upon us from on high

*Isa 42:1* I [God] have put my *s* upon him [God's servant]

*Ezek 3:24* Then the *s* entered into me [Ezekiel]

*Ezek 11:19* I [God] will put a new *s* within you

*Dan 6:3* because an excellent *s* was in him [Daniel]

*Joel 2:28* I [God] will pour out my *s* upon all flesh

*Zech 4:6* Not by might…but by my [God's] *s*

*Matt 5:3* Blessed are the poor in *s*

*Matt 26:41* the *s*…is willing, but the flesh is weak

*Mark 6:7* he [Jesus]…gave them [the disciples] power over unclean *s's*

*Luke 23:46* Father, into thy hands I [Jesus] commend my *s*…gave up the ghost

*John 3:5* Except a man be born of water and of the *S*

*John 4:23* worship the Father in *s* and in truth

*John 16:13* the *S* of truth [Holy Spirit], is come

*Acts 17:16* his [Paul's] *s* was stirred in him

*Rom 8:16* The *S* itself beareth witness with our *s*

*1 Cor 12:4* diversities of gifts, but the same *S*

*1 Cor 12:10* to another discerning of *s's*

*2 Cor 3:6* letter killeth, but the *s* giveth life

*Gal 5:16* Walk in the *S*

*Gal 5:22* fruit of the *S* is love, joy, peace, longsuffering

*Eph 4:3* unity of the *S* in the bond of peace

*Eph 6:17* sword of the *S*…the word of God

*2 Tim 1:7* God hath not given us the *s* of fear

*1 John 4:1* try the *s's* whether they are of God

*Rev 2:7* hear what the *S* saith unto the churches

## SPIRIT, FILLING OF, AT PENTECOST. Acts 2:1–21.

## SPIRIT OF GOD

*Gen 1:2* **S-o-G** moved upon the face of the waters

*1 Sam 11:6* And the *s-o-G* came upon Saul

*Job 33:4* The *s-o-G* hath made me [Job]

*Matt 3:16* Jesus…saw the **S-o-G** descending like a dove

*Rom 8:14* led by the **S-o-G,** they are the sons of God

*1 Cor 3:16* Know ye not…that the **S-o-G** dwelleth in you

*Eph 4:30* And grieve not the holy **S-o-G**

## SPIRIT OF THE LORD

*Judg 6:34* the *s-o-t-L* came upon Gideon

*1 Sam 16:13* the *s-o-t-L* came upon David

*Isa 11:2* the *s-o-t-L* shall rest upon him [God's servant]

*Isa 61:1* The *s-o-t-L* GOD is upon me [God's servant]

*Luke 4:18* The **S-o-t-L** is upon me [Jesus]

*Acts 8:39* the **S-o-t-L** caught away Philip

*2 Cor 3:17* where the **S-o-t-L** is, there is liberty

## SPIRITUAL [LY]

*Rom 8:6* to be **s'ly** minded is life and peace

*1 Cor 14:1* Follow after charity, and desire **s** gifts

*1 Cor 15:44* It is sown a natural body…raised a **s** body

*Eph 6:12* we wrestle…against **s** wickedness in high places

*1 Pet 2:5* Ye also, as lively stones, are built up a **s** house

## STAND [EST, ETH, ING]

*Ex 3:5* the place…thou [Moses] **s'est** is holy ground

*Ex 14:13* **s** still, and see the salvation of the LORD

*Job 19:25* my [Job's] redeemer… shall **s** at the latter day

*Ps 1:1* walketh not…nor **s'eth** in the way of sinners

*Ps 24:3* who shall **s** in his [God's] holy place

*Prov 12:7* the house of the righteous shall **s**

*Isa 40:8* but the word of our God shall **s** for ever

*Mal 3:2* who shall **s** when he [God] appeareth

*Matt 12:25* house divided against itself shall not **s**

*Acts 7:55* he [Stephen]…saw… Jesus **s'ing** on the right hand

*Rom 14:10* all **s** before the judgment seat of Christ

*1 Cor 10:12* thinketh he **s'eth** take heed lest he fall

*1 Cor 16:13* Watch ye, **s** fast in the faith…be strong

*Gal 5:1* **S** fast…in the liberty… Christ hath made us free

*Eph 6:11* able to **s** against the wiles of the devil

*2 Thes 2:15* Therefore, brethren, **s** fast

*Rev 3:20* I [Jesus] **s** at the door, and knock

## STATUTE [S]

*Ex 27:21* a **s** for ever unto their generations

*Lev 10:11* teach…Israel all the **s's**…the LORD hath spoken

*Lev 16:34* this shall be an everlasting **s** unto you

*Deut 5:31* I [God] will speak unto thee [Moses] all the commandments … **s's** … judgments

*1 Kgs 3:3* Solomon loved the LORD, walking in the **s's** of David his father

*Ps 19:8* The **s's** of the LORD are right, rejoicing the heart

*Ps 119:12* Blessed art thou, O LORD: teach me thy **s's**

*Ezek 20:19* walk in my [God's] **s's,** and keep my judgments

## STEDFAST [LY, NESS]

*Luke 9:51* he [Jesus] **s'ly** set his face to go to Jerusalem

*1 Cor 15:58* Therefore…be ye **s,** unmoveable

*Col 2:5* and the **s'ness** of your faith in Christ

*Heb 3:14* hold the beginning of our confidence **s** unto the end

**STEPHEN** (a believer who became the first Christian martyr when he was stoned because of his testimony). Acts 6:5–9; **7:55–60;** 8:2; 11:19; 22:20.

### STEWARD [S]

*Matt 20:8* lord of the vineyard saith unto his **s,** Call the labourers ... give them their hire

*Luke 16:8* the lord commended the unjust **s**

*1 Cor 4:2* required in **s's,** that a man be found faithful

*Titus 1:7* a bishop must be blameless, as the **s** of God

*1 Pet 4:10* good **s's** of the manifold grace of God

### STEWARDSHIP

*Luke 16:2* give an account of thy **s** ... be no longer steward

*Luke 16:3* my lord taketh away from me the **s**

### STONE [D, S, ST]

*Gen 31:45* Jacob took a **s,** and set it up for a pillar

*Ex 17:4* this people ... be almost ready to **s** me [Moses]

*Ex 31:18* two ... tables of **s,** written with ... finger of God

*Lev 26:1* neither shall ye set up any image of **s**

*Josh 4:6* What mean ye by these **s's**

*1 Sam 17:50* David prevailed ... with a sling and ... a **s**

*Ps 118:22* **s** which the builders refused is become the head **s**

*Eccl 3:5* and a time to gather **s's** together

*Isa 28:16* I [God] lay in Zion for a foundation ... a tried **s**

*Matt 4:3* command that these **s's** be made bread

*Matt 21:42* The **s** which the builders rejected

*Matt 24:2* There shall not be left here one **s** upon another

*Matt 27:66* they [soldiers] ... made ... sepulchre sure, sealing the **s**

*Mark 16:4* they [the women] saw ... the **s** was rolled away

*Luke 13:34* O Jerusalem ... which killest the prophets, and **s'st** them

*John 1:42* called Cephas ... by interpretation, A **s**

*Acts 4:11* the **s** which was set at nought of you builders

*Acts 7:59* they **s'd** Stephen

*1 Pet 2:8* a **s** of stumbling, and a rock of offence

*Rev 21:19* foundations ... garnished with ... precious **s's**

### STRAIGHT

*Isa 40:3* make **s** in the desert a highway for our God

*Luke 3:4* Prepare ye the way of the Lord, make his paths **s**

*Acts 9:11* go into the street which is called **S**

## STRANGER [S]

*Deut 10:19* Love ye … the *s*

*Ps 54:3* For *s's* are risen up against me

*Ps 69:8* I am become a *s* unto my brethren

*Matt 25:35* I was a *s,* and ye took me in

*Eph 2:19* therefore ye are no more *s's* and foreigners

*Heb 13:2* Be not forgetful to entertain *s's*

## STRENGTH

*Ex 13:14* By *s* of hand the LORD brought us [Israel] out from Egypt

*Ex 15:2* LORD is my *s* and song

*Job 12:13* With him [God] is wisdom and *s*

*Ps 18:2* my God, my *s,* in whom I will trust

*Ps 19:14* words of my mouth… be acceptable … my *s,* and my redeemer

*Ps 27:1* the LORD is the *s* of my life

*Ps 43:2* For thou art the God of my *s*

*Ps 46:1* God is our refuge and *s,* a … help in trouble

*Ps 71:9* forsake me not when my *s* faileth

*Ps 84:5* Blessed is the man whose *s* is in thee [God]

*Ps 90:10* if by reason of *s* they [days of our years] be fourscore years

*Ps 118:14* The LORD is my *s* and song … my salvation

*Isa 12:2* LORD JEHOVAH is my *s* and my song

*Isa 30:15* in quietness and in confidence shall be your *s*

*Isa 40:31* they that wait upon the LORD shall renew their *s*

*Hab 3:19* LORD God is my *s*

*Mark 12:30* love the Lord thy God … with all thy *s*

*2 Cor 12:9* my [Paul's] *s* is made perfect in weakness

## STRENGTHEN [ED, ETH, ING]

*Ps 27:14* he [God] shall *s* thine heart: wait … on the LORD

*Luke 22:43* there appeared an angel … *s'ing* him [Jesus]

*Phil 4:13* do all things through Christ which *s'eth* me [Paul]

*2 Tim 4:17* the Lord stood with me [Paul], and *s'ed* me

## STRIPES

*Isa 53:5* with his [God's servant's] *s* we are healed

*2 Cor 11:24* five times received I [Paul] forty *s*

*1 Pet 2:24* by whose [Jesus'] *s* ye were healed

## STRIVE [D, ING, TH]

*Luke 13:24* *S* to enter in at the strait gate

*Rom 15:20* so have I [Paul] *s'd* to preach the gospel

*1 Cor 9:25* every man that *s'th* for the mastery is temperate in all things

*Phil 1:27* one mind **s'ing** together for … the gospel

*2 Tim 2:24* the servant of the Lord must not **s**

## STRONG [ER]

*Deut 31:6* Be **s** and of a good courage, fear not

*Ps 24:8* The LORD **s** and mighty … mighty in battle

*Ps 71:7* but thou [God] art my **s** refuge

*Ps 89:8* who is a **s** LORD like unto thee

*Prov 18:10* The name of the LORD is a **s** tower

*Eccl 9:11* the race is not to the swift, nor the battle to the **s**

*Luke 2:40* child [Jesus] grew, and waxed **s** in spirit

*Rom 15:1* **s** ought to bear the infirmities of the weak

*1 Cor 1:25* the weakness of God is **s'er** than men

*2 Cor 12:10* when I [Paul] am weak, then am I **s**

*Eph 6:10* Finally, my brethren, be **s** in the Lord

## STUMBLINGBLOCK [S]

*Jer 6:21* I [God] will lay **s's** before this people

*Rom 14:13* no man put a **s** … in his brother's way

*1 Cor 1:23* Christ crucified, unto the Jews a **s**

*1 Cor 8:9* liberty … become a **s** to them that are weak

## SUBMISSION TO OTHERS IN THE LORD. 1 Pet 3:1–12.

## SUBMIT [TING]

*Eph 5:21* **S'ting** yourselves one to another … fear of God

*Eph 5:22* Wives, **s** yourselves unto your own husbands

*Jas 4:7* **S** yourselves therefore to God. Resist the devil

*1 Pet 5:5* ye younger, **s** yourselves unto the elder

## SUCCOTH-BENOTH (an idol set up in Samaria by the people who colonized the area after the Northern Kingdom fell to the Assyrians). 2 Kgs 17:29–30.

## SUFFER [ED, ETH, INGS]

*Ps 55:22* he [God] shall never **s** the righteous to be moved

*Matt 16:21* Jesus … must go … and **s** many things

*Matt 19:14* **S** little children, and forbid them not

*Luke 24:26* Ought not Christ to have **s'ed** these things

*Luke 24:46* thus it behoved Christ to **s**

*Acts 9:16* he [Paul] must **s** for my [Jesus'] name's sake

*Rom 8:18* **s'ings** … not worthy to be compared with the glory … revealed

*1 Cor 10:13* God … will not **s** you to be tempted above that ye are able

*1 Cor 13:4* Charity *s'eth* long, and is kind…envieth not

*Phil 3:10* the fellowship of his [Jesus'] *s'ings*

*2 Tim 2:12* If we *s,* we shall also reign with him [Jesus]

*Heb 5:8* learned he [Jesus] obedience by the things which he *s'ed*

*1 Pet 4:13* ye are partakers of Christ's *s'ings*

**SUKKIIMS** (an African or Ethiopian tribe allied with Pharaoh Shishak of Egypt when he invaded Judah). 2 Chr 12:3.

**SUN STANDS STILL AT AJALON.** Josh 10:12–14.

**SUSANNA** (a woman who provided food and lodging for Jesus). Luke 8:2–3.

**SWEAR**

*Lev 19:12* ye shall not *s* by my [God's] name falsely

*Matt 5:34* I [Jesus] say unto you, *S* not at all

*Mark 14:71* he [Peter] began to curse and to *s*

**SYCHAR** (a city of Samaria where Jesus talked to the woman at Jacob's well). John 4:5–42.

**SYCHEM.** See *Shechem,* No. 2.

**SYNAGOGUE [S]**

*Matt 4:23* Jesus went about all Galilee, teaching in their *s's*

*Mark 5:22* one of the rulers of the *s,* Jairus by name

*Mark 13:9* in the *s's* ye shall be beaten

*Luke 4:16* he [Jesus] went into the *s*…stood up for to read

**SYRACUSE** (a city in Sicily visited by Paul). Acts 28:12.

**SYRIA** (a nation northeast of Israel which was a persistent enemy of the Jews across several centuries). Judg 10:6 • 2 Sam 8:11–13 • 1 Kgs 20:1–34 • 2 Kgs 13:3–24 • Isa 17:1–3 • Luke 2:2 • Acts 15:23,41. *Aram:* Num 23:7.

**SYRIA-DAMASCUS.** See *Damascus.*

# -T-

**TABERNACLE BUILT IN THE WILDERNESS.** Ex 36:8–38:21.

**TABITHA** (a widow, also known as *Dorcas,* whom Peter restored to life). Acts 9:36–40.

**TABOR, MOUNT** (a mountain from which the judge Deborah sent Barak to defeat the Canaanites). Josh 19:22 • **Judg 4:6–14;** 8:18 • Ps 89:12 • Jer 46:18 • Hos 5:1.

**TAMAR** (Absalom's sister who was sexually assaulted by her half brother Amnon). **2 Sam 13:1–32** • 1 Chr 3:9.

**TARPELITES** (a tribe which colonized Samaria after the Northern Kingdom fell to Assyria). Ezra 4:9.

**TARSUS** (capital city of the Roman province of Silicia and the place where Paul was born). Acts 9:11,30; 11:25; 21:39; 22:3.

**TARTAK** (a pagan god worshiped by the Avites, a people who colonized Samaria after the Northern Kingdom fell to the Assyrians). 2 Kgs 17:31.

**TATNAI** (a Persian official who tried to stop the Jews from rebuilding the temple in Jerusalem). Ezra 5:3–17.

## TAUGHT

*Ps 119:102* thy [God's] judgements: for thou hast *t* me

*Isa 54:13* all thy children shall be *t* of the LORD

*Mark 1:22* he [Jesus] *t* them as one that had authority

*Mark 4:2* he [Jesus] *t* them many things by parables

*John 8:28* but as my Father hath *t* me [Jesus], I speak these things

*2 Thes 2:15* hold the traditions which ye have been *t*

## TEACH [EST, ETH, ING]

*Deut 6:7* thou shalt *t* them [God's commands] diligently unto thy children

*Job 21:22* Shall any *t* God knowledge

*Job 36:22* God exalteth by his power: who *t'eth* like him

*Ps 25:4* Show me thy ways, O LORD; *t* me thy paths

*Ps 51:13* Then will I *t* transgressors thy [God's] ways

*Ps 86:11* *T* me thy way, O LORD…walk in thy truth

*Ps 90:12* So *t* us to number our days

*Prov 16:23* heart of the wise *t'eth* his mouth

*Jer 31:34* they shall *t* no more every man his neighbour

*Matt 21:23* elders...came unto him [Jesus] as he was *t'ing*

*Matt 28:19* Go ye therefore, and *t* all nations

*Matt 28:20* **T'ing** them to observe all things

*Mark 8:31* he [Jesus] began to *t*...Son of man must suffer

*Luke 11:1* Lord, *t* us [the disciples] to pray

*Luke 12:12* Holy Ghost shall *t* you...what ye ought to say

*John 14:26* the Comforter...he shall *t* you all things

*Rom 2:21* Thou therefore which *t'est* another, *t'est* thou not thyself

*Col 3:16* *t'ing*...one another in psalms and hymns

*1 Tim 3:2* A bishop...given to hospitality, apt to *t*

**TEACHER [S]**

*Ps 119:99* I have more understanding than all my *t's*

*John 3:2* know...thou [Jesus] art a *t* come from God

*1 Cor 12:29* are all prophets? are all *t's*

*Eph 4:11* he [God] gave some, apostles ... some ... pastors...*t's*

**TEARS**

*Ps 6:6* water...couch with my *t*

*Ps 126:5* They that sow in *t* shall reap in joy

*Jer 9:1* Oh that my [Jeremiah's] head were waters, and...eyes a fountain of *t*

*Rev 21:4* God shall wipe away all *t* from their eyes

**TEKOA** (a fortress city near Bethlehem and hometown of the prophet Amos). 2 Chr 11:6; 20:20 • Jer 6:1 • Amos 1:1. *Tekoah:* 2 Sam 14:2,4,9.

**TEKOAH.** See *Tekoa.*

**TEL-ABIB** (a Babylonian city where the prophet Ezekiel lived with the other Jewish captives). Ezek 3:15.

**TEMPERANCE**

*Gal 5:23* Meekness, *t:* against such there is no law

*2 Pet 1:6* And to knowledge *t;* and to *t* patience

**TEMPERATE**

*1 Cor 9:25* And every man that striveth for the mastery is *t* in all things

*Titus 1:8* a lover of good men, sober, just, holy, *t*

*Titus 2:2* That the aged men be sober, grave, *t*

**TEMPT [ED, ING]**

*Deut 6:16* Ye shall not *t* the Lord your God

*Ps 78:41* Yea, they turned back and *t'ed* God

*Matt 4:1* was Jesus led...into the wilderness to be *t'ed*

*Matt 4:7* Thou shalt not *t* the Lord thy God

*Mark 8:11* seeking of him [Jesus] a sign ... *t'ing* him

*John 8:6 t'ing* him [Jesus] ... to accuse him

*1 Cor 7:5* Satan *t* you not for your incontinency

*1 Cor 10:13* God ... will not suffer you to be *t'ed* above that ye are able

*Heb 4:15* high priest [Jesus] ... was ... *t'ed* like as we are

*Jas 1:13* Let no man say ... I am *t'ed* of God

## TEMPTATION [S]

*Matt 6:13* lead us not into *t*

*Luke 4:13* when the devil had ended all the *t,* he departed from him [Jesus] for a season

*1 Cor 10:13* no *t* taken you but such as is common to man

*Jas 1:2* count it all joy when ye fall into divers *t's*

*Jas 1:12* Blessed is the man that endureth *t*

*2 Pet 2:9* Lord knoweth how to deliver ... out of *t's*

## TEMPTATIONS OF JESUS.
See *Jesus, Life and Ministry of.*

## TEN COMMANDMENTS.
Ex 20:1–17 • Deut 5:7–21.

## TERAH (father of Abraham).
**Gen 11:24–32** • Josh 24:2 • 1 Chr 1:26. *Thara:* Luke 3:34.

## TERTULLUS (a Jewish lawyer who accused Paul of

desecrating the temple). Acts 24:1–8.

## TESTIFY [IED, IETH, ING]

*Num 35:30* one witness shall not *t* against any person to cause him to die

*Isa 59:12* our sins *t* against us

*John 4:44* Jesus ... *t'ied* ... a prophet hath no honour in his own country

*Acts 20:21 t'ing* ... to the Jews, and ... Greeks, repentance

*Acts 23:11* Paul ... hast *t'ied* of me [Jesus] in Jerusalem

*Heb 7:17* he [God] *t'ieth,* Thou art a priest for ever

*1 John 4:14* we ... do *t* that the Father sent the Son

*1 John 5:9* the witness of God ... hath *t'ied* of his Son

*Rev 22:20* He [Jesus] which *t'ieth* ... saith ... I come quickly

## TESTIMONY [IES]

*Deut 6:20* What mean the *t'ies* ... which ... God hath commanded you

*Ps 19:7 t* of ... LORD is sure, making wise the simple

*Ps 119:24* Thy [God's] *t'ies* also are my delight

*Mark 6:11* shake off the dust ... for a *t* against them

*John 21:24* and we know that his *t* is true

*2 Tim 1:8* Be not ... ashamed of the *t* of our Lord

**THADDAEUS.** See *Judas.*

**THANK**

*Matt 11:25* I [Jesus] *t* thee...
Lord of heaven and earth

*Luke 18:11* Pharisee...prayed...
God, I *t* thee, that I am not
as other men

*Phil 1:3* I [Paul] *t* my God
upon...remembrance of you

**THANKS**

*1 Chr 16:34* give *t* unto the
LORD; for he is good

*Ps 92:1* It is a good thing to
give *t* unto the LORD

*Ps 107:1* give *t* unto the LORD,
for he is good

*Luke 22:19* And he [Jesus] took
bread, and gave *t*

*1 Cor 11:24* he [Jesus] had
given *t,* he brake it [bread]

*1 Cor 15:57* *t* be to God, which
giveth us the victory

*2 Cor 9:15* *T* be unto God for
his unspeakable gift

*1 Thes 5:18* In every thing give
*t*...this is...will of God

**THARA.** See *Terah.*

**THEBEZ** (a fortified city
where Abimelech was killed).
**Judg 9:50–55** • 2 Sam 11:21.

**THEOPHILUS** (a friend to
whom Luke addressed the
Gospel of Luke and the Book of
Acts). Luke 1:3 • Acts 1:1.

**THESSALONIANS, FIRST
AND SECOND EPISTLES
TO THE.** Two epistles written
by the apostle Paul to the
believers in the church at
Thessalonica. The theme of
both letters is the second coming of Christ.

**THESSALONICA** (a city on
the Macedonian coast where
Paul preached and founded a
church). Acts 17:1–13 • 1 Thes
1:1.

**THIEF [VES]**

*Matt 6:20* where *t'ves* do not
break through nor steal

*Mark 14:48* Are ye come out, as
against a *t*

*Mark 15:27* with him [Jesus]
they crucify two *t'ves*

*Luke 10:30* A certain man...
fell among *t'ves*

*Luke 19:46* ye have made it
[God's house] a den of *t'ves*

*John 10:10* The *t* cometh not,
but for to steal

*John 12:6* This he [Judas]
said...because he was a *t*

*1 Thes 5:2* the day of the Lord
so cometh as a *t* in the night

*2 Pet 3:10* the day of the Lord
will come as a *t* in the night

**THINK [EST, ETH]**

*Prov 23:7* as he *t'eth* in his
heart, so is he

*Jer 29:11* I [God] know the
thoughts that I *t* toward you

*Matt 6:7* heathen...*t*...they shall be heard for...much speaking

*Matt 24:44* such an hour as ye *t* not the Son of man cometh

*Luke 10:36* Which...of these... *t'est* thou, was neighbour

*John 16:2* that whosoever killeth you will *t* that he doeth God service

*Rom 12:3* not to *t* of himself... highly than he ought to *t*

*1 Cor 10:12* *t'eth* he standeth take heed lest he fall

*1 Cor 13:5* [charity] is not easily provoked, *t'eth* no evil

*Gal 6:3* For if a man *t* himself to be something, when he is nothing

*Eph 3:20* unto him [Jesus] that is able to do...above all that we ask or *t*

*Phil 4:8* if there be any praise, *t* on these things

**THOMAS** (a disciple of Jesus who insisted on indisputable proof that Jesus was alive). Matt 10:3 • Mark 3:18 • Luke 6:15 • John 11:16; 14:5; **20:24–29;** 21:2 • Acts 1:13.

**THORN IN THE FLESH, PAUL'S.** 2 Cor 12:7–10.

**THOUGHT [S]**

*Gen 50:20* ye *t* evil against me [Joseph]; but God meant it unto good

*Job 21:27* Behold, I [God] know your *t's*

*Job 42:2* no *t* can be withholden from thee [God]

*Ps 92:5* O LORD...thy *t's* are very deep

*Prov 16:3* Commit thy works unto the LORD, and thy *t's* shall be established

*Isa 55:8* For my [God's] *t's* are not your *t's*

*Jer 29:11* I [God] know the *t's* that I think toward you

*Matt 6:27* Which of you by taking *t* can add one cubit unto his stature

*Mark 7:21* out of the heart of men, proceed evil *t's*

*1 Cor 3:20* The Lord knoweth the *t's* of the wise

*1 Cor 13:11* I [Paul] understood as a child, I *t* as a child

*Phil 2:6* Who [Jesus]...*t* it not robbery to be equal with God

*Heb 4:12* the word of God...is a discerner of the *t's* and intents of the heart

**THRONE**

*Ps 45:6* Thy *t*, O God, is for ever and ever

*Ps 97:2* righteousness and judgment are the habitation of his [God's] *t*

*Prov 20:28* his [the king's] *t* is upholden by mercy

*Isa 6:1* I [Isaiah] saw also the Lord...upon a *t*

*Isa 66:1* Thus saith the LORD, The heaven is my [God's] *t*

*Jer 33:17* David shall never want a man to sit upon the *t* of the house of Israel

*Lam 5:19* thy [God's] *t* from generation to generation

*Matt 19:28* Son of man shall sit in the *t* of his glory

*Matt 25:31* shall he [Jesus] sit upon the *t* of his glory

*Luke 1:32* God shall give unto him [Jesus] the *t* of ... David

*Heb 4:16* Let us ... come boldly unto the *t* of grace

*Rev 4:2* one [Jesus] sat on the *t*

**THRONE OF GOD**

*Heb 12:2* Jesus ... is set down at the right hand of the *t-o-G*

*Rev 7:15* before the *t-o-G,* and serve him day and night

*Rev 22:1* water of life ... proceeding out of the *t-o-G*

**THYATIRA** (hometown of Lydia and site of one of the seven churches addressed by John in the Book of Revelation). Acts 16:14 • Rev 1:1; 2:18,24.

**TIBERIAS**

1 A city near the Sea of Galilee built by Herod Antipas and named for the Roman emperor Tiberius. John 6:1,23; 21:1.

2. Another name for the Sea of Galilee. See *Galilee, Sea of.*

**TIGLATH-PILESER III** (an Assyrian king who defeated the Northern Kingdom and carried Jewish captives to Assyria). 2 Kgs 15:29; 16:1–10. *Pul:* 1 Chr 5:26. *Tilgath-pilneser:* 2 Chr 28:20.

**TIGLATH-PILNESER.** See *Tiglath-pileser III.*

**TIMON** (one of the seven men chosen as "deacons" in the church at Jerusalem). Acts 6:1–5.

**TIMOTHEUS.** See *Timothy.*

**TIMOTHY** (a young believer, also called Timotheus, who traveled with Paul and briefly shared his imprisonment at Rome). **Acts 16:1–3; 17:14–15; 18:1–5;** 19:22; 20:4 • Rom 16:21 • 1 Cor 4:17; 16:10 • 2 Cor 1:1,19 • **Phil 1:1; 2:19,23** • Col 1:1 • 1 Thes 1:1; 3:2,6 • 2 Thes 1:1 • 1 Tim 1:2,18; 6:20 • 2 Tim 1:2 • Phlm 1 • Heb 13:23.

**TIMOTHY, FIRST AND SECOND EPISTLES TO.** Two short epistles of the apostle Paul to his friend and fellow missionary, Timothy. The first epistle is practical in scope, instructing Timothy on how to lead a church. In 2 Timothy Paul expresses tender affection for the young minister (1:1–2:26) and speaks of the possibility of his own execution (4:6–22).

**TIRZAH** (capital of the Northern Kingdom before Samaria was built). 1 Kgs 14:17; 15:21,33; 16:6–23 • 2 Kgs 15:14–16 • Song 6:4.

**TITHE [S]**
*Lev 27:30* all the *t* of the land ... is the LORD'S
*Deut 14:22* Thou shalt...*t* all the increase of thy seed
*Neh 13:12* Then brought all Judah the *t* of the corn
*Mal 3:8* have we robbed thee [God]? In *t's* and offerings
*Mal 3:10* Bring ye all the *t's* into the storehouse
*Luke 11:42* ye [Pharisees] *t* mint and rue and...herbs
*Heb 7:6* he [Melchisedec] ... received *t's* of Abraham

**TITUS** (a church leader and traveling companion of Paul). 2 Cor 2:13; 7:6–14; 8:6,16,23; 12:18 • Gal 2:1–3 • 2 Tim 4:10 • Titus 1:4–3:11.

**TITUS, EPISTLE TO.** A short epistle from the apostle Paul to Titus in which he deals with several practical church matters (1:5–16) and the behavior of Christians in an immoral world (3:1–11).

**TOBIAH** (an Ammonite who opposed Nehemiah's reconstruction of Jerusalem's wall). Neh 2:10,19; 4:3,7; 6:1–19; 13:4,7–8.

**TOLA** (a minor judge of Israel). Judg 10:1–2.

**TONGUE, POWER OF.** Jas 3:1–12.

**TONGUES, SPEAKING IN.** 1 Cor 14:7–40.

**TOOTH FOR A TOOTH**
*Matt 5:38* An eye for an eye, and a *t-f-a-t*

**TOPHET** (a place of human sacrifice in the Valley of Hinnom near Jerusalem). Jer 7:31–32.

**TOWER OF BABEL.** Gen 11:1–9.

**TRADITION [S]**
*Matt 15:6* commandment of God of none effect by your [Pharisees'] *t*
*Mark 7:5* Why walk not thy [Jesus'] disciples according to the *t* of the elders
*2 Thes 2:15* hold the *t's* which ye have been taught

**TRANSFIGURATION OF JESUS.** See *Jesus, Life and Ministry of.*

319

## TRANSGRESS [ED, ETH]

*Deut 26:13* I have not *t'ed* thy [God's] commandments

*Jer 2:29* all have *t'ed* against me, saith the LORD

*Matt 15:2* Why do thy [Jesus'] disciples *t* the tradition of the elders…wash not their hands

*1 John 3:4* Whosoever committeth sin *t'eth* also the law

## TRANSGRESSION [S]

*1 Chr 10:13* Saul died for his *t*…against the LORD

*Job 13:23* make me [Job] to know my *t* and my sin

*Ps 32:1* Blessed is he whose *t* is forgiven

*Ps 32:5* I will confess my *t's* unto the LORD

*Ps 51:3* I acknowledge my *t's*

*Prov 12:13* The wicked is snared by the *t* of his lips

*Prov 29:6* In the *t* of an evil man there is a snare

*Isa 53:5* he [God's servant] was wounded for our *t's*

*Amos 1:3* For three *t's* of Damascus, and for four

## TRANSGRESSOR [S]

*Ps 51:13* Then will I teach *t's* thy [God's] ways

*Prov 22:12* he [God] overthroweth the words of the *t*

*Mark 15:28* he [Jesus] was numbered with the *t's*

## TREASURE [S]

*Ex 19:5* ye [Israel] shall be a peculiar *t* unto me [God]

*Ps 135:4* LORD hath chosen… Israel for his peculiar *t*

*Prov 10:2* *T's* of wickedness profit nothing

*Prov 15:16* Better is little with the fear of the LORD than great *t* and trouble

*Matt 2:11* they [the wise men] had opened their *t's*

*Matt 6:20* lay up for yourselves *t's* in heaven

*Matt 13:44* kingdom of heaven is like unto *t* hid in a field

*Luke 12:34* where your *t* is, there will your heart be also

*2 Cor 4:7* we have this *t* in earthen vessels

*Col 2:3* In whom [Jesus] are hid all the *t's* of wisdom

## TREE OF KNOWLEDGE OF GOOD AND EVIL (a tree in the Garden of Eden declared off-limits for Adam and Eve by the Lord). Gen 2:9–17.

## TREE OF LIFE (a tree in the Garden of Eden whose fruit would bring eternal life). Gen 2:9 • Rev 22:2.

## TRESPASS [ED, ES]

*Ezra 9:15* we are before thee [God] in our *t'es*

*Ezek 15:8* they have committed a *t,* saith the Lord GOD

*Ezek 39:23* Israel went into captivity ... because they *t'ed* against me [God]

*Matt 6:14* if ye forgive men their *t'es,* your ... Father will also forgive you

*Mark 11:25* your Father ... may forgive you your *t'es*

*Luke 17:3* If thy brother *t* against thee, rebuke him

*2 Cor 5:19* God was ... not imputing their *t'es* unto them

*Eph 2:1* hath he [Jesus] quickened, who were dead in *t'es*

## TRIBULATION [S]

*Matt 24:21* then shall be great *t*

*John 16:33* In the world ye shall have *t*

*Rom 5:3* knowing that *t* worketh patience

*Rom 8:35* Who shall separate us ... shall *t,* or distress

*2 Cor 1:4* Who [Jesus] comforteth us in all our *t*

*Eph 3:13* I [Paul] desire that ye faint not at my *t's* for you

## TRIUMPHAL ENTRY OF JESUS. See *Jesus, Life and Ministry of.*

**TROAS** (a city on the coast of Mysia where Paul received a vision). **Acts 16:8–11;** 20:5–6 • 2 Cor 2:12 • 2 Tim 4:13.

**TROPHIMUS** (a believer who accompanied Paul on the third missionary journey). Acts 20:4; 21:29 • 2 Tim 4:20.

## TROUBLE [D, TH]

*1 Sam 16:14* an evil spirit from the LORD *t'd* him [Saul]

*1 Kgs 18:17* Art thou [Elijah] he that *t'th* Israel

*Job 14:1* Man ... is of few days, and full of *t*

*Ps 9:9* The LORD ... will be a refuge ... in times of *t*

*Ps 31:9* Have mercy upon me, O LORD, for I am in *t*

*Ps 38:6* I am *t'd;* I am bowed down greatly

*Ps 46:1* God is ... a very present help in *t*

*Ps 77:2* In the day of my *t* I sought the Lord

*Ps 90:7* by thy [God's] wrath are we *t'd*

*Ps 108:12* Give us help from *t*

*Prov 15:27* He that is greedy of gain *t'th* his own house

*Jer 8:15* We looked for peace ... and for a time of health, and behold *t*

*Matt 2:3* he [Herod] was *t'd,* and all Jerusalem with him

*Luke 1:29* she [Mary] was *t'd* at his [the angel's] saying

*John 12:27* Now is my [Jesus'] soul *t'd* ... what shall I say

*John 14:1* Let not your heart be *t'd* ... believe ... in me

*2 Cor 4:8* We are *t'd* on every side ... not distressed

*Gal 1:7* some that *t* you, and would pervert the gospel

*2 Thes 1:6* recompense tribulation to them that *t* you

**TRUE**

*Ps 19:9* judgments of the LORD are *t* and righteous

*Zech 7:9* Execute *t* judgment, and show mercy

*John 1:9* the *t* Light [Jesus]... lighteth every man

*John 6:32* my [Jesus'] Father giveth you the *t* bread

*John 15:1* I [Jesus] am the *t* vine...Father...the husbandman

*John 21:24* we know that his [John's] testimony is *t*

*Rom 3:4* let God be *t,* but every man a liar

**TRUE VINE, JESUS AS.** See *"I Am" Statements of Jesus.*

**TRUST [ED, ETH, ING]**

*Deut 32:37* Where are their gods...in whom they *t'ed*

*2 Sam 22:3* The God of my rock; in him will I *t*

*Job 13:15* Though he [God] slay me [Job]...I *t* in him

*Ps 13:5* I have *t'ed* in thy [God's] mercy

*Ps 16:1* Preserve me...for in thee [God] do I put my *t*

*Ps 26:1* I have *t'ed*...in the LORD...I shall not slide

*Ps 34:8* blessed is the man that *t'eth* in him [God]

*Ps 37:5* *t*...in him [God]...he shall bring it to pass

*Ps 56:3* What time I am afraid, I will *t* in thee [God]

*Ps 112:7* his heart is fixed, *t'ing* in the LORD

*Ps 118:8* better to *t* in the LORD than...confidence in man

*Prov 3:5* *T* in the LORD with all thine heart

*Prov 11:28* He that *t'eth* in his riches shall fall

*Mark 10:24* hard is it for them that *t* in riches to enter... the kingdom

*1 Tim 1:11* According to the glorious gospel...which was committed to my [Paul's] *t*

**TRUTH**

*1 Sam 12:24* serve him [God] in *t* with all your heart

*Ps 25:5* Lead me in thy [God's] *t,* and teach me

*Ps 33:4* all his [God's] works are done in *t*

*Ps 86:11* Teach me...I will walk in thy [God's] *t*

*Ps 100:5* his [God's] *t* endureth to all generations

*Ps 119:30* I have chosen the way of *t*

*John 1:17* grace and *t* came by Jesus Christ

*John 4:24* must worship him [God] in spirit and in *t*

*John 8:32* know the *t,* and the *t* shall make you free

*John 14:6* I [Jesus] am the way, the *t,* and the life

*John 16:13* the Spirit of *t*... will guide you into all *t*

*John 18:38* Pilate saith unto him [Jesus], What is *t*

*Acts 10:34* Of a *t* I [Peter] perceive that God is no respecter of persons

*1 Cor 13:6* [charity] rejoiceth in the *t*

*Gal 4:16* Am I [Paul] ... enemy, because I tell you the *t*

*Eph 4:15* speaking the *t* in love

*1 Tim 2:4* Who [God] will have all men ... come unto the knowledge of the *t*

*1 Tim 3:15* the church ... the pillar and ground of the *t*

*2 Tim 2:15* workman ... needeth not to be ashamed, rightly dividing the word of *t*

*1 John 1:8* If we say that we have no sin ... *t* is not in us

*3 John 4* no greater joy than to hear that my [John's] children walk in *t*

**TYRANNUS** (a citizen of Ephesus who allowed Paul to use his lecture hall). Acts 19:8–10.

**TYRE** (an ancient Phoenician city and thriving trade center north of Palestine). Josh 19:29 • 1 Kgs 5:1–12 • Joel 3:4–6 • Matt 15:21–28. *Tyrus:* Ezek 26:1–21; 27:1–36 • Amos 1:10.

**TYRUS.** See *Tyre.*

# -U-

## UNBELIEF
*Mark 9:24* Lord, I believe; help thou mine *u*

*Heb 3:12* lest there be in any of you an evil heart of *u*

*Heb 4:11* lest any man fall after the same example of *u*

## UNBELIEVERS
*1 Cor 6:6* brother goeth to law with brother...before the *u*

*2 Cor 6:14* Be ye not unequally yoked together with *u*

## UNBELIEVING
*Acts 14:2* But the *u* Jews stirred up the Gentiles

*1 Cor 7:14* the *u* husband is sanctified by the wife

*Titus 1:15* unto them that are defiled and *u* is nothing pure

## UNCIRCUMCISED
*1 Sam 17:26* this *u* Philistine [Goliath], that he should defy...the living God

*Ezek 44:9* No stranger, *u* in heart...shall enter into my [God's] sanctuary

*Acts 7:51* stiffnecked and *u* in heart and ears

## UNCIRCUMCISION
*1 Cor 7:19* Circumcision is nothing, and *u* is nothing

*Gal 5:6* neither circumcision availeth any thing, nor *u*

*Col 3:11* neither Greek nor Jew, circumcision nor *u*

## UNCLEAN [NESS]
*Num 19:11* He that toucheth the dead body...*u* seven days

*Isa 6:5* because I [Isaiah] am a man of *u* lips

*Isa 64:6* But we are all as an *u* thing

*Mark 6:7* And he [Jesus]...gave them [the disciples] power over *u* spirits

*Acts 10:14* I [Peter] have never eaten any thing...*u*

*Rom 1:24* God also gave them up to *u'ness*

*Rom 14:14* persuaded...that there is nothing *u* of itself

*Gal 5:19* works of the flesh are manifest...Adultery, fornication, *u'ness*

*1 Thes 4:7* God hath not called us unto *u'ness*

## UNDEFILED
*Ps 119:1* Blessed are the *u*... walk in the law of the LORD

*Heb 7:26* high priest [Jesus]... who is holy, harmless, *u*

*Jas 1:27* Pure religion and *u* before God and the Father

## UNDERSTAND [EST, ETH, ING]
*1 Kgs 4:29* God gave Solomon wisdom and *u'ing*

*Job 26:12* by his [God's] *u'ing* he smiteth...the proud

*Job 28:28* and to depart from evil is *u'ing*

*Job 32:9* neither do the aged *u* judgment

*Ps 119:27* Make me to *u* the way of thy [God's] precepts

*Ps 119:34* Give me *u'ing,* and I shall keep thy [God's] law

*Ps 147:5* Great is our Lord... his *u'ing* is infinite

*Prov 2:2* and apply thine heart to *u'ing*

*Prov 2:5* Then shalt thou *u* the fear of the LORD

*Prov 3:5* and lean not unto thine own *u'ing*

*Prov 4:7* and with all thy getting get *u'ing*

*Prov 10:13* a rod is for...him that is void of *u'ing*

*Prov 14:6* knowledge is easy unto him that *u'eth*

*Prov 17:28* he that shutteth his lips is...a man of *u'ing*

*Isa 40:28* there is no searching of his [God's] *u'ing*

*Isa 44:18* he [God] hath shut their eyes...and...hearts, that they cannot *u*

*Dan 9:22* come forth to give thee [Daniel] skill and *u'ing*

*Dan 10:14* make thee [Daniel] *u* what shall befall thy people

*Matt 15:16* Are ye [the disciples] also yet without *u'ing*

*Mark 8:21* How is it that ye [the disciples] do not *u*

*Luke 24:45* opened he [Jesus] their [Emmaus travelers'] *u'ing*...might *u* the scriptures

*Acts 8:30* Philip...said, *U'est* thou [Ethiopian eunuch] what thou readest

*Rom 3:11* none that *u'eth*... none that seeketh after God

*1 Cor 13:2* though I [Paul]...*u* all mysteries

*1 Cor 14:19* I [Paul] had rather speak five words with my *u'ing* ... than...unknown tongue

*Phil 4:7* peace of God, which passeth all *u'ing*

*Heb 11:3* we *u*...worlds were framed by the word of God

## UNDERSTOOD

*Job 13:1* mine [Job's] ear hath heard and *u* it

*Job 42:3* I [Job] uttered that I *u* not; things too wonderful

*Isa 40:21* have ye not *u* from the foundations of the earth

*John 12:16* These things *u* not his [Jesus'] disciples

*1 Cor 13:11* When I [Paul] was a child...I *u* as a child

## UNGODLY [INESS]

*Ps 1:1* man that walketh not in the counsel of the *u*

*Prov 16:27* An *u* man diggeth up evil

*Rom 1:18* wrath of God is revealed...against all *u'iness*

*Rom 5:6* in due time Christ died for the *u*

*Titus 2:12* denying *u'iness*... we should live soberly

*Jude 18* mockers... should walk after their own *u* lusts

## UNJUST

*Matt 5:45* he [God]... sendeth rain on the just and... *u*

*Luke 16:8* the lord commended the *u* steward

*1 Pet 3:18* Christ... suffered for sins, the just for the *u*

## UNKNOWN

*Acts 17:23* altar with this inscription, TO THE *U* GOD

*1 Cor 14:4* speaketh in an *u* tongue edifieth himself

*1 Cor 14:19* I [Paul] had rather speak... with... understanding... than... in an *u* tongue

## UNRIGHTEOUS [NESS]

*Ps 92:15* and there is no *u'ness* in him [God]

*Isa 55:7* Let the wicked forsake his way, and the *u* man his thoughts

*Rom 1:18* wrath of God is revealed from heaven against all... *u'ness* of men

*1 Cor 6:9* the *u* shall not inherit the kingdom of God

*2 Cor 6:14* what fellowship... righteousness with *u'ness*

*1 John 1:9* he [Jesus] is faithful... to cleanse us from all *u'ness*

## UNSEARCHABLE

*Ps 145:3* Great is the LORD... his greatness is *u*

*Rom 11:33* how *u* are his [God's] judgments

*Eph 3:8* I [Paul] should preach... the *u* riches of Christ

## UR OF THE CHALDEES (a city in Mesopotamia where Abraham spent his early life before going to Canaan). **Gen 11:28,31;** 15:7 • Neh 9:7.

## URIAH (a Hittite warrior whom David had killed after his affair with Uriah's wife). **2 Sam 11:1–26;** 12:9–10; 23:39 • 1 Kgs 15:5 • 1 Chr 11:41. *Urias:* Matt 1:6.

## URIAS. See *Uriah.*

## URIJAH (a prophet killed by King Jehoiakim for predicting God's judgment on Judah). Jer 26:20–23.

## URIM AND THUMMIN (two objects in the breastplate of the high priest which were cast as lots to help determine God's will). Ex 28:30 • Lev 8:8 • Num 27:21 • Deut 33:8 • Ezra 2:63 • Neh 7:65.

## UZ (a place west of the Arabian desert where Job lived). **Job 1:1** • Jer 25:20.

**UZZA** (an Israelite struck dead for touching the ark of the covenant). 1 Chr 13:7–11.

**UZZIAH** (a king of Judah who contracted leprosy as a divine punishment for assuming duties that belonged to the priesthood). 2 Kgs 15:13–34 • **2 Chr 26:1–23;** 27:2 • Isa 1:1; 6:1; 7:1 • Hos 1:1 • Amos 1:1 • Zech 14:5. *Azariah:* 2 Kgs 14:21. *Ozias:* Matt 1:8.

# -V-

## VAIN

*Ex 20:7* not take the name of the LORD ... in *v*

*Ps 2:1* Why do ... the people imagine a *v* thing

*Ps 60:11* *v* is the help of man

*Ps 127:1* Except the LORD build the house, they labour in *v* that build it

*Prov 31:30* Favour is deceitful, and beauty is *v*

*Matt 6:7* when ye pray, use not *v* repetitions

*1 Cor 3:20* The Lord knoweth the thoughts of the wise, that they are *v*

*1 Cor 15:14* if Christ be not risen, then is our preaching *v*

*2 Tim 2:16* But shun profane and *v* babblings

## VANITY [IES]

*Job 35:13* God will not hear *v,* neither...regard it

*Ps 31:6* I have hated them that regard lying *v'ies*

*Ps 39:5* every man at his best state is altogether *v*

*Ps 94:11* LORD knoweth the thoughts of man ... they are *v*

*Ps 144:4* Man is like to *v:* his days are as a shadow

*Eccl 1:2* *v* of *v'ies;* all is *v*

*Isa 41:29* they are all *v;* their works are nothing

*Acts 14:15* Sirs [people of Lystra] ... turn from these *v'ies*

*Eph 4:17* walk not ... in the *v* of their mind

## VASHTI (the queen of Ahasuerus of Persia who was replaced by Esther). Esth 1:9–12; 2:1–4,15–17.

## VENGEANCE

*Ps 94:1* God, to whom *v* belongeth, show thyself

*Isa 61:2* To proclaim ... the day of *v* of our God

*Luke 21:22* these be the days of *v* ... things ... may be fulfilled

*Rom 12:19* *V* is mine; I will repay, saith the Lord

## VICTORY

*Isa 25:8* He [God] will swallow up death in *v*

*1 Cor 15:55* O grave, where is thy *v*

*1 Cor 15:57* God ... giveth us the *v* through ... Jesus Christ

*1 John 5:4* this is the *v* that overcometh the world

## VINE [S]

*Judg 9:12* said the trees unto the *v* ... reign over us

*Song 2:15* the little foxes, that spoil the *v's*

*Mic 4:4* sit every man under his *v* and under his fig tree

*Luke 22:18* I [Jesus] will not drink of the fruit of the *v*

*John 15:5* I [Jesus] am the *v,* ye are the branches

**VINE OF SODOM** (a plant which produced a beautiful fruit that was unfit to eat—a fitting description of Israel's idolatry). Deut 32:32.

**VIRTUE**

*Mark 5:30* Jesus…knowing… that *v* had gone out of him

*Phil 4:8* if there be any *v*… think on these things

*2 Pet 1:5* add to your faith *v;* and to virtue knowledge

**VIRTUOUS**

*Ruth 3:11* all the city…doth know…thou art a *v* woman

*Prov 12:4* A *v* woman is a crown to her husband

*Prov 31:10* Who can find a *v* woman … price … above rubies

**VISION [S]**

*Prov 29:18* Where there is no *v,* the people perish

*Ezek 1:1* heavens…opened, and I [Ezekiel] saw *v's*

*Ezek 11:24* the spirit…brought me [Ezekiel] in a *v*…into Chaldea

*Dan 2:19* Then was the secret revealed…in a night *v*

*Joel 2:28* your young men shall see *v's*

*Hab 2:2* Write the *v,* and make it plain upon tables

*Luke 1:22* he [Zacharias] had seen a *v* in the temple

*Acts 16:9* a *v* appeared to Paul in the night

*Acts 26:19* I [Paul] was not disobedient unto the heavenly *v*

**VOICE [S]**

*Gen 22:18* thou [Abraham] hast obeyed my [God's] *v*

*Ex 5:2* Who is the LORD, that I [Pharaoh] should obey his *v*

*Josh 24:24* our God will we serve…his *v* will we obey

*1 Kgs 19:12* and after the fire a still small *v*

*Job 40:9* canst thou thunder with a *v* like him [God]

*Ps 27:7* Hear, O LORD, when I cry with my *v*

*Ps 66:8* make the *v* of his [God's] praise to be heard

*Ps 116:1* he [God] hath heard my *v* and my supplications

*Isa 40:3* The *v* of him that crieth in the wilderness

*Jon 2:2* and thou [God] heardest my [Jonah's] *v*

*Matt 3:3* The *v* of one crying in the wilderness

*Matt 3:17* a *v* from heaven… my [God's] beloved Son

*Mark 9:7* a *v* came out of the cloud…This is my [God's] beloved Son

*Luke 23:46* when Jesus had cried with a loud *v*

*John 10:27* My [Jesus'] sheep hear my *v*…I know them

*Acts 9:4* a *v* saying…Saul, why persecutest…me [Jesus]

*1 Cor 14:10* There are…so many…*v's* in the world

*Heb 3:15* To day if ye will hear his [God's] *v*

*Rev 1:10* I [John]…heard behind me a great *v*

*Rev 3:20* any man hear my [Jesus'] *v,* and open the door

**VOICE OF THE LORD**

*Gen 3:8* they [Adam and Eve] heard the *v-o-t-L*

*Deut 13:18* thou shalt hearken to the *v-o-t-L*

*1 Sam 15:22* Hath the LORD as great delight in…sacrifices, as in obeying the *v-o-t-L*

*Ps 29:4* the *v-o-t-L* is powerful… full of majesty

*Isa 6:8* I [Isaiah] heard the *v-o-t-L*…Whom shall I send

**VOW [ED, EST, S]**

*Judg 11:30* Jephthah *v'd* a *v* unto the LORD

*Ps 50:14* and pay thy *v's* unto the most High

*Ps 116:14* I will pay my *v's* unto the LORD

*Eccl 5:4* *v'est* a *v* unto God, defer not to pay it

*Jon 1:16* the men…offered a sacrifice…and made *v's*

*Jon 2:9* I will pay that that I have *v'ed*

# -W-

## WAGES

*Lev 19:13* **w** of him...shall not abide with thee all night

*Hag 1:6* earneth **w** to put it into a bag with holes

*Rom 6:23* the **w** of sin is death

## WAIT ON THE LORD

*Ps 27:14* **W-o-t-L:** be of good courage...strengthen thine heart

*Ps 37:34* **W-o-t-L,** and keep his way...he shall exalt thee

*Prov 20:22* **w-o-t-L,** and he shall save thee

## WALLS OF JERUSALEM REBUILT AFTER THE EXILE. Neh 6:15.

## WANDERING IN THE WILDERNESS BY ISRAEL. Num 14:20–35.

## WATCH [ED, ETH, ING]

*Job 14:16* dost thou [God] not **w** over my sin

*Ps 90:4* For a thousand years in thy [God's] sight are...as a **w** in the night

*Ps 141:3* Set a **w,** O LORD, before my mouth

*Matt 24:42* **W** therefore: for ye know not what hour

*Mark 14:37* couldest not thou [Peter] **w** one hour

*Luke 2:8* shepherds...keeping **w** over their flock

*Luke 12:37* Blessed are those... the lord...find **w'ing**

*Luke 12:39* goodman...had known...thief would come, he would have **w'ed**

*1 Pet 4:7* be ye...sober, and **w** unto prayer

*Rev 16:15* I [Jesus] come as a thief. Blessed is he that **w'eth**

## WATER [EST, ETH, S]

*Gen 1:2* the Spirit of God moved upon...the **w's**

*Gen 7:24* the **w's** prevailed upon the earth

*Gen 9:11* neither shall all flesh be cut off any more by the **w's** of a flood

*Ex 7:18* Egyptians shall loathe to drink of the **w** of the river

*Ex 14:22* **w's** were a wall unto [the Israelites]

*Num 20:11* Moses...smote the rock...and...**w** came out

*Josh 9:27* Joshua made them [Gibeonites]...drawers of **w**

*1 Kgs 18:38* fire of the LORD fell...and licked up the **w**

*Job 5:10* Who [God]...sendeth **w's** upon the fields

*Ps 1:3* like a tree planted by the rivers of **w**

*Ps 22:14* I am poured out like **w**...bones are out of joint

*Ps 23:2* he [God] leadeth me beside the still **w's**

*Ps 63:1* flesh longeth for thee [God] in a dry and thirsty land, where no *w* is

*Ps 65:9* Thou [God] visitest the earth, and *w'est* it

*Ps 69:14* let me be delivered... out of the deep *w's*

*Ps 119:136* Rivers of *w's* run down mine eyes

*Prov 5:15* Drink *w's* out of thine own cistern

*Prov 25:21* if he [one's enemy] be thirsty, give him *w*

*Eccl 11:1* Cast thy bread upon the *w's*

*Song 8:7* Many *w's* cannot quench love

*Isa 11:9* earth shall be full of the knowledge of the LORD, as the *w's* cover the sea

*Isa 40:12* Who [God] hath measured the *w's* in... his hand

*Isa 55:1* every one that thirsteth, come ye to the *w's*

*Jer 2:13* forsaken me [God] the fountain of living *w's*

*Jer 9:1* Oh that my [Jeremiah's] head were *w's*

*Ezek 7:17* all knees shall be weak as *w*

*Ezek 12:18* drink thy [Ezekiel's] *w* with trembling

*Amos 5:24* let judgment run down as *w's*

*Hab 2:14* earth... filled with... the glory of the LORD, as the *w's* cover the sea

*Mark 1:8* I [John the Baptist]... have baptized you with *w*

*Luke 8:24* he [Jesus]... rebuked...the raging of the *w*

*John 3:5* Except a man be born of *w* and of the Spirit

*John 4:14* drinketh of the *w* that I [Jesus] shall give him

*Acts 1:5* John... baptized with *w;* but ye shall be baptized with the Holy Ghost

*Acts 8:36* here is *w;* what doth hinder me [Ethiopian eunuch] to be baptized

*1 Cor 3:7* neither he that *w'eth;* but God that giveth the increase

*Rev 22:17* whosoever will, let him take the *w* of life freely

## WAY [S] OF THE LORD

*2 Sam 22:22* I have kept the *w's-o-t-L*

*2 Kgs 21:22* he [Amon]... walked not in the *w-o-t-L*

*Ps 18:21* For I have kept the *w's-o-t-L*

*Ps 138:5* they shall sing in the *w's-o-t-L*

*Isa 40:3* Prepare... the *w-o-t-L*

*Jer 5:4* they are foolish: for they know not the *w-o-t-L*

*Ezek 33:17* the... people say, The *w-o-t-L* is not equal

*Hos 14:9* for the *w's-o-t-L* are right, and... just

*Mark 1:3* Prepare... the *w-o-t-L,* make his paths straight

*Acts 13:10* wilt thou [Elymas]... pervert the right *w's-o-t-L*

**WAY OF THE SEA** (a road that ran from Phoenicia to Egypt, passing through Palestine). Isa 9:1.

**WAY, THE TRUTH, AND THE LIFE, JESUS AS.** See *"I Am" Statements of Jesus.*

**WAYS**

*Deut 10:12* what doth…God require…to walk in all his *w*

*1 Sam 18:14* David behaved… wisely in all his *w*

*2 Chr 7:14* If my [God's] people…shall…turn from their wicked *w;* then will I hear

*Job 34:21* his [God's] eyes are upon the *w* of man

*Ps 25:4* Show me thy *w,* O LORD, teach me thy paths

*Ps 128:1* Blessed is every one… walketh in his [God's] *w*

*Prov 3:6* In all thy *w* acknowledge him [God]

*Prov 14:12* the end thereof are the *w* of death

*Prov 28:18* he that is perverse in his *w* shall fall

*Isa 55:8* neither are your *w* my *w,* saith the LORD

*Lam 3:40* search and try our *w,* and turn…to the LORD

*Rom 11:33* how unsearchable are his [God's] judgments… his *w* past finding out

*Jas 1:8* A double minded man is unstable in all his *w*

**WEAK [ENED]**

*Ps 6:2* Have mercy upon me, O LORD; for I am *w*

*Ps 102:23* He [God] *w'ened* my strength in the way

*Matt 26:41* the spirit…is willing, but the flesh is *w*

*Acts 20:35* so labouring ye ought to support the *w*

*1 Cor 1:27* God hath chosen… *w* things of the world to confound the…mighty

*1 Cor 9:22* became…*w,* that I [Paul] might gain the *w*

**WEAKNESS**

*1 Cor 1:25* the *w* of God is stronger than men

*1 Cor 15:43* it [the body] is sown in *w*…raised in power

*2 Cor 12:9* my [Jesus'] strength is made perfect in *w*

**WICKED [LY, NESS]**

*Gen 6:5* God saw that the *w'ness* of man was great

*Gen 18:23* Wilt thou [God]… destroy…righteous with the *w*

*Job 4:8* they that…sow *w'ness,* reap the same

*Job 18:5* Yea, the light of the *w* shall be put out

*Job 27:4* My [Job's] lips shall not speak *w'ness*

*Ps 10:2* *w* in his pride doth persecute the poor

*Ps 34:21* Evil shall slay the *w*

*Ps 58:3* The *w* are estranged from the womb

*Ps 71:4* Deliver me, O my God, out of the hand of the *w*

*Ps 84:10* rather be a door-keeper...than to dwell in the tents of *w'ness*

*Ps 94:3* LORD...how long shall the *w* triumph

*Ps 106:6* committed iniquity, we have done *w'ly*

*Ps 129:4* he [God] hath cut asunder the cords of the *w*

*Prov 4:17* they [evil men] eat the bread of *w'ness*

*Prov 15:29* The LORD is far from the *w*

*Isa 53:9* he [God's servant] made his grave with the *w*

*Jer 4:14* O Jerusalem, wash thine heart from *w'ness*

*Jer 17:9* The heart is...desperately *w:* who can know it

*Hos 10:13* Ye have plowed *w'ness*...reaped iniquity

*Jon 1:2* their [Ninevites'] *w'ness* is...before me [God]

*Matt 16:4* A *w*...generation seeketh after a sign

*Eph 6:12* we wrestle...against spiritual *w'ness*

*Eph 6:16* able to quench all the fiery darts of the *w*

## WICKED ONE

*Matt 13:19* cometh the *w-o*...catcheth...which was sown

*Matt 13:38* the tares are the children of the *w-o*

*1 John 2:14* and ye have overcome the *w-o*

*1 John 3:12* Cain...was of that *w-o,* and slew his brother

*1 John 5:18* begotten of God...that *w-o* toucheth him not

## WILL OF GOD

*Mark 3:35* do the *w-o-G,* the same is my brother

*Rom 12:2* what is that good...and perfect, *w-o-G*

*1 Thes 4:3* this is the *w-o-G*...abstain from fornication

*1 Thes 5:18* give thanks...this is the *w-o-G* in Christ Jesus

*1 John 2:17* he that doeth the *w-o-G* abideth for ever

## WINE

*Job 32:19* my belly is as *w* which hath no vent

*Prov 4:17* they...drink the *w* of violence

*Prov 20:1* *W* is a mocker, strong drink is raging

*Isa 5:22* Woe unto them that are mighty to drink *w*

*Mark 2:22* no man putteth new *w* into old bottles

*John 2:3* mother of Jesus saith...They have no *w*

*Acts 2:13* men [believers at Pentecost] are full of new *w*

*Eph 5:18* be not drunk with *w*

*1 Tim 3:8* deacons be grave...not given to much *w*

*1 Tim 5:23* use a little *w* for thy stomach's sake

## WISDOM

*1 Kgs 4:29* God gave Solomon *w* and understanding

*Job 28:28* Behold, the fear of the Lord, that is *w*

*Job 34:35* his [Job's] words were without *w*

*Ps 90:12* number our days... apply our hearts unto *w*

*Ps 111:10* fear of the LORD is the beginning of *w*

*Prov 2:2* So that thou incline thine ear unto *w*

*Prov 4:7* **W** is the principal thing; therefore get *w*

*Prov 10:13* In the lips of him that hath understanding *w* is found

*Prov 23:4* Labour not to be rich: cease from thine own *w*

*Eccl 1:18* For in much *w* is much grief

*Isa 11:2* the spirit of *w* and understanding

*Jer 9:23* Let not the wise man glory in his *w*

*Luke 2:52* And Jesus increased in *w* and stature

*Acts 6:3* seven men... full of the Holy Ghost and *w*

*1 Cor 1:20* hath not God made foolish the *w* of this world

*1 Cor 1:22* Jews require a sign... Greeks seek after *w*

*1 Cor 3:19* *w* of this world is foolishness with God

*Col 3:16* word of Christ dwell in you richly in all *w*

*Jas 1:5* If any of you lack *w,* let him ask of God

## WISE

*Ps 19:7* testimony of the LORD is sure, making *w* the simple

*Prov 3:7* Be not *w* in thine own eyes: fear the LORD

*Prov 6:6* consider her [the ant's] ways, and be *w*

*Eccl 4:13* Better is a poor and a *w* child than an old and foolish king

*Isa 5:21* Woe unto them that are *w* in their own eyes

*Jer 9:23* Let not the *w* man glory in his wisdom

*Matt 2:1* when Jesus was born... came *w* men from the east

*Matt 7:24* a *w* man, which built his house upon a rock

*Matt 10:16* *w* as serpents, and harmless as doves

*Matt 11:25* thou [God] hast hid these things from the *w*

*Matt 25:8* foolish said unto the *w,* Give us of your oil

*Rom 12:16* Be not *w* in your own conceits

*1 Cor 1:20* Where is the *w?* where is the scribe

*1 Cor 1:26* not many *w* men after the flesh... are called

## WISE MEN VISIT THE CHILD JESUS. Matt 2:1–12.

## WITNESS [ES]

*Ex 20:16* not bear false *w* against thy neighbour

*Ps 35:11* False *w'es* did rise up

*Prov 19:9* A false *w* shall not be unpunished

*Matt 24:14* gospel … preached … for a *w* unto all nations

*Mark 14:56* many bare false *w* against him [Jesus]

*John 1:8* He [John the Baptist] … was sent to bear *w* of that Light [Jesus]

*Acts 1:8* and ye shall be *w'es* unto me [Jesus]

*Acts 22:15* thou shalt be his [Jesus'] *w* unto all men

*Rom 8:16* The Spirit itself beareth *w* with our spirit

*Heb 12:1* compassed about with so great a cloud of *w'es*

## WIVES

*Matt 19:8* Moses … suffered you to put away your *w*

*Eph 5:22* **W,** submit … unto your own husbands

*Eph 5:25* Husbands, love your *w* … as Christ … loved the church

*Col 3:18* **W,** submit … unto your own husbands

*Col 3:19* Husbands, love your *w* … be not bitter

*1 Tim 4:7* But refuse profane and old *w'* fables

*1 Pet 3:1* *w,* be in subjection to your own husbands

## WOMAN AT THE WELL TALKS WITH JESUS. John 4:5–42.

## WONDERS

*Ps 77:14* Thou art the God that doest *w*

*Ps 96:3* Declare his [God's] … *w* among all people

*John 4:48* Except ye see signs and *w,* ye will not believe

*Acts 2:43* *w* and signs were done by the apostles

*Acts 6:8* Stephen, full of faith and power, did great *w*

## WORD [S]

*Job 8:2* *w's* of thy [Job's] mouth be like a strong wind

*Ps 12:6* The *w's* of the LORD are pure *w's:* as silver

*Ps 19:14* Let the *w's* of my mouth … be acceptable in thy [God's] sight

*Ps 119:11* Thy [God's] *w* have I hid in mine heart

*Ps 119:81* I hope in thy [God's] *w*

*Ps 119:105* Thy [God's] *w* is a lamp unto my feet

*Prov 15:1* but grievous *w's* stir up anger

*Prov 15:23* a *w* spoken in due season, how good is it

*Isa 40:8* the *w* of our God shall stand for ever

*Jer 1:9* I [God] … put my *w's* in thy [Jeremiah's] mouth

*Dan 12:9* Go thy way, Daniel: for the *w's* are closed up

*Mal 2:17* have wearied the LORD with your *w's*

*Matt 12:36* That every idle *w* that men shall speak, they shall give account

*Matt 24:35* my [Jesus'] *w's* shall not pass away

*Luke 1:38* And Mary said…be it unto me according to thy [God's] *w*

*Luke 4:32* his [Jesus'] *w* was with power

*Luke 5:5* at thy [Jesus'] *w* I [Peter] will let down the net

*John 1:1* In the beginning was the *W*…*W* was God

*John 6:68* thou [Jesus] hast the *w's* of eternal life

*John 17:17* Sanctify them… thy [God's] *w* is truth

*Acts 8:4* they that…scattered abroad went every where preaching the *w*

*1 Cor 2:4* my [Paul's] preaching was not with enticing *w's*

*2 Cor 5:19* committed unto us the *w* of reconciliation

*Col 3:17* And whatsoever ye do in *w* or deed

*2 Tim 2:15* a workman… rightly dividing the *w* of truth

*Jas 1:22* doers of the *w,* and not hearers only

*1 John 3:18* let us not love in *w*…but in deed

## WORD OF GOD

*Prov 30:5* Every *w-o-G* is pure

*Luke 4:4* not live by bread alone, but by every *w-o-G*

*Luke 5:1* people pressed upon him [Jesus] to hear the *w-o-G*

*Luke 8:21* my [Jesus'] brethren are these which hear the *w-o-G,* and do it

*Acts 4:31* place was shaken… filled with the Holy Ghost… spake the *w-o-G*

*Rom 10:17* faith cometh by hearing…hearing by the *w-o-G*

*Eph 6:17* the sword of the Spirit, which is the *w-o-G*

*Heb 4:12* the *w-o-G* is quick, and powerful

*Heb 11:3* the worlds were framed by the *w-o-G*

## WORD [S] OF THE LORD

*Ps 33:6* By the *w-o-t-L* were the heavens made

*Amos 8:11* not a famine of bread…but of hearing the *w's-o-t-L*

*Acts 19:10* all…in Asia heard the *w-o-t-L*

*1 Pet 1:25* the *w-o-t-L* endureth for ever

## WORK [ETH, ING]

*Gen 2:2* on the seventh day God ended his *w*

*Ex 23:12* Six days thou shalt do thy *w*

*Neh 4:6* for the people had a mind to *w*

*Ps 8:3* consider thy [God's] heavens, the *w* of thy fingers

*Ps 77:12* I will meditate also of all thy [God's] *w*

*Ps 90:17* establish thou [God] the *w* of our hands

*Ps 115:4* Their idols are…the *w* of men's hands

*Eccl 12:14* God shall bring every *w* into judgment

*John 4:34* My [Jesus'] meat is...to finish his [God's] *w*

*John 5:17* My [Jesus'] Father *w'eth*...and I *w*

*John 6:29* the *w* of God, that ye believe on him [Jesus]

*John 9:4* night cometh, when no man can *w*

*John 17:4* I [Jesus] have finished the *w* which thou [God] gavest me to do

*Acts 13:2* Separate me Barnabas and Saul for the *w*

*Rom 8:28* we know...all things *w* together for good

*Rom 13:10* Love *w'eth* no ill to his neighbour

*1 Cor 3:14* If any man's *w* abide...receive a reward

*1 Cor 12:10* To another the *w'ing* of miracles

*Eph 4:12* perfecting of the saints...*w* of the ministry

*Phil 1:6* he [God] which hath begun a good *w* in you

*Phil 2:13* God...*w'eth* in you... to do of his good pleasure

*1 Tim 3:1* office of a bishop, he desireth a good *w*

*Heb 13:21* *w'ing* in you that which is wellpleasing in his [God's] sight

## WORK [S] OF GOD

*Ps 64:9* all men...shall declare the *w-o-G*

*Ps 66:5* Come and see the *w's-o-G*

*Ps 78:7* not forget the *w's-o-G,* but keep his commandments

*Eccl 7:13* Consider the *w-o-G*

*Eccl 8:17* Then I beheld all the *w-o-G*

*John 6:28* that we might work the *w's-o-G*

*Acts 2:11* hear them speak... the wonderful *w's-o-G*

## WORK [S] OF THE LORD

*Ps 77:11* I will remember the *w's-o-t-L*...thy wonders

*Ps 118:17* I shall...declare the *w's-o-t-L*

*Jer 48:10* Cursed be he that doeth the *w-o-t-L* deceitfully

*Jer 51:10* declare in Zion the *w-o-t-L* our God

*1 Cor 15:58* stedfast, unmoveable, always abounding in the *w-o-t-L*

## WORKERS

*Ps 6:8* Depart from me, all ye *w* of iniquity

*1 Cor 12:29* are all teachers? are all *w* of miracles

*Phil 3:2* Beware of dogs, beware of evil *w*

## WORKS

*1 Chr 16:9* talk ye of all his [God's] wondrous *w*

*1 Chr 16:24* Declare his [God's] glory...marvellous *w* among all nations

*Job 37:14* consider the wondrous *w* of God

*Ps 33:4* all his [God's] *w* are done in truth

*Ps 40:5* Many, O LORD…are thy wonderful *w*

*Ps 92:5* O LORD, how great are thy *w*

*Ps 143:5* I meditate on all thy [God's] *w*

*Ps 145:9* his [God's] tender mercies are over all his *w*

*Matt 5:16* see your good *w,* and glorify your Father

*Matt 13:58* he [Jesus] did not many mighty *w* there

*John 6:28* that we might work the *w* of God

*John 9:3* *w* of God should be made manifest in him [Jesus]

*John 14:12* greater *w* than these shall he do

*Gal 2:16* man is not justified by the *w* of the law

*Eph 2:9* Not of *w,* lest any man should boast

*2 Tim 3:17* That the man of God may be perfect…furnished unto all good *w*

*Titus 3:5* Not by *w* of righteousness…we have done

*Jas 2:17* faith, if it hath not *w,* is dead, being alone

*Rev 3:8* I [Jesus] know thy [church at Philadelphia's] *w*

**WORSHIP [PED, PETH]**

*Ps 95:6* *w* and bow down [before God]

*Ps 99:5* *w* at his [God's] footstool; for he is holy

*Jer 25:6* go not after other gods…to *w* them

*Dan 3:6* whoso falleth not down and *w'peth* shall…be cast into the…furnace

*Dan 3:18* we [Daniel's three friends] will not…*w* the golden image

*Matt 2:2* we [the wise men]… are come to *w* him [Jesus]

*John 4:24* they…must *w* him [God] in spirit and in truth

*Acts 17:23* Whom…ye ignorantly *w,* him [God] declare I [Paul] unto you

*Acts 17:25* Neither is [God] *w'ped* with men's hands

*Rom 1:25* Who [ungodly people] … *w'ped* … served … creature more than…Creator

*Rev 7:11* all the angels…fell before the throne on their faces, and *w'ped* God

**WORSHIP THE LORD**

*1 Chr 16:29* *w-t-L* in the beauty of holiness

*Ps 96:9* O *w-t-L* in the beauty of holiness

*Luke 4:8* *w-t-L* thy God, and him only shalt thou serve

**WRATH**

*Ex 32:11* why doth thy [God's] *w* wax hot

*Job 5:2* For *w* killeth the foolish man

*Ps 21:9* LORD shall swallow them up in his *w*

*Ps 90:7* by thy [God's] *w* are we troubled

*Prov 14:29* He that is slow to *w* is of great understanding

*Matt 3:7* warned you [Pharisee] to flee from the *w*

*Rom 5:9* we shall be saved from *w* through him [Jesus]

*Eph 4:26* let not the sun go down upon your *w*

*Eph 6:4* fathers, provoke not your children to *w*

*Rev 6:17* the great day of his [God's] *w* is come

## WRATH OF GOD

*Ps 78:31* The *w-o-G* ... slew the fattest of them

*John 3:36* believeth not the Son ... *w-o-G* abideth on him

*Rom 1:18* *w-o-G* is revealed ... against all ungodliness

*Rev 16:1* pour out the vials of the *w-o-G* upon the earth

# -Y-

## YIELD [ED, ING]

*Gen 1:11* earth bring forth grass, the herb **y'ing** seed

*Num 17:8* rod of Aaron...budded...**y'ed** almonds

*Ps 67:6* Then shall the earth **y** her increase

*Matt 27:50* Jesus...**y'ed** up the ghost

*Rom 6:13* but **y** yourselves unto God

*Rev 22:2* the tree of life...**y'ed** her fruit every month

## YOKE

*Deut 28:48* he [God] shall put a **y** of iron upon thy neck

*1 Kgs 19:19* Elisha...was plowing with twelve **y** of oxen

*2 Chr 10:14* My [Rehoboam's] father made your **y** heavy

*Jer 28:2* I [God] have broken the **y** of...Babylon

*Matt 11:30* my [Jesus'] **y** is easy, and my burden is light

*Gal 5:1* be not entangled again with the **y** of bondage

## YOUTH

*1 Sam 17:33* thou [David] art but a **y,** and he [Goliath] a man of war

*Ps 25:7* Remember not the sins of my **y**

*Ps 71:17* O God, thou hast taught me from my **y**

*Prov 5:18* rejoice with the wife of thy **y**

*Eccl 12:1* Remember now thy Creator in the days of thy **y**

*Matt 19:20* All these things have I kept from my **y** up

*1 Tim 4:12* Let no man despise thy **y**

# -Z-

**ZABULON.** See *Zebulun*.

**ZACCHAEUS** (a tax collector who met Jesus and vowed to give half of his wealth to the poor and make restitution to those whom he had cheated). Luke 19:1–10.

**ZACHARIAH** (a king of Israel who ruled only about three months before being assassinated). 2 Kgs 14:29; 15:8–11.

**ZACHARIAS** (father of John the Baptist). Luke 1:5–79.

**ZAMZUMMIMS** (a race of giants who lived in the region later occupied by the Ammonites). Deut 2:20–21.

**ZAREPHATH** (a coastal town of Phoenicia where Elijah restored a widow's son to life). **1 Kgs 17:9–24** • Obad 20. *Sarepta:* Luke 4:26.

## ZEAL
*Ps 69:9* the *z* of thine house hath eaten me up
*John 2:17* written, The *z* of thine house hath eaten me up
*Phil 3:6* Concerning *z,* persecuting the church

## ZEALOUS
*Acts 21:20* Jews…which believe…are all *z* of the law
*Acts 22:3* I [Paul]…was *z* toward God, as ye all are
*Titus 2:14* purify unto himself [God] a peculiar people, *z* of good works

**ZEBAH** (a Midianite king killed by Gideon's army). Judg 8:4–28.

**ZEBEDEE** (father of James and John, disciples of Jesus). Matt 4:21–22; 10:2; 20:20; 26:37; 27:56 • Mark 1:19–20; 3:17; 10:35 • Luke 5:10 • John 21:2.

**ZEBOIIM.** See *Zeboim*.

**ZEBOIM** (a city destroyed along with Sodom and Gomorrah because of its sin). Gen 10:19 • **Deut 29:23** • Hos 11:8. *Zeboiim:* Gen 14:2,8.

**ZEBULUN** (a son of Jacob and ancestor of one of the twelve tribes of Israel). Gen 30:20; 35:23; 46:14; 49:13 • Ex 1:3 • 1 Chr 2:1. The tribe of Zebulun settled in northern Canaan. Josh 19:10–16. *Zabulon:* Matt 4:13.

**ZECHARIAH** (a prophet after the Exile and author of the book that bears his name). Ezra 5:1.

**ZECHARIAH, BOOK OF.** A prophetic book of the Old Testament written to encourage the Jewish people during the difficult years after they returned from the Exile. Zechariah encouraged the people to complete the task of rebuilding the temple in Jerusalem.

**ZEDEKIAH** (the last king of Judah who ruled as a puppet king under King Nebuchadnezzar of Babylonia and who was often condemned by the prophet Jeremiah). **2 Kgs 24:15–20; 25:2–7** • 1 Chr 3:15 • 2 Chr 36:10–11 • **Jer 21–52.** *Mattaniah:* 2 Kgs 24:17.

**ZELOPHEHAD** (an Israelite whose five daughters petitioned for the right to inherit his property because he had no sons). Num 26:33; **27:1–8.**

**ZELOTES** (a political-religious party of Jesus' time whose aim was to overthrow Roman rule and establish a Jewish theocracy). Luke 6:15.

**ZEPHANIAH** (a priest and friend of the prophet Jeremiah and author of the book that bears his name). 2 Kgs 25:18 • Jer 21:1; 29:25,29; 37:3; 52:24.

**ZEPHANIAH, BOOK OF.** A short prophetic book of the Old Testament known for its portrayal of the certainty of God's judgment against the nation of Judah (1:1–2:15). The prophet Zephaniah also declared that God would spare a faithful remnant (3:13), through which His promise of a future Messiah would be accomplished.

**ZERUBBABEL** (a Jewish leader who supervised the rebuilding of the temple in Jerusalem after the Exile). Hag 2:21–23 • **Zech 4:6–10.** *Sheshbazzar:* Ezra 5:14. *Zorobabel:* Matt 1:12–13.

**ZIBA** (a former servant of King Saul who helped David locate Jonathan's son Mephibosheth). 2 Sam 9:2–11.

**ZIDON.** See *Sidon.*

**ZIKLAG** (a city where David hid from King Saul). 1 Sam 27:5–6.

**ZILPAH** (Leah's maid who became a concubine of Jacob and bore two of his twelve sons, Gad and Asher). Gen 30:9–13.

**ZIMRI** (a chariot commander who assassinated King Elah of Israel and assumed the throne). 1 Kgs 16:8–20.

**ZIN** (a desert wilderness near the Dead Sea through which the Israelites passed). Num 13:21; 20:1; 27:14; 33:36; 34:3–4 • Deut 32:51 • Josh 15:1–3.

**ZION** (another name for the city of Jerusalem, particularly used in the Psalms). Pss 48:2, 11–12; 102:13–21; 137:1,3; 149:2 • Lam 2:1–18. *Sion:* Rev 14:1.

**ZIPH** (a city where David hid from King Saul). 1 Sam 23:14–18.

**ZIPPORAH** (wife of Moses). Ex 2:21–22; 4:25; 18:2.

**ZOAR** (a city destroyed along with Sodom and Gomorrah because of its sin). **Gen 19:20–25** • Deut 34:3 • Isa 15:5 • Jer 48:34. *Bela:* Gen 14:2.

**ZOBAH** (a Syrian kingdom that warred against King Saul). 1 Sam 14:47. *Hamath-zobah:* 2 Chr 8:3. *Zoba:* 2 Sam 10:6,8.

**ZOPHAR** (one of the three friends who comforted Job). His speeches appear in Job 11:1–20; 20:1–29.

**ZOROBABEL.**
See *Zerubbabel.*